THE WAYWARD FLOCK

Mark Edward Ruff

THE WAYWARD FLOCK

Catholic Youth in Postwar West Germany, 1945–1965

THE UNIVERSITY OF NORTH CAROLINA PRESS

CHAPEL HILL AND LONDON

© 2005 The University of North Carolina Press
All rights reserved

Designed by Rebecca Giménez
Set in Quadraat by Keystone Typesetting, Inc.
Manufactured in the United States of America

The paper in this book meets the guidelines for
permanence and durability of the Committee on
Production Guidelines for Book Longevity of
the Council on Library Resources.

Library of Congress Cataloging-in-Publication Data
Ruff, Mark Edward.
The wayward flock : Catholic youth in postwar west Germany,
1945–1965 / by Mark Edward Ruff.
p. cm.
Includes bibliographical references and index.
ISBN 0-8078-2914-5 (cloth : alk. paper)
1. Church work with youth—Germany—History—20th century.
2. Catholic Church—Germany—History—20th century.
3. Youth—Religious life—Germany—History—20th century.
I. Title.
BX2347.8.Y7R84   2005
259′.23—dc22
2004013683

09 08 07 06 05   5 4 3 2 1

TO MY FAMILY

CONTENTS

∞

ACKNOWLEDGMENTS

༚

THIS BOOK is the product of more than two years of research in nearly
two dozen archives and libraries and two different academic institutions.
It never would have come to fruition without the generous support of
many individuals and institutions on both sides of the Atlantic.

The Deutscher Akademischer Austauschdienst (German Foreign Exchange Service) provided funds for a ten-month stay in Germany in 1994
and 1995 and subsequently extended my funding for ten months to allow
me to continue my research into the summer of 1996. The Institut für
Europäische Geschichte and the Max Planck Institut für Geschichte in
Göttingen provided funds for three summer sojourns in 2000, 2001, and
2003, and here I would like to thank Prof. Dr. Rolf Decot and Prof. Dr.
Hartmut Lehmann for their support.

I have accumulated many debts to many archives in Germany and the
United States. My most sincere thanks extend to the staff of the Historisches Archiv des Erzbistums Köln, who generously supported my re-
quests during nearly a year of research. Special thanks must go to Josef van
Elten, Wolfgang Schmitz, Brigitte Torsey, Joachim Oeppen, and in particular, Dr. Ulrich Helbach. I am equally indebted to Dr. Norbert Kandler of
the Diözesanarchiv Würzburg; Bernd Börger, archivist at the Bund der
Deutschen Katholischen Jugend headquarters in Düsseldorf; Dr. Georg
Pahlke of the Jugendhaus Hardehausen in the archdiocese of Paderborn,

who commented on nearly all of the chapters; and Franz Hucht, who provided many of the photos for this book. I would also like to thank Erika Kösters of the Christliche Arbeiterjugend in Essen, Franz Lüttgen at the Kolpinghaus in Cologne, and the staff of the Bundesarchiv in Koblenz. Josef Rommerskirchen granted me access to his papers in the Konrad-Adenauer Stiftung as well as a five-hour interview at his home near Bad Godesberg. Dr. Felix Raabe, of the Zentralkomitee der Deutschen Katholiken, commented extensively on several papers I presented in Germany and provided me with important critical feedback.

I am particularly indebted to several groups of scholars in Germany who graciously welcomed a young American into their midst and provided indispensable guidance. At the Kommission für Zeitgeschichte in Bonn, I would like to thank Dr. Karl-Heinz Hummel, Margit Linsday, Wolfgang Dierker, Christoph Brohl, Petra von der Osten, Dr. Christoph Kösters, and in particular, Dr. Wolfgang Tischner, who read the manuscript from cover to cover. I would also like to thank the Arkeitskreis für kirchliche Zeitgeschichte in Münster and especially Professor Dr. Wilhelm Damberg and Dr. Antonius Liedhegener, who in addition to their friendship provided forums for me to present my work and commented extensively on several chapters. I have greatly profited from their expertise in the history of Catholicism and the structure of Catholic organizations.

On this side of the Atlantic, I would like to thank the archivists at Catholic University and the National Archives and my friends and colleagues from my time in Providence, including Ted Bromund, Alan Petigny, Jim Sparrow, Father David Lewis Stokes, and Jonathan Wiesen. I would like to thank my dissertation committee, including David Kertzer, Tom Gleason, and most importantly, my advisor, Volker Berghahn, now of Columbia University, who provided the proper mixture of encouragement and criticism. At Concordia University, Portland, I would like to thank Matt Becker, Chuck Kunert, Norm Metzler, and Gerd Horten. Larry Falkowski of St. Stephen's Episcopal Church provided feedback on the chapters and valuable computer assistance. I would also like to thank Michael Geyer, Doris Bergen, Anna Dzirkalis, and Christof Morrissey for a number of valuable suggestions on how to revise the work for publication.

At UNC Press, I would like to thank Amanda McMillan, Charles Grench, Ron Maner, and Stephanie Wenzel for their patience and valuable suggestions on rewriting the manuscript.

This work, finally, is dedicated to my family. This project began through many long conversations with my father, a Lutheran minister, about the future of the church and changes in Christianity. My family has watched the project take shape over many years. My brother Michael offered valuable help with the proofreading. They and my new wife, Lynnae, have provided tremendous support during years of work and research.

Bund, Bünde: literally, league(s), but with the sense of binding oneself and one's allegiances to the larger group. This was a common organizational form in the Catholic youth movement.

Bund der Deutschen Katholischen Jugend (BDKJ): The League of German Catholic Youth, a superstructure created in 1947 by Ludwig Wolker, which was an amalgamation of parish youth organizations (*Pfarrjugend*) and individual organizations (*Verbände*), including Kolping, the Christliche Arbeiterjugend, and Quickborn

Bund Deutscher Mädel (BDM): League of German Girls

bündisch: adjectival form of *Bund*

Bund Neudeutschland: The League of New Germany, an organization for male Catholic high school students attending the *Gymnasien*, the elite German academic high schools

Christliche Arbeiterjugend (CAJ): The Young Christian Workers, an organization brought to Germany in 1947, an offshoot of the Jeunesses Ouvrières Catholiques

Deutsche Jugendkraft (DJK): German Youth Force, a union of Catholic sporting organizations

Deutscher Sportbund (DSB): League of German Sport

Freie Deutsche Jugend (FDJ): Free German Youth, a Communist-led youth organization

German Youth Activities (GYA): an American youth organization

Heliand: organization for female academic high school students, the counterpart to Bund Neudeutschland

Jeunesses Ouvrières Catholiques (JOC): an organization founded in Belgium by Josef Cardijn

Jugendpflege: care for youth, youth work

Katholische Arbeiterbewegung (KAB): Catholic Workers' Movement, an organization for male workers which formed some groups for youth

Katholische Landjugendbewegung (KLJB): Catholic Rural Youth Movement, a movement that took shape in the 1950s to prevent an erosion of the Catholic milieu in the agrarian regions of Germany

Katholischer Jungmännerverband: the major youth organization in the 1920s

Kolping: an organization for young male artisans

Marian congregations: organizations mainly for women, although some were for men, which usually emphasized Marian traditions and forms of piety

Pfarrjugend: "ordinary" parish youth organizations

Quickborn: organization founded by Romano Guardini in 1921 that emphasized *bündisch* forms

Verband, Verbände: national organization(s) that brought together and united many individual *Vereine*. It can refer to the attempt to organize everyone in *Vereine*. This term is usually used quite negatively.

Verein, Vereine: club(s) or organization(s) at the local level, usually with a president (*Vorsitzender*), vice president, and treasurer. This was the typical form of organization in Germany, with deep roots in the nineteenth century.

Vereinsmeierei: a situation where individual *Vereine* battled for turf, or simply an exaggerated emphasis on the importance and significance of the *Vereine*

Wandervögel: one of the earliest groups in the German youth movement

Protestant theologians displayed a much greater openness to the liberal ideals of the Enlightenment and even modified their theological understanding to coincide more closely with contemporary science (and arguably declined because of this), the papacy rebuffed all such attempts at compromise.[7] It issued blanket condemnations of liberalism in the "Syllabus of Errors" and infuriated liberals by proclaiming such doctrines as papal infallibility and the Immaculate Conception of the Virgin Mary. Significant religious revivals only intensified this antimodern spirit. Thousands of the Catholic faithful flocked to pilgrimage sites, and enraptured young women reported apparitions of the Virgin Mary, events that to liberals seemed to be the embodiment of superstition and reaction.[8]

Galvanized by the pressures of state persecution and industrialization and succored through religious revivals, Catholicism in Germany took on its distinctive character as a discrete, tightly unified subculture. One of the chief features of this Catholic milieu was defense: it strove to protect Catholics from what was perceived to be a hostile outside world. To a certain extent, the oppositional identity of this subculture has been a feature of many institutions, sacred and secular. It seems to be a universal trait to define oneself by what one is not as much as by what one is. Certainly, many religious institutions, Christianity included in its early years, gave themselves a clearer identity through such an oppositional identity.

Although its critics naturally took delight in deriding it as a ghetto, the Catholic milieu was anything but a simple relic of antimodernism. To protect their own flock more effectively, Catholic leaders deliberately adopted the strategy of using modern weapons to fight the modern world. Almost from the outset, they appropriated the most current forms of organization—political parties, clubs, and the ubiquitous *Verein*, the prevailing organizational model in nineteenth-century bourgeois society. They then sought to fill these forms of organization with an antimodern message.

It might seem that using "modern means to fight modernity" would have ensured the survival of the Catholic milieu for many decades.[9] But this strategy proved insufficient to sustain the Catholic milieu in the postwar era, a period when society was undergoing rapid cultural and social change. To account for the erosion of the Catholic milieu after 1945, one has to pose a somewhat different question: why was this strategy amiss in the changing culture of the Federal Republic?

The 1950s and early 1960s were an era in which economic prosperity and the spread of technology were changing the face of German society, less so in the early 1950s than from the late 1950s to the early 1960s. Prior to the 1950s, industrialization had largely been a phenomenon affecting persons in or adjacent to cities. In contrast, economic growth in the postwar years spilled over to the countryside and led to a significant increase in the number of daily commuters between urban and rural areas. Although the daily lives and social status of all Germans were not immediately transformed by the increased use of dishwashers, washing machines, and motor vehicles, technology began to change expectations and mentalities. Televisions, the cinema, and motorcycles ensured that even inhabitants of remote agrarian regions were exposed to new "modern" trends. An ethic of consumption was beginning to take root.[10]

Perhaps no portion of society was affected by these changes in culture more than youth. For as observers noted, young persons were, in general, far more receptive to changes in culture and society—new technologies, new employment possibilities, new ways of thinking, and opportunities outside the church worlds—than their elders. Indeed, a new youth culture was taking shape during the 1950s, a world of jazz aficionados, rock 'n' roll revelers, motorcycle riders, and hobby clubs.[11] Although this new youth culture was largely apolitical, it was centered around a new ethos of individualism and consumption—the right of individual young persons to choose to take part in those activities that were of the greatest appeal and interest.

For church leaders, on the other hand, the new youth culture of the 1950s and 1960s was a source of trepidation. Youth leaders feared that the glamour and appeal of this new culture would lead to a mass exodus from traditional youth groups of the teenagers and young adults who alone could sustain this Catholic milieu for another generation. Others recognized that this new ethic of individualism was corrosive to traditional youth work, which was centered around principles of leadership and hierarchy. Although some youth leaders took pains to protect their young flock from this new, modern culture, others recognized the futility of this strategy. Because society was changing so rapidly, they argued, it was essential to integrate the new youth culture—mass entertainment, hobby clubs, and jazz festivals—into activities for their teenagers.

Yet in spite of their best efforts, Catholic youth leaders never genuinely succeeded in appropriating the new youth culture of the 1950s and 1960s for their own ends. Why were they unable to take advantage of this new, modern culture and use it to fight modern society? After all, this strategy of making use of the prevailing forms of youth culture had reaped a substantial harvest even as late as the 1920s and 1930s, when Catholic youth leaders appropriated the forms of the bourgeois German youth movement and *bündisch* youth groups and, in turn, brought more than 1.5 million young men and women into the ranks of the church. Why were they able to hold together their ranks in the face of ruthless persecution from the National Socialist state and yet be unable to withstand an onslaught of Harley Davidsons, Elvis Presley records, and makeup twenty years later? Why did Catholic youth leaders find it difficult to come to terms with a youth culture that was increasingly predicated upon individualism and consumption?

The answers to this question will form the core of this book. It will focus on several factors that contributed to the erosion of youth work in the 1950s and, in turn, to the erosion of the Catholic milieu: generation gaps between the leadership and the young persons during the late 1940s and 1950s and the difficulties in upholding the antimodern ideological heritage from the nineteenth century. It will also examine the often deadly effects of internecine struggle between conservative integralists, who sought to keep the flock cut off from the outside world and its temptations, and moderate reformers, who attempted to adapt themselves to newer cultural norms, at least halfway.

EXAMINING THE EROSION of the Catholic milieu during the 1950s and 1960s allows one to modify three existing sets of historical and sociological narratives: interpretations of the 1950s, larger accounts of twentieth-century German history, and finally, recent debates on theories of secularization.

Many interpretations of the 1950s depict this era as static.[12] For conservative historians, the 1950s and early 1960s represented a golden age in German history, a decade of full employment and cultural and political stability after years of totalitarian rule and social upheaval.[13] More recently, a number of English-language historians have attached to this picture of stability a more negative value judgment and emphasized the conservative, quasi-authoritarian patriarchal and restorationist features of the era. They assert that the peculiar circumstances of postwar Germany—the black market, military occupation, the return of veterans and prisoners of war, prostitution, and the shortage of men—gave rise to this unique discourse on power, sexuality, gender, and politics. Yet while these works continuously refer to the enormous power of social conservatives in shaping this discourse, they rarely examine more than fleetingly the many nuances and, above all, significant changes within the religious world of West German social conservatives of the 1950s. In some cases, religion is left out altogether.[14]

In this book, in contrast, I attempt to turn both of these interpretations on their heads. By showing that even the conservative heart of West Germany was subject to rapid and unprecedented changes, I argue that the larger society of the 1950s was marked by subtle but unmistakable change beneath the placid surface. The erosion of the Catholic milieu, and especially its waning influence among the young, is evidence enough that the larger structures of authority came under question during this time, even where the rhetoric of some Catholic politicians and church leaders might leave the impression that they had, indeed, succeeded in their program of a conservative cultural restoration. Antecedents for the challenges to authority in the late 1960s existed already in the 1950s. In this book I will also argue that German Catholicism was less monolithic than is portrayed in the recent literature. There were many competing voices and discourses within the church.

This work can thus fit into an expanding body of recent literature on the 1950s that emphasizes the significant impact of the growing culture of consumption on German society. It was the power of this new culture that, perhaps more than any other factor, led a number of younger Catholics to posit alternative visions for youth work. I agree with current arguments put forward, especially by Uta Poiger, that leading voices in Germany abandoned their once-scathing indictments of mass culture and even embraced consumerism. Leading Catholics, however, did so for reasons quite different from those of Cold War liberals.[15]

The erosion of the Catholic milieu, secondly, has a much greater significance for the larger trajectory of German history. Any history of twentieth-century Germany has to confront two fundamental challenges: how to explain how Germany moved first toward and then away from National Socialism. On the level of politics, culture, and society, it has to account for both upheaval and stabilization, for the convulsions and tumult of the German Empire and the Weimar Republic as well as for the path to stability that characterized the Federal Republic, particularly by the 1960s.

German society was bitterly divided along the lines of class, region, and confessions from the second half of the nineteenth century through the 1950s. These rifts were so gaping that a number of historians and sociologists created a new terminology to account for this fragmentation. This new lexicon postulated the existence of independent subcultures, or milieus. It appropriated the phrase "Catholic milieu" from a Catholic publicist in the 1960s, Carl Amery, who used it pejoratively to call attention to the insularity and backwardness of Catholic communities.[16] Sociologist M. Rainer Lepsius first brought it into widespread currency in the historical profession. While analyzing election results and German political cultures of the late nineteenth and early twentieth centuries, Lepsius used the word "milieu" to denote four major groupings within German society as they emerged in the late nineteenth century: Catholics, Socialists, liberals, and East Elbian conservatives. For Lepsius these milieus were "unified social entities, which were formed by a coming together of many structural dimensions such as religion, regional tradition, economic conditions, cultural orientation and social structure of its elites. The milieu is a sociocultural construction, which is determined by the specific relation of such dimensions within a particular segment of the population."[17] The use of the term "Catholic milieu" has since aroused many controversies, and a number of historians have modified Lepsius's original conceptions or provided alternative formulations.[18]

The trajectory—the formation and erosion—of the Catholic and Socialist milieus, in particular, decisively influenced the larger contours of German history and the decisions made at key junctures, such as 1918, 1933, and 1945. Making larger interpretations more difficult is the reality that both the Catholic and the Socialist subcultures eroded in fits and starts in the course of the twentieth century because of the discontinuous nature of the challenges they had to face. Already in the first two decades of the twentieth century, men from some Catholic working-class communities were beginning to desert church institutions for those of Socialist rivals. This process was accelerated in the 1920s as the forces of mass culture tore away at the Catholic milieu.

Yet both during the German Empire and in the 1920s, both subcultures offered visions of politics and society that were often more democratic than those of rival conservatives and even many liberals. But they frequently inspired these fearful and threatened opponents on the right to subvert democracy and to violate civil liberties in their fight against these perceived threats. Faced with the breakdown of the political system, many Germans turned to the National Socialist Party, outsiders with radical and violent political visions, in the hopes of restoring unity to a nation torn asunder.[19] Catholic complicity in the events of 1933 can be linked, simultaneously, to fears of another Kulturkampf and Bolshevism and to the recognition of weakness in the face of internal divisions in the wake of secularization.

The impact of Nazism on the Catholic milieu was utterly equivocal, dependent on region, class, and gender. The Gestapo, ss, and Hitler Youth destroyed the extensive network of Catholic Vereine, sent many priests to their grave, and provided young persons with alternative values (especially on questions of sexuality). Many Catholics, however, found their commitment to the church strengthened during these years of duress.[20] Deadlier than the encroachments of the National Socialist state were the dislocations brought on by the war, which destroyed entire cities and led to vast population transfers that changed the confessional landscape in many regions. In spite of unprecedented upheaval, the Catholic milieu reconstituted itself with astounding speed after 1945.[21] The subsequent decade was an era of restoration, in which the church rebuilt nearly all of the organizations destroyed in the preceding twelve years. In some areas the milieu flourished well into the 1960s.[22] Here a confluence of two factors led to the stabilization of West German society. By the 1950s and 1960s, both the Catholic and the Socialist subcultures had entered the social and cultural mainstream and became driving forces politically through representatives in the CDU and the SPD (Social Democratic Party), bringing their more democratic traditions with them into the postwar era. At the same time, both subcultures eroded, diluting their dogmatic ideological heritage from the nineteenth century; the fissures described by Lepsius and others no longer dominated Germany as they had in the 1920s.

What emerged instead by the 1960s was a homogenized German culture and society, a transformation that was brought about, in part, by increased prosperity and the power of consumption.[23] By the end of the decade, Catholics had begun to leave the church in droves. One might even refer to the 1960s as the time of a second foundation of the Federal

Republic: the social and cultural rifts that had plagued German society for nearly 100 years had finally been overcome.

Thirdly, examining the erosion of the Catholic milieu allows one to modify existing theories of secularization. Sociologists of religion have recently engaged in often bitter debates over questions that were of interest nearly a century ago to Max Weber and Émile Durkheim and restated in the 1960s: do modern society and its processes of modernization necessarily undermine religious belief and religious institutions? Although there have been many voices in these debates, two major positions have emerged. On one side have been the defenders of the traditional secularization thesis, which asserts that modernization necessarily erodes religious beliefs and institutions. On the other side have been the advocates of "rational choice theory," which insists that the demand for "religious goods" has not necessarily waned. Instead, the suppliers of religious products in much of Western Europe have inadequately met the demand.[24]

But these debates have operated with a host of weaknesses. They have consistently lacked a sound empirical basis and have frequently bordered on the ahistorical. Scholarly exchange has been bogged down in quibbles over semantics and terminology. Most importantly, most of the theorists of secularization from the 1960s and 1970s applied these processes indiscriminately to almost all European nations, regardless of differing national and religious traditions. In this work I will attempt to correct such weaknesses. In the conclusion, I will draw parallels between the erosion of the Catholic subculture in Germany and the collapse of the Catholic milieu in Switzerland and the Catholic "pillar" in the Netherlands, the two countries that are most similar to Germany.[25] The conclusion will subsequently—and briefly—contrast these patterns with processes of secularization elsewhere in Europe and the United States.

HOW DOES ONE analyze the erosion of the Catholic milieu empirically? The massive tomes on secularization provide surprisingly little help. They often fail to distinguish between religious belief and religious behavior. Outward commitment is not always an adequate measure of religious belief. Catholic leaders often discovered to their chagrin that many parishioners in rural villages attended mass solely out of habit and not out of deep-seated religious convictions. Religious belief, moreover, is difficult to measure in any quantitative sense. Many surveys attempt to provide an objective framework for measuring belief by asking carefully framed questions—Do you believe in God? Do you believe in life after death?—but the shortcomings of these polls should be obvious. The same polls can assess religious behavior much more easily through a different set of questions—Do you attend church on a given Sunday? Are you a card-carrying member of the Catholic workers' organization? Do you attend its annual banquet?

Studies that purport to analyze religious behavior nonetheless often concentrate almost exclusively on one variable—church attendance—and do not address the full range of religious behavior. To overcome these difficulties, at least partially, I have constructed a model that casts religious behavior in the shape of a pyramid. The most rudimentary forms of religious observance—Christian burial, baptism, and marriage—sit at the bottom of the pyramid. The most rigorous and exclusive—entry into the priesthood and Catholic orders—are at the top. In the middle lie a series of religious behaviors, each more demanding than the last and, by extension, finding fewer practitioners: Christmas and Easter Communion, occasional Communion, regular attendance at mass, extra participation in religious organizations, and finally, leadership roles in these organizations.

The erosion of the Catholic milieu, according to this system, can be understood as the erosion of this pyramid. Religious observances that asked more of the adherents spiritually, emotionally, and physically were hit first (and hardest) by the decline in participation; those that required less time and energy continued to be well attended. To give but two examples, many young Catholics continued to attend mass regularly but stopped participating in youth organizations. The number of candidates for the priesthood, similarly, dropped by nearly two-thirds between 1939 and the late 1950s.

This model does not always, of course, correspond perfectly to changes in actual spirituality—some young men and women continued to "believe" in Catholic teachings, even as they stopped attending mass regularly—but that a general connection exists is beyond dispute. It underscores the erosion of one underpinning of religious faith among Roman Catholics: the belief in the authority of the church to transmit the teachings of Christ and to lay claim to the ways in which individuals structured their daily lives. This book will concentrate on the erosion of the top of this pyramid—of the network of Catholic Verbände and the increasing reluctance of young men and women to assume leadership roles within these organizations.

The focus on *Verbände* will allow this investigation to go beyond those studies that have concentrated almost exclusively on church attendance as a measure of the relative strength of Catholic communities.

The loss of youth was critical in this process of erosion. To survive, religious institutions depend either on waves of conversion and revival—phenomena strikingly absent in postwar Germany—or on successful youth work. As an old adage tellingly put it, "Who has the youth has the future." It was relatively rare for adults in their forties and fifties to quit church organizations suddenly or to suddenly stop attending mass (one exception would be the departure of men from the church during the early years of National Socialist rule; another would be the reluctance of refugees to attend mass in their new areas of settlement). The erosion of the Catholic milieu, to a substantial degree, began with the decisions by young men and women in their teenage years or early twenties to stop attending mass or to leave their youth groups, even if they had been raised in the church or instructed in the rudiments of the faith. Young men and women, in other words, had to decide how far up the pyramid they wished to go.

This work examines the erosion of a vast network composed of more than twenty Catholic youth organizations. This once-proud network brought as many as 1.5 to 2 million young persons together during its heyday in the late 1920s and 1930s. To contemporaries, it conjured up images of well-built young men in white shirts and short pants confidently marching through the streets of German cities, of romantic hikes through the local woods, of pious young women with straight hair gathering for evening devotions, and of festivals celebrating the virtues of home and village. The Nazi state put an end to many of these organizations later in the 1930s, but after the war, church leaders immediately went to work to restore the "Catholic Youth," as they called it, to its former grandeur. On the surface, it appeared as though they succeeded. By the mid-1950s, Catholic groups numbered more than 1 million members, while organizational leaders spoke "in the name of the Catholic youth" to effect political changes. Catholic leaders claimed to have enrolled at least 30 percent of all Catholic youth into their groups.[26] Although they regularly bemoaned the absence of the other 70 percent, they succeeded in enlisting, at least formally, a higher percentage of young persons than their rivals in Socialist and Protestant youth organizations.

In reality, however, many of these groups lacked the verve, excitement, and sense of purpose of two decades earlier. Above all, by the late 1950s they were unable to sustain their membership, as thousands of young men and women refused to join new groups or, more commonly, left their groups as teenagers. Traditionally, many young men and women most active in youth work went on to assume leadership positions in other Catholic lay organizations as adults or to enter the priesthood. The disintegration of many groups thus meant that Catholic institutions were often denied a new generation of leaders.

Until the 1970s, Catholic youth groups retained an intricate organizational apparatus. They were divided along the lines of region, gender, class, occupation, and age. Youth work for boys and girls, for instance, was rigorously segregated; groups existed for boys between ages 10 and 14, 14 and 18, and 18 and 25 and for girls between 10 and 14, 14 and 18, and 18 and 28 (although in some cases older women remained active in their groups). Traditionally, the groups of 10- to 14-year-olds were the largest and the groups for 18- to 25-years-olds the smallest, as members entered the workplace, were married, or simply lost interest.

Youth groups were also organized along diocesan, deanery, and parish lines—with several exceptions. Groups for young artisans and students existed for all of Germany and frequently crossed ecclesiastical borders. This richness in texture provides the historian with a remarkable opportunity to differentiate the process of erosion on the basis of the most important categories of historical analysis: region, class, occupation, generation, historical memory, and everyday life. The methodology reflects the reality, all too often overlooked, that all of these categories are ultimately interrelated. One cannot examine regional changes without bringing in gender or class, and vice versa.

Each chapter is accordingly structured on the basis of one of these variables. Chapter 1, "Generation Gaps," focuses on the role of historical memory in shaping Catholic youth after 1945. It describes the decisions and conflicts confronting prominent laity and clergy as they sought to rebuild Catholic youth organizations following the collapse of National Socialism. In spite of widespread opposition, they attempted to build a single giant structure uniting the many Catholic youth organizations that had hitherto existed independently. They strove to imbue the new edifice, the League of German Catholic Youth (Bund der Deutschen Katholischen Jugend) (BDKJ) with the ideals and traditions of the Catholic youth movement from the 1920s and 1930s. The principal architect was Bavarian monsignor Ludwig Wolker, who singularly dominated youth work and serves as a common thread throughout subsequent chapters.

Chapter 2, "Where the Boys Are," provides an account of the everyday life of local parish groups—including their activities, processions, and festivals—and argues that the emerging recreational and entertainment industries posed often insurmountable difficulties for these organizations by the end of the 1950s. Chapter 3, "Where Have All the Young Girls Gone?" concentrates on gender and how changes in values—regarding marriage, career, makeup, dancing, and relationships—led to the exodus of many young women from Catholic youth organizations. Chapters 4 and 5 examine the roles played by region and class. Chapter 4 analyzes groups for young workers and artisans in the most industrialized diocese in Germany, the archdiocese of Cologne. Chapter 5, in contrast, examines rural youth there and in one of the most rural dioceses, Würzburg, and scrutinizes the effects of socioeconomic change on youth work. Chapter 4 looks primarily at two Catholic Verbände, Kolping and the Young Christian Workers (Christliche Arbeiterjugend) (CAJ); Chapter 5, at general parish groups and the Catholic Rural Youth Movement. Verbände played a less significant role within Catholicism in Lower Franconia than in the Rhineland or Westphalia, where the network of Vereine was highly developed.

Chapter 6, "A League of their Own," brings together all of these variables—historical memory, class, gender, and region—in an examination of a schism that emerged over an independent Catholic sporting organization in the Ruhr, the German Youth Force (Deutsche Jugendkraft) (DJK). By examining youth organizations in the dioceses of Cologne, Würzburg, Münster, and Paderborn (through the fight over the DJK), all strongholds of German Catholicism, this work can reasonably claim that its conclusions represent most of Germany and are not merely the product of regional peculiarities.

Two methodological caveats are, finally, in order here. This study is based on materials from nearly two dozen archives in Germany and the United States.[27] Even within these vast materials, there are few reliable statistics for membership in the BDKJ and for church youth groups. Leaders often inflated their membership in order to receive greater financial support from the federal government, which apportioned funds on the basis of numbers. Local statistics are equally untrustworthy. In some parishes, priests tallied all young persons in the parish between ages fourteen and twenty-five, whereas others counted only those who had joined groups and sworn an oath of allegiance to the BDKJ.[28] Nonetheless, one can discern larger membership trends, in part, based on the attendance at national festivals and on the subscription rates to national youth magazines. Several individual *Verbände*, such as Kolping and the CAJ, carried out regular and reliable membership surveys. In any case, a clear downward trend is evident in all of the statistical information available from the mid-1950s onward; even in the mid-1950s, membership did not come close to that of the mid-1930s, the heyday of the Catholic youth movement. In 1954 the membership in the male and female *Stämme* (main organizations) of Catholic youth work was estimated at 863,000; by 1964 this number had decreased to 450,000. This figure did not include membership in many ancillary organizations, such as the CAJ or Kolping, and so the total was little more than 1 million in 1954 and approximately 550,000 by 1964. But even these figures were probably somewhat overestimated.[29]

Secondly, while this book examines Catholic youth in the postwar era, it concentrates primarily on the young men and women in Catholic youth organizations and those who had recently left these groups. The documents from these organizations focus on, quite naturally, group members, who comprised, at most, 30 percent of German Catholic youth. A more comprehensive study of all Catholic youth remains methodologically difficult, if not impossible. A more exclusive focus on organization members still allows one to draw much larger conclusions about the erosion of the Catholic milieu in the postwar era.

ONE

Generation Gaps:
Catholic Youth Work
and the Dialogue
with the Past

IN THE WAKE of Germany's surrender in May 1945, it appeared that the Catholic milieu had crumbled under the pressures of war and systematic persecution. Churches had been reduced to piles of stone, thousands of priests had perished in concentration camps, and a once-thriving network of ancillary organizations had been forcibly disbanded by the Gestapo. Within this context, bishops, politicians, former youth leaders, and even the most humble parish priests resurrected organizations that had lain dormant for years and brought groups that had been driven underground back into the open. Although these individuals shared the common goal of "organizing" the Catholic faithful into groups or movements of some sort and nurtured deeper hopes of pulling the tattered Catholic milieu back together, they could not agree on how best to breathe new life into their once-thriving subculture. Some sought to rebuild the extensive network of organizations and associations and the old Center Party, while others wished to start anew, turning their backs on the models from the past, which in their eyes had failed the decisive tests of the 1930s.

At first glance, these conflicts—"restoration or a new beginning"— were but a reiteration of the old theme, one central to German Catholicism since the nineteenth century: should the church remain a hermetic, insular institution, or should it, through its ancillary organizations, assert itself within modern society?[1] These debates, more significantly, reflect the impact of historical memory, but it was the Weimar past and not just the twelve years under National Socialism that became the object of attention. Catholic historical memory remained fixated on 1933, as prominent spokesmen asked themselves whether their forms of organization had limited the church's influence vis-à-vis National Socialism during the last years and months of Weimar. Like the rest of German society in the late nineteenth and early twentieth centuries, Catholic Germany had been ravaged by vast rifts between aristocrats, artisans, peasants, and workers; these fissures had weakened the church in the face of the encroachments of the National Socialist state. Following the Second World War, Catholic leaders resolved to build "unified" institutions that would be strong enough to overcome these internal divisions and to withstand challenges from political extremists on both the left and the right of the political spectrum. This quest to achieve unity especially dominated youth work, where some leaders sought to create a giant superorganization that would bring all Catholic youth together into one fold and serve as a bulwark against potential Communist threats. These efforts culminated in 1947, when, with much fanfare, youth leaders launched the BDKJ. The church's blueprint for reconstruction was a product of long-standing fears of secularization and of its understanding of the recent past.

This chapter will trace the complex story of Catholic youth work from the late nineteenth century to the late 1940s. The outcome of these structural debates from the mid-1940s was decisive in setting the tone and agenda for Catholic youth work for the next twenty years. The youth leaders of 1947 were to discover years later and much to their chagrin that many youth had responded to their efforts with indifference or apathy, a reflection of the old maxim that even the best-laid plans have unforeseen consequences.

FROM THE OUTSET, the German Catholic milieu was characterized by its insularity. It was possible for a Catholic to be born in a Catholic hospital, attend religious schools, participate eagerly in pilgrimages with thousands of equally ardent wayfarers, marry a fellow Catholic, and receive a Catholic burial, having "breathed Catholic air" from the cradle to the grave. At virtually every corner was a rich and ever increasing number of ancillary organizations (*Vereine*) in the years after 1871, the so-called formative phase of the Catholic milieu.[2] By the turn of the twentieth century, a typical Rhenish or Westphalian parish of several thousand was home to a mothers' club; a workers' organization; a *Verein* for artisans, journeymen, and apprentices (*Gesellenverein*); a St. Boniface *Verein*; a farmers' association; a Marian congregation for boys and one for girls; and a charity or "Caritas" association.

After having withstood several rounds of state persecution during the Kulturkampf, Catholics began adopting the strategy of using the most modern means possible to fight the modern world. They borrowed the organizational form of the *Verein* from bourgeois society with the intent of protecting the flock from the very real dangers of the outside, "modern" world.[3] In contrast to the old guilds, the *Vereine* were less hierarchical and more egalitarian; any individual could join or leave the organization at will. In large parishes in rapidly industrializing areas, these associations served as the link that bound Catholics to the church. Before long, central committees were up and running on the national level, and by the 1880s more than 80 percent of German Catholics were voting for their own Center Party.

Youth organizations were, surprisingly, relative latecomers into this subculture. Catholic youth work did not resemble its modern shape until the end of the nineteenth century, when industrialization and urbanization radically transformed formerly rural Catholic communities in the Rhineland and Westphalia.[4] It took time for leading voices in German society to discover the potentially disruptive potential of "adolescence," a new concept in academic and sociological circles.[5] As life expectancies increased and the workplace became increasingly separated from the home, young men and women suddenly found themselves in an awkward position between childhood and adulthood. These youth, especially in industrializing regions, were seen by political and religious authorities as vulnerable to subversive and radical influences. Even as bourgeois reformers introduced legislation that provided care for youth (*Jugendpflege*), Roman Catholic leaders began to provide for the young people under their charge. They gave youths games to play and encouraged them to attend lectures and speeches delivered by leading clerics and laity. Many farsighted Catholics realized, most importantly, that the teenage years were critical for cementing the loyalty of youth to the church. A favorite saying proclaimed, "Who has the youth, has the future."[6]

Within Catholic Germany, several types of youth organizations existed alongside one another, a mixture of the old and the new. Brotherhoods, congregations, and sodalities tended to be narrowly religious in character, dating back in some cases to the Counter-Reformation. Most were little more than prayer and mission societies—reflections of local customs and popular piety—run by adult clergy. The Marian congregations for young maidens (*Jungfrauenkongregationen*) underwent a renaissance in the nineteenth century (see Chapter 3). If the congregations represented a retreat from the world, a narrow "ghetto mentality" fashioned through decades of Kulturkampf, ultramontanism, and crusades against liberalism, other organizations attempted to carve out a space for Catholics within the world. Already at midcentury, Rhenish cleric Adolph Kolping had begun to build organizations for young men. Kolping was a former artisan who feared that his onetime colleagues were no longer finding a place within the church and might be lured away by the emerging Socialist movement. These groups, which came to be known as *Gesellenvereine* or *Kolpingsvereine*, not only provided religious instruction but also offered practical training and skills for their trades. The *Kolpingsvereine* often had their own meeting places in the *Kolpingshaus*, where young artisans had a chance to socialize, discuss personal and vocational problems, and above all, put down beers.[7]

The burgeoning *Vereine* rapidly crossed parish, deanery, and diocesan lines after 1871 to become national organizations with bureaucracies and power structures as centralized as that of the church itself.[8] Every organization within Germany was required by law to register with the civil authorities as an *eingetragener Verein*, or *e.V.*. Each organization was ordered to appoint a board of directors (*Vorstand*) and hold at least one full assembly each year. As a result, many organizations were under the control not of the bishops but of a figure known as the *Generalpräses*, who was almost always a priest but had a legal status independent of the bishops and frequently was not mindful of instructions given to him by the church hierarchy.

Some organizations, moreover, began to compete against one another for members. Within large parishes (often in industrializing regions), workers' associations, Christian trade unions, and Kolping groups frequently became bitter rivals. Such *Vereinsmeierei*, a sometimes comical, exaggerated sense of self-importance on the part of many members, was often seen as an intrusive and disruptive element in parish life.[9] By the 1920s, as a result, many *Vereine* were subjected to withering reproofs from critics in the episcopate. They painted a bleak picture of soused *Junggesellen* who played Skat at the local watering hole and engaged in turf battles with the members of Catholic workers' associations.[10] For them, Catholic organizations had become too worldly, overly political, and undisciplined—indistinguishable from the mass society around them.[11]

Such clerical indignation was in keeping with the spirit of the times. In the years after the First World War, Catholic Germany was overspread by a potent sense of crisis, politically, culturally, and spiritually.[12] Already at the turn of the century, perceptive observers had begun to notice that young men, in particular, were less receptive to the message of the church. One cleric from the Rhineland estimated in 1916 that a mere 10 percent of young men stuck with Catholic organizations, youth or adult, following their graduation from school at age fourteen.[13] Many feared, not without good reason, that their young men would be drawn into Socialist organizations. In fact, male Catholic workers indeed began to cast their votes for the Communists or Social Democrats, and the number of candidates for the priesthood sank to an all-time low in many dioceses, a phenomenon that cannot be solely attributed to a decline in the numbers of young men as a result of the war.[14] Industrialization had clearly opened deep rifts throughout German society that the Catholic milieu was no longer capable of withstanding as successfully as it had in the 1870s and 1880s.[15]

To make matters worse, Catholic leaders found themselves in a confrontation with the emerging mass culture of the 1920s. Leading clerics realized that the new mass entertainment had the potential to undermine an ethic of hard work, modesty, self-sacrifice, renunciation, and submission to authority. As a result, the bishops drew up lists of behaviors and items that, they argued, placed Catholics in grave danger of succumbing to sexual temptation: alcohol and tobacco consumption, the movies, public swimming pools, public performances by women gymnasts (öffentliches Schauturnen), wild dancing, and jazz. By the mid-1920s, denunciations of immorality, sexual deviance, and promiscuity were commonplace in the sermons and public writings of the bishops. Such jeremiads tended to be aimed at women, who were regarded as more vulnerable to the siren songs of consumption and sexual promiscuity and who were seen as likely to take advantage of the fuller range of opportunities available to them in Socialist institutions and depart from the Catholic fold.

Thus it became painfully obvious to many youth leaders by the early 1920s that neither the Verbände nor the tradition of Jugendpflege was adequate to reach young persons at a time of tremendous societal and cultural upheaval. In response to this sense of crisis, youth leaders desperately sought alternatives. Carl Mosterts, head of the Katholische Jünglings-vereinigungen, embarked on a modest program of centralization.[16] He began to transform the loose confederation of groups in the tradition of *Jugendpflege* into a more unified organization, the Katholischer Jungmän-nerverband. In 1920 Mosterts helped form the DJK, a union of Catholic sporting organizations that had hitherto existed independently of one another.[17]

Yet in spite of Mosterts's best intentions, the efforts at renewal that proved to be most successful were those that arose spontaneously. Of these, the youth movement and the liturgical movement fundamentally transformed Catholic youth work—and German Catholicism as a whole—by the late 1920s. As is so often the case in the history of German Catholi-cism, ideas and impulses from outside tended to enter Catholic society belatedly. But then, as if to compensate for their tardy arrival, they made their presence felt especially intensely. The Catholic youth movement was no exception. Where bourgeois youth had been organizing itself into groups of *Wandervögel* prior to the First World War, not until the early 1920s did the youth movement began to flourish in Catholic Germany.[18]

Initial efforts had begun more than a decade earlier by a little-known chaplain in Mainz with a burning interest in theology and philosophy. Romano Guardini, who in spite of his name was German by birth, turned a fledgling Catholic organization named Quickborn into a centerpiece for renewal.[19] Members of this small group, which never tallied more than 20,000, were drawn to the romanticism of the youth movement. They donned uniforms and short pants and carried flags for rambles in the German countryside. Quickborn was characterized by a *Gemeinschafts-ideologie*, that is, an implicit rejection of specious bourgeois values (the so-called *Gesellschaft*) in favor of the purity of a tightly knit community in touch with nature.[20] Youth were no longer the mere object of youth work, faithfully obeying the commands of adult leaders, but steered, planned, and countenanced groups themselves. They chose their own leaders—a slap in the face to those clergy who insisted that youth organizations should be run along the lines of the congregations, that is, by adults.

Guardini, remarkably enough, also served as the guiding light for yet another movement of renewal, the Liturgical Movement.[21] As its name suggests, this movement concerned itself with the intricacies of liturgy: antiphons, hymns, prayers, and versicles. But its main significance lay elsewhere. The Liturgical Movement redefined the relationship between young persons and the church. It sought to transform each parish from a perfunctory administrative center into an organic community of true believers. The church thereby took on a new meaning as the Corpus Christi *mysticum*, the mystical body of Christ. The altar became the center of the *Gemeinschaft* of young persons, a community of those called through baptism to receive Holy Communion at the altar of the Lord. Groups of young persons gathered at their local parish to celebrate the mass, often early in the morning with a favorite chaplain. In a radical departure from existing practice, many groups of young persons performed the mass in the vernacular and made use of their own liturgical innovations. These small groups of adherents defined themselves first and foremost as Catholics and only secondarily as workers, peasants, or students. "We want to be Catholic to the hilt," heralded a leitmotif from "The Fulda Confession" from 1924.[22]

It did not take long for observant leaders within Catholic youth circles to discover the power and excitement that these new approaches exerted over youth. Like Guardini, Carl Mosterts had insisted that Catholic youth organizations had to be marked by a renewed Catholic consciousness, a pride in being Catholic. Mosterts's successor, Ludwig Wolker, took these initiatives and, more than any other individual, began to transform the desultory assortment of *Vereine*, *Kongregationen*, and *Bünde* in the tradition of Catholic youth movement into a more coherent entity unified by a common identity and purpose.

Ludwig Wolker was the decisive figure in the Catholic youth work of the twentieth century. He called the shots not just in the late 1920s and 1930s but for five to ten years immediately after the war. The forms that youth work took after the war were Wolker's. He shaped and inspired an entire generation of Catholic youth and assumed a near-legendary status for those who came of age during the interwar years.

Wolker was born in 1887 to an interconfessional middle-class Bavarian family. His Protestant father was a high-ranking customs official; his Catholic mother was the daughter of a brewer.[23] His ideals and aspirations were no doubt the product of his bourgeois upbringing. They embody many of the same contradictions and longings articulated most poignantly in the middle-class youth movement then taking shape across Germany. He went to university initially intending to study medicine, but after several semesters he secretly switched to theology. Wolker took his priestly vows in 1912, and in 1915 he was appointed to the chaplaincy at a parish in Munich, where he was put in charge of a group of young artisans. There he discovered—almost by accident, it seems—just how effectively the spirit of the youth movement could transform barren Catholic *Vereine* into groups distinguished by their élan and energy.[24] Membership in Wolker's group soon more than doubled from 100 to 250, and it was not long before he was appointed *Vereinspräses* and, after 1925, head of the union of Catholic organizations for young men in Munich. In 1926 he took over the helm of the Katholischer Jungmännerverband, then located in Düsseldorf.

Wolker's rotund appearance—he was none too tall, but stout, with a round head and a protruding nose—belied his charisma and volatility. Friends and detractors alike likened him to a volcano ready to erupt. He was of an imperious nature and typically barked out orders in a Bavarian dialect that was scarcely intelligible to his subordinates.[25] Before long, he had earned the nickname "the General" (short for *Generalpräses*), with which his colleagues even addressed him in correspondence. For those with whom he was on more familiar terms, he was known simply as the GP. According to all reports, Wolker was a first-rate orator, peerless within Catholic circles. The Catholic youth center at Düsseldorf even issued recordings of speeches he had delivered in the 1930s, including one of his most fiery displays of oratory, "We will fight."[26] To today's ear, his oratory sounds bombastic and full of pathos, but it was precisely these qualities that mesmerized many young Catholics. To many young people, his august manner embodied leadership at its fullest. To no one's surprise, a cult of personality quickly took shape around him in Düsseldorf.

Once at the helm of the Katholischer Jungmännerverband, Wolker launched an ambitious program for renewal to bring the spirit of the youth movement to a "musty" headquarters.[27] He dismissed several long-standing employees of the *Jugendhaus* when he first visited in 1926 and began to realign the Katholischer Jungmännerverband along lines pioneered by Quickborn earlier in the decade.[28] Wolker unveiled a new ideological platform on which Catholic youth work was to rest for subsequent decades: "The kingdom of God, the kingdom of youth, and the German kingdom" (*Gottesreich, Jugendreich, Deutsches Reich*).[29] Wolker's edifice for youth work was hierarchical. In making subordination (*Unterordnung, Überordnung*) the foundation of these "kingdoms," he merely accentuated what to a Catholic would be obvious: that authority and obedience provide the underpinning of society. Wolker naturally under-

Monsignor Ludwig Wolker, the leader of Catholic youth
work in the second half of the 1920s, the 1930s, and
the immediate postwar years (Courtesy of
Diözesanarchiv Würzburg)

stood God, the church, and the secular authorities as indisputable authorities, but to these he surreptitiously added the charismatic leader of
the youth kingdom, the position that he himself hoped to occupy. In both
theory and practice, then, a cult of leadership occupied a central place
within the Catholic youth movement of the interwar years.

Thus the face of youth work was completely changed at the grass
roots. Wolker sought to cast parish groups in the form of a *Bund*. The
term *Bund* comes from the word *verbinden*, which means, literally, to tie or
to bind. Each group of young boys was to be bound together; the group
itself was to lay a higher claim on the behavior, values, and daily life of its
members. Through rituals and symbols such as uniforms, flags, and
banners, the *Bund* was designed to forge ties that would last for life. Upon
their induction into the groups, for instance, individuals assumed a wide

range of obligations. They pledged to remain loyal to the group, church, and fatherland and to fulfill all the commands of their superior, the *Jungführer*, as he was called through the 1960s.

Wolker, in turn, discovered images and rhetoric that not only reinforced these messages of authority and leadership but also magnetized youth. Here the word "rediscovered" is probably more accurate, for many of these images looked back to a romanticized, heroic Middle Ages.[30] Wolker, for instance, frequently exhorted Catholic youth to pattern their lives after Michael, the archangel who slew the dragon; in so doing, they could become modern-day Christian knights and fight for God, Christ, and the German fatherland. The leading magazine for Catholic youth was titled *Michael!*[31] The figure of Christ was likewise transformed from the mawkish and suppliant sufferer to the triumphant Christ the King.[32] Wolker had clearly turned his back on the forms of piety of the nineteenth century; the sentimentality of the Heart of Jesus movement had little place within the Catholic youth movement.

But as even these few examples make clear, the new forms were almost strictly male in their orientation. With only several exceptions, female groups retained the outward trappings and internal content of pious congregations. These *bündisch* forms mirrored the larger cultural climate of 1920s and 1930s Germany, as authority, heroism, and masculinity were seen as central to any regeneration, religious or national. At the same time, images of masculinity, as all-pervasive as they were in the 1930s, took on meanings unique to German Catholics. Younger Catholics looked back aghast at the "weak" religious practices of the nineteenth century that reflected the preponderance of women in the pews. But it was precisely these qualities that led many members of the Hitler Youth to dismiss Catholics as weak and effeminate and to place the blame for Germany's national weakness on the shoulders of "feminized" Catholic institutions. The exaggerated images of masculinity—the "breast of steel," the phallocentric rhetoric, and the disciplined marching—were undoubtedly an attempt to compensate for past traditions and to swell the ranks of men in the church.

At the center of the *bündisch* forms that Wolker (and indeed many non-Catholic youth groups of the 1920s and 1930s) espoused lay the theme of identity. Wolker, too, believed that a powerful religious identity alone could overcome the tremendous fragmentation taking place within the Catholic milieu between workers, farmers, artisans, and students. He repeatedly used the word "unity" to describe his larger goal of creating a single unified organization that would bring together all Catholic youth in one fold.[33] Wolker may have unconsciously been trying to create an antipode to the weak and fragmented Weimar state. At a time when the state had won the hearts of very few, Wolker and his young crusaders within their youth kingdom may have looked for an alternative to the unifying function that the state was supposed to fulfill. In overcoming these divisions based on class, occupation, and geography, Wolker undoubtedly hoped to provide a shining example to all Germans of how to achieve a *Volksgemeinschaft*, a goal that he tirelessly and enthusiastically supported. He ultimately strove to place Catholic youth squarely within the mainstream of German society and even sought to recast German society along Catholic values and lines.

By the early 1930s, Catholic youth leaders had asserted their claim to shape German state and society, and their organizations began to display their distinctly Catholic identity in the public arena. The waning years of Weimar were something of a golden age for politicized youth organizations, not just for militant Nazi and Communist youth movements but for Catholic youth organizations. A popular slogan from the time urged all *Jungführer* to go "to the front."[34] Thousands of young Catholics, in turn, faithfully assembled for mass rallies and rousing assemblies. The most demonstrative of the Catholic youth organizations took the name *Sturmschar* (the storm host) and routinely held marches with drummers, mass rallies, and processions.[35] Such moves were designed not just to intimidate ideological opponents elsewhere but to generate political support for Heinrich Brüning, the chancellor from the Center Party.

This pattern did not disappear in 1933 when the Center Party was disbanded. The signing of the concordat actually led to something resembling euphoria in many Catholic quarters, not least in youth circles, where many of the most influential leaders believed that they would be able to shape the new German state decisively. New slogans at the time called for "Christ's kingdom and a new Germany" and "Everything for Germany, Germany for Christ"—optimistic but naive embodiments of long-standing hopes to make national values fundamentally Catholic and Christian.[36] In a phrase that would have many distinct echoes after 1945, Wolker, in particular, began once again to urge Catholics to "gain influence" in as many public institutions as possible.[37] Perhaps as a result, the Catholic youth movement did not ebb in 1933, as one might assume, but actually continued to grow in strength and influence into the mid-1930s. It succeeded in bringing vast numbers of young men back to the church. The number of young seminarians, an excellent indicator of this process, had more than doubled by the mid-1930s.[38]

One would have thought that the episcopate would have welcomed these movements for renewal and, above all, those that made the institution of the church the object of faith and devotion. Yet some of the most prominent men in the church hierarchy soon became deeply suspicious of both movements. In Wolker they saw a clear rival for ecclesiastical power, one whose charisma had already brought him a mass following among adults and youth alike. Rumors that he was out to usurp power dogged him until his death in 1955.[39] As we shall see, many German clerics harbored deep reservations about the very fundamentals—form and content—of both the youth and liturgical movements.

By the late 1920s and early 1930s, leading clerics had begun to develop their own plans for renewal. They seized upon a model pioneered in Italy in the mid-1920s in an attempt to draw the lines between the church and the Fascist state. This model, named Catholic Action, was officially introduced to German Catholics in 1928 by Papal Nuncio Eugenio Pacelli (who later became Pope Pius XII) in a speech at the Katholikentag in Magdeburg. Catholic Action had two basic characteristics: it was both an ideology of renewal and a method of organization.[40] It was to lead the church to a new era by sending lay representatives "into the world" to carry out tasks that priests were unable to do there. Energetic young Catholics were to go into coal mines, to sit on the boards of directors of industrial firms, and to rise to leadership positions in national sporting organizations to fulfill the missionary work of the church and expand Catholic influence.[41]

Catholic Action also served as an organizational model. Catholic parish life in Italy revolved around four (or sometimes six) large pillars from which lay activities and Catholic social life emerged: a group for adult men, one for adult women, one for male youth, one for female youth, and where applicable, organizations for male and female students.[42] These pillars were organized, not as in the German context through a centralized Verbandsstruktur, but strictly along diocesan and parish lines. Control was thereby in the hands of the parish priest and ultimately the bishop. "Nothing without the bishop," ran a popular slogan of Catholic Action proponents in Germany.[43] It was often described as "the participation of laity in the apostolic mission of the church but not in the hierarchy itself." Catholic Action was often understood in terms of ideological purity—the return to fundamentals at a time of crisis. The four pillars—men, women, boys, and girls—were intended to resemble a family. They were a rediscovery of the basics of life: the authority of the church and the family.

Many German bishops thus embraced Catholic Action as a tool with which to chasten and discipline traditional *Vereine*. They argued that this system lent Catholic organizations a unity that the dozens of quarreling *Vereine* were unable to achieve. Some even envisioned using Catholic Action to do away with the network of *Vereine* altogether. Wilhelm Böhler, one of the most prominent men within the Cologne episcopate, sought to invest power in the hands of a diocesan representative appointed directly by the bishop and to remove it from the *Generalpräses* of Kolping or the *Volksverein*.

The promise of Catholic Action, however, was not immediately realized throughout Germany. Pacelli himself admitted that Catholic Action would have to be severely modified in order to work in the German context. For many Catholics, particularly those already in the *Verbände*, Catholic Action's call to arms was nothing new; it represented precisely what the *Verbände* had already been doing for more than seventy-five years.[44] It seemed that Catholic Action was but another form of *Gleichschaltung*, this time undertaken not by Nazi leaders but by their own bishops and priests. The church hierarchy, however, found that it could neither dissolve the *Vereine* in one fell swoop nor replace the leaders of the *Vereine* with their own handpicked officials. Implementing a program of Catholic Action, moreover, meant placing even more responsibility in the hands of priests who were already horribly overburdened by such basic duties as performing masses, burials, and marriages in parishes that often included more than several thousand members.

By 1934 matters had reached an impasse. The bishops had neither the clout nor the will to push through Catholic Action against the opposition of the *Vereine*. They took pains to insist that they had no plans to dissolve or even limit the scope of the traditional *Vereine*. Nor had Wolker, on the other hand, achieved his goal of bringing all Catholic youth into one fold. Catholic youth organizations, despite having been instilled with a new consciousness and pride, still remained fragmented, divided into more than twenty separate *Bünde*, *Kongregationen*, and *Verbände*. The youth movement had hardly set foot in many rural regions of Westphalia, to say nothing of the agrarian heartland of Bavaria, regions where the traditional forms of youth work—*Jugendpflege* or congregations—still predominated.[45]

The repression and restrictions imposed by the National Socialist state inadvertently brought about the unity for which Catholic leaders had striven in vain for years. The concordat of 1933 stipulated that the Catholic ancillary organizations were to be retained; only activities and organizations that were expressly political were to be prohibited. As a result, Catholic youth organizations, with the notable exception of the DJK in 1934, were not immediately banned. The Hitler Youth instead exerted other forms of pressure—peer pressure—to convince Catholic youth to shift allegiances. Participation in Catholic youth activities, however, actually increased in many places, and so the National Socialist regime was soon forced to take more draconian measures. In 1935 and 1936, the Gestapo, the SS and the Sicherheitsdienst (security service of the party) issued edicts that dissolved individual *Verbände*. The remaining organizations were restricted to activities strictly religious in nature. Members were forbidden to wear uniforms, march, sing in public, and go on hikes. By 1939 the Nazi police state had eliminated nearly all Catholic organizations. More than 150 Gestapo agents dealt the final blow. They seized the center for Catholic youth work in Düsseldorf, confiscated all assets, and dissolved the Katholischer Jungmännerverband. Priests who dared to disagree with these policies were slapped with heavy fines or prison sentences or, in some cases, were dragged off to concentration camps.[46]

This increasingly hostile atmosphere ultimately provided the bishops with an opportunity (and an excuse) to put through their agenda of Catholic Action and shift the locus of youth work from the *Verbände* to the individual dioceses. In 1936 they convened a commission to draw up new statutes for youth work. The commission consisted of members from six dioceses and the largest youth organizations as well as representatives from a committee on Catholic Action that had been operating since the early 1930s. Although the drafters avoided language that seemed to deprive the *Verbände* of their autonomy, their product—*Die Richtlinien von 1936* [The guidelines of 1936]—did precisely that.[47] The new guidelines arranged for future youth work to be carried out from the dioceses. Individual parish priests were given the call to constitute parish youth groups, or *Pfarrjugend*, as they were labeled. Most dioceses soon appointed leaders to oversee the youth work in their dioceses. Some dioceses even went to the expense of creating entirely new structures—*Diözesanjugendämter* (diocesan youth offices)—to run youth work. In this way, the Catholic organizations could more easily avoid allegations that their activities were other than purely religious.

Wolker's hand can be clearly discerned in these guidelines, even though he stood to lose considerable power were they to be implemented. In these statutes he no doubt saw the opportunity to achieve his old dream of unifying all Catholic youth and spreading the ideals of the youth and liturgical movements into all parishes, large and small. The statutes expressly called for leading as many young people as possible into a "conscious, joyful life within the church in the form of a community to last for life." Since the Nazi regime had forbidden Catholic youth organizations from carrying out any activities outside church walls, Wolker sought to ensure that all parish groups would take on as many of the trappings of the liturgical movement as possible, such as new liturgy and masses planned and countenanced by the youth. Otherwise, he feared that the *Pfarrjugend* groups would have little appeal to youth, even as the Hitler Youth often provided more attractive alternatives. Between 1936 and 1938 local bishops gradually put the *Richtlinien* of 1936 into place in their dioceses. The bishops, with Wolker's blessing, had succeeded in bringing Catholic Action to youth work.

The results, at least initially, exceeded the wildest expectations of youth planners. Throughout many dioceses (but by no means all), the newly appointed leaders vigorously set out to cultivate the new forms of worship for youth inspired by the liturgical movement. Many young persons appear to have responded enthusiastically to their efforts. The number of participants in "spiritual exercises" and "days of reflection" increased dramatically, from 38,000 in 1934 to 60,000 in 1938 in the diocese of Münster alone.[48] Other youth formed personality cults of sorts around charismatic bishops such as Cardinal Faulhaber in Munich and Cardinal von Galen, the bishop of Münster, who became the most outspoken opponent of the Nazi euthanasia program.[49] The deeper meanings of these cults, though perhaps unclear to Clemens August von Galen and others of like mind, were quickly grasped by state authorities. Many youth had rejected the authority of National Socialist leaders and were intent, instead, on upholding the legitimate, God-given authority of "their" bishops.[50]

Wolker and many of the bishops clearly hoped that extinguishing the

Verbände would put to rest the intermittent scuffles over youth work that had marred the successes of the preceding dozen years. Here, too, they were to be bitterly disappointed. The rift deepened between friends and foes of the new parish groups over questions of style and substance, of liturgical reform that they were charged with promoting. One official from the archdiocese of Paderborn recounted the difficulties in trying to spread the ideals of the liturgical movement against determined opponents: "The efforts of the youth ministers to incorporate thoroughly the bishops' directives into the lives of youth had, as a consequence, that we not seldom had to fight on two sides, on fronts inside and outside the church."[51]

The youth and liturgical movements alarmed conservatives who were committed to upholding a hierarchical vision of society. Conrad Gröber, the cantankerous archbishop of Freiburg, emerged as the most vocal critic.[52] His criticisms in the 1930s, during the war, or afterward almost always revolved around the theme of how laicism had brought about widespread degeneration. Laicism, he was fond of saying, was the "plague of our time." He claimed that new liturgical forms destroyed hundreds of years of orthodoxy and tradition; the mysticism and "irrationalism" of the liturgical movement threatened the neoscholastic and neo-Thomist base on which church dogma rested.[53]

Gröber took aim at the traditions of the youth movement that he regarded as emancipatory. He particularly disliked the practice of having boys take charge of youth groups. The maxim that "youth leads youth" he took as a direct challenge to the rank and privilege on which ecclesiastical authority rested. Always something of a curmudgeon, Gröber undoubtedly nurtured an idealized image of passive youth who did little more than pray and meditate. One of Gröber's opponents summed it up best: "Out of fears of this sovereignty, of this revolution by youth, the church doors were closed rather tight and iron bars were placed across them."[54]

Gröber's criticisms paved the way for skirmishes between friends and foes of the youth and liturgical movements. Some remained behind closed doors; others were waged in full view of an astonished public. These reached their apogee, bizarrely enough, in 1943, during the middle of the war, when Gröber published a vitriolic manifesto titled *Mich beunruhigt* [I am disturbed]. Gröber's criticisms, which he laid out in seventeen points, were by now familiar and included the overemphasis on liturgy and the obligation to introduce the *Gemeinschaftsmesse*.[55] For many clerics, his manifesto confirmed their own misgivings regarding these movements, and many refused to carry out the new forms of youth work that they had been charged with promoting under the guidelines of 1936. Many young persons, in response, hurled invective at their elders. Gröber particularly disliked the characterization of him as an "old fogey" and even made this epithet the focus of one of his seventeen points.[56] The situation became so bad that some contemporaries began to speak of two distinct churches: one orthodox (or reactionary), stodgy, closed-minded and old, and the other progressive, open-minded, and young.

The abuse at the hands of the National Socialist regime and the church itself inevitably took its toll on Catholic youth work. Even as youth work flourished in rural areas where the youth movement until then had not set foot, so, too, did it drop off precipitously in urban regions that were confessionally mixed; there the oppression from the authorities was often more severe, and Catholic youth fell prey more easily to peer pressure from Protestants.[57] Some priests and chaplains were intimidated by the threats from the local police and were unwilling to sponsor youth groups. In other parishes, priests who had been hostile to the new forms of youth work from the outset simply informed young people that they were no longer permitted to meet within the church. Catholic youth leaders also bemoaned a new spirit of sexual permissiveness that they believed had resulted from the war. In response, older leaders sought to turn youth work inward to meet needs at a time of temptation and vice. The situation required, one manual explained, self-denial, an examination of the conscience, and an ethos of asceticism.[58] The youth work that remained was often little more than a surrogate for religious instruction, what American youth would receive during Sunday school classes.[59]

Youth work thus became precisely what Wolker most feared: a joyless set of religious obligations, prayers, and remembrances stripped of the spirit and élan of the great Catholic movements for renewal. As one young woman noted, "We were only allowed to [do] pious things, sing pious songs, which we, of course, did not do."[60] In these instances, the Pfarrjugend reverted to what essentially was Jugendpflege. This term was no longer used (it had been replaced with the designation Jugendseelsorge), but the content was the same.

Under attack from both church and state and unwilling to accept the strictures of local clergy (which many representatives of the old school enthusiastically supported), young people who were still committed to the ideals of the Catholic youth movement eventually took matters into their own hands. Some young leaders took their groups underground and arranged clandestine trips to nearby cities or local woods. This trend was most pronounced in rural regions like Lower Franconia, where Catholic institutions enjoyed the unbounded support of the local populace.[61] But even large cities such as Berlin witnessed the emergence of small, courageous youth cells inspired by the ideals of the liturgical movement. For the first time, many of these groups consisted of young women, who until then had not partaken of the spirit of the youth and liturgical movements.[62]

The impact of National Socialism on both youth work and the Catholic milieu was, thus, ambiguous, at least until the late wartime years. On one hand, Catholic youth work retained an elite cadre of dedicated volunteers who were even more inspired by the ideals of the youth and liturgical movements than the young people of 1933. But at the same time, youth groups lost a sizable number of members who had participated with a lower level of engagement—the so-called masses, in the parlance of that time.[63] The guidelines of 1936 were part and parcel of a larger process that worked to bind youth more tightly to the institution of the church (ein Verkirchlichungsprozess); church leaders, in turn, attempted to return to religious fundamentals.[64] This bears out the picture of the Catholic subculture in Bamberg described by Werner Blessing, in which many nominal Catholics left the church, but the commitment of those who remained was actually strengthened.[65]

Yet the wartime years were ultimately as decisive in shaping the trajectory of Catholic youth work for the postwar years as either this process of binding the youth more tightly to the church or the earlier waves of state persecution. The regime indeed stepped up its efforts at persecution, but the dislocations brought on by the war were even more deadly to Catholic institutions. Most of the Jungführer were drafted into the army, where a disproportionate number fell in battle.[66] The Nazi regime conscripted many young clerics and deliberately placed them in exposed positions on the front, where as intended, they became the victims of enemy fire. Even many young women were called into duty to distribute mail, clear rubble, or nurse wounded soldiers. Youth leaders could only shake their heads in frustration. Reports from the time depict the situation in near-catastrophic terms: "In the entire German region, conditions are such that there no longer exists the possibility for an ordered youth ministry, one which corresponds—even partially—to the task at hand."[67] Subsequent accounts depict an even bleaker situation. Again in 1944, "the conditions of the youth of the church, which we had to observe with so much concern in the past years, have become even more grave as a result of the developments of the preceding year."[68]

The loss of an entire cohort of youth leaders, lay and clerical, drove a giant wedge into youth work from which it never fully recovered. Those who would have been teenagers between 1941 and 1945 came of age without ever being exposed to the rudiments of a Catholic education. As one report put it, "Even the most simple forms of preaching the gospel to young men and women, who are coming of age, can hardly be fulfilled."[69] This development proved devastating to groups in many locations, since the approaches to youth work introduced by the youth movement depended on young people rising through the ranks to assume leadership positions and, in turn, recruit new members. Most parish groups in the archdiocese of Cologne, for instance, never again attained the membership figures of the 1930s, even long after the war had ended.[70] Some contemporaries estimated that roughly 20 percent of Catholic youth, at best, remained "organized" within parish groups.[71] In other locations, Catholic youth work simply ceased to exist.

The end of hostilities gave way not to the sobering reality that youth work lay in tatters but to a surprising mood of triumphalism. Many church leaders took great pride in the fact that the church had survived the trials of the "church struggle" with its institutions largely intact. Joseph Frings, the archbishop of Cologne who as chair of the Fulda Bishops' Conference soon became one of the most powerful figures within German Catholicism, openly declared, "The Catholic Church proved itself to be the strongest bulwark against National Socialism."[72] It is difficult to imagine that the top brass of the church perceived the end of the war as anything resembling a "ground zero." This notion would have implied that a dramatic break was about to take place with the past.[73] The bishops certainly envisioned nothing of the sort. The disruption of the war notwithstanding, their world was marked by continuity, not the radical change that characterized other German institutions at this time. There had been only a modest turnover in personnel at the highest levels of the episcopate; few clergymen on the local level had been dismissed for having collaborated with National Socialist institutions.[74]

Youth work bore out this pattern. The bishop charged with overseeing youth work for all dioceses, Albert Stohr of Mainz, urged Frings to put Wolker back at the helm. Wolker had remained involved in youth work even during the darkest days of persecution, when he had retreated to his home in upper Bavaria. He had founded a brotherhood called the Johannesbruderschaft to keep himself and others abreast of the latest developments in youth work. It was with little hesitation, then, that he accepted Frings's offer to run the national youth center at Altenberg, a historic cathedral with an adjacent monastery located in a narrow valley twenty-five miles east of Cologne.[75] With Wolker came Hermann Klens, a pious priest from the Catholic Sauerland who had been guiding the youth work for women ever since 1915.[76] Klens, about whom more will be said in Chapter 3, was entrusted with running the female youth center at Altenberg. One can safely say that "the men of the last hour were the men of the first hour."

The bishops urged Wolker and Klens to stay the course. This meant operating under the guidelines of 1936 and keeping youth work organized strictly along diocesan, deanery, and parish lines.[77] In a conference held in Werl in June 1945, the West German bishops insisted that it was necessary to retain and extend the template of Catholic Action they had adopted in the 1930s.[78] This meant keeping groups arranged in only two columns, one for boys and one for girls. Two months later the bishops stipulated that the Catholic youth, the body of all active young Catholics, was to be a well-ordered unity of male and female.[79] Wolker was well aware that these plans precluded old Verbände from reestablishing themselves, but he insisted that it was far more important to keep the parish— and not the Verbände—as the basis for Catholic unity. This position came to be known as the Pfarrprinzip, which invested a higher spiritual quality in structures centered around the individual parish.

The plans assembled by Wolker and the bishops placed the highest priority on retaining the unity of all Catholic youth, a development that they believed the guidelines of 1936 had brought about. The bishops clearly held on to their old fears of Vereinsmeierei: "We do not want various organizations and Bünde competing with each other, side by side. A loose amalgamation or alliance of organizations and Bünde that are fully independent is also not suitable."[80] Wolker, on the other hand, saw in the unity of Catholic youth the chance to realize his old dream of spreading the ideals of the youth movement to the farthest reaches of Germany. He turned once again to his grandiose conceptions from the 1930s: "And I will turn to the word, which once was coined in the youth movement and which received such a full, large and beautiful meaning in the lives of the youth of the church: the word of *Jugendreich* (youth kingdom)."[81] He proposed bringing all parish groups together to constitute a giant *Bund*—yet another echo of old visions.

Wolker undoubtedly issued these bold plans to challenge hostile representatives from the so-called old church. He was enraged by clerics who had openly flouted the charge placed on them in 1936 to lead youth to a "joyful life" within the church and instead had turned their groups into tired and sterile entities. "Never and nowhere may the Catholic youth be a kingdom of boredom," he thundered. "Boredom kills joy and life."[82] In a passage certain to raise the ire of Gröber, he decried the "clericalism" of the preceding years.[83] Some of his supporters described the purely religious youth work of the preceding years in even more blunt terms as an outright heresy. Wolker instead strove to lift all restrictions that had been placed on Catholic youth groups and to provide them with a breath of fresh air. Calling himself the "crier from Altenberg," he openly proclaimed his vision of the promised land to 5,000 youth gathered at the University of Cologne: "All portals of the joy of life must be opened to our young people. Forest and meadow, mountain and sea, they shall once again be ours. Nature and art, music and song, games and jest, the stage and dance, gymnastics and sport, the spinning room and the private garden, mirth and happiness, camaraderie and friendship—be joyful—all this shall be ours. Be joyful, everything is ours."[84]

These remarks betray Wolker's earnest, and ultimately naive, conviction that youth would continue to be receptive to the call of the youth movement as long as the proper structures—a *Bund*—were in place; or to put it somewhat differently, "If you build it, they will come." Wolker himself expected that a new generation of youth would arise to provide a renaissance for his youth kingdom, just as it had after the First World War, when returning soldiers revived the German youth movement from the turn of the century through martial and *bündisch* forms. Thus in 1945 he anticipated that returning soldiers and the younger generation would unite to rejuvenate the youth movement. In this vein, Wolker spoke of "two dynamics," one consisting of veterans of the Catholic youth movement from the 1930s and the other of boys under eighteen who were just coming of age. To quote the youth leader from Cologne, Klaus Koch, "Movement! An often named word! There must be movement for the stratum of Catholic youth between 18 and 25. . . . This generation will once again grab hold of the outdoors with fists, when it is freed from its paralysis."[85]

As one perceptive young observer pointed out, however, there were few signs that young Germans were mobilizing to carry on the traditions of the youth movement. Eighty-five percent of Catholic youth was not *bündisch*, the same youth worker pointed out.[86] Several small *bündisch* groups were indeed showing signs of revival throughout Germany. Arno Klönne has argued that the youth movement experienced a renaissance of sorts directly after the war, but one that was short lived and limited in scope.[87] These indications may have bolstered Wolker's hopes that young people were ready to revive the youth movement. It became increasingly clear, nonetheless, that the broad masses of German youth were hardly prepared to buy into Wolker's vision of a giant *Bund* in the tradition of the Catholic youth movement. The irony of the situation was not lost on some observers from the time. Adults from the generations of 1914 and 1933 were in the rather precarious position of trying to launch a new movement for the youth of 1945.[88]

This is but one indication of the difficulties Wolker was to encounter in trying to realize his vision of young Catholics arrayed by parish and diocese into a unified youth movement. Various forces and groups repeatedly stepped forward to assail the plans emerging from Altenberg. The ensuing struggles centered on questions of organizational form and reopened the by now familiar rifts between leaders of the old *Verbände*, representatives of the old church, and others. This new round of mudslinging would scarcely be distinguishable from that of the 1930s were it not for the fact that it raised for the first time the question of how the experiences of the recent past were to be understood. The memory of the past significantly altered the understanding of the present, and the exchanges over youth work were frequently read as a dialogue between past and present. Prominent Catholics directed their reflections toward that issue that, pragmatically enough, was foremost in their concerns after the war: the weaknesses that they perceived to be crippling religious institutions. Most leading Catholics harbored very real fears that their institutions lacked the muscle to hold their own against ideological foes on both the left and the right of the political spectrum. The triumphalist rhetoric of 1945 notwithstanding, Catholics concerned about Germany's political future were in reality haunted by the sudden and unexpected capitulation

The Catholic youth movement (Courtesy of
Diözesanarchiv Würzburg)

of the Center Party in 1933 and by the inability of Catholic institutions to
mount a united defense against the National Socialist colossus.

Even Catholics who honed in on the mistakes made in the fatal days of
1933 argued that their institutions had become weak because too many
believers had left the fold. These leaders thus molded their understanding of the past around the church's long antipathy toward liberalism and
materialism.[89] They argued that the moral impotence, spiritual flabbi-
ness, and political strife that were the hallmark of Weimar had driven
many Catholics from the church and left a collapse of some sort inevita-
ble. Secularization, of which sexual emancipation, political turmoil, and
atheistic socialism were but symptoms, was now identified as the culprit
behind the national misfortunes of the preceding two decades. Many
leaders ascribed the twelve years of National Socialism to divine retribu-
tion for secularization, just as the children of Israel were repeatedly pun-
ished for having turned their backs on the Lord.[90]

Many of these same Catholics in the postwar era saw in the upheaval the echoes of the violent last years of Weimar. The political scene was certainly troubled; many commentators have described the 1949 elections in the Federal Republic as the last Weimar election. At the same time, millions of young Western Germans seemed to be succumbing to lures of the black market, prostitution, and American soldiers. It is not at all surprising, then, that Catholic plans for action took on a renewed militancy; they were geared, above all, toward strengthening Catholic institutions and values against enemies real and imagined. The images and rhetoric used betray these deeper aspirations and apprehensions: the need for vitality, strength, and action (masculinity) and fears of decadence, weakness, and softness (femininity).

Seemingly arcane discussions of the proper organizational forms for youth work could not but assume deeper and more troubling meanings in light of these understandings of the past. Wolker's choice of a Bund to unite all Catholic youth into one fold was, in light of these considerations, not merely an echo of old dreams. It was intended to instill in all Catholic youth a united sense of identity and purpose—in short, to overcome the perennial problem of fragmentation within the Catholic milieu, which, he now argued, had prevented Catholics from joining ranks in the critical days of 1933. Had there been a single youth organization in 1933, and not a motley array of more than thirty separate Bünde, Verbände, and Kongregationen, youth leaders might have rebuffed the attacks by the Hitler Youth. As Willy Bokler, Wolker's successor as the leader of Catholic youth, put it in a speech from 1954, "And the mistakes lay in the fact that everything was side by side. The pennants were depended in front of one another, instead of swinging together in the great war against the one common enemy and for the one great goal, namely, the deliverance of German youth. And there a formulation was found which has since remained authoritative: unity of the youth ministers, unity of action, a united body under a united leadership. Whereby, however, leadership is—obviously—bound to the central leadership and not to the individual persons and the 'Lebensgemeinschaften.' "[91]

This position explains Wolker's scarcely veiled antipathy toward the associations that were on the verge of reestablishing themselves. Although he was proud of proclaiming, Einheit in der Vielfalt (unity through diversity—a slogan that would have granted the other associations a place within the ranks of Catholic youth), it is doubtful whether Wolker truly intended to live up to his own promises. "Not everything that once was, shall exist again," he warned those who might be considering reviving old organizations. "Not all groups still have a right to exist."[92]

But it was precisely these unwanted *Verbände* that rose from the ashes with unprecedented speed, much to the consternation of the leadership in Altenberg. At the same time, young people who had taken their groups underground now reappeared to swell the ranks of Kolping, Quickborn, and Bund Neudeutschland, with whom some of them had been loosely associated. All three groups doggedly resisted calls by Altenberg to dismantle their organizations and align themselves according to parish and diocese.[93] They brought with them an understanding of the past that differed substantially from that of Altenberg, based as it was on their unique experiences under the Nazis. The stage was set for years of acrimony, which frequently defied the best efforts of the church leadership at resolution.

One direction subsequent debates were to take was prefigured by none other than Guardini himself in a letter to Stohr. Guardini began to voice his concerns during the summer of 1945, even before his Quickborn groups had been able to reconstitute themselves.[94] He was of course concerned with the forthcoming plans for youth work that threatened to leave little or no room for smaller organizations like his. To Guardini the manner in which youth leaders intended to implement their directives was eerily reminiscent of the coercion of the Nazi regime:

> And it is perhaps not unnecessary to consider that the personalities working in the church remain products of their time. I want to say that the methods of force that were practiced for more than twelve years and that disregarded the problems, rights, and needs and that wanted to achieve everything through dictates and prohibitions, also could have rubbed off on us. I have heard pronouncements by spiritual leaders that distinguished themselves from those of National Socialists only by the fact that they took place in a religious environment and from religious offices. The warning of perspicacious men about the "National Socialism" in the church, this way of treating one's fellow human beings, seems not to be taken lightly.[95]

Guardini was one of the few prominent Catholics who described the tragedy of the preceding twelve years overwhelmingly in terms of the loss of individual freedom and dignity. He decried the overemphasis on subsuming the individual in larger collectives. Most other accounts by churchmen, in contrast, painted a picture of apostasy (how the Nazi doctrine of race—the "new heathendom"—had replaced Christian theology) or demonstrated outrage (the Nazi regime had dared to wage an all-out struggle for control over the church).[96] Some church accounts did bewail the loss of civil liberties generally but tended to focus on the encroachments on the churches' freedom of action. Guardini left the conclusion of his letter to Stohr unstated but unmistakably clear: every Catholic organization had the right to exist freely.

Other organizations were quick to employ this argument against the efforts of the bishops to circumscribe youth organizations into a program of Catholic Action. One small youth organization, Bund Neudeutschland, founded in 1919 for boys at the academic high school (*Gymnasien*), took the lead. Like other small *bündisch* groups, it registered a period of extraordinary growth directly after the Second World War and reached nearly 40,000 members, but many church leaders were none too happy with this growth.[97] In a set of plans from 1945, Frings ordered this group to dispense with its unique organizational system, which divided districts into *Gauen* and *Marken*, and to redraw its boundaries to conform to diocesan and deanery lines. He demanded that the group appoint one cleric per diocese to supervise local chapters, that person to be subject to the authority of the bishop.[98] The bishop of Trier refused to recognize Bund Neudeutschland's existence until 1946. Gröber, unsurprisingly, banned all groups from his archdiocese.[99] This association also ran into considerable opposition from clerics at the parish level who were none too happy to see this self-proclaimed elite drain the best and the brightest from "their" parish groups.[100]

In desperation, leaders of Bund Neudeutschland took their case to the supreme authority, Pope Pius XII, and urged him to support their cause. They received a laudatory, though nonetheless generic, letter in response, which they forwarded to Frings, who still refused to budge.[101] But Frings also could not afford to alienate an organization that had a trump card to play. A significant percentage of seminarians had emerged from the ranks of Neudeutschland and cited their experiences there as the inspiration behind their decision to take the priestly vows. Frings and Wolker hesitated to take severe action against this group and, in turn, cut a lifeline to the church's future. So the situation remained at a stalemate until 1947, interrupted only by verbal jabs from both sides. Supporters of

Neudeutschland were dismissed as "fanatical Jesuit boys"; they, in turn, labeled Altenberg "command headquarters."[102]

At first glance, it might seem that these petty but nonetheless doggedly waged skirmishes were a peculiarity of the Catholic milieu in Germany. Yet not only Catholic institutions had to wrestle with the questions of how to position and guide their organizations in a changed postwar era. Socialist organizations were confronted equally with the dilemma of whether ideology (Marxist dogma) or more pragmatic concerns were to dictate the direction of the organizations within their milieu. Socialist youth organizations, like their Catholic counterparts, appeared sui generis after the war. One report likened their reappearance to "mushrooms that sprout up after a fresh rain."[103] As was the case with the Catholics, in 1945 many of the leaders of the Red Falcons, as the Socialist youth were called, were far older than the organization's members. Many leaders had been youth themselves in 1933 and had taken their groups underground after the Nazi seizure of power. After the war, these leaders were forced to determine how to align their organizations: should they return to the pre-1933 pattern of conflict with their Catholic rivals, or should they bury the hatchet and cooperate with non-Socialist organizations, at least to a limited extent?[104] This was nothing less than the old question of whether to leave the Socialist ghetto. These considerations were complicated by the founding of the Freie Deutsche Jugend (FDJ), a communist-led youth organization strongest in the Soviet zone of occupation. Membership was essentially compulsory, but the organization had also taken root within the western zones and found some support from young workers in old Communist strongholds.[105]

The Catholic leaders within youth work sounded the alarm instead over the emergence of both the Red Falcons and the FDJ.[106] They were especially concerned with altercations—usually taunting and name-calling, but occasionally full-fledged brawls—that had broken out between young persons from the Socialist and Catholic camps. Many Catholic groups were ordered by their pastors to keep a safe distance from the subversive radicalism of young workers. Fears that a workers' revolution was brewing became so great among the bishops that they broke with their doctrine of keeping the number of Verbände limited and drew up plans to form a special organization for young German workers, the CAJ.

As fearful as the bishops were of the Communist peril, they argued that the degenerate moral climate of the postwar years placed German youth equally at risk. They maintained that Nazism had left a moral vacuum in its wake—a miasma of skepticism, apathy, and despair that had hit youth the hardest. Wolker described this mood in a letter to Frings: "The worst result of the National Socialist system (but also of the current propaganda in the world), was that it made the German people, including the youth, dishonorable."[107] Embittering were not just the experiences of total war and absolute defeat, but the palpable sense of betrayal—that twelve years of indoctrination into an ideology of race, national glory, and authority of the state had just been revealed as a web of lies.[108] Wolker concluded that young people had lost the capacity to believe and to trust, not just in the proclamations of politicians, but more ominously, in all institutions and authorities. Wolker's observations were indeed born out by many of his contemporaries. Sociologist Helmut Schelsky called national attention to a new "skeptical generation" and described in great detail the unwillingness of the young to give their loyalty to larger collectives.[109]

Stohr claimed that this new, invidious spirit was best observed in roving gangs of youth that often went by the name Edelweiss Pirates. These cliques of so-called wild youth typically consisted of seven to fifteen young men and women who bore Edelweiss insignia on their breasts. They had existed since the early 1940s and had been bitterly persecuted by the Nazis, in part because they took great pleasure in assaulting vulnerable groups of Hitler Youth.[110] Albert Stohr described them as dangerous agents of emancipation, probably because they included teenagers of both sexes. "They extend not just among working youth, but also among students and they have a surprisingly destructive conduct in sexual relations, and they aggressively mock us."[111] As this statement suggests, Stohr was quick to combine ominous symbols of chaos with traditional fears of sexual emancipation. Changing gender norms, he argued, threatened to upset the very balance of society. Reconstructing German society meant restoring the nuclear family to its rightful place, "since the family is the cornerstone of our people (Volksfamilie) and without it the main support for reconstruction is absent."[112]

It might seem, then, that the bishops were painting two contradictory portraits of German youth. On one hand, young people were nihilistic, prone to sexual libertinism, individualistic, and suspicious of all authority —"Everything is a fraud."[113] On the other hand, they were lending their support to Socialism and Communism, a de facto submission to authority and higher ideals. This apparent contradiction, however, made sense as part of what amounted to a full-fledged theory of history, which many Catholic intellectuals shared. Stohr provided an excellent summation of this theory in a pastoral letter from October 1945. Ever since the Enlightenment, he argued, liberalism and individualism had defined European thought and behavior. Liberalism, by its very nature, sought to free the individual from larger collectives, such as religious institutions and the domination of the nobility: "The individual is everything, the community is nothing." He argued that this one-sided emphasis on the rights of the individual generated its own antithesis in the form of an exaggerated ideology of collectivism: "The collective is everything, the individual is nothing." Both dogmas had created false gods and were equally destructive of religious authority. "According to the first way of error, the individual is deified and even the most appropriate ties to human society are denied. According to the second way of error, it is the other way around: the free, independent personality is so absorbed, that almost nothing is left of it."[114] Stohr described the history of the preceding two centuries as a moving back and forth between these two extremes. Weimar represented the apotheosis of individualism; Soviet Russia and Nazi Germany, the deification of collectivism. The Edelweiss Pirates embodied nihilism; the FDJ, collective totalitarianism.

Many leading Catholics began, as a result, to search for a so-called third way between these two extremes of unbridled individualism and untrammeled collectivism. They sought new systems of authority that would bind German citizens to larger collective structures—the church and the state—while still guaranteeing them a degree of individual freedom. These quasi-philosophical discussions naturally found their way into youth work. Youth leaders, too, were driven by the conviction that structures for their work needed to properly balance freedom and authority. Josef Rommerskirchen, who was elected lay leader of the BDKJ in 1947, articulated the views of most of his colleagues when he exclaimed that untrammeled freedom could only lead to chaos—a none-too-subtle reminder of the fate of Weimar.[115] Wolker's proposed Bund promised to place the proper line between freedom and authority in the institution of the church: "The church is a kingdom of freedom, but one which is ordered. It is anchored in this holy order. . . . Ordering means fitting in and subordination (Einordnung und Unterordnung)."[116] According to Wolker, freedom was to be found through submission to authority.

In light of the competing pressures coming from the bishops, the old *Verbände* and *Bünde*, and the youth leadership at Altenberg, a final decision on how to "organize" Catholic youth had to be postponed until early 1947. All of these parties convened in March in the Cistercian monastery, Hardehausen, to resolve this question once and for all. It was Wolker who finally provided the delegates at Hardehausen with the architecture that finally won acceptance. After two days of little progress, Wolker abruptly withdrew from conference proceedings and reappeared hours later with a blueprint for the BDKJ.[117] This plan offered concessions to all sides. The bishops were pleased by the fact that the parish groups were to be kept intact and that the diocesan youth offices were to retain their hold on local groups. Only on the highest administrative level were these groups to be brought together in the form of two large columns (*Stämme*). One of these pillars, the *Mannessäule*, was to be for male youth; the other, the *Frauensäule*, for young women. Wolker envisioned these two columns as the foundation of the *Bund*. They were to unify Catholic youth and provide young people with a common ideology and sense of purpose. The assortment of independent *Bünde* and *Verbände* were to be placed adjacent to these pillars, as appendages (*Gliederungen*). These groups were to retain their own administrative apparatuses but were expected to participate as full-fledged members within the *Bund*. Wolker clearly intended that the BDKJ would be more than an umbrella organization that did little more than hold otherwise independent organizations loosely together (*ein Dachverband*). He anticipated that young people would develop a lasting allegiance to this organization (hence his choice of the word *Bund*). His brainchild—a giant Catholic youth kingdom on earth—was to be endowed with its own ceremonies, uniforms, oaths, medals, pledge words, guardian angels, and patron saints.

The sheer force of Wolker's personality helps explain why this plan won the day. For the younger members present, he assumed an almost legendary presence; he had endured several arrests and interrogations by the Gestapo but had never given up hope for the future of Catholic youth. The proceedings from the conference also make it clear that there were no viable alternatives. Father Johannes Hirschmann, a Jesuit priest associated with Bund Neudeutschland, called for the right of all organizations to coexist freely. But this plan was not entertained seriously by the majority of the delegates.[118] Wolker's plans also paid lip service to Catholic

Action; the two *Stämme* sufficiently resembled the two main columns of Catholic Action to appease some potential critics.

Wolker's plan, as shaky as it might have been, resonated with the delegates at a far deeper level. It resolved the difficulty with which Catholics had wrestled for years over how to position themselves within the modern world. Wolker's solution attempted to place Catholic institutions at the forefront of power and influence. "Break open the ghetto," he cried, spurring his fellow travelers to action; "advance into the ranks of the German people."[119] Observers noted that one of his arguments proved most convincing to delegates: the strength of Catholic youth lay in numbers. "If we all stand together, then we are 750,000, the largest youth organization that exists in Germany."[120] The haste with which the male and female youth organizations were joined together undoubtedly stemmed from his desire to provide a public show of strength. Disunity was taken as weakness, an inauspicious reminder of the fragmentation of the 1920s.

Wolker and Rommerskirchen were already involved in serious discussions with non-Catholic youth leaders from throughout Germany, including Erich Lindstädt (the leader of the Red Falcons), Erich Honecker (the head of the FDJ), and representatives from the Protestant youth organizations.[121] They hoped to create an umbrella organization for all German youth organizations (*Bundesjugendring*). A similar organization had existed during the Weimar Republic; its mission had consisted largely of distributing largesse from the national state to its members. Wolker and Rommerskirchen hoped that the *Bundesjugendring* would play a more extensive role and, indeed, chart the larger course for all German youth organizations. It was a significant triumph for Catholic youth leaders when they succeeded in ejecting the FDJ from the *Bundesjugendring*. Wolker reasoned that the *Bund* would be operating in a polarized and contentious political and cultural climate not unlike that of the 1920s and 1930s. It was thus necessary to go "into the world" to defend one's own interests—the same cry from the 1920s and 1930s to "win influence" in secular society.

On the other hand, Wolker's plan allowed individual youth leaders the option of keeping the boys and girls under their charge cut off from the outside world almost entirely. The *Pfarrjugend*, based on the so-called *Pfarrprinzip*, was in many ways a reflection of the notion of the *Heimat*, a theme that dominated discussions of postwar German society. Those who emphasized this motif hoped that German youth, after years of upheaval, would rediscover the healing power of the familiar—of home and hearth. Wolker's proposals appeased many conservatives by promising to keep youth untainted from corrupt influences, such as prostitution and licentious films, that they might encounter in the world.[122] Wolker's plans, in short, offered the best of both worlds: interconfessionalism at the highest echelons of youth work and a strict sectarianism at the local level.[123]

Catholic youth work subsequently took on a new mission for the postwar era. Many Catholic leaders, Wolker not the least, equated building the BDKJ with reconstructing postwar German society. Wolker saw his task in Manichean, even apocalyptic terms. He evoked images of light and darkness, of the struggle between Christians and Satan, of despair and hope. "Everything is at stake, the existence or non-existence of our people—one could almost say, all of humanity." In this context, he saw the Bund as a source of light (symbolized in the torches, the hikes by candlelight, and the candles within chapels) that would counter the overwhelming darkness in German society (many homes lacked power and heat). These utterances should not be dismissed as inflated rhetoric, for Catholic leaders sincerely hoped to rebuild German society with Christian values and traditions. Just as they attributed the hardships of the preceding decades to the curse of secularization, so, too, did they argue that re-Christianizing German society would place it back on the proper path. They had to instill the Catholic values of the Christian West into the hearts and souls of all Germans. The commitment to the Pfarrjugend, which formed the cornerstone of the Bund, may have represented nothing less than the resolve to rebuild Germany from the parish upward and to place the parish at the center of village and city life. Rebuilding the Catholic youth—and the Bund in particular—was a precondition for the "rebirth of the soul of the German people."[124] Through the interconfessional work of Catholic leaders, Catholic values could be transmitted to all organized German youth.

There was one more significant reason why Wolker's plan was so readily adopted, an explanation that is not directly addressed in any document. The continued opposition from a handful of clerics, bishops, and youth leaders to the liturgical and youth movements not only added numerous obstacles but achieved the opposite of what they set out to accomplish: they convinced Wolker of the righteousness of his path and strengthened his own resolve to bring his plans to fruition. At least four bishops had gone so far as to prohibit Wolker from making public appearances within their dioceses; in some of these regions the youth movement had made little or no headway.[125] Their opposition was not strong enough to derail Wolker's efforts altogether but was significant enough to blind him to alternatives.

By 1948, then, Catholic youth work in the western zones of Germany had taken on a distinctive character. The BDKJ served as the official association for all "organized" Catholic youth. Under its wings flourished more than a dozen smaller youth organizations—Neudeutschland, Quickborn, Kolping, the CAJ, Marian congregations, the Pfadfinder, Die Schar, and Heliand (to name but a few). Each organization emerged with a mission shaped both by traditions that had existed prior to 1933 and by the manner in which it made sense of the experiences of the intervening twelve to fifteen years. The traditions and ideals of the youth movement continued to hold sway in some of these organizations, including Bund Neudeutschland, the Pfadfinder, and many parish groups.

It became quickly apparent that Wolker's brainchild, the BDKJ, would have difficulty realizing the vast hopes that had been invested in it. On paper, it was a mass organization with more than 1 million members by 1954. Over time, however, it evolved into that which Wolker had sought to avoid: a mere amalgamation of individual Verbände with little remaining of the élan of the youth movement or a unified Catholic consciousness. Wolker was never able to resolve many pressing administrative and organizational questions. Representatives from the individual Verbände almost immediately set out to reduce their dependence on the central administration in Altenberg and to increase their share of power within the BDKJ.[126] Wolker's quest to bring unity to Catholic youth was ultimately an attempt to gainsay a fundamental truth: that the Catholic milieu was, in fact, heterogeneous, divided along the lines of region, class, and gender. This is not the place to provide an official organizational history of the BDKJ.[127] Subsequent chapters will, instead, examine the response of youth to the concrete initiatives and broader religious and cultural visions that defined Roman Catholic youth work in the era after the Second World War.

TWO

Where the Boys

Are: Catholic Youth

Groups and the

Competition of Mass

Entertainment and

Modern Culture

UNTIL THE LATE 1950s, much of the Catholic youth work for boys was anchored in the traditions of the youth movement. As such, it conjures up idyllic images of summer camp: tents in the woods, banners, pennants, campfire, hikes, songs, devotions, ghost stories, and groups of young boys wearing white shirts and short pants. At the same time, it evokes the spirit of organization: mass rallies, lectures, uniforms, oratory, weekly meetings, and in rare cases, marching.[1]

As early as the late 1940s, however, youth leaders began to recognize that these approaches to youth work from the 1920s and 1930s no longer commanded the same power to move and inspire young people as they had in the past, save in remote villages where the movement was just taking root. New options for entertainment and relaxation—sporting organizations, dance halls, clubs, cinema, automobiles, and vacations abroad—undercut the privileged role of the church and meant that Catholic youth groups lost their monopoly on entertainment and recreation.

Faced with a seemingly unbeatable foe, many youth leaders resorted to the tried and true strategy of appropriating modern means to fight the modern world. In a number of venues, priests and lay leaders attempted to countenance in their groups a more modern idiom, such as film, dance, music, or relaxation. By the late 1950s, Catholic youth leaders had adopted and in some small villages pioneered new initiatives: the club-house model (Häuser der offenen Tür), discussions, and even fashion shows and rock 'n' roll and dance parties, approaches that had been formerly despised as part of mass culture and some of which American occupation authorities had championed. Young Catholics, they insisted, had to be both Catholic and modern.

Yet the efforts to clothe the youth movement of the 1920s and 1930s in a more modern garb fell short of expectations. In this chapter I examine why it proved so difficult to reconcile the ideals of the Catholic youth movement to an individualistic culture of consumption. I begin by analyzing the educational and pedagogical goals of Catholic youth work after 1945. I then provide an account of the activities of Catholic youth groups —how the young men and women spent their time, and how the groups functioned and the conflicts they encountered. I subsequently examine why the old forms of the youth movement sputtered by the 1950s and how Catholic youth work took on an individualistic flavor that its leaders had hitherto rejected, particularly in the realms of film, dance, and music.

THE RETURN TO THE
CATHOLIC YOUTH MOVEMENT

Until the early 1960s, Catholic youth work was decisively shaped by the traditions of the Catholic youth movement from the 1920s and 1930s. The romantic notion of a youth kingdom—Jugendreich—continued to dominate the thought of top leaders. To quote from a 1946 speech Wolker delivered to 5,000 young men in Cologne: "I look before me to the day which is given to you, to the day which will come to you and proclaim to you the kingdom of the Catholic youth, your kingdom of youth, as a kingdom of freedom and truth, a kingdom of life and hope."[2]

To cement the loyalty of young persons, Wolker turned back to the symbols of the youth movement. Members were outfitted with special uniforms: bright green shirts and short pants for the boys, white dresses for the girls. Some groups presented their members with an official identification card, which listed age, parish, and the date of induction into the group. All young men were required to swear an oath of loyalty publicly on the day of their induction. This ceremony usually took place in spring and was accompanied by widespread festivities that included banquets, flowers, and a special mass.[3] Like the Boy Scouts, members who performed outstanding service to the Bund were awarded a badge of honor, the most distinguished in gold and silver.

Youth leaders also imposed yearly dues, an annual offering (Opfer) of 1 mark. The top leadership at Altenberg took this step not just to instill a sense of sacrifice within young men and women but also to defray the cost of publishing more than a dozen youth magazines at a time of fiscal emergency.[4] By the early 1950s, every member automatically received the newspaper appropriate to his or her age group and sex. Two magazines, Der Jungführer and Die Jungführerin, gave leaders guidance in planning activities for their groups and provided a forum to discuss difficulties that they were likely to encounter. Some of these magazines were holdovers from the 1930s, as their titles—Michael and Die Wacht [The watch]—suggest.

The youth center in Altenberg (moved to Düsseldorf in 1954) also sponsored national festivals. The largest of these took place in Dortmund in 1954, a mass spectacle involving nearly 100,000 young men and women.[5] This gathering carefully followed prescribed rituals. It began with a procession through the center of this industrial center in the Ruhr in which individual Catholic organizations—Kolping, the CAJ, Bund Neudeutschland, and diocesan groups from Swabia, Lower Franconia, and Münster—proudly carried their pennants and banners (most of which were twice as large as the boys). The gathering subsequently featured orchestral music, a cabaret, and a sport festival held in a nearby stadium. These were followed by a series of grandiloquent speeches by church leaders, who proclaimed the platform of the BDKJ—its goals, politics, and mission to the German nation. The gathering culminated in an open-air mass led by the bishops in the central square of Dortmund. Such festivals obviously sought to instill in their participants an enraptured sense of belonging to a greater whole. But they were also a demonstrative show of strength in the public arena, an attempt to intimidate the ideological opponents of the Bund. In one incident, "ambassadors" from the FDJ took the podium to extend greetings from the Soviet zone and were promptly escorted out of the pavilion by Catholic guards. These festivals were a continuation of the rituals of the early 1930s, of the militance of organized youth groups in the last years of Weimar.

The leaders at Altenberg ultimately aimed to influence the behavior and conduct of young people in all of the domains of life—the workplace, friendships, and group life—at this impressionable and formative stage.

They claimed the entire human being—thought, free time, values, aspirations, and maturation—to prepare youth for the rigors of family life and career.[6] This was the theme of mastery of the challenges of life. As leaders were quick to point out after 1945, they did so not through compulsory brainwashing, as they argued was the case in the FDJ and the Hitler Youth, but through gentle encouragement, mild social pressure, and an array of joyful activities.

To do this, the leaders cast group life at the center of their youth work, for they hoped that the group would wield authority over the lives of its members. They envisioned a vast network of individual youth groups, each with its own duly anointed leader under the guidance of the local curate or pastor. These groups were to be organized solely along parish, deanery, and diocesan lines. Occasionally, all of the groups within a deanery or diocese would convene for a joint celebration of the mass. To help the groups, most dioceses retained the administrative apparatuses they had established in the late 1930s—the youth ministry centers—as part of the response to the restrictions imposed by the National Socialist state in the 1930s. These centers periodically sponsored seminars and schools to train youth leaders and printed newsletters and magazines that complemented the publications of the national center in Altenberg.[7]

Within each parish, youth work was broken down according to the age and sex of the participants. For the boys and young men, the Jungschar (young host) united the 10- to 14-year-olds; the Jungenschaft, 14- to 18-year-olds; and the Junge Mannschaft, 18- to 25-year-olds. A similar pattern existed for the girls and young women. The Frohschar (happy host) brought together the 10- to 14-year-olds; the Mädchenjugend, 14- to 18-year-olds; and the Frauenjugend, 18- to 28-year-olds. Many parishes, as a result, often had as many as six to ten or twelve, in the case of large urban parishes, youth groups. Although the groups of 10- to 14-year-olds had far more members, they were given less weight than the groups for the older boys and young men. In the eyes of top leaders, the younger groups were stepping-stones, formative units for the other two organizations that were considered to be the foundation of the Bund, the site where the "real" process of rearing full-blooded and true-blue Catholic men was to take place.[8] For Wolker, youth work was about forming strong men. This was a holdover from the 1920s ideal of the Männerbund, the comrades and the sense of togetherness that originated in the trenches of the First World War.[9] Not everyone shared his opinion; the women's work found forceful advocates among both laity and clergy. (See Chapter 3.) But the *Bund* nonetheless succeeded in its early years in portraying itself to the public as a masculine organization of strength, vitality, and virility.

How did youth groups function at the grass roots, and did they live up to the high expectations that Wolker and others had invested in them? Some groups held on to the old adage "Youth leads youth." There the young men and women themselves—not the clergy—chose their leader, generally that person who was most charismatic and most active in the group. It was more common, however, for the clergy to appoint leaders for the younger groups.[10] For the boys aged 10 to 14, they often chose an older boy from the *Jungenschaft*. This was typically one of the more engaged and committed members, one whom they also felt would have a good rapport with the younger boys.

The activities that the clergy and leaders planned for their young people were designed to instill a sense of group allegiance. One evening per week, members gathered to play games, carry on discussions, and socialize. These meetings (*Heimabende*) generally followed set formulas.[11] The groups convened at 7:30 P.M. in a room in the parish hall or within the church's own youth center. The curate opened the meeting with a prayer, after which the youth leader led the group in song. As a rule, the boys and girls used accordions or guitars; the youth movement gave a high status to these instruments, as it associated them with folk music and the authentic voice of the German people. The group subsequently turned to administrative and organizational matters, such as ordering newspapers and planning upcoming activities. When all of these concerns had been addressed, the leader moved on to the most important and weighty part of the evening: the group discussion. The leader generally tried to choose topics relevant to the lives of the participants—the opposite sex, school, and problems at work—but the topics were often as far ranging as politics, the missionary work of the church, or issues of theology. On some occasions the pastor or a representative from the diocese gave a full lecture. The group leader also might tell stories to the younger children. Once the topic of discussion was exhausted, the fun and banter began. The younger children might engage in raucous games of hide-and-seek; the older ones might play charades or even create their own games. The group leader or priest was finally called upon to conclude the evening with a song and prayer.

Parish groups often joined neighboring organizations in their diocese in building massive tent villages that could house hundreds. These were ambitious undertakings that required the logistical and financial support of many men and women. A priest was on hand for the duration of the trip; women provided and served the standard bread, coffee, pea soup, and sausage. A 1955 account of a diocesan youth festival in Cologne provides glimpses into how these retreats functioned.[12] Like most of these gatherings, this retreat took place in mid-June to coincide with Pentecost. On Thursday night more than 250 boys between the ages of fourteen and eighteen traveled by train and bicycle to the shores of a lake in a rugged corner of the Eifel, the mountainous southwest corner of the Rhineland. At 8:00 the next morning the boys, some of whom had arrived after 1:30 A.M., were awakened to celebrate the mass. This mass was followed by a round of singing and an address by the diocesan youth leader, who spoke of the great decisions that awaited the boys in the coming years—decisions about marriage, about whether to enter the priesthood or an order, and about whether to succumb to the lures and temptations of mass society. After lunch the boys played an old favorite, capture the flag. On Saturday they were treated to a motorboat ride across the lake and were given a talk by a local forest ranger, who proclaimed the wonderful works of creation of God in nature. During the evening the boys screened an adventure film that also dwelled on religious themes. On Sunday, finally, they were divided into small groups to discuss issues with which they were confronted on a regular basis: relationships, alcohol, nicotine, girls, and films. The retreat concluded with groups of young boys putting on a vaudeville show. With a prayer of thanksgiving, the chaplain finally pronounced his blessing upon the group, and the boys went home.

Far more important than these major retreats and annual Pentecost tent camps was the degree to which the boys and girls within a group were able to bond with one another during the often tumultuous years of adolescence. When the group jelled, the ties often lasted for life, as the example of an organization from the old inner city of Cologne illustrates.[13] In 1960 this group from the parish of St. Severus commemorated its ten-year jubilee, a rare feat for Catholic groups, which usually existed only for several years. For this celebratory occasion the leader compiled a chronicle that detailed his experiences leading the group for more than a decade.

In 1950 the curate of St. Severus appointed a slightly older boy, Lam-

Members of Die Schar, a small organization in the
tradition of the youth movement located predominantly
in the archdiocese of Paderborn, on the way to their
Pentecost gathering. Note the banners and uniforms.
(Courtesy of Jugendhaus Hardehausen)

bert Sombert, to lead a group of ten- to eleven-year old boys. Lambert had
only recently graduated from the *Jungschar*. As he described it, there was
no group to start with, just a ragtag assortment of practical jokers, imps,
and dirty and disheveled lads from the inner city. His initial attempts to
run the group proved disastrous. For the evening socials he relied on
lesson plans and topics for discussion that had been presented to him at
one of the seminars for youth leaders, then run at Altenberg. He immediately discovered that these approaches fell flat. Desperate for anything
that worked, he indulged his charges instead with raucous games and
"uproarious songs" rather than discussions, lectures, and religious worship. What sustained him during these difficult early years, he admitted,
was the unusually strong support of his chaplain, who frequently took
him aside to bolster his confidence.

The tide turned when the boys undertook their first camping trip into the countryside. On one trip over Pentecost in the Bergisches Land, the boys ate so much that Lambert had to dip into his own pockets and even take out a small loan at a local bank to pay for the trip back home. Shortly thereafter the boys took for themselves the name St. Michael, in honor of the patron saint of Germany. At this point Lambert began to engage the boys in one-on-one conversations. Many of the parents were wary of him and wanted to know about the misdeeds of their boys but came to see in him a comrade and fellow counselor who was bringing about something positive in the lives of their boys. By the same token, the boys overcame their initial skepticism and distrust of Lambert and regarded him as a confidant and friend to whom they could reveal their innermost secrets.

Lambert described the early teenage years as those of the greatest difficulty. As the boys finished school at fourteen and entered the work world or academic high schools and discovered girls, some left the group, never to return. "It was difficult for a group of boys in a large city with all of its attractions, temptations to remain decent and clean." At this point the group undertook its most ambitious adventures: rambles through the Eifel, a bicycle tour along the entire length of the Moselle River, and a hike through the Black Forest from Freiburg to Lake Constance. In his chronicle Lambert sweetly reminisced about the powerful emotions during these lengthy sojourns. He recounted taking still rambles at night under the rain or in the moonlight, spending jovial evenings in youth hostels, keeping watch in front of the tents on a starry night, and celebrating Holy Communion outdoors in the wee hours of the morning. With justified pride he concluded, "So we have grown together to be a sworn community, which also will have a future for every individual. Today, boys have become men, who will carry on their professions, who will stand in the middle of life and have mastered it."

St. Michael provides an example of how a Catholic group could succeed in achieving its goals: ushering young boys, step-by-step, into manhood and developing in them a "full Catholic personality" through encounters with nature, social events, deep discussion, and conviviality. Yet as the editor of the newsletter in which this chronicle appeared admitted, St. Michael was a rarity among Catholic groups. Even in the best of times, the number and membership of groups for young men between fourteen and eighteen and, above all, between eighteen and twenty-five, were relatively small. As men and women began adolescence and entered the

The cover of a group digest put together by high school boys
from Bund Neudeutschland to recount their achievements. Their
attempt to reconcile tradition and modernity is depicted in the
contrast between the city of Cologne, characterized by a
mixture of modern skyscrapers and churches, and
the tent camp near the lake. (Courtesy of
Bund Neudeutschland)

workplace, many fell by the wayside and, as we shall see, developed
interests and passions elsewhere. Others married, at which point their
interest in single-sex youth work usually ceased.

These problems were in no way endemic exclusively to Catholic organizations. Within most German youth groups, members increasingly
dropped out as they grew older. In the mid-1950s, officials from the
national ring of German youth organizations, which included Protestant,

bündisch, and Socialist organizations, reported that no more than 30 percent of the German youth had been organized.[14] In spite of their differing ideologies, these leaders agreed that the broad masses of unorganized youth posed a clear and present danger to German society. They believed that young men and women needed a firm moral underpinning, which only an organization could provide. They were appalled by the youth riots that had broken out in many large cities in the mid-1950s, evidence in their eyes of the spreading nihilism and juvenile delinquency.

Some of the difficulties that Catholic youth groups encountered after 1945 were those of youth groups of any time and age. Youth work rarely flourished when too many adults were present. Groups thrived, instead, when young persons had greater freedom and autonomy and when charismatic leaders magnetized younger boys and girls. Other groups suffered from poor or nonexistent leadership. In many smaller rural parishes, for instance, there were simply too few young men or women to take charge of groups.[15] When a boy between the ages of fourteen and eighteen was put in charge of a group of ten- to fourteen-year-olds, the older boys lost their most committed and engaged member, who likely would have served as their leader. Youth leaders who had to work or to study for exams often had little time to devote to their groups. Groups often ran into difficulties when their leaders fell in love.[16] Catholic groups were, by definition, exclusively for boys or girls, and frequently the remaining boys felt betrayed when their leaders suddenly began to spend their time and energy elsewhere. Once-dynamic groups often fell apart when a gifted and charismatic leader stepped down and was replaced by one less skilled or more reserved; on the other hand, inspiring leaders often succeeded in rejuvenating long-dormant groups. The most common problem was the lack of training for youth leaders. To redress this situation, most dioceses began to sponsor seminars and workshops to better equip their young leaders.[17] But even these events were often far removed from the day-to-day realities of individual groups. Much of the instruction was written at a highly intellectual and abstract level by older clergy or youth leaders and offered few concrete suggestions for how to run groups.[18]

In addition, the degree of support given or withheld by the clergy could make or break groups.[19] Enthusiastic young chaplains and curates galvanized the young men and women; curmudgeons likewise could easily send young persons running. In one parish in Lower Franconia, three young curates donned hats, false noses, neckties, makeup, and striped shirts for Carnival and masqueraded as clowns before their young audience—and were greeted by wild enthusiasm.[20] Another curate in the Rhineland sacrificed most of his salary during the month of the currency reform to help finance a tent camp for his youth group.[21] The deanery leadership for the region of Hassfurt in Lower Franconia reported that the arrival of a new priest in the parish of Gädheim caused the youth group to break up.[22] The previous priest had enthusiastically supported the youth and had made enemies of many of the adults in the parish. In contrast, the new priest embraced the adults and alienated the youth. In another instance within the archdiocese of Paderborn, church officials ordered the removal of a showcase that the youth group had spent months building.[23] The local curate, who had supported his young parishioners throughout, was eventually transferred to another parish. In response the youth groups held a mock burial for their beloved showcase. For young persons, the priest was both an authority figure and a friend, a predicament that not all groups were able to resolve. Some young men complained that their priests behaved like civil servants: they were authoritarian and distant and refused to allow others to enter their domain of authority. Many priests responded that it was impossible for them to be "everything to everybody." Ideally, the priest was to be the ultimate authority on life, one who "could give answers to the very last questions."[24]

The most difficult conflicts between clerics and youth groups involved clergy who viewed dynamic groups as a threat to their authority. Some priests were strong believers in Catholic Action and insisted that it was their duty to maintain control of youth work. For them, the adage "Youth leads youth" was pure heresy. One pastor from Zell am Main, a parish near Würzburg, was outraged that his youth groups were shirking their responsibilities toward adult parish life and indulging instead in tomfoolery.[25] He blamed the collapse of the church choir on the refusal of young persons to participate. In a thinly veiled reference to the Hitler Youth, he exclaimed, "The sentence, youth leads youth, has shown itself to be untenable. Youth needs the guidance of adults. Today's youth may especially need to be subordinated to church authority and its own process of education." In the parish of Wörth (in the diocese of Würzburg) the curate denounced the youth leader as a rascal unfit to be a member of the Catholic youth, let alone a youth leader. In a show of his own command, he refused to recognize the authority of this boy and vowed to lead the two parish groups himself.[26] These cases were, of course, exceptional.

They required the intervention of outsiders (usually from the diocesan youth centers) but nonetheless underscore some of the difficulties that groups encountered. In contrast, priests who had participated in the Catholic youth movement in the 1920s and the 1930s often treated young men and women far more sympathetically.

In many locales the more serious problem was not the bullheadedness of clergy but the absence of clergy from youth work altogether. In one parish in the archdiocese of Cologne, a forty-five-year-old curate refused to lead youth work because he deemed himself too old.[27] In many smaller parishes only one priest was available to manage all of the daily masses, women's groups, men's groups, marriages, and funerals. In larger parishes curates were required to spend more than thirty hours per week providing religious instruction within the schools, in addition to their normal obligations. In some large parishes that had a myriad of *Vereine* and *Verbände*, curates were expected to tend to as many as twelve youth groups. As a result, it was often extremely difficult, if not impossible, for them to provide the necessary degree of guidance. Under these conditions, clergy who were committed to helping their groups were forced to toil day and night or to turn the lion's share of work over to the boys and girls themselves.[28] The quality of Catholic youth work, as a result, varied widely from parish to parish and village to village.

The more serious challenges, however, stemmed from the fact that many Catholic youth groups had drawn too heavily from the *bündisch* forms and antibourgeois spirit of the German youth movement between 1900 and 1933. Already in the late 1940s, officials from the American military government foresaw difficulties ahead for the Catholic youth groups as a result. Some officials were especially perturbed by the spread of *bündisch* forms, such as banners, flags, uniforms, and marching, which they associated with the militarism of the Hitler Youth. In their determination to stamp out the spirit of militarism, they outlawed in several instances the banners and pennants that Catholic groups planned to use.[29] The Americans, in particular, recoiled from the language used by the Catholic groups, especially terms such as *Jungführer*. In their eyes this word was irrevocably tainted. Not only had it been appropriated by the Hitler Youth, but it could not but remind them of the former dictator. This critique was shared not solely by the Americans and their British allies. Many Catholic laity and clergy expressed grave concerns that the Catholic youth had come to resemble the Hitler Youth.[30] Others complained that new uniforms would merely renew the ideological and political conflicts of the early 1930s.[31] Faced with mounting criticism, the leadership in Altenberg maintained that the Hitler Youth had brazenly misappropriated the heritage of the German and Catholic youth movements, and not the other way around. "National Socialism, in order to bend the thinking and way of the German population around to its own way of thinking, misused the German language in an outrageous manner. The words *Jungführertum* and *Jungführer* are property of the Catholic youth and have been used for two decades under the recognition of the church."[32]

In defending the new uniforms for younger boys, youth leaders sought to distinguish between uniforms that were used for military purposes and those that symbolized an idea or a way of life.[33] They claimed that the military uniform was intended for camouflage and for carrying munitions. The Catholic uniforms, in contrast, were an outward manifestation of inner values, just as the white collars and black shirts of priests helped shape identity and a sense of group belonging. In an argument that would become widespread by the 1950s, advocates claimed that the uniform would prevent boys from yielding to the lures of mass society: "The uniform is a protection for boys. With a uniform, it is more difficult to stand before a kiosk, to go to a dubious film, to smoke or to cheat in school. . . . The uniform educates!"[34]

The American critique of Catholic organizations went further. Military officials chastised the Catholic group for being too undemocratic.[35] They disliked the fact that the clergy occasionally appointed youth leaders or that the most dynamic and charismatic lad automatically became the leader. One American official noted that the youth leaders frequently ran their groups in a dictatorial and authoritarian manner.[36] The Americans insisted that youth groups should hold free elections instead,[37] and they urged German youth organizations to launch more individualistic approaches. Drawing on what they called the "clubhouse models," they urged parishes to build "houses of the open doors" (*Häuser der offenen Tür*). They constructed more than 100 such youth centers where boys and girls could use the facilities at will, play table tennis, browse the youth library, and socialize with their friends more freely. The Americans held up to the German youth leaders their own youth organization, the German Youth Activities (GYA), as a model.[38] In the GYA the Americans sought to realize their approach to reeducation: fun and games, free elections, and the chance for youth to gather informally. Many of the adults in the Catholic

Affairs Branch of the military government who were also involved in youth work no doubt had favorable recollections of Catholic youth organizations in America, which according to many reports operated quite differently. Young German men and women who participated in exchange programs in the late 1940s and early 1950s enthusiastically noted, for instance, that young persons and figures of authority in America were closer; for example, priests would play basketball with the boys.[39]

The response from German youth leaders to these new approaches was predictably skeptical. They insisted that American models, however successful in the United States, could not simply be imposed in a foreign cultural and national context.[40] Although they were more than happy to receive material assistance from American soldiers—tent deliveries, sites for sporting events, food, paper, and money—they not infrequently refused to take part in activities sponsored by the Americans.[41] In Würzburg the Catholic youth declined to participate in a dance put on by the Red Cross club that would have allowed American solders to meet young German women.[42] The GYA, moreover, had little support at this time within Germany. It succeeded in signing up only a very small percentage of young Germans and was routinely lambasted for its shallow and naive approaches to youth work.[43]

The failure of the GYA notwithstanding, the criticism by the Americans was, nonetheless, prophetic. The Americans reproached the German youth organizations for willfully living in the past. One report from 1948 described German organizations as existing between "yesterday and tomorrow." According to the author, they desperately sought to recapture the glories of yesterday, when "they never had it so good," but were making tentative steps toward an uncertain tomorrow, a process that the emerging East-West conflict was making more difficult. "Some young Germans have made their choice between these two forces, but the great majority is still waiting and watching—not so much out of indecision as because of the fact that they don't want to be 'wrong' again in three, five or ten years."[44] More generally, in the late 1940s and early 1950s it was premature to pioneer new approaches for youth work but too late for the old models to replicate past successes.

As incisive as the American critique was, it would take indigenous authorities who recognized that the youth movement was past its prime to change Catholic youth work. By the late 1940s many leading Catholic newspapers had begun to question whether the youth movement was capable of reaching the younger generation in the changed cultural climate of the postwar era.[45] In private correspondence, Rommerskirchen noted that many of Wolker's approaches were now dated. "After there is no longer the way of conduct: 'The leader orders, we follow,' the dictate, 'The general orders, we follow' has become very questionable to the young. It is not easy to communicate that to the older ones."[46] One article noted that the protests against the philistine bourgeois world, which had characterized the youth movement since the turn of the century, had receded. In observations echoed by many Catholic youth leaders, sociologist Helmut Schelsky observed that young Germans were rushing to join middle-class society and achieve a degree of stability in their lives.[47] In his picture of a "skeptical generation," he argued that young men and women sought careers and distrusted grand dreams and ideology, attitudes that many young persons from 1900 or 1933 would have mocked. One youth worker described the young person of 1960 as "sober, free of illusions, objective, critical, concrete, reluctant to enter into unforeseen institutional attachments, but still open to instructive social sensibility."[48] Subsequent historians have since modified Schelsky's description of the youth of the 1950s as thoroughly apolitical and disengaged, but few have taken issue with his accounts that youth felt an acute sense of betrayal and were unwilling to commit immediately to new organizations and ideologies.[49]

It was clear by the late 1940s that the generation gap between those who had come of age prior to the Second World War and those whose formative years lay in the subsequent era of upheaval, scarcity, and dislocation sounded the death knell for the youth movement.[50] Some contrasted the fervid mass rallies of the early 1930s with the lackadaisical and tired gatherings of the late 1950s. The church newspaper in Cologne printed dire accounts of young men who were ignorant of—or unwilling to learn—the proper way to carry out hikes and run a tent camp. Before the war, the article noted, the boys would inevitably hang a boot or hat on top of the flagpole at the center of the tent camp, a sign of enthusiasm; now boots and hats, alas, remained in their proper place in front of the tents.[51] The article also noted that the boys had to be told exactly what to bring and how to use it. To make matters worse, many boys simply found these tent camps too exhausting and demanding. "Their choice of words says it all. Before, everything was 'colossal.' Today, this word is no longer used. Now everything is 'in order.' The weather is 'in order,' a meal is 'in order,' a trip is 'in order,' an evening social or a bonfire are 'in order.'"

The reasons for the decline of the youth movement after 1945 are not difficult to ascertain. In contrast to the aftermath of the First World War, few German soldiers returned home with calls for further struggles, discipline, and the restoration of the high idealism and grand destiny of the German nation. The harsh realities of unconditional surrender and total defeat made it impossible to sustain another "myth of the war experience."[52] Veterans could hardly be expected to restore the youth movement to health, even had they wished to do so. Harsh combat experiences on the eastern front in temperatures that had plunged to −40 degrees Fahrenheit and the bitter winters of 1946 and 1947, moreover, had stripped much of the romanticism from nature.

Older Catholic leaders inveighed against newly emerging trends in travel.[53] The youth magazine Die Wacht denounced travel by hitchhiking as "degenerate trips" and as a violation of the unofficial codes of the youth movement.[54] To hitchhike, leaders argued, meant to renounce solitude, the stillness of nature, and the togetherness of a group; to hitchhike was to indulge in an ethic of selfish individualism.[55] Although young men and women continued to go hiking, their rambles were devoid of the deeper sense of purpose that had characterized the youth movement. As if to emphasize this very point, some groups wore blazers, ties, and dark sunglasses and carried sleek walking sticks while strolling arm in arm through the countryside.[56]

Other groups, bored with the short duration of traditional excursions, undertook more ambitious trips abroad. Some went to Rome, a customary destination for Catholic groups, while others visited the Swiss or Italian Alps; still others went to Scandinavia. Many went by train and, in some cases, motorcycle. In these trips young persons were emulating their elders. Longer excursions were part of a larger trend in which many Germans began traveling abroad for relaxation and fun, a development that increases in holiday and vacation time and a shorter workweek had made possible. Older youth leaders, however, denounced these trips as egoism.[57] Others saw these journeys as a betrayal of the German nation; young persons should first discover the beauty and wonder of their homeland and Heimat and only then explore regions abroad. Pope Pius XII issued a statement titled "Christian Conceptions of Travel."[58] In it he condemned those who traveled for pleasure and called for Christians to practice what he called an "asceticism of travel." The Christian wayfarer was to be a man of character. He was to toughen the body and strengthen the soul, to heighten the power of resistance against the obstacles that inevitably arise during longer excursions.

What ultimately confounded Catholic efforts to uphold the forms and spirit of the youth movement were changes in how young persons spent their free time. According to surveys from the early 1950s, young persons preferred to read, socialize (a nebulous category that included going to the movies and hanging out with friends), play sports, and in some cases, join informal "hobby clubs."[59] There were clubs for avid readers and photo enthusiasts—by the late 1950s, between 30 and 40 percent of young Germans owned a camera. On the weekends, these surveys reported, young persons preferred sleeping in, going to the movies, hanging out in taverns, or simply being bored. At the same time, German youths were increasingly able to partake of the offerings of the mass society and culture around them. Theaters, new magazines such as Bravo, which targeted teenagers, and dance halls were within easy reach of most young Germans, particularly those in urban areas. Many young Germans were, moreover, infatuated with mopeds and motorcycles, even if only a very small percentage actually owned one.[60] The activities German youth preferred were individualistic, unconnected to larger ideological, religious, or political purposes, even if West German conservatives attached to them a dangerous political stigma. Young persons often just wanted to have fun, even as their elders were bewildered by what they described as the "problem of free time." They were disconcerted by young men who, on weekends or during the holidays, loitered on street corners, a sign of boredom and too much free time.[61]

It was also clear just how powerfully the rise of a new youth culture could put traditional youth groups at a disadvantage. In the past, many young persons participated in Catholic groups simply because there were few other recreational activities available. In many small villages, for instance, youth leaders noted that young persons continued to join the Catholic groups but showed signs of boredom or simply wanted to hang out with their buddies. In the direct aftermath of the war, the occupation authorities prevented most nonreligious events from taking place on Sunday mornings, ensuring that the churches had a monopoly on the free time of West German citizens. Sport organizations lacked adequate facilities, many theaters had been bombed, and curfews limited the hours when young persons could be outside. As West German society rebuilt itself by the early 1950s, however, alternatives to the religious groups reemerged. To be sure, many of these options had already existed in the 1920s. But by the late 1950s, Germans from all walks of life—proletarian, Catholic, Protestant, rich, and poor—and not just from wealthier families could afford to go to the movies or enjoy longer vacations.

Catholic groups and institutions, in the face of such competition, were frequently barely able to keep their heads above water. Nowhere can this pattern be seen more clearly than in the collapse of more than a dozen Catholic periodicals by the 1960s. Between 1955 and 1960 their circulation took a nosedive.[62] *Scheideweg*, the magazine for 10- to 14-year-old boys, saw its readership plummet from 58,210 to 31,100, a fall of 46 percent. *Voran*, for 14- to 18-year-old boys, likewise saw its circulation drop from 45,445 to 30,946, a decline of 32 percent. The two magazines for girls in these age brackets fared no better. Subscriptions for *Die Bunte Kette*, for 10- to 14-year-olds, declined by 22 percent from 48,441 to 37,446, while the circulation for *Morgen* dwindled from 62,565 to 50,003, a loss of 20 percent. Only the magazines for older youth picked up readers during this time, in part because several other publications for that age group— *Michael* and *Die Wacht*—went under in 1955.[63] The subscriptions for *Der Jungführer* declined by 37 percent, from 16,939 to 10,568, although the net readership of *Die Jungführerin* actually rose by 24 percent, from 13,262 to 17,569.

What caused the fortunes of Catholic youth magazines to ebb so rapidly in such a short time? To begin with, these publications were plagued by organizational problems. The audience for several of the magazines overlapped. More significant, however, was the fact that these periodicals were often unappealing to young readers, who were becoming increasingly choosy by the late 1950s.[64] These publications were printed on rough paper, were poorly laid out with an antiquated, unattractive typeface, and all too often dwelled on narrow religious topics. Several of these magazines lacked a clear sense of purpose. They were intended to serve as the official voice of the BDKJ and thus cover meetings and provide the latest information on upcoming events. But they were also supposed to engage younger readers, a difficult proposition in any case. Once *Bravo*, the acclaimed popular newsmagazine for teenagers, hit the newsstands in 1956, the fate of the Catholic publications was sealed. Some tried to adopt a more modern format in the early 1960s, but they were ultimately unsuccessful. By the late 1960s almost all were forced to cease publication.

Even worse was the reality that the structures built in 1947 had met with dwindling interest and loyalty even by the mid-1950s. Catholic youth leaders noted that young men and women repeatedly failed to fulfill their obligations to the Bund.[65] Many young members refused to remit their annual dues, and more ominously, others chose not to participate in mandatory masses for youth, special services that took place once a month. Even more shocking to the national leaders of the BDKJ was the reality that young men and women had developed little, if any, allegiance to their organizations. In 1958 a survey of forty-four male Jungschar leaders, twenty-five of whom were between 14 and 16 years old, eighteen of whom were between 16 and 20, and another who was 28, was carried out to determine what they knew about their organizations.[66] The results were distressing to the national leaders. Not one of these forty-four young men could name the youth leader for the archdiocese of Cologne. Only 8 percent knew the name of the national leader of the BDKJ. Apparently two-thirds could recite the official prayer and repeat the slogan of the Bund—"Long live God in Catholic youth!"

By the early 1950s, Catholic newspapers were forced to confront publicly the difficulties in their youth work. In 1953 the youth digest for the archdiocese of Cologne printed an account of a group on the verge of collapse. In a slightly mocking tone reminiscent of the children's poem "Ten Little Indians," the author described the painful process by which the members, one by one, left their once-flourishing group. The group, Michael, consisted of twelve boys between the ages of fifteen and sixteen. The leader, Hermann, had led the group for three years and was regarded as a "great guy." The difficulties set in when two of the boys were called to serve as youth leaders for the younger boys. In one fell swoop, the most committed boys were gone: "Jupp and Döres still wanted to belong to their group, but they just can't do it, for they are first and foremost preoccupied with their own group, leadership seminars, etc." Things got worse when Peter suddenly discovered a passion for hockey. He joined a hockey club and took his best friend with him. "OK, a youth group can't offer everything, even when the group leader played more than just soccer with his group." At this point Fridolin found the love of his young life, Kunegunde. There's no stopping love, he claimed, and quit attending the evening meetings. Worse was yet to come: Hermann suddenly ran out of ideas. For three years he had been leading the most exciting activities: boxing tournaments, wrestling matches, smuggling games, charades, games where you had to think on your feet, and sessions telling bone-chilling ghost stories by candlelight. Since only four or five boys were still showing up, he stopped preparing for the evening events. At least two more boys stopped coming, since the evenings were too dull. One day only three stalwarts were left. The author ended with a cry for help. Were there too many groups? he asked. Is the entire system of groups no longer viable? How can we help groups that lack competent leaders?[67]

The response by youth leaders took several forms. Catholic leaders stepped up their efforts to protect youth from dangerous and immoral influences. They crusaded against indecent literature, licentious films, and excessive alcohol consumption. These initiatives led to the formation of several committees and minor pieces of legislation. This tough line represented a change from the rhetoric of the mid- to late 1940s. Although fears of nihilism and rampant immorality were never far from anyone's mind directly after the war, church leaders were wont to speak in more conciliatory and sympathetic tones of the desperate circumstances confronting youth: unemployment, lack of shelter, and conscription to work in coal mines.[68]

For many youth leaders, however, these renewed efforts to protect young persons from the dangers of the outside world were too shrill, bombastic, and negative and were likely to drive young persons from religious institutions altogether or to kindle their interest in immoral activities. Leaders realized that if the church denied teenagers the chance to participate in activities dearest to them, they would look elsewhere to meet their needs. These leaders chose a more positive tactic: they began to integrate into their own programs the recreational activities that young persons enjoyed most. They urged groups, depending on the interests of the members, to set up circles for reading, photography, singing, stamp collecting, and playing chess and to sponsor activities for musicians, radio and television enthusiasts, and cinema devotees.[69] They likewise encouraged groups to establish a club to build and maintain a showcase where young photographers and artists could display their work. To attract younger boys to the tent camps, they recommended that a group put out promotional advertisements. A select few were to scout out the planned site (and even travel by motorcycle, if possible) and take alluring pictures of nearby castles and of the forest where the boys would play. The pictures were to be the weekly highlight of the group's showcase.[70]

Youth leaders likewise took steps to curtail the increasing numbers of young men and women who were leaving their groups to travel abroad with their friends, often with the help of a growing commercial travel industry.[71] By the late 1950s the church had begun to establish vacation centers for young persons in the more popular tourist destinations. The archdiocese of Cologne reserved rooms in pensions and private homes in the Black Forest and on the southern shore of the Chiemsee and offered them to young men and women between the ages of eighteen and twenty-five at affordable prices for up to two weeks. As one advertisement explained, "It is the express goal of these vacation centers to offer low prices and high quality especially to those who cannot or do not wish to travel with a youth group."[72] These centers differed from the stricter youth hostels, which often placed restrictions on how long young persons could stay and which were becoming increasingly unpopular among the youth.[73] For the younger boys and girls the church provided stays in youth hostels and youth centers in upper Bavaria, along the North Sea or the Belgian coast, and in the mountains of northern Italy.

In addition to these vacation centers, the church began to offer guided tours to Greece, the lakes of northern Italy, Florence, Rome, and the Belgian coast, among other destinations. Some were intended for young married couples or newlyweds on their honeymoon, but most targeted young singles between eighteen and twenty-five. As late as 1957 the editorial board of the newspaper *Mann in der Zeit* continued to discourage young men and women from vacationing together.[74] But by 1960 the church had been forced to change its policies regarding coed travel for youths older than eighteen. "To prevent a migration of our Catholic young people to other establishments, the Catholic vacation center for the archdiocese of Cologne has allowed itself to depart from decree #51 of the diocesan synod of 1954 and, as an experiment, introduce joint trips for youth of both sexes."[75] Church leaders, of course, ensured that the young men and women were under constant supervision and, to prevent too many lascivious thoughts from emerging, made sure that all destinations were of religious and cultural significance.

They soon realized, however, that even these steps were not enough. Many families or young persons continued to take extended vacations in campgrounds or hotels far removed from the influence of the church. Realizing that these vacationers were unlikely to attend mass while on holiday, the church dispatched clergy to campsites with instructions to hold regular Sunday masses—and to provide the church with a toehold at sites where it previously had little visibility or influence. These policies required a major change in thinking. Church leaders began to speak of the importance of free time and recreation for the well-being of men and women, topics that hitherto had received almost no attention.[76] They emphasized that free time, such as evenings of relaxation, travel, and holidays abroad, was part of the natural rhythm of life. They underscored how important it was for young men and women to recuperate (Erholung) and even set up centers where they could recover from the stresses of daily life (Erholungswerke).[77]

These newer approaches to youth work were a capitulation to the preferences of a younger generation, an attempt to retain the traditional forms of youth work by including more modern and up-to-date activities. Catholic leaders thus inadvertently put into place the suggestions made by the Americans nearly a decade earlier. In 1950 the American GYA centers were turned over to German authorities, and some clamped down on the permissive approaches brought in by the Americans. But as the economy picked up in the early 1950s, parishes and local municipalities were able to finance the construction of local youth centers. In the city of Cologne in 1953, 11 youth centers were finished, 18 were under con-struction, 28 were largely completed but needed further expansion, and 28 were in temporary quarters.[78] Of 92 parishes, 85 had established some form of a youth center. Many of these were modeled after the American clubhouse. They had a central room where large groups could congre-gate. But they also had many smaller annexes and rooms where groups of five or six could carry on smaller projects. Some rooms were designated for crafts; others were for chess, table tennis, and badminton.[79] One room was set aside for a library. Most were well equipped with comfort-able furniture so that the youngsters could relax and socialize with one another.

It became increasingly clear, however, that many church leaders were exceedingly uncomfortable with the new direction youth work was taking. The critics of these new approaches were not always just aging, embittered veterans of the youth movement who refused to admit that their time had passed. Many farsighted group leaders recognized that attempts to repli-cate the offerings of the outside world raised more problems than they solved. According to these critics, most Catholic groups were simply not capable of providing youth with everything they wanted. They lacked adequate facilities, well-trained leaders, and the glitz and glamour of the modern entertainment industry. As one youth worker explained, "Who is to equip the reading rooms with books and newspapers? Who is available for dance courses, hours of training, the screening of films, to give advice on books, for vacations, for time to relax?"[80] One group leader wrote to the youth magazine for the archdiocese of Cologne to voice his criticism of how Hermann, the above-mentioned leader, was running his group. Taking note of the activities Hermann had sponsored, he observed, "With this way of leading a group, it is not at all surprising that the boys . . . look elsewhere for their fun, since they have much better offerings elsewhere. I believe that the group described above has missed its actual goal." He argued that Hermann's activities had their place in breaking the ice, but to make them the centerpiece of the group was a cruel delusion.[81] Catholic groups had to play to their strengths by providing young men and women with answers to fundamental questions of life: how to behave around members of the opposite sex, how to develop a relationship with God and the church, and how to deal with the secular workplace. The group was to provide young persons with an ethical foundation at an impressionable stage in their lives. Indeed, the experiences of many groups bore out these observations. This same writer pointed out that in his group, all members gladly participated in more traditional group activities because they sensed that the questions that the group examined in discussions and lectures were of tremendous importance to their lives.

At the same time, youth leaders were quick to note the strong aversion among many young persons to activities that were perceived to be religious in nature. According to these reports, young men and women regarded such programs, such as learning how to kneel properly, studying the Bible, and analyzing the holy mass, as insipid, irrelevant, and tiresome. In a survey of more than 1,200 young men and women, young persons overwhelmingly wanted "less religion" in their groups and more fun.[82] To no surprise, these developments alarmed church leaders, who feared that youth work would rapidly lose its religious substance. But many older church authorities failed to recognize that the criticism by their youngsters was directed as much at how the church provided religious instruction as at the actual ideas it put forward. Where young persons were given the chance to participate in a dialogue and to shape their own activities in a manner relevant to their lives, they continued to participate with enthusiasm. But where they were forced to listen to lengthy monologues and lectures by older leaders, they quickly grew disenchanted and were more apt to leave.

In cinema the church found a force that it could not ignore. According to church statistics, by the early 1950s West Germans were going to the movies nearly eleven times a year; the figure was much higher for England and the United States.[83] For Bavaria alone, church leaders estimated that more than 1 million persons saw films each week.[84] Church leaders noted, "Never before in the history of mankind has a force of such power been available to the masses as the modern film."[85] Since persons between ages eighteen and twenty-five were more likely to go to the movies than those in other age brackets, it is not surprising that discussions of cinema repeatedly made their way into Catholic youth work in the 1940s and 1950s.

The Catholic response to cinema sums up the ambiguous relationship between the church and modernity in the twentieth century. The church never condemned this new medium of communication outright but warned instead of the potentially invidious purposes to which it could be put.[86] Church leaders feared not only that film might advance political agendas as it had under National Socialism and in the Communist East but that it might undermine traditional attitudes and values, particularly among impressionable young men and women.

Church leaders, not surprisingly, denounced films that they deemed immoral and subversive—those that, in their words, made the deviant the norm. They wanted to take a particularly tough line against gangster films, where young persons all too easily identified with the villains and which might evoke violent, carnal desires among impressionable adolescents.[87] Church leaders also denounced films that encouraged sexual improprieties, especially in the aftermath of the war, when many women resorted to prostitution to secure enough food and money for themselves and their families. In this context, church leaders reacted vehemently against the film *Die Sünderin* in 1951 because it seemed to legitimate a vast array of reprobate behaviors: prostitution, adultery, common-law marriage, and, still worse, suicide and euthanasia.[88] Frings himself voiced his opinion on this movie to the interior minister in Düsseldorf: "The film *Die*

Sünderin shows not only individual scenes which are risqué but puts forward the thesis that prostitution, free love, suicide are allowed, if not even heroic deeds, when they take place for love."[89] In another, less celebrated example Cardinal Frings wrote to the British occupation authorities to express his concern that a British military car "filled with German girls" bore the inscription "A night of love." Brigadier John Barraclough subsequently informed Frings that this placard was an advertisement for a film being shown in Cologne based on the Émile Zola novel *Un Page D'amour*. In this case, Frings accepted the explanation with good grace.[90]

It was not just films with explicitly immoral scenes or titles that met with disapproval. Even romantic films with happy endings triggered the anger of church authorities. For many critics, such cinematic fantasies overromanticized life, created illusions of unparalleled power, and glossed over the less sanguine realities of life. "The person who runs uncritically every week to the movies loses all too easily the joy of what is real, of his life. He will become—think for a moment of so many of your colleagues at vocational school—somehow dissatisfied, envious, listless, a poor worker [who] is at odds with himself and the world."[91] Such films, according to critics, could lead to higher divorce rates by depicting overromanticized notions of marriage.

In light of these fears and of the reality that they could not ban films altogether, church officials proposed, directly after the war, establishing an organization whose goal was to bring about a rebirth of a German film industry under the guiding light of the church.[92] This proposal noted that film producers within Catholic nations such as Poland, Hungary, Spain, and Italy had, in the past, been too weak to guarantee the steady production of films with a religious content. The church, as a result, had to take the lead in building its own film industry. The advocates of a religious film industry optimistically pointed out that there were more than enough Catholics in the world to make such an enterprise viable and, even more importantly, able to unify Catholics throughout the world. This was, in many respects, an echo of plans to rebuild the Christian West against the onslaught of materialism and Bolshevism. These high hopes, however, were illusory. Church leaders underestimated the difficulties, financial and technological, of competing with Hollywood studios. It is hardly surprising that a thriving Catholic cinema failed to materialize.

Unable to compete with American and even indigenous European film production, the church was forced to take a different approach. The church launched a film bureau that rated individual films.[93] The idea of a Catholic film commission, oddly enough, stemmed from the United States, where the church had set up the Catholic Film League and Legion of Decency.[94] These initiatives were rather successful. Select laity and clergy went to the opening of a film, put together a brief description of its content and theme, and decided whether it was appropriate for Catholic viewers and, if so, for which age brackets. Once the official list was compiled, it was sent to parishes, where it was posted on message boards, read aloud from the pulpit, or printed in bulletins. Through this approach, clergy hoped to capitalize on the potential purchasing power of millions of Catholics. As they sought to make clear to the major film studios, a thumbs-down rating could cost producers tens of thousands of dollars; a positive appraisal, on the other hand, could help fill the coffers. In reality, they noted, only about 5 percent of films, mostly gangster films, were given the red light. The masterminds behind the Catholic film bureau realized that it was too much to ask even loyal Catholics to attend only pious films with religious motifs and the goal of spiritual uplift. "That would probably be boring," they admitted.[95] Churchgoers could—and even should—go to films that depicted sin and vice but only so long as the films communicated outrage at the immoral acts being committed.

For certain especially indecent films, church leaders advocated forceful protests. The high-minded bourgeois ideals of tolerance are desirable, one manual explained, but such tolerance cannot be extended to all criminal and immoral acts: "Dogmatically and morally, Christians have before them the teachings of Christ, who loved the sinner and hated the sin. There is only one way: for or against. Neutrality, not taking a stance, does not exist, also not within film."[96] With this philosophy, youth groups occasionally took action against cinema owners who showed films deemed immoral. In Düsseldorf fifteen young men disrupted several screenings of Die Sünderin. Under the tutelage of their priest, Carl Klinkhammer, they timed their protest to coincide with the first nude scene in postwar German cinema. Precisely at the moment when Hildegard Knef shed her clothes, the boys set off more than forty stink bombs and forced the patrons to flee the theater. A demonstration several days later against the film turned violent. Klinkhammer was arrested, and a crowd of more than 300 supporters chanted in protest: "The police protect prostitutes, the police protect smut and filth, down with the police!"[97]

But by the late 1950s, this philosophy had begun to shift. Some young leaders of Catholic youth groups perceived past responses to films—the protests and the constant warnings—as too negative. Others believed that these approaches were likely to turn off young men and women who were genuinely interested in film. One former group leader recounted how he and his associates arrived at a new understanding of film.[98] Over glasses of beer late at night, one of his mates muttered that he never went to the movies, since "there was never anything decent playing." Hearing this remark, one of the other young men became irate. He spoke glowingly of international film festivals, Federico Fellini, the best films of the year, and the international Catholic film bureau. To everyone's astonishment, he turned out to be the founder of the local film club. Every Wednesday evening his group of almost twenty boys met to decide which film to see on the weekend. During the meeting they played music from detective films while discussing the films they had already seen. Perceiving great potential, Der Jungführer encouraged group leaders to form their own film clubs. It recommended selecting films that were substantive but entertaining. Fellini's La Strada was probably on too high a level for most groups, but Gary Cooper's Friendly Persuasion would do just fine. To arrive at a decision, film clubs were to study the verdicts of the Catholic film service sentence by sentence. The real work, however, occurred when the boys returned from their film. They were to sit down and discuss it: how it was put together; the camera angles; the music; the message; its positions on love, family, and marriage; and the motivations of the characters.[99] In short, the boys were to become film critics. They were to deconstruct the film and place a critical distance between themselves and the screen.

These new approaches to viewing films were emblematic of how many younger Catholics came to respond to mass culture by the early 1960s. They mirrored the heightened interest within West European society in film—in film festivals and in new aesthetics. But more importantly, church leaders ultimately sought to transform mass culture into an elite culture, to set themselves up as the arbiters of what was critically acceptable and what was not. In so doing, they intended not only to render mass culture harmless but also to actively put it to work for their own ends. As Der Jungführer explained, "The boys were to see at the end how superficial and unsatisfying it is to see films the way they normally do."[100] The advocates of these new approaches realized that the task ahead—teaching critical thinking—was daunting, but they argued that the process of disciplining the mind would ultimately train a new generation of Catholic youth.

By the late 1950s, church leaders had reappraised popular music in much the same way they had reevaluated film.[101] Music, too, was an arena of conflict between older youth leaders and younger teenagers. From the outset, debates over popular music took on an alarmist yet remarkably unfocused tone. Church leaders, whose musical training—if they had any at all—was limited to classical music, rarely differentiated between specific forms of popular music, such as swing, bebop, Dixieland, or German hit songs (Schlager). To church leaders, these forms were all more or less the same, even if some were of American or African origin and others were the products of indigenous German singers. What triggered the often anguished discussions about popular music was the timeless "problem" of dancing. These concerns had, to be sure, surfaced already in the 1920s, as American popular music began to make itself heard throughout Western Europe. They, moreover, did not go away during the twelve years of National Socialist rule, even when Nazi officials launched tirades against degenerate "Negro music."[102] But it was only during the postwar years that the discussion of popular music and dancing took on such an extremely dissonant tone among many church leaders.[103] Many of their most powerful fears—of out-of-control sexuality, reversed gender roles, the loss of moderation and restraint, the stultifying effects of mass culture, and changes in village life—found their first expression in diatribes against dancing and popular music. Even though surveys from the time indicated that dancing was not the most popular pastime of most German youth, conservative church leaders frequently acted as though dancing to jazz or rock 'n' roll was an obsession for the majority of young persons.[104]

The subject of dancing had long been fraught with difficulties for religious leaders. Well into the twentieth century, most clerics held to Augustinian notions that elevated the soul to a position of supremacy over the body. For them, dancing threatened to kindle sensual desires and awaken a dormant sexuality. Most clerics, however, realized that it was impossible to ban dancing altogether. Dancing, mostly folk dancing, was so ingrained in the local culture, particularly in regions that enthusiastically celebrated Carnival, that church leaders never would have succeeded in stamping it out.[105] In the new forms of American dance music of the 1920s, however, they saw an ominous challenge to these carefully circumscribed approaches to dancing. To them, jazz represented anarchy, disarray, and radicalism. Although racial categories certainly informed some critiques of jazz, church leaders were far more apprehensive about the impact of the music itself on young men and women. One youth leader, Ottilie Mosshammer, described in alarmist terms the dreadful consequences of dancing to popular music: "The exclusiveness of a pair who moves to the hammering rhythms of jazz music, of pop-songs, whose texts are frivolous and blunt—this can insidiously lead to experiences becoming more superficial and coarse and degenerates to a revolting pushing and shoving or a sticking together of the partners. The measure of time and space breaks down, the people lose their sense of moderation and lose control of themselves."[106] As we shall see in the next chapter, church leaders also believed that popular music pushed gender boundaries one step too far by masculinizing women and feminizing men.

Yet another reason why Catholic clergy had so many qualms about popular music lay in the changing texture of village life. By 1946 and 1947 the reports by clergy reiterated the same theme: "the city had entered the village." The teenagers in the villages, they claimed, were possessed by a "dance-fury."[107] They even coined the word *Tanzwut* (literally, dancing madness) to describe this phenomenon.[108] Such frenetic dancing may have been, in part, a natural response to years of hardship during the war. Young persons found in wild dancing an outlet for years of pent-up frustration; they simply wanted to "live" again. Most clergy and older youth leaders, however, did not see this trend in this light. One youth leader in charge of a tent camp in 1947 in Lower Franconia complained vociferously to the diocesan youth leadership for Würzburg about the ruckus when a group of guests from Wuppertal began singing the most "despicable" popular songs. "When I forbade them from singing these songs, they became infuriated and promptly sang church hymns." Things, however, grew worse, for those "Tango-youths from the darkest pubs of a city neighborhood" began singing their songs before the entire public, with the hopes of "enticing the girls to flirt with them."[109] Other reports from this time depict groups of young men and women who sang songs from the youth movement only when prodded—and then grudgingly. When given the chance to sing their own more modern songs, however, they suddenly sprang to life and sang with great joy—much to the dismay of their leaders.

Two photos in *Michael*, the Catholic newspaper for older teenagers, summed up all that church leaders believed to be wrong with popular music.[110] The first depicted two young male jazz enthusiasts. One was wearing a tie and a suave sport-coat, a popular fashion at the time. Above him stood an effeminate-looking younger man strumming a guitar, his mouth open and his glazed eyes staring absently toward the ceiling. The second photo featured two wholesome-looking Catholic girls with high cheekbones, their hair pulled back as they smiled broadly. The caption read, "The ecstasy of these jazz fans, which a large share of the youth indulges in, stands in sharp contrast to the healthy cheerfulness of the boys and girls who want to be simple, natural, and genuine. It is easy to decide with whom our people can build its future." In a subsequent article, *Michael* identified the more effeminate boy as Adolf, born in 1933.[111] He was an apprentice, loved motors, and had already excelled in "soap-box derbies." Like all boys of his generation, he joined the Nazi organization for ten- to fourteen-year-olds, *Das Jungvolk*. The national capitulation, however, brought disillusionment; his mother sobbed uncontrollably at the time of defeat. Adolf now refused to participate in any organized youth groups. He turned instead to jazz music, to the mambo and boogie-woogie, "as if they were the most beautiful of songs." To conclude their description of young Adolf, the editors appended a cryptic footnote: "Jazz Fan Adolf, class of '33, feels quite at home on civilian turf; march music is not (yet) his cup of tea." In so doing, they not only equated jazz music with the refusal to commit to larger collective organizations but, once again, subtly placed the responsibility for the rise of National Socialism and Communism on materialism and mass culture. East German leaders tellingly denounced the boogie as part of the evils of "the culture of the Christian West."[112]

In response to the challenges posed by jazz, church leaders took steps to preempt the appeal of popular music. As early as the 1930s, they granted young men and women the opportunity to go dancing—in very restricted situations. Carefully selected groups of young men and women (they were, of course, kept apart from one another) were allowed to form their own singing and dance circles. These dances, however, were a far

A "musical week" for the girls of the archdiocese of Paderborn, 1955 (Courtesy of Jugendhaus Hardehausen)

cry from the freer forms of jazz. A series of guidelines from 1933 for Catholic groups in the archdiocese of Cologne, for instance, called for the young women to "march in" in an orderly manner to march rhythms, which would have been in 4/4 time.[113] The girls were likewise to depart from the dance floor "in closed ranks." These guidelines also insisted that during "all performance, we ask that the most stringent discipline and control be maintained. All unnecessary speaking and giggling endangers the nobility of our event. We adhere to these instructions not just because we are being observed (by the public) but because we want to develop self-control and decency for ourselves."

Yet most church leaders realized that even these steps would never sate the appetite of young persons for more popular dances. By the late 1940s the youth center at Altenberg had begun to sponsor "social evenings" for men and women in their twenties. But even these events featured traditional dances such as the waltz, foxtrot, and polka. Not until later in the 1950s did church leaders begin to shed their hostility toward these newer forms of music and dance—the samba, mambo, and rumba—and incorporate them into their own group activities. As was the case with modern films, they no longer saw chaos and disorder in jazz and the new dance

Rock 'n' roll arrives in Catholic youth work. These boys were competing in a battle of the bands in 1965. Youth work now attempted to appropriate more modern forms. (Courtesy of Jugendhaus Hardehausen)

forms. Instead, they began to note the unique rhythmic and melodic structures of these dances. Young persons might dance to a different drummer, but at least there was a drummer who lent these dances rhythmic precision and order. Some leaders noted that the South American and African dances posed greater challenges, since the rhythmic forms were far more subtle, but even here they argued that proper musical training would ensure that the music and dance did not degenerate into "an indiscriminate, pounding mess" or "an unaesthetic madness and formlessness."[114] One chaplain pointed out that modern dance was, in and of itself, a beautiful thing; the danger emerged only when "unrestrained" individuals corrupted these forms.[115] Dance also taught virtue: respect for one's partner, tact, harmony, attentiveness, and appreciation of larger forms of order.

To arrive at this new understanding of modern dance and music, church leaders were forced to shed the undertones of racism that had informed criticisms of African American dance music in the past. Instead of deriding jazz as Negro music, they located its roots in African American spirituals, which they extolled as the indomitable voice of a long-suffering people. Catholic youth magazines urged leaders to introduce spirituals to their groups; one young chaplain exclaimed, "Finally, there's something going on in the church."[116] This same priest pointed out that many of the profane dances had religious roots: the samba was originally a fresh, joyful dance of thanksgiving performed at the time of harvest. "That this dance form has been ruined has nothing to do with the fact that it stems from people with a darker skin color. It is our sad distinction that it has been pounded to death by our countrymen through their ignorance."[117] By identifying jazz with African villages, church leaders were able to link popular music to genuine folk music—and thus show that what many regarded as degenerate, barbaric music for the masses was as authentic as homegrown German folk music.

Some youth workers soon began to offer courses in modern dance to all young persons in their parishes.[118] One advertisement for a Catholic dance class was titled, "Born to Dance!"[119] For these courses they brought in trained professional dance instructors who, in some cases, taught young men and women directly after Sunday mass. The boys and girls spent hours mastering basic dance moves and even began to practice with members of the opposite sex. The benefits from these dance courses, church leaders noted, were multifold. Some argued that these classes gave young persons a positive way to spend their free time. By holding dance courses in parish halls instead of dance studios, "where a distinctly heathen climate reigns," they believed that they would be able to maintain control of their young people and prevent them from becoming tainted by the anticlericalism of modern society.

Some parishes began to celebrate the mass with jazz music, in so-called jazz masses.[120] One chaplain even sponsored a dance party in the "house of the open door" in Cologne in 1957 and advertised it under the provocative title, "Is the church against rock 'n' roll?" This party helped earn him the nickname "the dance-chaplain."[121] In the diocese of Würzburg many groups held workshops to scrutinize the quality of pop songs. Hit songs were not all bad, one brochure explained, as it really depended on the manner in which individual songs dealt with basic human themes such as love, separation, mirth, and loneliness. To be avoided were songs that were egotistical—"Baby, you're mine"—and that showed no regard for other human beings. But songs that addressed basic questions of life with style, humor, wit, or tenderness were to be taken seriously. One brochure praised songs that evoked powerful feelings of betrayal or lost

An advertisement from 1962 for "jazz and spirituals" to be followed by an hour of prayer. "The meaning of work is in glorifying God." (Courtesy of Jugendhaus Hardehausen)

love: "Why are today so many so lonely, so many so alone, no one thinks any more of others, why must it be like this?"[122] In this respect, hit songs resembled folk songs. They examined fundamental questions of life in a direct, simple, and authentic manner.

Yet even as these religious leaders succeeded in creating a new intellectual and religious justification for their reevaluation of popular music and dance, many of their initiatives quickly foundered. The 1957 rock 'n' roll festival gave some indication of the difficulties they were to encounter. The chaplain in charge intended to give his young audience a musical tour of popular music; he began with marches and moved step by step to the foxtrot, swing, blues, boogie-woogie, and spirituals. During this time, however, some of the lads became impatient. They demanded that he "turn the record-player off" and bellowed, "We want rock 'n' roll" (*Drieh dä Kasten av! Mir wollen Rockenroll!*). One commentator noted that these young men had paid attention only to the last four words of the chaplain's advertisement, "Is the church against rock 'n' roll?" This party, moreover, met with equal resistance from the other side. Diocesan officials in Cologne scribbled in large black letters on a newspaper account of the evening, "Scandal! Shortage of priests? Curate must go!"[123] Such events were often the worst of both worlds. They alienated more conservative officials within the church, and as a result, few other clergy were willing to go forward with similar initiatives.[124] This chaplain admitted that he was one of the few clerics who was willing to undertake such events. At the same time, they offered too little to teenagers who were not particularly interested in providing an exegesis of modern music. They simply wanted the product and often did not know why. The newspaper account of the dance festival concluded with the following observation: "To the question, 'why do you so like to dance to Rock, in particular?' came no answer." Only one girl said apathetically, "That will probably be a thing of the past as well." Although many groups enthusiastically embraced jazz and even founded their own elite Catholic jazz clubs, young persons were not receptive to their quest to transform rock 'n' roll into elite music. The church was unable to co-opt rock 'n' roll to its own ends.

CONCLUSIONS

By the early 1960s, Catholic youth leaders had embraced mass culture. They had dropped their resistance to popular forms of entertainment such as film, jazz, and hit songs. They tried to co-opt the latest forms of recreation and leisure—book clubs, film clubs, and dance parties—into their own groups and sponsored activities that were vastly more individualistic than those of the 1930s. Catholic youth work by the late 1950s was characterized by the attempt to wed new approaches to old forms. It was clear to almost everyone that the spirit of the Catholic youth movement from the 1920s and 1930s was dead. Youth leaders, in response, retained the outward forms of the youth movement—groups, social evenings, tent camps, and hikes—and tried to give them a more modern edge. Like their elder brothers and uncles from the 1930s, the youth leaders of the early 1960s retained an elitism, a sense that they had been chosen to carry out lofty goals. But unlike the generation of 1938 or 1914, they no longer sought to separate themselves from mass culture by retreating into romantic forests or into a fictitious kingdom of youth. They set out, instead, to harness and become the masters of mass culture itself.

Uta Poiger argues that such changes were part of a much larger and more complex reevaluation of mass culture and American popular culture occurring within liberal opinion in West German society at the height of the Cold War. According to Poiger, West German authorities embraced consumption, leisure, pleasure, jazz, rock 'n' roll, and American film as weapons with which to expose the inferior economic and political system of the East. They, too, sought to transform mass culture into elite culture.[125]

Catholic authorities underwent much the same process of reevaluation as Cold War liberals but did so for different reasons. On the local level in Germany, they sought primarily to ensure the survival of their own institutions and were only secondarily concerned with fighting the Cold War, even where a militant anti-Communism still figured high in their rhetoric. They began to realize that by retaining an implacable antagonism toward mass culture, they risked driving many young men and women from the church and into the arms of dance hall owners, media magnates, and the new youth culture of the 1950s. Even worse, they risked making themselves look like anachronisms. But equally significant on the larger level was the climate of reform that accompanied the rise of John XXIII to the papal throne and the temporary loss in influence of more conservative voices within the church. In this euphoric moment, many church leaders sought to bring about a rapprochement with modern society and end a long-standing hostility toward mass culture, a step that cannot always be linked to Cold War tensions. This changing climate of opinion culminated in the landmark reforms of the Second Vatican Council of 1962 to 1965, which in many regions swept away hundreds of years of traditions.

Yet these new approaches of the late 1950s and early 1960s, which were really only half-measures, never manifested the hopes invested in them. They did not even succeed in keeping up the membership rosters. The same pattern was to be observed in the national youth festivals. The gathering in Düsseldorf in 1954 brought together more than 100,000 young men and women. By 1959 the number had dropped to 80,000, and by 1965 it was a meager 30,000.[126] This tremendous decline in participation took place even as the youth festivals became more individualistic and more in tune with modern styles. In 1959 and 1965, for instance, the festival featured jazz music and individual workshops—"modern" forms of participation.

Why did the attempts at reform later in the 1950s fall short of their goals? In developing jazz clubs, film clubs, and Catholic vacations, youth leaders ultimately tried to compete with the modern entertainment and recreation industries, an effort that was inevitably futile. Some youth workers recognized at the time that they, given their limited financial resources, had no chance of bringing the same glamour and enticements to Catholic groups. They were, moreover, always one step behind the times—they could merely duplicate what the modern world had to offer and could never be on the cutting edge. The elitist nature with which Catholic groups attempted to appropriate popular culture undoubtedly limited their mass appeal. At the same time, the competition from the outside, modern world also forced youth leaders to downplay religious and spiritual topics in a bid to win the hearts of young persons.

More importantly, these youth reformers were the victims of unintended consequences. By entering a dialogue with the modern world, they set themselves up to be transformed by the forces they hoped to master. By allowing young persons to be exposed to films of all types, even those with which they disagreed, they helped sanction and give legitimacy to values that often conflicted with those of the church. Training young persons in critical thinking was a double-edged sword, as it inadvertently gave a younger generation a weapon with which to question fundamental beliefs and doctrines. The appropriation of an ethos of consumption likewise undermined the authority of the church. In an era of consumption, individuals are free to choose which elements of the faith to adopt, rather than accepting the authority of the church and its leaders wholesale.

As such "cafeteria Catholicism" became the norm, the authority of church leaders was increasingly questioned, especially on issues of gender, as we shall see in the next chapter. A mere five to ten years later, a more radical cohort of young persons set out to turn basic church teachings on sexuality, faith, and politics on their head, much to the consternation of these "elite" reformers of the early 1960s. The leaders of the BDKJ adopted an anticlerical platform that frequently owed more to Marxism and the New Left than to Catholicism and included protests against the Vietnam War, denunciations of imperialism, and calls for solidarity with the Third World. The "oppositional" Catholic identity that had once been directed against liberalism and socialism was now turned against the church itself.

By the late 1960s, then, the system of Catholic youth work, including the uniforms and formal leadership, had fallen like a house of cards. The last vestigial ties to the youth movement were cut. The *Jungführer* model was abandoned, youth groups became coed, and youth work became increasingly professionalized. The BDKJ evolved into an umbrella organization, a loose confederation of associations including Kolping, the CAJ, and the Katholische Junge Gemeinde (the new name for the parish youth groups). The *Bund*, as the leaders from 1947 had envisioned it, had ceased to exist.[127]

THREE

Where Have
All the Young
Girls Gone?

℘

BETWEEN 1953 AND 1959, Catholic youth organizations for women lost more than 40 percent of their members in North Rhine–Westphalia. According to figures released by authorities, 255,335 young women and 233,139 young men were members of Catholic youth organizations in the province in 1953. By 1959 membership had plummeted. Only 148,917 young women and 198,128 young men claimed membership in Catholic youth organizations, a drop of 15.8 percent for the young men and an astounding 41.2 percent for the young women.[1] These figures are all the more remarkable in light of the fact that the total number of young persons actually increased in these six years by 260,000. Of these, at least half were nominally Catholic.[2] These changes signaled the end of a long-standing pattern in which the number of young women in youth groups typically exceeded the number of young men by between 20 and 30 percent.[3]

This unprecedented decline of more than 40 percent cannot be attributed to modest increases in female employment.[4] As many Catholic youth leaders were quick to point out, working hours rarely conflicted directly with group activities, which typically took place during the early evening, on Saturday afternoons, or after mass on Sundays. Only in cases of increased mobility—where young women left their hometowns to find work in neighboring cities—does this explanation hold up.[5]

In this chapter I argue, instead, that questions of gender, however indirectly, influenced the decision of many young girls to leave Catholic organizations. A casual glance at Catholic literature of this period attests to how pervasively gender dominated discussions and debates during the 1950s. Articles with such revealing titles as "Why I Don't Run Around with Girls While I Am Still Young" or "There Are No Longer Any Upstanding Girls" remained a mainstay of church encyclicals, sermons, religious handbooks, and youth newspapers well into the 1960s.[6]

Yet church positions on gender were far from monolithic. Numerous voices within the church, in fact, vied for the chance to shape church doctrines on questions of sexuality and gender. Behind the scenes many theologians and even low-ranking youth leaders drafted their own counterpoints to official church encyclicals. Even when the church appeared to be speaking with one voice, the "official position" was often derived from contrasting traditions, including neoscholasticism from the late nineteenth century and the youth and liturgical movements of the 1920s and 1930s. By the 1950s many youth leaders based their ideas, in part, on the emerging youth culture imported from America, which included Elvis Presley, rock 'n' roll, jazz, and "modern fashions." To speak of an unqualified hegemony and to restrict one's gaze to a "dominant discourse," as have recent accounts of West German society, is to overlook the impact of alternatives on official church policies.[7]

In this chapter I begin by examining the role played by gender in shaping Catholic values from the late nineteenth century into the early twentieth century and the manner in which youth leaders incorporated issues of gender into their institutions. I subsequently chronicle a series of conflicts in the 1950s that emerged between groups of young women and church authorities over questions of morality and values. Finally, I argue that these struggles actually helped lead to declines in the youth work for women during this time.

One caveat is in order here. The declining rate of female participation was far more extreme in North Rhine–Westphalia than in Baden-Württemberg or Bavaria, a trend that is borne out by figures released from the BDKJ headquarters in Düsseldorf, which indicate a modest 10 percent decrease for all of Germany. Youth leaders in the agrarian regions of southern Germany were, to be sure, confronted with many of the same issues as their counterparts within western Germany, but the social structures and cultural climate were far different within a region such as Lower Franconia from that in the Rhineland. As a result, the church in southern

Germany was able to absorb far more successfully the mounting criticism of its stance on questions of gender and values.[8]

GENDER AND THE CATHOLIC CHURCH

In the nineteenth century, church teachings on gender assumed a new form as part of a process that has been described as one of feminization.[9] The neoscholastic moral theology of the church originated in the nineteenth century, coinciding with rapid industrialization. Many men left their families and farms to find work in factories and coal mines, where they were exposed to liberal and Socialist influences. As men ceased to participate in the activities sponsored by the church, women, by default, became the mainstay of support for the church. They filled the pews on Sunday mornings, comprised the majority of participants on pilgrimages and processions, took their children with them to mass, and taught them the fundamentals of the faith. Forms of religious piety underwent a major transformation at this point. They became maudlin and cloying in their sentimentality; they emphasized, for instance, the bleeding heart of Christ and the sorrows of Mary.

It is no coincidence that the church began to cultivate a new image of women as pious, sexless, celibate, and motherly. In the Middle Ages these characteristics had been reserved for saints alone; ordinary women were seen as weak and easily susceptible to sexual temptation. Theologically, this new emphasis on female piety drew on Marian traditions, which underwent a renaissance in the second half of the nineteenth century. These traditions exhorted young women to model their values and behavior after those of Virgin Mary, the incarnation of virgin and mother: purity, humility, chastity (except for the purpose of procreation within a divinely sanctioned marriage), fertility, love, motherliness, selflessness, and above all, unrelenting self-sacrifice. Some church leaders insisted that the responsibility of women to love and serve others entailed an obligation to "everything living, and for all domains of life in the world."[10]

Women were, however, given responsibility only for the private, domestic sphere; men ruled the public sphere. According to these conceptions, masculine qualities that were to predominate in the public sphere, such as hardness, toughness, nobility, dignity, resolve, reverence (*Ehrfurcht*), and decisiveness, needed to be counterbalanced in the private sphere by the feminine attributes of motherliness, tenderness, love, charity, and piety. Theologians and proponents of natural law assumed that society could function harmoniously only when both men and women adhered to the roles assigned to them by God, where women felt called to be women in the very fullness of their being. It comes as no surprise that most Catholic social theorists adamantly rejected calls for equal rights between men and women. They emphasized, instead, that men and women were of equal worth and value before God; attempts to make men and women fundamentally equal would destabilize the natural order of society designed by God. This position—a doctrine of "separate but equal"—remained at the heart of Catholic teachings until the Second Vatican Council.[11]

This division of the world into male and female spheres found its logical expression in Catholic conceptions of the family, the unit that served as the anchor for many Catholic theories of society. Catholic social theorists sought to apply the model of the holy family to all institutions within German society. They described, for instance, the church as a large family, and the nuclear family as a small church. As we shall see, they envisioned the family as a bulwark against forces of individualism, collectivism, and materialism. As late as 1959, advocates of the Catholic Familienpolitik put together a National Exhibition of the Family in which one exhibit was titled, "Mothers and Families as Bulwarks against Bolshevism."[12]

While these norms reflect a nostalgia for the large, traditional agrarian families, these standards were also derived from the Catholic response to industrialization. The growth of cities and of factories detached the home from the workplace and made it easier for Catholic theorists to draw a sharp line between the male public sphere and the female private sphere. In defining women's roles as domestic, Catholics were far from alone. Despite their mutual enmity at the time of the Kulturkampf, Catholics and Liberals frequently put forth remarkably similar ideas on gender. Both groups saw the existence of the female-led domestic sphere as a precondition for stability within society.[13]

But when industrialization led to an increase in female employment outside the home (and women were suddenly placed into the public sphere), Catholic leaders responded with vitriolic attacks on changing gender norms. Between 1895 and 1939 the number of women working outside the home rose from 3.8 million to nearly 9 million.[14] Many of these jobs were initially in factories and subsequently in offices. As a result, Catholic leaders claimed that the lines separating male and female spheres had become blurred. They insisted that men had become feminized and women had become masculinized as a result of working together. Catholic newspapers began to pillory weak men and hardened women, who worked like men, smoked like men, dressed like men, campaigned for equal rights, and looked something like Marlene Dietrich. The church particularly denounced the women's movement, which it regarded as hostile to the church and a harbinger of secularization. The church's hostility toward the modern world frequently found its first expression in a litany of complaints about declining values and decadence, a synonym for changing gender norms.

The church responded by reviving an old symbol of decadence, corruption, and temptation: Eve. By the 1920s, Catholic leaders had begun to compare the modern "emancipated" woman with the figure of Eve. They argued that the modern woman, like Eve, portended a return to unhappiness and destruction. Ottilie Mosshammer, a youth leader from Regensburg who compiled several widely read and influential training manuals for youth leaders, stated, "An often heard word from girls and women is, 'I would like to have my own life.' That is the new language of Eve, who failed miserably. With no power to sacrifice one's heart, no selfless love, life becomes so unbearable for many that they say, 'That is truly no life anymore.' "[15] Catholic leaders juxtaposed this picture of Eve with that of Mary, who according to their theology was sent into the world to help redeem mankind from the sins of her predecessor, Eve.

As organizations explicitly designed to steep young Catholics in the basics of the faith, Catholic youth groups for women, more than any other organizations within the church, took on the prevailing attitudes toward gender in the first half of the twentieth century.[16] They brought together the feminine forms of piety that stemmed from the Marian tradition, the hopes to maintain separate spheres for men and women, and above all, the desire to protect young women from the corrupting influence of the world around them—from the siren songs of the women's movement and the temptations of the workplace, bars, and sporting events.

The so-called Marian maiden congregations, without a doubt, most directly embodied these gender norms from the late nineteenth century. Although the congregations dated back to the Counter-Reformation, their numbers increased significantly with the advent of industrialization

in the second half of the nineteenth century.[17] As one might have sus-
pected, they became associated with the feminine forms of piety at that
time. The young members gathered in the evenings to sing Marian
hymns, pray, and meditate in the local chapel. In addition, the congregations imposed a wide range of obligations on their members, who were
given a trial membership for several months to see if they were capable of
living up to the high standards required. Members were expected to pray
the rosary and to express regret for sins they might have committed
during the preceding day, and they were urged to avoid contact with all
persons with a bad or dubious reputation. They were required to examine
their consciences at least once a day, to recite the prayers of the congregation regularly, and to receive Holy Communion at least twice a month.[18]
For these acts, members were rewarded with indulgences, which would
lessen their time in purgatory. Members were entitled to a complete
indulgence if, upon their deathbed, they were to kiss or caress a medal-
lion given to them by the head of their congregation upon their day of
induction.[19]

The maiden congregations, as they were called, were explicit about
their goal of cultivating feminine virtues. As one brochure explained,
"The veneration of Mary illuminates what it means to be a woman." The
young maidens were urged to strive toward a life of holiness, a model
religious life, to the "full and continuous dedication of one's self to the
service of the most holy virgin and mother of God." Another brochure
urged young women to "place themselves under the special protection of
Mary and to see in her the model for how to be a girl."[20]

These exclusive communities of true believers consciously aimed to
protect young women from the pernicious world outside. Until the days
of the liturgical and youth movements, most congregations sought to
isolate young Catholics not just from mass society and unsavory liberal
and Socialist influences but from the opposite sex. This separation was
premised on the belief that young women and young men should be kept
as far apart as possible until they had reached adulthood. Although Marian congregations also existed for young men, they met in different locations at different times and retained separate administrative apparatuses.
In their attempts at theater, young men adopted falsetto voices, put on
skirts, and played the roles of women. During the celebration of the
mass, men and women typically sat on opposite sides of the church.[21]

Underlying the belief that boys and girls were to be separated until

After 1945 the Catholic youth movement brought together
not just young men but young women. In this photo, singing
girls follow their leader, Klaus Hermans, into the diocesan youth
center for the archdiocese of Paderborn at Hardehausen in 1946.
The guitar was one of the instruments of choice for the youth
movement. (Courtesy of Jugendhaus Hardehausen)

adulthood was far more than simple prudery, although Catholic leaders
certainly held on to old fears that illicit sexual activity might corrupt
youth. By the turn of the century, many Catholic social workers were
postulating theories of adolescence and of human development that
maintained that men and women reached true adulthood only by remaining apart from the opposite sex. Youth training manuals typically explained that boys would be made "soft" and feminine and that girls
would adopt masculine characteristics were too much contact between
the sexes to take place too soon.[22] One such article, "Why I Don't Run
Around with Girls While I Am Still Young," put forward ten theses that
condemned flirting. In this article from 1952 the author chose the word

poussieren, which even at the time had an old-fashioned ring to it, instead of the more modern *flirten.*[23] Flirting, the author explained, undermined true love, which was only to be found in marriage. "I don't flirt because I am waiting for 'my' girl whom God has preordained for me." The author differentiated between the "true" higher values, such as love, and the false, specious world of appearances, to which flirting belonged. In 99 cases out of 100, he informed young readers, the object of flirting, *das Poussiermaedchen,* will not be the future wife. The author even claimed that flirting would eventually undermine the entire system of law upon which church authority rested. Flirting was a violation of the sixth commandment (adultery); the seventh commandment (it would encourage young boys to steal money to pay for dates; "I have to respect my wallet"); the eighth commandment (lying); the ninth and tenth commandments (coveting); and the fourth commandment (by flirting, one no longer respected one's parents and authority).

That this article targeted young men might suggest that the church presented young men and young women with what was essentially the same course of moral instruction and education. In reality, however, the church directed its concerns about degenerate behavior and declining moral standards disproportionately toward women. Church leaders were far more fearful of the impact of "practical materialism" on women and of "dialectical materialism" on men. As Gertrud von LeFort, one of the most widely read Catholic authors of the time, explained, "The fallen girl is fundamentally more fallen than the fallen boy. Just as the fallen angel is more horrible than the fallen human being, so too is the fallen woman more horrible than the fallen man. As a result, the girl bears a particular responsibility for the boy. Eve is the temptress (the enticer) and Adam falls with and through Eve."[24]

The individual who charted this course for women's youth work from 1910 through the early 1950s was Hermann Klens, a priest from one of the most staunchly traditional areas of Westphalia, the Catholic Sauerland. Klens's attitudes and values were an unmistakable product of this insular Catholic world. He was one of nine children; his father was a shoemaker, and his mother stayed at home to care for the children. Klens admitted that he based the ideas that underlay his pedagogy for women on his mother, a woman who, in his words, lived plainly and simply from her Catholic faith. "I never saw anything in her which I could not have but honored. For my later life work, she was the reliable model for a woman and a mother."[25] Within such a staunchly Catholic region, it was taken for granted that a young lad as talented as Klens would enter the priesthood. In 1905 he took his vows and was immediately sent to a parish in Dortmund, then one of the fastest-growing cities within Germany. Klens was horrified by what he regarded as the debilitating and disorienting impact of industrialization on the young women, most of whom were recent arrivals from the countryside, in his parish. Given charge of a maiden congregation, he set out to provide the more than 400 young women with a "slice of home," an attempt to replicate agrarian structures and values within the industrial world. The congregation blossomed under his care. Its membership increased dramatically, and he became recognized nationally as a pioneer for female youth work in Germany.[26]

In what was to become his life's work, Klens began to extend his success in Dortmund to other parishes, first within his home diocese of Paderborn and, subsequently, for all of Germany. Just as many of his colleagues created national networks of workers' organizations and political parties, so, too, did he do the same for the maiden congregations. By 1915 he had created a national ring of congregations (Zentralverband der katholischen Jungfrauenvereinigungen Deutschlands). For the time, this was a bold step. Most priests simply took the presence of women within the church for granted and opposed putting in extra hours to minister to women's groups. Klens's initiatives, furthermore, took place at a time when no national organizations within the church existed for any youth organizations, male or female. Klens's efforts long predated— and even inspired—Mosterts's and Wolker's crusades to unify male youth organizations throughout Germany.

Klens, more than any other Catholic youth leader, embodied the mixture of conservatism and modernity that characterized female youth work during the first half of the twentieth century. The values that he sought to instill in young women—sacrifice, service, humility, piety, and reverence —were unabashedly traditional. In his sermons and public statements he emphasized these virtues to such a degree that by the late 1940s some of his colleagues had come to regard him as hopelessly out of touch with reality.[27] Yet Klens deliberately set himself against other currents of the time. He continually maintained that women needed a space within the church free from the domination of men. Just as women needed their own separate sphere within society, within the so-called motherly professions (nursing, social work, and teaching), so, too, did he strive to carve out a separate sphere for women in the church. Many of the women to whom he ministered praised him effusively and bestowed upon him the title "the advocate of women."

By the late 1920s, however, there were signs that Klens's approaches were losing their luster. Many youth leaders became aware that as young women discovered alternatives to the austere congregations, traditional feminine forms of piety no longer inspired them. The challenge to the traditional forms of youth work came from several directions, both within and outside the church. The Catholic youth and liturgical movements undercut the appeal of many of the more traditional congregations. Although neither movement set out to reconfigure the church's teachings on gender (both actually sought to revitalize traditional gender norms), both inadvertently transformed the attitudes of many young Catholics toward gender relations. The challenge to the traditional feminine norms of the church came from a new militant right that sought to replace what it regarded as weak, feminine forms of piety from the nineteenth century with more dynamic models.

One youth leader associated with the youth movement, Ludwig Esch, sought to transform the image of Mary from that of a suffering and weeping woman to a strong matriarch: "The picture of Mary had been misrepresented through softness, sweetness and pious blathering. As a result, I, as a boy who made a point of not showing any weaknesses (at least publicly), did not want to have anything to do with it. So I turned away, until Mary was portrayed as the strong woman. Then I gladly served." But as Irmtraud Götz von Olenhusen has pointed out, only male identity underwent a significant transformation during this period. The organizations for young women remained mired in the old traditions. The church continued to make its case for the "polarity of the sexes," or as Hermann Klens put it, "The most noble, most womanly young women for the best, most manly young men."[28]

More significantly, some young women in the 1930s and 1940s began to organize themselves into small youth cells independent of the local clergy. These groups were deeply committed to the traditional views of the church regarding the role of women in society and were dedicated to a rigorous asceticism: abstinence, teetotaling, and above all, the duty to heal the world by spreading feminine virtues of love, selflessness, and charity. Yet they were characterized by a militance and an independence of action that directly contradicted the passivity of the old congregations.

Many of these groups organized and carried out their own hikes, picked their own leaders, which they called *Jungführerinnen* (a word adapted from the male youth movement), and put on their own theater events and social hours. During the war many of these groups met clandestinely in local woods or abandoned farmhouses. After the war many of them continued their activities as before. One young woman, Christel Beilmann, carried out her leadership role with such zeal that she aroused the suspicion of conservative male church leaders.[29] One leader described the attitudes and disposition of Beilmann as "symptomatic of the confusion, and unfortunately, for the lack of reverence of many of our youth and female youth leaders (thank God, however, of only a small proportion)."[30] These youth groups for women had appropriated the outward forms of male youth work, a reversal of gender roles that was profoundly unsettling to many church leaders. Some church leaders were horrified by the tent camps that some young women had set up. Camping, they argued, contradicted the true essence of women.[31]

As nonplussed as church leaders were by the effects of the liturgical and youth movements on the congregations by the late 1930s, even they recognized that the greater challenge to the gender norms they sought to uphold came from the National Socialist state.[32] By the mid-1930s the regime had made participation in the League of German Girls (Bund Deutscher Mädel) (BDM) mandatory. In many locations, BDM leaders deliberately set out—as Catholic leaders were all too aware—to drive a wedge between young women and the clergy and, as a result, dissolve traditional allegiances to the church. Children were encouraged to denounce their parents to the authorities and to ridicule the religious values of their elders.[33] The BDM, moreover, frequently sponsored enticing activities that church leaders might otherwise have forbidden: swimming, gymnastics, and hiking. To no surprise, Catholic leaders claimed that the BDM had led to a masculinization of women. They were horrified by the manner in which the Nazi regime openly mocked church teachings on sexuality, abstinence, and virginity.[34] Girls who hoped to enter a Catholic order or who sought to delay marriage and childbearing, for instance, were often the target of brutal abuse. Although church leaders were not unsympathetic to the Nazi state's campaign for family values, they were alarmed by the state's willingness to sponsor coed activities for youth in the hopes of raising fertility rates. Some referred to the BDM with derisive nicknames such as *Bubi Drück mich!* (Boy, Hold Me Tight!) or *Bund deutscher*

Milchkühe (League of German Milk Cows).³⁵ After the war, many Catholic leaders were determined to reeducate girls along traditional lines. As one youth leader declared, "The word maiden [Jungfrau, which also means virgin] must be allowed to be said again without inducing sneers, as was the case in the preceding decades."³⁶

Some church leaders went still further and argued that the rise of National Socialism and the outbreak of the Second World War were the direct results of female emancipation. According to this interpretation, women were the embodiment of love, motherhood, and service to others and normally counterbalanced the more barbaric impulses of men. In giving up their roles as nurturers, German women had caused society to become masculinized and barbarized. According to Mosshammer, "Much of what took place in these years—the mass murders and the concentration camps, the tragedy of Stalingrad, a war waged in utter disregard of the civilian population—would have been unthinkable, if women in the appropriate places had exerted their moderating and soothing influence upon men. Men, at this time, became so degenerate, their manhood so out of control, because of the absence of women and because women had failed in their womanhood."³⁷

By the end of the war, church leaders were struggling to adjust to a time when it appeared that traditional gender norms had crumbled. They were all too aware that millions of men remained interred in POW camps and that, as a result, German women had taken charge of clearing rubble and holding together broken families. The church's response to this changed climate, however, was not always uniform. On one hand, many leaders were quick to praise women for their part in helping German society to recover physically and morally from the destruction caused by the war and even claimed that only women could put Germany back on the path to healing. One of Klens's favorite sayings from the time was "All necessity cries out for Mother!"

On the other hand, many leaders insisted that German women were fundamentally incapable of coping with chaos and destruction of this magnitude. To quote Hermann Klens from 1946, "The general destruction and lack of order is borne least by women. In their weaknesses, they are particularly vulnerable to these conditions. As a result, women become most easily unrestrained and disordered."³⁸ Such fears were fueled by the realities within many German cities, where prostitution was rampant and thousands of robust and well-fed American soldiers were proving too alluring for many Germany *Fräuleins*.[39] In light of their widely held ideology that the materialism of the Weimar years had paved the way for the national disasters that lay ahead, many church leaders believed that the renewed signs of decadence—dancing (*Tanzwut*), prostitution, and strong women—portended yet another disaster to come. Stabilizing the Catholic milieu and providing order to the chaos of postwar society meant cultivating traditional gender norms for youth.

CATHOLIC YOUTH WORK FOR
YOUNG WOMEN AFTER THE WAR

Many of the same difficulties—whether to judge women as temptresses, harlots, mothers, healers, or victims, strong or weak—plagued leaders as they strove to chart a new path for women's youth work after the war. As a result, Catholic youth work emerged as a bundle of contradictions, a set of assumptions about the nature and roles of women that were not always immediately congruous. Women such as Beilmann, who had been inspired by the liturgical and youth movements, sought to instill a renewed sense of Catholic conscience within young women—of pride in being Catholic, of independence of action and thought, and even of a certain militance (if only to reinforce traditional values). They often replicated the activities of male youth organizations, such as theater presentations, hikes, sporting events, and *Heimabende*. Many church leaders strove to assist young women in the transition from childhood to adulthood, to develop the full, mature Catholic personality. Of course, many conservative church leaders saw their task as one of protecting young women from the corrupt, seductive world around them. Church leaders even established agencies explicitly charged with keeping young persons, in particular young women, safe from corruption and vice. By the mid-1950s, their list of potentially dangerous influences had grown to include dancing, cinema, smoking, coed camping, beauty pageants, coed sporting events, gymnastics meets, provocative advertisements and billboards, alcohol, circuses, Carnival, and racy comics.[40]

In the years immediately after the war, youth leaders were also confronted with the difficulty of dealing with the millions of young women who, as a result of the conflict, were unlikely to find a spouse. Traditionally, youth organizations for women had based their membership on marital status. Women were permitted to remain members of the Catholic youth organizations until the day of marriage, unless they had disgraced themselves through immoral or unseemly conduct. Those who did not marry were permitted to remain members until their death. In some congregations, as a result, women in their sixties and seventies served as *Jungführerinnen*. In one congregation in Bavaria, for instance, an eighty-two-year-old spinster was the youth leader.[41]

By 1946 and 1947, Catholic leaders had become acutely embarrassed by this situation. Some noted with grave concern that younger women were being scared away from Catholic youth groups whose leadership was in the hands of their aunts or even great-aunts. In light of the fact that the number of unmarried women had swelled during the war, most youth leaders concluded that some action had to be taken. They, however, failed to agree on precisely how to rectify the situation. Some suggested setting a cutoff age at twenty-five or thirty years and establishing new groups for older women. Others urged that older women be permitted to remain, in accordance with congregational bylaws. Other church leaders offered to place these unmarried women within groups for married women with children. According to one survey of thirty-six parishes within the archdiocese of Cologne, fourteen continued to place unmarried women within the groups for maidens. Eleven transferred them to the organizations for mothers, while the remainder either arranged for clerics to minister to the women independently or had found other solutions.[42]

Catholic youth leaders were thus forced to reexamine traditional conceptions of gender and, specifically, to weigh the relative importance of two potentially irreconcilable ideals: that of the virgin and that of the mother. Unmarried women, in particular, resented their second-class status in a church that celebrated motherhood. One young woman, for instance, was outraged by church teachings that declared that women could find fulfillment only through marriage and childbirth. "We Christians," she argued, "know or should in any case know, that the value of a woman is fully independent of her attachment to a man." This woman even compared the position of the church to that of the National Socialist regime, which attacked unmarried women as persons hostile to the state and its population policies.[43] Returning to an old tradition within Catholic theology, educators sought to reconfigure Marian ideals so as to place the status of the virgin on a par with that of the mother. They urged unmarried women to transfer the spirit of motherhood to other domains of life where they would be in a position to realize the high ideals of sacrifice, love for others, and reverence.[44] Klens encouraged unmarried women to seek motherly vocations, such as nursing, teaching, and charity work, so that they could regard their potentially unhappy situation not as an evil destiny but as a higher calling.[45] In this vein, Ottilie Mosshammer cited the example of a female doctor, unhappy at remaining single, who dedicated her life to healing her patients and, in the process, caught an illness and died a martyr's death.[46] Yet it seems doubtful whether alternatives such as the celebration of the virgin offered much consolation to these young women. Klens ultimately repeated old platitudes that were increasingly detached from the concrete needs of individual women.[47]

It should come as no surprise, given this diversity of goals and approaches to women's youth work, that leaders found themselves at odds over whether to integrate female youth organizations into the fledgling BDKJ. Once again, questions of gender decisively shaped the outcome of these struggles: the merger of these once-independent organizations on the administrative level but continued separation at the parish level. Ludwig Wolker initiated the efforts to bring together male and female youth organizations as part of his larger quest to forge a giant organization for all Catholic young persons. Wolker, moreover, harbored conceptions of gender different from those of most of his colleagues. At a time when the German bishops continued to hold fast to guidelines they had drawn up in the 1920s to regulate the length of skirts, Wolker actually sought to relax prohibitions on issues of sexual ethics and gender norms. On more than one occasion he accused Klens of beating to death his message of self-sacrifice, humility, and motherliness.[48] Young women, he observed, no longer needed to be reminded incessantly of the importance of Marian virtues. In 1942 Wolker even drew up a set of guidelines that, among other things, called for masturbation to be regarded as a venial and not a mortal sin.[49] He believed that a renewed religious identity ultimately had to transcend all limitations of class and gender, an agenda inimical to Klens, who emphasized the peculiarities and need for the separation of the sexes.

After a series of hard-fought battles, Klens acceded to Wolker's plans, but not because he believed that his female youth organizations would profit from these steps. Rather, Klens assumed that the presence of women within the top leadership of the Bund would benefit male youth leaders. He, too, believed that the worst atrocities of the preceding decade had come about because women had failed in their mission to counteract the barbaric behavior of men. By integrating Catholic youth organizations, he envisioned that the BDKJ might restore feminine virtues to male institutions and serve as a beacon for all German institutions.[50] The bishops appear to have operated from more practical considerations. Although many were skeptical of Wolker's plans, they reluctantly agreed to this merger primarily to cut costs. Many bishops warned that the men and women in such a tight-knit environment would succumb to sexual temptation, fears that were not unfounded. In fact, rumors spread that Wolker engaged in affairs with his female colleagues in Altenberg.[51] This situation ultimately gave the bishops grounds to dismiss him in 1951.

Yet Klens presciently realized that integration would inevitably lead to a loss of autonomy for women.[52] Within the BDKJ, women continually played second fiddle to men. Although the number of women enrolled in the Catholic youth organizations in 1950 was still substantially larger than that of men, the women's organization received considerably less money than its male counterpart.[53] Still more irksome to the women in the BDKJ was the fact that the men ran the show. The female leaders of the Bund complained that they had been "steamrolled" by the male leaders, in particular by Wolker. "Our hopes for the possibility of a fair treatment for the women's organizations have completely disappeared within the Bund," they wrote in an angry letter to Frings.[54] They urged the bishops to grant them a greater role not just within the Bund—to hire and fire their own personnel—but within public life in general. The situation, however, did not improve after Wolker's death. Years later, the women at the helm of the BDKJ noted that Wolker's successor, a priest from Limburg, Willy Bokler, treated women as subordinates and not as coworkers.[55] One woman stated bluntly that years of being surrounded exclusively by male colleagues had left Bokler incapable of interacting successfully with women.[56]

Put more generally, conceptions of gender that portrayed women as weak and in need of separate spheres afforded women greater autonomy than conceptions that aimed for integration and that downplayed questions of morality and values. Masculinizing Catholic identity, a cornerstone of Wolker's vision ever since the 1920s, was necessarily accompanied by eliminating, or at least starkly reducing, female spheres within the church.

This pattern was not confined to the top leadership of the Bund. Young women who were ardently committed to spreading traditional, Catholic values to their peers often found themselves rejected from all sides. They were unable to gain the support of church leaders because of the zeal with which they carried on their activities and of the lingering suspicions of conservatives. More tragically, because of their continued allegiance to what many of their friends and colleagues regarded as old-fashioned notions, they often failed to win over the young women whom they had targeted for membership in their groups.

The history of a group of eight to ten young women from Essen in the late 1940s illustrates this predicament. These women were determined to form groups for young women from the working class in the tradition of the CAJ. They hoped to clean up what they regarded as a climate of moral filth in the workplace: dirty jokes, promiscuity, and anticlericalism. They believed that the presence of morally pure women would suffice to cleanse the degenerate atmosphere and restore Christian values to a pagan environment. "We have to convince our (female) colleagues of the power of love." The group summarized its philosophy in particularly telling terms: "The activity of women never presumes that women are equal to men; women rule by serving, but they also serve by ruling in the right way."[57] With this philosophy in mind, group members distributed leaflets to young women at work, held weekly group meetings, routinely visited sick or troubled colleagues, and approached women they perceived to be at risk—most of whom were involved in the black market or laden with familial problems in the wake of the war.

The path that lay ahead was to be rockier than they had imagined. Klens, who believed that women should not be pursuing careers in factories or coal mines, took steps to block the formation of local CAJ groups for women.[58] Wolker, similarly, remained opposed to the CAJ as a whole, for both men and women, committed as he was to uniting all Catholic youth organizations. Convinced that they needed stronger clerical support, the women in Essen appealed to the bishops to appoint a Jesuit father of whom they were particularly fond.[59] Frings, however, denied their request, citing issues of jurisdiction. The group, by now extremely angered, fired back a letter deploring the church's lack of sensitivity toward women's and workers' issues. To make matters worse, the women in Essen found little support from their supposed benefactors: male CAJ leaders. After a national conference of the CAJ, for instance, the women bitterly noted that their concerns had been completely overlooked.[60]

The response from the women in the Ruhr to whom they ministered, however, was dismissive. The women who ran the group were, for the most part, not blue-collar factory workers but, rather, white-collar work-ers—secretaries and office workers within the large industrial conglom-erates, Krupp and Thyssen.[61] A few were kitchen workers; others were kindergarten teachers or managerial assistants. Given the bourgeois or lower middle-class background of these women, it is hardly surprising that many of their efforts ended in failure. They had, for instance, set up a sewing circle that met with utter disbelief from young working-class women within the industrial heartland of the Ruhr who had neither time for nor interest in such traditional activities.[62] The women's incessant calls for service and self-sacrifice likewise were treated with skepticism and disdain. Some group members concluded that their philosophy of service was, in reality, little more than egoism and self-indulgence.[63] Others complained that they had defined their goals too broadly; rather than try to help all women and men, they should concentrate, they ar-gued, only on those with personal connections to the group.[64] By 1950 the group in Essen was on the verge of disintegration. Several of their leaders had reportedly been seen smoking, and fights had broken out among the members.[65] Unable to recruit a new generation of leaders, the group had ceased to exist by 1951, the idealism of its members seemingly dashed.

The fate of the group in Essen illustrates the dilemma in which many groups of young women found themselves after the war: how could they reconcile the official teachings of the church pertaining to values and gender with the realities of postwar German society that they encountered in their everyday lives? The church set its ideals so high and demanded so much of its members that young women, particularly those of a more sensitive disposition, were traumatized when they realized that they were unable to meet these expectations. Christel Beilmann claimed that many top-ranking Catholic youth leaders suffered tremendously later in life as a result of their experiences within youth circles. According to her, they had been brought up to regard marriage as something sacred—or as Klens would put it, as the crown of life.[66] Given the importance that the church vested in the sacrament of marriage, many young women were surprised to discover—and indeed were disillusioned by the fact—that marriage frequently failed to meet the standards of excellence and blessedness that the church had promised. Several marriages ended in divorce, and one youth leader even took her own life.[67]

The changed realities of the postwar era—the surplus of women, in-creasing prosperity, and the spread of consumerism—led many young women to question church teachings on morals and values. Young women found themselves unsettled not just by the church doctrines on fundamental questions of marriage, love, and careers but by many smaller issues, such as flirting, dancing, and gymnastics. The degree to which these issues resonated with young women can be seen in hundreds of letters written to the editors of Catholic newspapers in which young women themselves voiced their opinions. Some supported the church positions; others were hostile. In no case, however, did these young women show signs of outright rebellion. The statements they made in church newspapers evinced, rather, a latent dissatisfaction with church teachings that was similar to forms of passive resistance. Young persons simply disregarded church teachings and, in doing so, ultimately eroded the authority of the church to speak on these questions.

The church's stance on female employment, in particular, alienated many young women. Ever since the 1920s, Catholic leaders had noted the rise in female employment with grave concern. Klens and other leaders had tried to counter this trend by exhorting young women to enter only those professions appropriate to the female sex: teaching, social work, and charity work. Yet young women continued to stream into jobs that were rapidly being created in factories and small companies in medium and large cities. Catholic newspapers noted with great concern that the number of women entering more traditional fields—the so-called social and motherly professions—was slowing to a trickle.[68] Even low-paying jobs such as secretaries had a glamour that few Catholic girls could resist; the women who held these jobs were often depicted as fashion conscious (most wore makeup and shorter skirts). For many young women, working in traditional professions, such as being a housewife or a maid in another person's household, conferred a second-class status.

Of career-related concerns, working as a maid in the homes of other families (der Haushaltsdienst) provoked the most discussion. In 1951 a young woman who had served for more than eleven years as a maid wrote to the editorial board of the church newspaper for the diocese of Cologne to voice her dissatisfaction with her profession. She noted bitterly that she had been poorly paid and treated as a third-class citizen, even though her work required as much energy, sweat, and toil as factory or office labor. "It is quite understandable that young girls say that only idiots go to work as a maid."[69] This letter opened the gate for a torrent of responses that flowed in for more than two years. Defenders of this profession generally extolled the lessons in humility, sacrifice, and modesty that it imparted to younger girls. One woman from Cologne argued that service as a maid was part of a young woman's larger schooling in life "to place the ego aside and adapt yourself to other human beings."[70] Another woman's account of her experiences as a maid reads almost as a confessional: "I was often dissatisfied and tortured myself, asking why, until I finally realized that the source of my dissatisfaction lay with me, and namely my lacking will to serve."[71] In less emotional terms, others maintained that working as a maid provided excellent training for how to be a housewife and mother, the future profession of every woman.[72]

The opponents of working for other families, in contrast, spoke primarily of their unpleasant experiences. One woman described working as a maid as the "epitome of everything horrible": scrubbing, cleaning, cooking, toiling from 5:30 A.M. to 11:00 P.M., and getting frayed nerves but never a kind word from the host family.[73] Another woman argued that conditions were so degrading that many housewives preferred to work elsewhere and pay others to perform household work for them. She argued that service as a maid had to be seen for what it really was: not merely as a service of caring love but as a profession that lacked the protections that other jobs had, such as fixed and limited working hours.[74] In fact, conditions for housewives in some rural parts of Germany were so poor that death rates for women over age fifty, according to estimates by the Catholic Caritas organizations, were 25 percent higher than for men; for every 100 men over sixty-five in the countryside, there were only 89 women.[75]

Put more generally, far more devastating to the Catholic milieu than scathing attacks launched by critics and intellectuals in the 1960s were the negative everyday experiences of young persons. When better alternatives arose—in the case of employment opportunities this meant the more glamorous factory work and secretarial positions—many youth simply ignored the polemics of the church to find their fortunes elsewhere. Throughout the 1950s, Catholic newspapers continually bemoaned the exodus of young women from rural regions into larger metropolitan areas. Through their new jobs in factories and offices, young Catholic women were exposed to a climate that allowed them to flirt with young men and mingle with Protestant and Socialist colleagues in a place where the church wielded little or no influence.

As the discussion of maid service makes clear, many young Catholics had begun to bristle at the strictures under which they were being raised. Faced with mounting pressure to change such situations, one youth leader, Heidi Carl, who headed the BDKJ's "column for female youth," gave a speech in 1953 titled "Be Modern, Catholics!" In this address, which was reprinted in Catholic youth newspapers, she caricatured popular conceptions of Catholics:

> Let us ask ourselves, how do other Germans look at us Catholics today? Are not being Catholic and being modern contradictions in terms? According to one view, being modern means: beautiful, with makeup, well-groomed, efficient, social, secure, dancing boogie, hanging abstract art on the wall, having unsymmetrical furniture, being charming and good at making conversation, friendly, flirtatious, with-it, mundane. Being Catholic, in contrast: somewhat prudish, traditional, serious, unpleasant, old-fashioned, narrow, shy, inhibited and insecure, bashful, inefficient, somewhat silly, being a wallflower, and backward. Isn't there even a derogatory expression out there— Boy, you are Catholic?[76]

Carl maintained that the church had to make its traditional values more palatable to young persons or risk losing them altogether. She urged young persons to adopt modern standards of dress while retaining core Catholic values. In the same speech, for instance, she asked Catholic youth, "Can I wear three-quarter length pants and wear makeup and still be Catholic? Why not, as long as you have the proper attitude." She summed up her ambitions: "Our goal is to ensure that every girl within our groups is both modern and Catholic." These pronouncements were enthusiastically greeted by young women but evoked prolonged controversies. One young woman from rural Bavaria, for instance, wrote to Cardinal Frings deploring the speech. Frings, apparently equally astonished by the tenor of Carl's remarks, pledged to take her to task.[77] Carl put it prophetically: "Our inner enemy will, however, fight back: the traditional Christianity of grandmother's time. According to this, merely sitting in on the Sunday morning service and murmuring back the rosary would suffice for one's personal Christianity."[78]

As Carl had foreseen, the issue of makeup ignited discussions that lasted for nearly a decade throughout Catholic Germany. Makeup had, of course, been around for decades, and in the 1920s it became widely identified with the "modern women's" movement.[79] Church leaders condemned it not just out of fear that it would lead to sexual improprieties but because it had originated in the working classes. Their target was ultimately mass society and mass culture: they feared that their Catholic women would devolve into human beings who had lost their individuality in an era of mass production, industrialization, and mass society. Along these lines, many Catholic youth leaders, in particular those who had been active within the youth movement of the 1920s and 1930s, drew a sharp distinction between their elite values of honor, duty, self-sacrifice, and asceticism and the more seductive false values of the mass society around them. They repeatedly used the words "real" and "unreal" (echt and unecht) to distinguish between a true spiritual essence and the superficial appearances of mass culture. In their eyes, makeup covered up one's true essence and ran against the deeply rooted Catholic ideal of naturalness. True beauty, they insisted, is always connected with the soul and not with the body.[80]

For both sides, then, makeup raised deeper questions regarding the extent to which external appearance reflects inner worth and to which traditional values can be reconciled with those of modern society. Carl, as well as most women voicing their opinions in the Cologne church newspaper, maintained that makeup posed little risk to girls so long as they retained inner Catholic values. She essentially offered a spirited defense of the core Catholic virtues of faith, moderation, valor, and love. Like many young Catholic women, she asserted that modern women had little choice but to wear makeup, for girls who looked and behaved like their grandmothers were often considered ridiculous. This argument underscored the fact that the Catholic milieu was no longer as isolated as it had been even twenty-five years earlier. Even the smallest villages now contained significant numbers of Protestant refugees, commuters to nearby cities, and theaters, all of which exposed young persons to new trends and made them far more self-conscious about their appearance and behavior.

Critics asserted, not without reason, that parts of a fundamental Catholic self-understanding were being lost, an identity that throughout the preceding century had been based on opposition to modern society. Such critics regarded makeup as the first in a tumbling row of dominoes.

Concessions on makeup would undermine church doctrines on sexuality, which for better or for worse remained at the core of Catholic teachings. Religious conservatives insisted on maintaining the proper lines between fashion, modern society, and religious beliefs and asserted that form and content were not to be separated.

One additional example should suffice here: an extended debate titled "Krach mit Lieselotte." In 1952 the editorial board of the church newspaper in Cologne printed a letter from a young man named Peter who had just terminated his relationship with his girlfriend of more than two years, Lieselotte.[81] The reason for Peter's decision: on a hot, sultry day, Lieselotte fluttered about wearing nothing but a short, deeply cut, sleeveless dress. Peter denied being jealous; rather, he insisted (in rather overblown rhetoric) that no decent girl behaved in this way. "I don't understand why our girls as well imitate those starlets who, in almost every illustrated magazine and in countless films, make themselves the trendsetters for what is a lack of dignity and who are being dragged along by styles that (and here I simply have to be blunt) look like they have been chosen by women of ill repute, who are using their charms and attractiveness to bring in men in order to earn their money for the day." Peter issued an ultimatum to his girlfriend: she could clothe herself like a wholesome Catholic girl or lose his friendship and trust forever.

Peter's seventy-year-old Uncle Wilhelm quickly entered the fray. He condemned the iniquitous moral standards of Lieselotte's generation and rejected her arguments that low-cut, sleeveless dresses could ever be morally acceptable. "I am of the opinion that what was improper back when I was young must still be regarded as such today."[82] Lieselotte angrily wrote back to say that she did little more than what most girls in the city had already done. "I am certainly no weeping Willow [Trauerweide, an old-fashioned, dour lady], and I simply have to go along with the latest fashions. I don't find anything wrong when girls wear sleeveless dresses. If you and people like you find something wrong with it, then you only have yourselves to blame!" She concluded her letter to Peter with a thinly veiled accusation: "If you want to make our future truly dependent on a question of clothing, then you have never truly loved me."[83]

This exchange brought in, over a period of four months, hundreds of responses not just from the Rhineland but also from America and Africa, of which only a fraction were printed. Most of the letters that subsequently appeared took Peter's side. One nineteen-year-old pledged her admiration for Peter's forthrightness; women needed men with strong, unyielding characters. Marriage, she maintained, needed the proper alignment of roles, in particular, subordination (*Unterordnung*). A group of Boy Scouts went further and argued that gender determines national destiny. "A people (*Volk*) arises and falls on the basis of its women and girls. Can you explain why the German people has fallen to such depths?"[84]

Most letters reproached Lieselotte for her stubborn unwillingness to face reality. Any half-witted girl should be able to make the connection between revealing clothing, prurient male desires, and the dignity and purity of women, even when standards of dress were no longer the same as they had been in 1900. One self-proclaimed city girl observed that external appearance served as a mirror of the soul; clothing reveals one's inner ambitions, dreams, manners, and beliefs.[85] Another letter-writer expressed the same views far more negatively. "When a woman, whose privilege and holy obligation is to protect everything fine, chaste, and tender, exposes so much of her body, as this dress does, she is speaking to other persons, without words, as she has undoubtedly noticed from the looks she has received from boys."[86] One woman maintained that sleeveless dresses could only serve as objects of temptation, which would in turn lead many otherwise wholesome young men and women down the path to ruin. "Who destroys blossoms, harvests no fruit," according to an old saying.[87] Yet another woman inadvertently revealed a deep source of anxiety for many Catholics who feared the long-term consequences of the women's movement: a shortage of priests. As she bluntly put it, "Do you really believe that a women with her lips full of red lipstick and red fingernails and wearing such deeply cut clothes could be the mother of a priest?"[88] In a final blow, the staff of the newspaper condemned Lieselotte for encouraging others to lead degenerate lives.[89]

Lieselotte and the persons who sprang to her defense saw the situation differently. They echoed the statements made by Heidi Carl: far more important than one's external appearance is the fact that one remains—internally—a good Catholic. One woman summed it up: "There is no such thing as indecent clothing. There are only people with indecent thoughts, feelings, and perceptions. I can't include all women wearing sleeveless dresses and bold décolletage in this category of people. One's conscience alone is decisive."[90] Others noted that Lieselotte, her choice of clothing notwithstanding, had remained a loyal member of her youth group; she had even met Peter at a party sponsored by her parish. Most of the women who voiced their opinions in the church newspaper for Cologne—even those who sharply criticized Lieselotte—dismissed Uncle Wilhelm as an old geezer who was unwilling to recognize that style and fashion changed throughout the decades. One girl averred that Uncle Wilhelm's commentary was sheer nonsense; to condemn a human being solely on the basis of her choice of clothing was simply unconscionable. Another respondent asserted that the real issue in this debate was not gender but class. She maintained that sleeveless dresses were only viewed as immoral since many women from the working classes wore them; in the past, she noted, the church had never voiced any grievances when women from the nobility wore such dresses.[91]

Such debates evoked feelings of euphoria and empowerment among young Catholic women. As open dialogues within a conservative environment, they gave young persons the chance to voice their opinions on fundamental questions of morals, values, relationships, and gender, often for the first time. Young persons responded with such fervor that even the editors, at the conclusion of this debate, admitted their astonishment not just at the sheer volume of the responses but at the fact that they continued to stream in for more than a year.[92]

For the first time, moreover, Catholic publicists began, however indirectly, to question the conduct not just of women but of men. At the end of the exchange, Peter himself came under fire from the editorial board. As they put it, he needed a thorough schooling in tact, wisdom, and Christian love.[93] For the same reason, a group of young women also took him to task. "Dear Peter," they wrote, "Do you know persons who can take such a strong critique and in the form you have put it, an ultimatum?"[94] Even though the church newspaper immediately pulled back its own punch, claiming that the matter was not important enough to warrant elaboration, this issue resurfaced in subsequent debates on the theme of marriage. Even in the early 1950s, many girls writing to church newspapers began to question the high ideals and conceptions of gender that Catholic theorists had invested in the institution of marriage. Many young girls noted that their own family life failed to live up to these standards of the "holy family." Some girls pointed out instances of spousal abuse—a taboo subject among most Catholics in the 1950s. Others began to suspect that the incessant calls for self-sacrifice that were directed solely at women were, in reality, a way for men to avoid grueling labor. As one woman noted, men get their evenings off; women receive yet more chores.[95] Others simply bemoaned the often joyless nature of marriages; they hoped to marry "for love," not out of duty.

By the early 1960s, Catholic conceptions of the roles within marriage had fundamentally changed. Catholic literature now called for men to play a greater part in family life and for a truer partnership. No longer was the woman to serve alone as the "heart" of the family, but she was to receive moral support from her husband. Instead of advocating separate spheres for men and women, educational tracts, lectures, and even seminars for young farmers urged cooperation. Partnership in the family became the model for a healthy society. As one 1964 brochure observed, "All areas in which men and women stand together in a healthy and moral relationship take on a family-like atmosphere and form the nucleus of a larger whole."[96] The dogma of equal worth was replaced by a doctrine of equal rights. Church leaders exhorted young women to enter the public sphere and the workplace and urged young men to assume greater duties and responsibilities at home. As one booklet explained, "The goal of being a good and virtuous housewife is insufficient for today. On the other hand, women must help men to win back an interest in the domains of life, from which they have distanced themselves for too long: familial and social questions."[97] These Catholics were reversing 100 years of church teachings. They were calling for men to take on more feminine roles and were accepting, however grudgingly, the more masculine roles that women had already assumed.

The word "love" assumed a much more prominent place in the vocabulary of Catholic moral theologians and, correspondingly, discussions of marriage. Church leaders, as we have seen, had throughout the 1950s derogated pop songs about love; now they appropriated the concept of love itself and made it a mainstay of their educational philosophies.[98] Church leaders urged young Catholics to marry for love and, instead of emphasizing the authority of parents, spoke of the "authority of love."[99] Parents were described as "partner of children"; the mother, as the best friend of children.[100] Although these concepts frequently lacked more precise definition, they spelled the end of traditional Catholic moral doctrines that celebrated sexless ideals of self-sacrifice and personal renunciation within marriage.

Responsible for these changes was, in part, a shift in the Catholic guard. A generation of conservatives began to retire. Pope Pius XII was replaced by the more progressive John XXIII. Within Germany, representatives of the traditional Catholic *Familienpolitik* such as Wilhelm Böhler either died or stepped down from their positions. The Second Vatican Council, of course, served as an enormous catalyst for change and elicited euphoria from many Catholics. Yet the reasons behind these transformations went far deeper. Catholics were, above all, not alone in making these changes. In the youth work of Protestant denominations in the United States, church leaders and educators spoke equally of the power of love. To a certain extent, they were consciously seeking to make the fount of religion less one of authority and obedience, concepts that were gradually taking on negative associations, but of healing, community, faith, and love, ideas that they hoped would renew the church. They rejected what they saw as a preoccupation with sin and the perceived negativity of traditional Catholic moral education. They were reacting to—and contributing to—the changing cultural climate of the late 1950s and 1960s. Authority was out, and love was in. Who, after all, could argue with the Beatles? "All you need is love!"

THE EROSION OF TRADITIONAL YOUTH WORK FOR YOUNG WOMEN

To what extent did this latent dissatisfaction with the church's positions on morals, dancing, and flirting lead to the exodus of young women from Catholic youth organizations by the late 1950s? And to what extent did the steps taken by leaders like Carl succeed in preventing a further decline?

The delay in bringing about change was responsible for a significant erosion of church authority and the collapse of many youth groups. The startling drop-off in the numbers of young women active in Catholic youth organizations throughout North Rhine–Westphalia can be read as yet another confirmation of the historic time lag within the Catholic church. Developments, ideas, and trends that originated elsewhere entered the ranks of the church only much later. Reformers like Carl were few and far between. They wielded relatively little influence outside youth work, and their proclamations were often bitterly contested by local clergy and religion teachers, who in any case, played a far greater role in the day-to-day life of young Catholics.

In some cities and small towns, youth work gradually changed with or without the knowledge of church superiors. Although youth work for young men and women under age eighteen was supposed to remain

Displaying a new spirit of conviviality, this gathering in 1949 brought together both young men and young women. Most activities until then had been segregated by sex. In this case, the participants are clearly older and dressed conservatively in suits and long dresses. (Courtesy of Jugendhaus Hardehausen)

strictly segregated by gender, many groups carried out activities jointly. Some groups were combined for secret hikes in the woods; others, to build showcases for their parishes.[101] The taboo on premarital sexual activity remained firmly in place, although many young women apparently walked down the wedding aisle visibly pregnant.

That most young women showed a distaste for the outdated mores forced on them by church superiors can be seen most clearly in the nearly complete disintegration of the Marian congregations by the 1950s. Although the congregations had entered a period of decline by the 1920s, the intervening twelve years of National Socialist rule led to a far more prodigious loss of membership. In some parishes in the archdiocese of Cologne, congregations lost five-sixths of their members. One youth worker for the diocese of Münster pointed the finger at the National Socialist ideology, which, in his words, deified the body and slighted the soul.[102] Other youth leaders blamed the character of the congregations themselves. In many parishes, all fourteen-year-old girls who had just finished their primary schooling were automatically inducted into the congregations, given a decorative membership badge, and presented with a long list of prayers and obligations.[103] Many of these groups, as a result, had ceased to be congregations in all but name. Instead of carrying out mandatory devotions, they put on plays, organized hikes, and held social hours—the usual activities for Catholic youth groups. Another observer reported that many groups were still carrying out their monthly prayer and meditation ceremonies but approached their obligations in such a perfunctory manner that they had lost the original spirit and intent of the congregations' founders. Since diocesan leaders were still unwilling to set age limits on members, some groups were dominated by elderly women. The youth leader of the diocese of Mainz, as a result, described the congregations there as "almost without exception, visibly stagnating entities." The name alone, he asserted, "horrifies young persons."[104] Even the Marian forms of piety, others noted, were in grave danger of disappearing.

These developments alarmed church officials who sought to make the Marian ideals embodied in the congregations the basis for rebuilding society after the war. To abandon the congregations, they argued, meant renouncing fundamental Catholic values. As one cleric put it, "One can hardly conceive how a leading Christian can reject the ideals of the Marian congregations; they are certainly the Catholic ideals!"[105] In response, high-ranking church officials searched for ways to resurrect all that was Marian: cults, orders, congregations, and virtues of humility, obedience, chastity, and motherhood. These initiatives came, for the large part, from above. Pope Pius XII, who particularly cherished the church's Marian traditions and heritage, issued an encyclical in 1948, Bis Saeculari, in which he called for young Catholics throughout the world to constitute new elite communities and rejuvenate old congregations. After proclaiming the new doctrine of the assumption of Mary in 1950, he ordered all devout Catholics to observe 1954 as a "Marian year."

German church leaders obediently set out to enact the wishes of the papacy. Throughout the late 1940s and early 1950s, various committees and work groups were set up to discuss how to restore Marian traditions. One group, whose members included Klens as well as the leader of the female youth organizations for the archdiocese of Cologne, embarked on an ambitious and highly idealistic crusade to restore the congregations to the preeminent position they had once enjoyed. Yet even the members in this group were not of one mind in how to achieve this goal. Some naively believed that they could turn back the clock and restore the mass model of the congregations from the turn of the century—an approach destined to fail.[106] Others sought to transform the congregations into a self-selected elite whose members would fulfill even more rigorous ideals of asceticism, moral purity, saintliness, and obedience.[107] They anticipated that this elite would energize the masses of the otherwise unorganized youth within the parish and serve as youth leaders for other parish youth groups.[108] These plans, however, never came to fruition. As late as the mid-1950s, the advocates of the congregations could still not agree on how to position their groups within the BDKJ.[109] Wolker placed numerous obstacles in the way. Proponents of the new form of the congregations even spoke of a "fight against the congregations" and the lack of support from church leaders, even those sympathetic to Marian ideals.[110]

Although the advocates of the congregations succeeded in overcoming the opposition of Wolker, the majority of young women continued to shun these groups. In the archdiocese of Cologne, approximately 600 congregations had been founded at the turn of the century. According to an estimate by diocesan youth officials in 1957, only 100 of these continued to induct new members and perform the normal obligations.[111] Most of these congregations were indistinguishable from regular parish groups.[112] Diocesan officials were able to name only one parish where the clergy had established a congregation in the new form. As a result, church leaders contemplated setting up congregations that would serve entire deaneries and even dioceses; at this point young women began to complain about the difficulty in arranging for transportation to locations often fifty kilometers distant.

Much to the embarrassment of church leaders, it became unmistakably clear by the mid-1950s that they had signally failed to rejuvenate the church's Marian heritage.[113] Nowhere can the ultimate futility of these efforts be seen more clearly than in the attempts of diocesan leaders in Cologne to bring about a Marian revival in 1953. In what they billed as the major religious event of the year, they brought to the archdiocese of Cologne numerous Marian icons and relics—the Peregrinatio Maria—from the village of Fatima in Portugal, where many young women reported that they had seen apparitions of the Virgin Mary in 1917. Church leaders transported these figures of Mary from village to village by truck and unloaded the statues in front of hundreds, sometimes thousands of intrigued observers. As pilgrimages and processions took place, they

Another Pentecost gathering, this time from 1955. The women are still dressed traditionally, a sign that the fundamental forms of youth work had yet to change. (Courtesy of Jugendhaus Hardehausen)

reported tremendous excitement and curiosity.[114] Yet scarcely one year later they sadly noted that the fervor had waned; the Peregrinatio Mary had apparently been a short-lived wonder with little "long-term success."[115] In retrospect, these events of the early 1950s—the Peregrinatio Maria and the calling of the Marian year—represent a "last gasp" of such feminine forms of religious piety and not the start of a movement for renewal.[116]

Although these developments disproportionately affected the Marian congregations, ordinary Catholic parish groups were equally frustrated by the reluctance of young women to commit to a life of asceticism. The data gathered in several surveys of Catholic youth organizations is particularly revealing. In 1955, 1,200 young persons between ages fourteen and eighteen, all of whom had jobs, were asked why they had left their groups.[117] Approximately half responded that they no longer had the time to take part in group activities. Twenty percent admitted that they had problems with the leadership of a group or had failed to gain parental permission to participate. At first glance it appears that practical considerations and not deeper questions of morality or gender were relevant to the decisions of many young persons to leave their groups. A more careful look at the results of this survey, however, indicates that many young persons were simply fed up with traditional teachings. Many respondents, for instance, complained that the activities sponsored by their groups consisted of little more than insipid lectures, many of which dealt almost exclusively with gender and values. Typical presentations were titled "Marriage: The Crown of Life!" or "The Way of the Family." Already in 1949 the leader of Catholic youth work for women, Ludgera Kerstholt, noted that many young Catholic women were becoming averse to programs and events that focused too narrowly on uniquely feminine qualities. As she put it, "Perhaps we have overdone educational themes such as 'The woman' and 'the girl.' "[118] Many young persons wanted less religion and more fun—sports, dancing, gymnastics, music, and singing. One woman wrote to Die Jungführerin, a newspaper designated for young female youth leaders, to voice her concerns about this development. "Is it not strange that we are so frighteningly determined to avoid any semblance of special piety in our group work? Every group leader will then say, 'no one will come to them.' "[119]

Another example, involving a group of sixteen- and seventeen-year-old girls from Langenfeld, a small city halfway between Cologne and Düsseldorf, illustrates the extent to which many young women had become dissatisfied with their groups. These self-proclaimed dance aficionados were planning to celebrate Carnival by taking part in a large dance festival sponsored by another parish. Although girls from neighboring parishes had already made plans to attend, the local priest in Langenfeld refused to give them permission to join the party, since the majority of the girls were still under eighteen. The group, clearly disappointed, appealed to Cardinal Frings to override the decision of their priest.[120] At the end of their letter the girls appended a brief warning: "Or is it better if we spend these hours going to the movies or going to dance halls in local bars?" A spokesman for the diocesan headquarters in Cologne immediately wrote back to inform them that attending the festival would violate diocesan rules. He encouraged them to celebrate Carnival in their own youth center —and to try to have some fun in the process.[121]

This case was unusual in that the group took the rare step of voicing its concerns to officials within the church hierarchy; most other groups would undoubtedly either have jumped ship and gone dancing anyway in secular establishments or, as other reports indicate, simply have disintegrated. As the mass culture of the 1950s spread and more attractive alternatives arose, groups either tried to match the offerings of the modern world or were met with dwindling enthusiasm and declining participation. When church leaders dug in their heels, they ultimately paid the price. Young persons either sullenly toed the church's line (where the Catholic milieu was still strong enough to exert considerable pressure on young women) or simply disregarded the church's warnings and polemics and took part in the new mass culture of the 1950s. Once youth began to decide for themselves which part of the church's message to heed, the authority of the church began to crumble. The result was a demystification of authority. To be sure, young persons were not openly challenging or rebelling against church leaders, as was to be the case by the early 1970s. Church authority, nonetheless, was brought down from the pedestal on which it had previously rested by disagreements on such innocuous questions as dancing and makeup, in turn setting the stage for the rebellions of a generation later.

To sum up, many Catholic women found themselves caught between two positions that, to them, often appeared to be polar opposites. On one hand, they remained subject to lofty, idealistic demands for sacrifice and service—traditional Catholic roles from the nineteenth century. On the other hand, they were tremendously attracted to the more modern society around them, where single women had the opportunity to work in occupations deemed inappropriate by the church, go to the movies, and participate in many sporting events, to mention but a few possibilities. Young women who were unable to resolve the tension between religious ideals of asceticism and the lure of the society around them were racked by guilt; many subsequently voted with their feet and left their youth groups altogether. Aware of this situation by the early 1950s, perceptive reformers like Carl sought to convince young women that Catholic ideals were not incompatible with those of modern society. In taking these positions, however, Catholic leaders found themselves in a dilemma.

Young Catholic women receive training in how to use cosmetics in a newly created "school for brides and mothers," ca. 1965 (Courtesy of Jugendhaus Hardehausen)

They realized the necessity of making concessions to the changing tastes and styles of youth (and this involved revising some of the church's prohibitions on dancing, clothing, and dating, or at least softening their rough edges). Yet in presenting young women with a new degree of openness, they ultimately encouraged them to question received beliefs and mores—in particular, the understanding that women had certain gender-specific roles to play within society.

Reformers such as Heidi Carl may, in fact, have brought about the opposite of what they hoped to achieve. As the debates in church newspapers over makeup, the length of dresses, and careers make clear, young persons were able, for the first time, to question fundamental church teachings on the issues most important to them. The answers that they received from church officials, however, were unfailingly conservative, often a simple repetition of the phrase young persons were all too wont to hear: "You may not do that." Carl, ultimately, aroused expectations that clergy could not meet, for they were frequently unwilling to change their approaches to youth work. In most regions, the old traditions remained the norm. By pledging openness but not following up with new programs and changes in attitudes, Catholic youth leaders inadvertently paved the way for increased resentment and disillusionment. In response, young women left the musty and atrophied Catholic milieu faster than the church was able to adapt its doctrines to the modern world.

It is something of a paradox that these modernizers were upset by the changes that would take place in Catholic youth work with a vengeance by the 1970s, such as demands for sexual emancipation, left-wing political activism, and the turning of the doctrines of the 1950s on their heads. Individuals like Carl were not revolutionaries attempting to overturn the entire system but, rather, mild reformers aiming to update traditional doctrines in hopes of preserving them. The 1950s might be summed up in the image of a young girl standing inside a church portal with both feet firmly planted on a historic mosaic while she gazes intently and somewhat longingly at the other girls dancing at a jazz festival just 100 meters away. In the 1950s the Catholic church in Germany took its first steps toward relinquishing its heritage from the nineteenth century: its carefully delineated conceptions of gender, its "feminine" forms of piety, and its insistence on unfailing obedience to church authority. As one Catholic newspaper noted, "There no longer exists a sheltered agrarian or bourgeois world."[122] Another female youth leader added, "The bourgeois ideals of women of past times are destroyed."[123] With this dictum in mind, they were beset with an even deeper uncertainty: how to redefine questions of gender, sexuality, and piety within the context of modern society and mass culture.

To speak of a pure restoration or even a decade of unadulterated conservatism in the 1950s is to attribute to these social conservatives a power that they did not have. Their efforts to define national morals were ultimately a statement of powerlessness, futile attempts to stave off social and cultural change. The marriage of social conservatism and economic modernization in the early years of the Federal Republic was to be a short-lived partnership.

FOUR

Youth Work in the
Industrial Heartland:
The CAJ and Kolping
in the Archdiocese
of Cologne

TRADITIONAL RELIGIOUS institutions flourished less easily in the city than in the countryside. Until very recently, both historians and contemporaries viewed the German industrial heartland in the Rhineland and the Ruhr as an increasingly secularized and Socialist bastion. Yet as a growing number of historians have shown, Catholic leaders until the early twentieth century proved remarkably adept at founding new parishes, workers' clubs, Christian trade unions, youth organizations, sporting organizations, theater troops, singing clubs, and Kolping groups for young artisans. In short, they built the framework for a thriving milieu in the industrial centers of Germany. Catholic clergy and laity accomplished what their Protestant colleagues could not: they transplanted rural structures to industrial city neighborhoods. The city parish thus took on the same functions it had in the country. It served as the nexus of neighborhood life, particularly in those areas of the Ruhr that were home to large numbers of miners, who retained something of a preindustrial nature.

During the twentieth century, however, this new Catholic subculture in the cities began to crumble. Many workers turned to ideological alternatives such as the Communists and the SPD. All too aware of their own precarious influence, church leaders set out to win young workers back to Christ and took steps to shore up their authority in those proletarian regions of Germany where the church still maintained a shaky hold over young men and women. With much fanfare, they introduced the Young Christian Workers (CAJ), a movement from Belgium.[1] Likewise, Kolping, which had originated in the Rhineland nearly a century earlier, renewed its efforts to reach young artisans. Although ordinary parish youth groups continued to enroll a majority of young persons, more specialized organizations such as Kolping and the CAJ were stronger here than in any other region of Germany, save for the archdiocese of Paderborn and the diocese of Münster. Some ordinary parish groups were, in fact, subsidiaries of national youth organizations.[2]

In this chapter I examine why Kolping and the CAJ, the linchpins in this series of initiatives to stabilize and restore the Catholic milieu in this crucial region of Germany, ultimately did not meet the high expectations vested in them in the late 1940s and 1950s, the years of the Cold War. I also link the difficulties in retaining young workers to the peculiar geography of the archdiocese. Gender, region, and class are, in this instance, inextricably bound together.

ODE TO COLOGNE:

THE GEOGRAPHY OF THE ARCHDIOCESE

The archdiocese of Cologne, which covers significant portions of the Rhineland, is utterly heterogeneous. It includes a significant number of Protestant enclaves, regions that were confessionally mixed, and other areas exclusively Catholic. It is a mélange of urban and rural, of the lonesome hills of the Eifel, of the old industrial cities of the Bergisches Land, and of the ancient Roman outposts on the Rhine, Cologne, Bonn, and Neuss. Until 1957 it included several cities in the Ruhr—Essen and individual neighborhoods of Duisburg and Oberhausen—when the German bishops carved out the diocese of Essen from parts of the dioceses of Cologne, Münster, and Paderborn. The Rhine divides the archdiocese confessionally. The regions to the west were, with few exceptions, overwhelmingly Catholic; the cities to the east were likewise largely Protestant. The archdiocese retained its Catholic majority through the 1950s, although the number of Protestants slowly grew.[3] In 1938 there were 2,502,084 Catholics and 1,754,106 Protestants in the archdiocese. By 1953 the figures were only slightly different: 2,737,769 Catholics and 2,099,449 Protestants.[4]

Yet the industrial structures of the region differed significantly. The

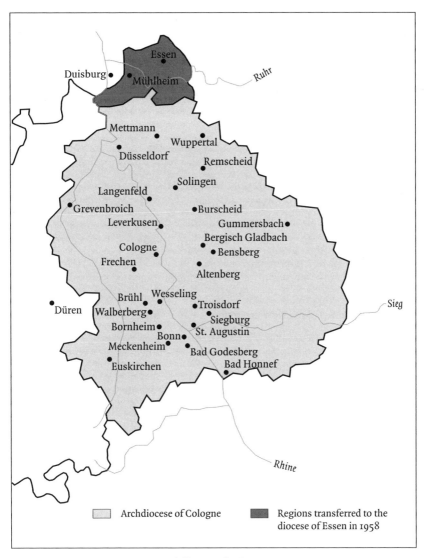

Essen

Duisburg • • Mühlheim   *Ruhr*

Mettmann
                • Wuppertal
        Düsseldorf
                • Remscheid

            • Solingen
    Langenfeld
        •
•Grevenbroich   •Burscheid
    Leverkusen •   Gummersbach •
                        Bergisch Gladbach
        Cologne   • Bensberg
    Frechen •
        •   • Altenberg

        Brühl Wesseling
•Düren Walberberg •   •Troisdorf   Sieg
        Bornheim •   •Siegburg
            Bonn • St. Augustin
    Meckenheim •
            • • Bad Godesberg
    Euskirchen •   Bad Honnef
                        •

                                Rhine

☐ Archdiocese of Cologne   ■ Regions transferred to the
                              diocese of Essen in 1958

Archdiocese of Cologne

cities along the Ruhr were world-renowned for coal and steel. Solingen and Remschied were known for electrotechnology, cutlery, machinery, and optics; Leverkusen had its pharmaceutical and chemical industry; and Düsseldorf was famous for its many metal processing factories and as a center for the banking, insurance, and fashion industries.[5] Cologne, the poor cousin of the swanker Düsseldorf, was home to Ford automobile plants. The southern suburbs along the Rhine became, after the war, the site for various oil refineries. To the west the industrial structures changed.[6] For a broad swath from Euskirchen in the south to Bedburg and Bergheim in the northwest, brown-coal mining dominated the terrain. Throughout the rural regions of the archdiocese, mostly in the southwest and southeast, small enterprises—glass factories, bottle plants, and textile mills—supplemented revenues from farming.

With more than 4.2 million inhabitants, the region was one of the most densely populated parts of Germany. The number and size of parishes were in keeping with the demographics of the region. The archdiocese had more than 600 by the early 1950s, and throughout the decade, new parishes continued to be formed. Some of the smaller congregations had fewer than 600 members.[7] Larger parishes often numbered as many as 10,000 members, particularly in areas that had undergone rapid industrialization at the turn of the century. Many of the parishes were home to large numbers of artisans, workers, and farmers, who continued to grow crops even in industrialized regions. One such parish, Herr Jesu in Leverkusen-Wiesdorf, was home to a Kolping group, workers' organizations, and mothers' clubs in addition to a vast array of youth groups.[8] But in spite of a membership of more than 10,000 in 1954, it had one pastor and two curates to tend the entire flock; diocesan leaders were forced, as a result, to subdivide it into three independent parishes by the end of the decade.[9] Smaller congregations frequently lacked curates. It is no surprise that clergy frequently complained of being overworked; simply performing the requisite daily masses, marriages, and funerals, to say nothing of managing an entire network of ancillary organizations, was more than many priests could handle.

Between 1918 and 1945 the Catholic milieu in many urban centers of the archdiocese began to crumble. After an unprecedented wave of revolutionary ferment and agitation between 1918 and 1923, many male workers deserted the Center Party, in many cases not for the Social Democratic Party but for the Communists.[10] By the late 1920s the Center Party was receiving only 20 to 30 percent of the votes in hard-core urban neighborhoods such as Altenessen in Essen, where the Communists and Social Democrats were tallying more than 50 percent.[11] These figures would have been much lower had women, who supported the Center Party more strongly than men, not been given the vote in 1918. In cities such as Cologne, many Catholic groups, particularly the workers' organizations, were beginning to disintegrate. Their leaders and members were rapidly aging and out of touch.[12]

The Second World War, more importantly, tore apart the heart of the Catholic milieu.[13] The Rhineland, because of its concentration of heavy industry and high population density and closer proximity to English airfields, was a favorite target of Allied bombers. In cities such as Cologne, Essen, and Düsseldorf, up to 80 percent of the housing stock went up in flames. Church leaders noted a mood of apathy, thriving prostitution, the black market, and mixed marriages, which they took as signs of moral collapse. The church faced a shortage of priests, since many curates had been arrested and sent to concentration camps or had perished in the war.[14] The number of seminarians, an excellent indicator of the degree of commitment of young persons to the church, rose from 52 in 1931 and 57 in 1932 to 84 in 1935 and 1936 to reach a peak of 116 in 1939. Then it fell drastically to a mere 1 in 1943 as a result of the war. This number never recovered to its prewar high, rising to 16 in 1948 and to an average of 35 by the early 1950s.[15]

Many male groups had been completely destroyed; their leaders had died or languished in POW camps. Teenagers in the first half of the decade had little exposure to a religious education, a result of the obligations imposed by the Hitler Youth and the state. The membership of most groups thus never returned to prewar levels. In 1946, diocesan leaders estimated that participation by young women was only 60 percent of prewar levels.[16] By 1947 the membership had increased to nearly 44,000.[17]

One year later, youth groups enrolled approximately 22 percent of the Catholic young persons between ages ten and twenty-five and 28 percent of boys ages ten to fourteen.[18] This phenomenon cannot be attributed solely to wartime casualties, since the cohort of teenagers in the 1950s had suffered few losses during the war. Diocesan statistics for more than 600 parishes in 1933 and 1954, the only two years for which statistics are available during this time, indicate that group membership in 1954 almost never exceeded the totals from 1933, male or female. In most parishes, the membership in 1954 was half or, at best, two-thirds of what it had been in 1933.[19]

Church leaders were even more frightened by what they perceived to be the rampant hostility of young workers toward religious institutions. In sweeping terms, they believed that the future of the church—and of the German nation—depended on their ability to bring young workers back to the church and defuse the revolutionary potential of young proletarians. Fritz Eink, youth leader for the archdiocese, concurred: "The social question has become the deciding question and the future of the people depends on how it is resolved. The decisions for the future no longer will fall in the bourgeois world, but in the masses of workers."[20] Father Johannes Leppich, a blustery Jesuit, similarly argued that the church stood on the brink of disaster: "It is five minutes to twelve. A worker, however, told me at the workplace, 'It is already five minutes after twelve.' That must not be!"[21]

Church leaders were, nonetheless, not of one mind as to how to reach young workers.[22] While Wolker sought to unify all Catholic youth into one organization, other church leaders, inspired by the social theorists from the time of Leo XIII, wanted to create special ministries for the working class. The organization that eventually took root in Germany was an offshoot of an association that had sprouted in Belgium earlier in the century, the Jeunesses Ouvrières Catholiques (JOC). This group, which had been founded by a charismatic and driven Flemish priest, Joseph Cardijn, had already inspired similar movements in England and France. The international Young Christian Workers movement, based in Brussels, made great strides in reaching young workers in France and Belgium and soon became a darling of Pope Pius XII. It was an initiative that, its proponents claimed, easily fell within the parameters of Catholic Action.[23] For these reasons, Pius XII put pressure on the German bishops to bring the JOC to Germany, even though it was clear that the German bishops had serious doubts about this foreign import.[24] The bishops nonetheless invited Cardijn in February 1947 to the national conference of youth leaders at Hardehausen. Dazzled by Cardijn's charisma and not at all put off by his limited German, conference participants pledged to support Cardijn's movement in Germany, which would bear the title Christliche Arbeiterjugend (CAJ). Father Leppich subsequently barnstormed major German cities. In his whirlwind tour he roused thousands of young Catholics with fiery speeches titled "Christ or Chaos" and "Rome or Moscow."[25]

Shortly thereafter, representatives from Belgium and France arrived to train their German counterparts in the methods of the Young Christian Workers. Belgian specialists headed for the industrial regions of Germany in the north and west, while the French generally remained in the southern zones.[26] These specialists had a highly specific program. The

CAJ was to be the antithesis of traditional German *Vereine*. It was to be a movement of action and not a sterile organization with a board of directors, annual assemblies, and weekly drinking bashes. It was based around small cells of three to fifteen young workers who would build friendships, live together, and discuss ways to improve their lives.[27] Responsible for the growth of the cells were the so-called forefighters (the German designation was *Vorkämpfer*; the French spoke of *militants*), who were to arrive months earlier to prepare the way.[28] Within the cells, the members were to visit the sick and to launch their own newsletters. Evening meetings were designed to get members to bare their souls and discuss candidly the problems they encountered at home and at work. The philosophy of the CAJ—"see, judge, act"—was an effort to lead young workers themselves to identify the causes of working-class militancy and to convince their comrades to return to the fold.

CAJ leaders believed that the masses of workers could be spurred to action only through an elite vanguard of militant fighters and not through a mass organization such as the BDKJ.[29] Individual forefighters were to win over individual workers through friendship and trust.[30] It was to be an organization of laity and only secondarily of clerics. Organizers believed that young workers enjoyed a far greater credibility among their peers than older clergymen. Fritz Eink, for instance, had long argued that the most important goals of the church were to address the pressing daily needs of young workers in the streets, factories, and mines and to stave off criticism that the church was too bourgeois. CAJ leaders claimed that the romantic traditions of the bourgeois youth movement had little chance of reaching hardened working-class lads.[31] But by the late 1940s, disagreements had broken out over whether to incorporate pageantry, hikes, and banners into CAJ groups.[32] Leaders eventually combined elements of both sobriety and heraldry in their groups. They developed insignia and unfurled their banners in grand fashion during a 1957 pilgrimage to Rome, where German CAJ members and 30,000 of their comrades from all over the world united for festive speeches and parades and to pay homage to their hero, Cardijn, around whom an unmistakably romantic mythology had emerged.[33] The organization also, on the other hand, retained a reputation for consisting of garrulous, chain-smoking activists committed to rational analyses of the situation at the workplace.

It quickly became apparent, however, that the CAJ would have great difficulties realizing the lofty expectations vested in it. The unceasing infighting, organizational bickering, and inadequate funding were so marked that the saying "The CAJ has failed" became common among church leaders. Even CAJ leaders themselves were forced to admit that their organization had not achieved any substantial success.[34] The CAJ's membership statistics bore out this sorry picture. In 1956 fewer than 9,000 young workers in all of Germany were enrolled in the CAJ, and of these, a mere 805 resided in the archdiocese of Cologne.[35] By 1958 these figures had plummeted, once the cities of Essen and Oberhausen were placed under the jurisdiction of the newly appointed bishop of Essen. In 1959 there were a paltry 138 members left in the archdiocese and 911 in the diocese of Essen.[36] By contrast, the largely agrarian dioceses of Würzburg and Eichstätt each had more members in the CAJ than Cologne with 291 and 351, respectively. The diocese of Münster had 2,450 members in 1958, a number that increased to 9,694 by 1964, but it appears that this apparent success stemmed from enormous subsidies granted by Bishop Michael Keller, an ardent supporter of organizations in the tradition of Catholic Action.[37] To give the appearance of greater membership totals, diocesan leaders apparently declared normal parish groups to be CAJ cells.

By 1962 the situation had improved somewhat. The diocese totaled 208 *Vorkämpfer*, 272 cell members, and 325 members of the Young-CAJ (for those younger than eighteen years), for a total of 805 members. The membership remained concentrated along the Ruhr. The city of Essen, whose members continued to be tallied alongside those of the archdiocese of Cologne, had 255 members; the city of Cologne, 78; Solingen, 27; Düsseldorf, 18; Neuss, 51; Duisburg, 70; Troisdorf, 25; Siegburg, 30; Rheinbach, 5; and Mettman, 5. Even so, these were clearly not the membership totals of a thriving organization.

The CAJ's difficulties began at the moment of inception. Wolker feared that the group would endanger the unity he was struggling to bring to Catholic youth organizations.[38] In 1948, Altenberg, faced with massive financial woes, cut the funding so sharply that CAJ leaders considered selling American cigarettes on the black market to raise funds (one pack fetched nearly five marks); the JOC-Central in Brussels was apparently prepared to donate the necessary cigarettes.[39] Karl Sroka, the good-natured but somewhat hapless leader of the CAJ, was forced to take his case directly to the bishops and beg for funds. To his dismay, however, Sroka found that there was no strong support behind the CAJ, the expressions of goodwill from the bishops notwithstanding.[40] As late as 1952, CAJ leaders continued to complain that they had been "stabbed in the back" by Altenberg.[41]

In addition, the new organization almost immediately generated the mistrust of leaders of both Kolping and an older organization for workers, the Catholic Workers' Movement (Katholische Arbeiterbewegung) (KAB), which began to compete with the fledgling organization for new members. The rivalry was most marked between the KAB and the CAJ. The aging KAB was looking for a few good men younger than twenty-five for its own youth organization, which, leaders hoped, would provide recruits for the adult KAB and revitalize its ranks.[42] By 1954, according to one estimate, there were more than 4,000 Young-KAB members in the archdiocese alone.[43] The KAB claimed that CAJ members all too frequently refused to join the KAB once they turned twenty-five; they were, as a result, endangering their organization. The CAJ, on the other hand, feared that a closer association with an organization with a reputation for senility might diminish its appeal among young workers.

The bishops were forced to take action. In 1955 Frings presented all three organizations—the KAB, the CAJ, and Kolping—with a clear set of orders.[44] The CAJ was to be the single Catholic organization for young workers. Young workers between ages 14 and 17 were to join the Young-CAJ; those between 18 and 21 were to enter the CAJ and were permitted to remain there until a maximum age of 25. The KAB was forbidden to recruit members under 21; in return, the CAJ members were expected to join the KAB either on their 25th birthday or when they married. The Young-KAB was to consist of workers between ages 21 and 25. Yet even these guidelines did not resolve the problems completely. In 1957 it was reported that Kolping was again recruiting members for the Young Kolping groups in the region in flagrant violation of the bishops' directives.[45] Such constant internecine strife sapped the energy of CAJ leaders (and of the other organizations as well) and diverted attention and resources from the effort necessary to make greater inroads into the German working classes.

Organizational conflicts alone, however, cannot explain the CAJ's conspicuous lack of success. In its early years, the CAJ was hampered by its foreign origins. In a memorandum from 1947, Cardijn himself noted that the JOC leaders in Belgium had to avoid giving the appearance of interfering in the affairs of the German CAJ: "The J.O.C. in Germany will be

German or it will not exist at all," he averred.[46] Cardijn, nonetheless, did not always practice what he preached. In 1948 he wrote to Frings to voice his dissatisfaction with the bishops' choice of a national director for the CAJ, noting, among other issues, that it was important to maintain the authenticity of the JOC methods that were tried and true in Belgium and France; the German leader, he implied, had not been adequately schooled in JOC procedures.[47] Once appointed, this director, whose nomination Cardijn had opposed, took Cardijn's line and attributed the CAJ's lack of success to the inability to implement the JOC's methods properly. Yet the practices that worked in France and Belgium did not necessarily work in Germany, since, for instance, German workers enjoyed a higher standard of living than their European counterparts.[48] Even as Belgian leaders continued to insist on maintaining the authenticity of their methods, German youth leaders threw up their hands in frustration at their inability to master the JOC's educational philosophy.[49]

It was hardly surprising that many young German workers came to regard the CAJ as an undesirable foreign import. The movement's French and Belgian origins were anathema to many workers in the Ruhr, who had witnessed the dismantling of factories and the shipments of large quantities of coal to Belgium and France.[50] They took umbrage at the reparation payments to France and Belgium, much as their elders had resented the French occupation in 1923. Under these circumstances, existing CAJ cells frequently became bogged down in discussions of whether foreign models were appropriate for Germany.[51] Rumors spread that the CAJ was being funded by the French JOC and the French military government.[52] Some of the French and Belgian "specialists" overstayed their welcome and began to foment trouble in their new communities.[53] There was little that German leaders could do to alter these unfavorable perceptions of the CAJ. Frings wrote to Cardijn, urging him to remove the most troublesome of the French assistants. Not until later in the 1950s, when nationalist fervor had subsided and reparations payments had ceased, did the CAJ finally shed its image as a foreign occupation force.

As if these problems were not enough, the CAJ rarely was able to win over priests to its cause. In some parishes, overworked clerics simply refused to minister to the CAJ.[54] Working with the CAJ was, moreover, labor intensive. The CAJ chaplain for the diocese reported in 1958 that he worked with one group every day for more than three months, a task for which the majority of clerics had neither the time nor the inclination.[55]

Most older clergy—most of whom did not come from working-class families—had received little training in how to minister to the working classes; such clergy often had little sympathy for social ministries.[56] For them, the CAJ embodied anticlericalism, especially in light of the powerful role given to the lay Vorkämpfer and individual cell leaders. Other clergy were put off by Cardijn's militant rhetoric, such as "We are not starting a revolution; rather, we are the revolution."[57] (The CAJ newspaper was titled Liberation [Die Befreiung].) Such priests claimed that the new organization had abandoned the apostolic mission of the church in favor of a Marxist doctrine of class struggle. To some clerics, the very mention of the word "worker" raised a red flag. A priest in Brühl-Heide, a region where brown coal predominated, forbade parish members to introduce cells from the KAB on his turf.[58]

This situation was exacerbated by the unwillingness of diocesan leaders to place individual priests at the disposal of the CAJ. Sroka struggled for months with Frings to get just one priest freed up for the diocesan headquarters of the CAJ in Cologne.[59] Frings ultimately acceded to the request, earning the nickname "The Protector" of the CAJ in the process, but the situation did not otherwise improve. In the early 1950s, one priest and one secretary were assigned to the CAJ in the archdiocese.[60] In contrast, the JOC in Belgium had more than 250 priests at its disposal, and the JOC in France had nearly 200, whereas in Germany a mere handful of priests were assigned to the CAJ, even though the working-class population there far exceeded that of its neighbors.[61] The German church hierarchy may have been put off by conflicts within the French worker-priest movement, which received widespread publicity in German church circles.[62] Apparently under pressure from Rome, the French episcopate took disciplinary action against French worker-priests who had participated in strikes. The worker-priests were forbidden to reside in workers' quarters and were placed in monasteries or rectories instead; their workweek amidst the workers was likewise reduced to three days.

If the CAJ was thus too radical for traditional clerics, it was too conservative for young workers. One group in Essen wrote church authorities in 1950 to point out the monumental gap between the world of the church and that of workers. Young workers, they observed, often perceived the church as too bourgeois and claimed it merely sought to defend private property and the interests of the capitalist elite. They laughed at outdated titles such as Herrn or Hochwürden. "In their funny black frocks . . . they look as if they were left over from the last century. The lads simply laugh at this old-fashioned stuff: you can't trust persons who look as though they came 200 years too late. How can he (the priest) bear a joyful message when he looks like he just came from a funeral?"[63] According to this group, many young workers saw the church as a museum artifact. Even in the late 1950s, many workers continued to regard churchmen as, at best, old fogies or, at worst, agents of reaction.[64] Some workers took offense at the church's ceaseless denunciations of materialism. Church leaders, they argued, were unwilling to grant to the lower classes what those from the middle and upper classes had enjoyed for years.[65]

Some workers were put off by the CAJ's puritanical attitudes. Throughout the 1950s the CAJ often understood the concept of re-Christianization to mean the cleaning up of what is regarded as the dissolute moral atmosphere of the workplace. According to CAJ surveys from the 1950s, male workers frequently indulged in vulgar conversations about girls, told dirty jokes, and scratched crude depictions of naked women on bathroom stalls. Die Befreiung angrily attacked, for instance, an article and photospread of Brigitte Bardot and "Comrade Bouché" in the newspaper of the major German trade union as denigrating the value of working women.[66] The CAJ groups for women likewise sought to convert and redeem "fallen girls," young working-class women who were allegedly promiscuous. Putting the organization at odds with many young workers were its denunciations of mass culture such as dancing, rock 'n' roll, and movies, which were popular pastimes for many working youths.

Church leaders thus found that if they made concessions to young workers regarding attitudes, dress, and manners, they risked allegations of anticlericalism, revolutionary activism, and abandoning the faith. Yet by clinging to their past, they became the laughingstock of young workers. CAJ members, as a result, had to put up with scorn from many fellow workers who mocked them as goody-goodies.

CAJ leaders also found it difficult to organize workers, since the industrial structures in the region were too diverse. CAJ groups were rarely organized by workplace—cells did not serve individual factories—but by city or village. Leaders quickly discovered that the archdiocese was too unwieldy to instill a collective sense of identity among most Catholic workers. When church leaders brought together brown-coal miners from Bergheim, steelworkers from Essen, and anthracite miners from the Ruhr, they often found that these workers had little in common. They preferred not to be identified as workers per se but by their specific occupations (machinists, welders, or drillers), a sign of diminished class-consciousness.

The success of the CAJ, as a result, varied from city to city. There were far more willing participants in Essen, where workers from individual neighborhoods often labored in the same industries, than in Cologne, where industrial structures were more heterogeneous.[67] In many villages that were home to large numbers of commuters to nearby industrial centers, local clergy failed to recognize the enormous social transformations that had taken place. In villages such as Duisburg-Mündelheim or Neunkirchen, between 50 and 70 percent of the young men were working in factories, but even there, the clergy refused to take notice. "There are no workers here," was a common refrain, according to one report. A curate in Oberhausen, for instance, insisted that his parish was not a "workers' parish" and that the CAJ was therefore superfluous.[68] Such attitudes help explain why many industrial regions surrounding the city of Cologne—areas such as Godorf—had no CAJ groups. In other locations, the CAJ had difficulty distinguishing between blue-collar and white-collar workers.[69] The CAJ groups for women in the archdiocese, for instance, consisted almost exclusively of white-collar workers. One group evinced great embarrassment when a young working-class woman attended a group event and was confronted with eighteen better-dressed white-collar workers.[70]

The CAJ's ultimate difficulty, however, lay in the fact that church leaders had misunderstood the attitudes and aspirations of young workers at a time of rapid socioeconomic change. CAJ leaders believed that workers were well versed in radical Marxist ideology and posed a revolutionary threat. In reality, workers simply wanted better living and working conditions. In the Third Reich, Social Democratic observers had already reached that conclusion, as they noted the passivity of most workers in the wake of the destruction of Socialist and Communist institutions. This unwillingness to fight for revolutionary causes did not change after 1945. The greatest segment of workers, another historian has concluded, showed a marked disinterest in politics and ideology in the postwar years.[71]

This declining political activism made the task not just of the CAJ but of the Social Democratic Party and its youth organizations more difficult. By the late 1950s the SPD itself was forced to turn its back on Marxist ideology, a sign that the Socialist milieu was undergoing a similar process of erosion. As historians have noted, the German proletariat was disappearing.[72] Those conditions—poverty, overcrowded living conditions, and mistreatment in the workplace—that had given the German proletariat its unique identity no longer existed as they had fifty years earlier. A new generation of younger workers, in other words, was no longer decisively shaped by the old Catholic and Socialist workers' culture but by higher salaries, a shortened workweek, relative prosperity, mobility, and mass culture.[73]

As such, the CAJ's revolutionary rhetoric—"We are the revolution"—had little appeal to young workers who rejected calls for revolution by Communist Party leaders. One priest noted that young workers who had become content with the rising standard of living had little interest in attempts to point out the dismal realities of working-class life.[74] Even church leaders began to speak of a "leveled middle class society" and predicted that the working class would eventually disappear. Such theories, in turn, gave priests an excuse to ignore ministering to the working classes, even as the CAJ reported a slight upswing by the late 1950s.[75] The national chaplain of the CAJ lamented this development: "As a result, one hears erroneous opinions that the CAJ is superfluous with the improved economic position of the working class."[76]

By the late 1950s, many young workers had become indifferent to the church—a sign, perhaps, that the process of secularization had proceeded one step further. In one survey carried out by CAJ leaders, young workers were asked how people spoke of religion and the church at the workplace.[77] Twenty-eight percent responded, "with reverence"; 25 percent responded, "with rejection, scorn, or hatred"; and 47 percent replied, "with indifference." To a similar question, "What is said about the church and priests," 11 percent responded, "good things"; 17 percent asserted, "bad things"; 21 percent gave no answer; and 51 percent maintained that workers did not talk about these subjects. The same survey noted that workers preferred to talk about sports, entertainment, girls, and only secondarily—and rarely—politics and working conditions.

By the end of the 1950s, the CAJ had changed its tactic, realizing that its stance on issues such as mass culture had alienated many potential recruits. It began to sponsor rock 'n' roll and dance festivals with far greater enthusiasm and verve than most other Catholic groups. It put itself at the forefront of mass culture, at which point its fortunes began to pick up.[78] In spite of the organization's improving fortunes by the 1960s, the grim realities remained. Many young workers had long left the church and were not receptive to appeals to class consciousness to win them back. There was, moreover, too little support within the church for the organization to succeed. So the CAJ's successes in the archdiocese of Cologne, after the regions in the Ruhr were transferred to the diocese of Essen in 1958, tended to be confined to areas where most residents were already practicing Catholics and the local clergy were sympathetic to young workers.[79] One membership survey carried out by CAJ leaders indicated that the majority of CAJ members came from two-parent households whose members attended church regularly, and not from the masses of unchurched workers. The CAJ chaplain for the archdiocese admitted that the best group in the region in the 1950s was in Troisdorf, a small Catholic city on the eastern bank of the Rhine.[80] The CAJ's strength, in other words, lay in areas where the Catholic milieu was most intact. CAJ leaders were preaching to the choir.

KOLPING

As the CAJ struggled to re-Christianize segments of society long lost to church leaders, Kolping groups remained a bastion of the traditional Catholic milieu—of the small artisans, journeymen, and apprentices who continued to make up a significant share of the Catholic population in the western regions of Germany. Kolping was one of the oldest Catholic organizations in Germany, dating back to 1847. Over time, Kolping became the quintessential Catholic *Verein*. It was an organization of the lower middle classes—the petty bourgeoisie Marx so despised—and it was firmly rooted in an ideology of the small, independent artisan whose fortunes were threatened by industrialization and automation. It offered lecture series, continuing education courses for its members, and technical training for young apprentices and journeymen. Kolping gained fame —and notoriety—for grandiose assemblies, flag waving, acrid squabbles with rival *Vereine*, and beer swilling at the weekly *Stammtisch*. It was, in short, an organization that bore all of the hallmarks of Catholic associations from the nineteenth century. It drew on bourgeois forms of organization, and it was rooted in an ideology of work, family, society, and insularity.[81]

Although Kolping groups in the dioceses of Münster and Paderborn outnumbered those in the Rhineland, the archdiocese of Cologne was, in many respects, the true home of the Kolping movement. Its founder, Adolf Kolping, hailed from Kerpen, a small city in the northwest corner of the archdiocese. His first groups were in Elberfeld, one of the first regions in Germany to undergo industrialization. Groups in Düsseldorf, Siegburg, and Cologne followed, and well into the first decades of the twentieth century, Kolping continued to expand.[82] These associations were originally intended for younger journeymen, an exclusively male clientele, but many recruits remained members until death, a situation that forced Kolping leaders to divide groups by age. Old Kolping was for those who were over thirty-five, married, or had formed their own business; General Kolping was for those under thirty-five, single, and not yet independent.[83] At the heart of the organization lay what was called the family principle; the prefect, or head, was the spiritual father of the organization.[84]

By the early 1920s, Kolping, like other Catholic associations at the time, found itself at a standstill.[85] Its membership declined as many young men discovered the appeal of the youth and liturgical movements.[86] To these young men, Kolping was a relic from the nineteenth century. It was reactionary, authoritarian (its structure remained hierarchical), philistine (it drew on bourgeois forms of organization from the mid-nineteenth century), and crass (its members refused to forswear alcohol and tobacco).[87] Kolping leaders found themselves challenged, above all, by militant Socialist and Communist youth organizations that proclaimed that the proletariat—and not skilled craftsmen, the despised petite bourgeoisie—would determine the future of the nation.

The manner in which Kolping leaders responded to this crisis decisively shaped the trajectory of the organization for the next forty years. Some groups appropriated the spirit of romanticism and of the youth movement. In the mid-nineteenth century many aspiring artisans undertook an arduous journey of several years during which they would wander from village to village in search of opportunities to ply their craft at the hands of a skilled master. This tradition of the so-called wandering journeymen was revived in the 1920s and was practiced by more than 10,000 participants throughout Germany. New groups, or families, as they were called, continued to be formed throughout the archdiocese, and the membership rose.[88]

Kolping soon found its future threatened by the National Socialist state. But even before the Gestapo and SS applied direct pressure to the organization, divisions opened in the Kolping ranks over how groups should position themselves in the changed political climate.[89] While some leaders vowed to remain apolitical, others chose to accommodate themselves to—and collaborate with—the new political powers in Germany. On 23 March 1933 one of the top leaders, Johannes Nattermann, without consulting the episcopate, announced his intention to work with the new state's leaders. It is perhaps because Kolping turned to the right that the punishment meted out to it during the National Socialist era was relatively light. In contrast to its retaliation toward other Catholic organizations, the Gestapo dissolved only some of the Kolping groups. In 1931 there were 1,777 Kolping groups in Germany, of which the Gestapo took action against 945. In 1945, 832 groups were still active, and 329 were immediately brought back to life.[90] The leadership of Kolping also remained remarkably intact. As a result, Kolping had a strong base on which to rebuild at the end of the war. Between 1946 and 1950, 32 new groups were formed in the archdiocese of Cologne alone (out of a total of more than 140).[91] Kolping leaders estimated that 26,000 new members between ages eighteen and twenty-four joined between May 1945 and March 1947 throughout the nation.[92] Kolping's favorable position stood in marked contrast to that of organizations such as the KAB, whose leadership had been decimated by the Gestapo.[93]

In most regions of Germany, Kolping was most strongly represented in cities and villages with fewer than 20,000 inhabitants. In the diocese of Münster, which included large areas of the Ruhr, 65 percent of Kolping members came from towns and villages with fewer than 10,000 people. For the archdiocese of Cologne, however, the pattern was the reverse. Fifty-eight percent of Kolping members lived in cities with more than 100,000 inhabitants, and less than 20 percent resided in villages of fewer than 10,000.[94] These figures indicate not just the high degree of urbanization in the area, but the fact that many skilled craftsmen were employed in large factories. The boundaries between laborers and skilled craftsmen were often difficult to discern. The occupational groups most heavily represented were, respectively, carpenters (13.55 percent), metalworkers (12.9 percent), and salesmen and shop owners (10.84 percent), followed by electrical workers and electricians (6.38 percent), bakers (5.69 percent), and painters (4.63 percent).[95] Of these members, 78 percent were said to be skilled manual workers (Handwerker); the remainder were farmers, students, unskilled workers, civil servants, salesmen, and shop own- ers. That many members were not self-employed artisans but employees in large manufacturing enterprises had long bedeviled Kolping leaders. They wanted to hold on to their doctrine of self-sufficiency for skilled workers but recognized that they could not exclude employees in large industrial firms if their organization were to survive.[96]

Why did Kolping attract so many young craftsmen after the war, and how did they find their way to the organization? According to one survey of 200 artisans from 1956, 64 percent were persuaded by friends and family to join.[97] Others were inspired by rallies, assemblies, or publica- tions. Of those who joined, 86.5 percent sought "human contact," 75.5 percent wanted to take advantage of Kolping's educational opportunities, 56.5 percent were motivated by religious convictions, 34 percent wanted professional advancement and the chance to improve professional skills, and 22.5 percent sought assistance and "relief in a foreign region" (these were probably refugees from the east). Of the members, 31 percent came from families in which the father was also a member, 12 percent were products of the Young Kolping groups, and 45 percent came from other Catholic youth organizations.

For members for whom professional concerns were most important, Kolping offered enticing opportunities to improve professional skills, which Kolping leaders regarded as central to their spiritual mission. According to one conference report from 1946, "The goal is the further education of a quality worker who regards himself as working in the Christian sense. . . . Every Kolping son must make it his task not only to be a valiant journeyman but also to become a valiant master in his field."[98]

To these ends, Kolping offered young artisans continuing education courses; some were in conjunction with German trade unions, and others were led exclusively by Kolping brothers. Some consisted of lecture series that reiterated traditional Kolping teaching: "The Master and Teaching," "Artisans in the Economy," and "Adolf Kolping and the Social Task in His and Our Time." Most courses, however, targeted specific trades and pro- fessions, such as electricians, metalworkers, carpenters, and bakers. These courses were intended to fill a void in the training of many young men. After completing their formal education at age fourteen or eighteen (from the *Berufsschule*), many young craftsmen still had not mastered—or been given an opportunity to learn—subjects essential for their future success, such as technical or business writing, bookkeeping, and shorthand.[99] These courses, which prepared young men for the examinations to become masters, enjoyed tremendous popularity in the 1930s until they were banned by the Nazis.

Kolping leaders also launched a major effort to teach new trades and crafts to men who had suffered debilitating injuries in the war—and, no doubt, to enroll them in Kolping groups and increase the organization's membership.[100] These courses were not just for the individual who had already been trained as an apprentice and had long been planning a career as a skilled craftsman, but for the veteran with little or no professional training whose education had been put on hold during the war. These veterans made easy recruits.

There were initial difficulties. Kolping lacked both the personnel and an adequate physical plant, as many buildings had been destroyed in the war.[101] Kolping organizers also discovered that these courses were ill suited to young artisans in the countryside, for whom a commute of even 15 miles was prohibitive while rail lines and roads still lay in ruin. For some, these courses presupposed too much prior knowledge. Other young craftsmen moved from one work station to another and did not remain in a location long enough to complete these courses. For these would-be artisans, Kolping introduced correspondence courses for those preparing for their examinations in fields such as baking, metalworking, principles of buying and selling, shorthand, English, and business writing. Kolping assessed a fee of sixteen deutsche marks or more, depending on the course of study, and it is difficult to determine to what extent the tuition deterred some young artisans from taking advantage of these opportunities.[102]

Yet it is possible to overestimate the degree to which these courses were responsible for the explosive growth of Kolping after the war. Another set of statistics yields different explanations for why young persons signed up for Kolping groups in droves after the war.[103] Only 25.7 percent of those who joined between 1945 and 1949 cited Kolping's professional opportunities as their primary reason, and only 47.9 percent mentioned general educational opportunities. For those who joined after 1950, these figures changed little—to 21.7 percent and 47.1 percent, respectively. The majority of new recruits were inspired by the convivial, "familylike" atmosphere and hoped to make friends and meet others of like mind in the organization. Some joined specifically because of the sporting events and theater productions, but the number of young men who highlighted these reasons remained between 5 and 15 percent. It seems that many young men were drawn to the weekly *Stammtisch*, where they and their brothers engaged in drunken revelry. Newspaper reports often recounted how Kolping members staggered home the morning after a long night of hard drinking and heavy dancing during Carnival.[104] Kolping's reputation for debauchery was such that a saying from the time proclaimed, "The Catholic Workers' Movement is dying of senility; Kolping is dying at the tap."[105] To young German males, Kolping offered a beloved community of brotherhood, merrymaking, and professional contacts. For many returning German soldiers, it offered the camaraderie they had known on the front.

But by the mid-1950s there were already signs of trouble ahead. The membership continued to increase, but at a much slower pace than in the years directly after the war. Between 1947 and 1957 the number of Kolping "families" in the Cologne archdiocese rose from fewer than 160 to not quite 180.[106] In 1958 the number of families dropped to 146, once the diocese of Essen was created, and remained at that level for the next ten years. The number in the General Kolping groups (which did not include the older members) increased hesitantly until 1947, reached a plateau at slightly fewer than 8,000 members, dropped by nearly 2,000 in 1958, and declined steadily to just slightly more than 2,000 by 1968.[107] As early as 1952 the number of new recruits dropped sharply. Although the number of new members varied substantially from year to year (from a high of 800 in 1952 to a low of 300 in 1954), the median number of recruits fell from approximately 600 in the early 1950s to 375 by the late 1950s and early 1960s. (This decline included those lost to the diocese of Essen in 1958.) By the late 1960s the number of new recruits scarcely exceeded 250.[108]

In their analysis, Kolping leaders blamed changing demographics for their membership slump. Teenagers in the mid- to late 1950s were part of a cohort that was considerably smaller than its predecessors, since fewer children were born during the wartime years. Kolping leaders also noted that groups consisted of older and younger men, since the generation of men in their thirties had borne the brunt of casualties during the war.[109] This situation had apparently given rise to tensions and conflicts in some Kolping families. Yet the decline in membership began before 1955 and continued through the 1960s, by which time the membership would have had a chance to recover. Put simply: Kolping's offerings no longer corresponded to the needs and interests of many young men in an era of mass culture, mass entertainment, and economic prosperity.

That Kolping was unable to tailor its offerings to a more demanding clientele can be seen in the total collapse of the wandering journeyman movement. Kolping leaders defended this tradition in much the same way that the leadership of the BDKJ continued to uphold the traditions of the youth movement. They insisted that boys in their late teens, by wandering from village to village in search of work from local masters, had the chance to get in touch with nature, to experience the joys of the countryside, and above all, to become resolute men. According to one proponent of the movement, "Wandering is a form of travel which is possible only in the years at the end of puberty. In this period, an inwardly secure and valiant man must emerge out of the boy."[110] Likewise, it was an antidote to the ills of modern society:

Modern man is in danger of being completely distanced from nature. Because man is, however, also a piece of nature, he will degenerate if he loses too much contact with nature. Wandering by foot brings him into the closest contact with nature. Now the increasing strength (of the boy) must be offered a field of action, otherwise it will be lost in the world of appearance in the movies, in the sensation of the athletic field, or in the alluring world of sexuality. . . . Now we have to fight against the mass appearance of modern times, with its superficiality, and the loss of higher human values.[111]

After the war, Kolping leaders attempted to reinvigorate the wandering journeyman movement. At least initially, their efforts met with some success, even if the number of participants never came close to the 10,000 per year who took part in the early 1930s.[112] President Theodor Heuss lent his support to the movement and encouraged young artisans to undertake this journey.[113] In 1952, 544 "wander-books" were ordered—a fairly reliable indicator of the level of participation. In the coming years, purchases shrank to 289 in 1954, 127 in 1958, 40 in 1961, 2 in 1967, and none thereafter.[114] The numbers were considerably smaller in the archdiocese of Cologne, as the largest share of the wandering journeymen came from the diocese of Münster, where Kolping groups were strongest. Eleven young men in 1951 and seven in 1954 from the archdiocese set out on their years of travel.[115]

By the early 1950s, most young artisans were unwilling to meet the heavy demands and reap the meager rewards of wandering journeymen. To embark on a three-year tour, one young man noted, a craftsman needed a full wallet.[116] Although participants were guaranteed food and lodging with Kolping brothers and in Kolping houses, even these were subject to restrictions—a maximum of thirty overnight stays in the first year, a number that in exceptional circumstances could be raised to forty or fifty.[117] The same man noted that participants stood out "like beings from another world." They were expected to attend mass daily, if possible, and observe a strict curfew; they were to arrive at their quarters by 9:00 P.M. (8:00 P.M. in winter). For others, the travel by foot was too strenuous. One Kolping leader urged members to travel by bicycle, car, or even airplane, if necessary, but these suggestions were frowned upon by the leader in charge of the program as antithetical to the spirit of wandering.[118] Traveling by foot rather than by bike or car, he argued, allowed the young person to get a fuller sense of the countryside. In response, the critic warned about living in the past: "We have not done our job, if we continue to speak of the golden past, which craftsmen once had." Most disastrous for this tradition was the reality that there were few compelling reasons for aspiring craftsmen, particularly those who worked in factories, to undertake a journey as rigorous as that of the wandering journeymen. For most craftsmen, employment opportunities beckoned in villages and cities during the years of full employment in the 1950s.

The popularity of Kolping's continuing education courses also sagged by the late 1950s. The number of courses in German correspondence, for instance, plunged from 692 in 1949 to 152 in 1964. Several courses of study —building, baking, and pastry making—had to be canceled altogether. The number of courses in bookkeeping dropped from 289 in 1949 to 68 in 1964.[119] Full employment and the increase in educational opportunities from the state undercut the appeal of continuing education programs.

Faced with declining demand for their products, Kolping leaders attempted to boost their membership by introducing Young Kolping groups for boys between fourteen and eighteen years old. These organizations immediately provoked the ire of the BDKJ leadership as well as that of the bishops.[120] In 1946 Kolping leaders had explicitly agreed not to recruit members younger than eighteen, even as they began to form Young Kolping groups.[121] In introducing these new organizations, they deliberately incensed the BDKJ leadership, who, they argued, had failed to give them a powerful voice in making decisions.[122] In a terse statement Kolping avowed, "The German Kolping Family will never recognize the charter of the BDKJ which was passed in 1946 and renewed in 1954 as valid for

Kolping."[123] Kolping leaders credibly noted that the majority of Young Kolping members had not been reached by ordinary parish groups. Kolping, they pointed out, was the only Catholic organization capable of attracting unorganized young men to the church.[124] Yet it is doubtful whether the Young Kolping groups realized the hopes of their founders. In 1962, for instance, the number of Young Kolping members in the archdiocese peaked at approximately 900 for teenage boys between fourteen and eighteen and did not increase substantially thereafter.

The history of Kolping demonstrated that it was still possible to reactivate and revitalize the traditional Catholic milieu after the war. In the case of Kolping, this milieu took the form of an insular organization of skilled craftsmen from the lower middle classes—an organization that cultivated an atmosphere that resembled that of an American college fraternity. Young persons joined to take advantage of the chances for career advancement and, above all, to have a good time. In this context, religion was not insignificant. Some young persons cited religion as an important, but not their primary, reason for joining, but religion frequently took a back seat to social and educational priorities such as rallies, banners, and evenings of beer and wurst. The reasons for Kolping's decline in the 1960s was foretold by one member in the 1950s: "When changing eras bring about new relationships, trade, and crafts, one can easily make the mistake of despairingly setting one's well-preserved traditions, which no longer fully correspond to new times, against everything new."[125]

More generally, the success of Catholic organizations in the archdiocese depended on the degree to which the Catholic milieu continued to influence young persons. Where the milieu had already crumbled, young persons were not receptive to movements to re-Christianize and convert. Workers in the cities, with some exceptions, resisted the efforts of clerics and their Christian colleagues to lead them back to the fold through the CAJ. Where a traditional Catholic way of life continued to exist, church leaders were far more successful, at least for a time. Class alone, of course, did not determine the allegiances of young persons to religious youth organizations (and by extension, to the church), but a strong connection existed between class, patterns of daily life, and the degree to which young persons remained receptive to the message and authority of the church.

FIVE

The Catholic Rural

Youth Movement in the

Rhineland and Lower

Franconia

IN THE GOLDEN SOIL, church leaders believed, lay the foundation of the German church.[1] Those who tilled the soil, they fancied, were more in touch with the divine than were those who toiled in the cities. Yet by the late 1950s, clerics closest to the realities of life in the countryside in the Rhineland directly after the war and in Lower Franconia had concluded that this vision of faith and soil was chimerical. Slowly but surely, these church leaders argued, village youths were being overcome by insidious influences once found exclusively in cities: mass sports, frenzied dancing, and indecent films. To them, the erosion of religious authority in the countryside was even more alarming than the loss of young workers in the cities, for this meant that their stronghold—rural Catholic communities—was now under siege.

Out of the conviction that the future of the church hinged on a religious renaissance in the countryside emerged the Catholic Rural Youth Movement (Katholische Landjugendbewegung) (KLJB). This was a movement with foreign origins, like the CAJ, but which, in contrast, drew on movements and traditions firmly rooted in native German soil. The KLJB was conceived not as simply another *Verein* or youth organization but as a movement to stir the heart and rouse young persons to action. To the delight of its founders, the KLJB succeeded in breaking new ground in rural villages throughout the 1950s and was credited with sowing the seeds of a religious revival.

In this chapter I begin by comparing the structures and geography of rural Catholic life in Lower Franconia with those in the archdiocese of Cologne.[2] I subsequently examine the rapid economic transformations in both regions in the postwar era and explain why the KLJB succeeded beyond all expectations, at least for the generation that came of age in the 1950s and early 1960s.

ON THE SURFACE, the patterns of daily life and religious practice in the rural regions of the archdiocese of Cologne and the diocese of Würzburg would appear to have little in common. As we have seen, the archdiocese of Cologne was marked by the ubiquitous presence of industry. By the early 1950s, one article in the Catholic newspaper for the archdiocese noted, of the sixty-four deaneries in the region, only thirty could be described as rural in character, and even in these, industry made its presence felt. Half of the industry in the archdiocese, the authors estimated, was located in the countryside.[3] In addition, more than 40,000 men and women commuted regularly to the city of Cologne, more than 30,000 went to Düsseldorf, nearly 18,000 traveled to Essen, and more than 10,000 went to Bonn, according to estimates from 1950. Duisburg, Oberhausen, Remscheid, Neuss, Solingen, and Mülheim received smaller, though by no means insignificant, numbers of commuters.[4] Some resided in villages between ten and twenty miles and, in some cases, even thirty miles distant. Nor was the flow from the country to the cities one way. Many city dwellers owned property in rural villages, where they spent their Sundays cultivating small gardens.[5] The outskirts of villages, once prime farmland, were filled with new developments in which Protestants often resided.[6] The conclusion of church leaders was unanimous: in no other diocese were the links between city and country as extensive as in the archdiocese of Cologne, and within the rural population, farmers were in danger of becoming a beleaguered minority.[7]

In contrast, church leaders in Lower Franconia administered a territory that industrialization had largely passed by. It extends from just west of the city of Aschaffenburg almost to the portals of Bamberg in the east. It juts down little farther than the city of Würzburg in the south but continues much farther to the north, encompassing the cities of Bad

Neustadt, Bad Kissingen, and Schweinfurt. This was a region of small farms. With ample sunshine, the banks of the Main and some of its feeders historically provided an important site for extensive grape and wine cultivation. In many other regions of Lower Franconia, however, the soil was considerably less fertile and the farms were smaller. The terrain becomes increasingly rugged and more densely forested as one travels farther from the Main toward the Spessart in the west. The Rhön, an isolated, sparsely populated, hilly region, straddles the border with Thuringia, and the Steigerwald is yet another mountainous forest in the south and east. In these regions of stony soil, the small peasant farmers were often barely able to eke out a living. Many had fewer than seven hectares at their disposal, a product of the system of partible inheritance; in the poverty-stricken regions to the east around Ebern, some farmers had less than one hectare.[8]

What little industry existed was concentrated in Schweinfurt (made famous by its ball-bearing plants during the Second World War), Aschaffenburg, and the western regions of the diocese. The city of Würzburg remained first and foremost an administrative and religious center. As late as the mid-1950s, 25 percent of the population was directly engaged in agriculture, as opposed to 20 percent for the rest of Bavaria and 16 percent for the Federal Republic as a whole. Some figures place the percentage of the population in Lower Franconia involved in agriculture as high as 30 percent for 1950.[9] Lower Franconia was, in short, a region without a sizable middle or educated upper middle class. Its population consisted primarily of small artisans and peasant farmers and, in only a few locales, workers. As one indication of the socioeconomic basis of the population, there were only twenty-two academic high schools (*Gymnasien*) for a total population of more than 900,000 in the region in 1950, a figure that increased to thirty-three by 1962; many of the older *Gymnasien* were associated with particular monastic orders.[10]

Lower Franconia was one of the most confessionally homogeneous regions of Germany, almost uniformly Catholic, similar to the western regions of the archdiocese of Cologne. According to diocesan statistics from 1948, 81 percent of the population was Catholic.[11] Some localities were more than 90 percent Catholic. Only a few areas were confessionally mixed. Cities such as Bad Kissingen, Kitzingen, Ochsenfurt, and Schweinfurt were only 50, 48, 54, and 66 percent Catholic, respectively, in 1948. Not surprisingly, Lower Franconia remained a stronghold of political

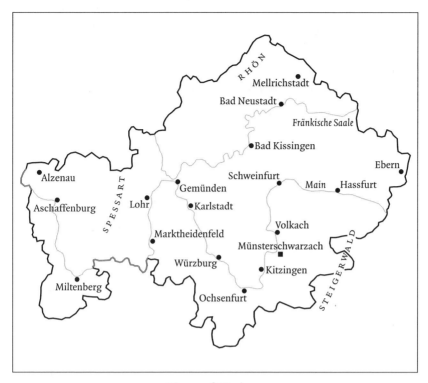

Diocese of Würzburg

Catholicism. In many regions, the CSU received more than 70 percent of the votes cast after 1945.

As late as the 1950s, outsiders had a sense of entering a world apart, where traditions had been handed down for centuries. Even the region's Catholicism remained distinct from that of other areas of Bavaria, to say nothing of the Rhineland or Westphalia. It was an enclave of Marian piety, a mélange of monasteries, pilgrimages, and processions. Even today it is not uncommon to see nuns in their habits and priests in their collars walking the streets of Frankish cities and villages. Its parishes were small and numerous. The diocese of Würzburg, with fewer than 900,000 total inhabitants and 730,000 Catholics, had slightly more than 500 parishes, roughly the same number as the archdiocese of Cologne, whose population was approximately 2.9 million, of whom 1.9 million were nominally Catholic.[12] The relatively small size and homogeneity of the parishes meant that there was little need to develop a vast network of *Vereine* for groups of workers, artisans, or farmers. Some pastors who were fond of a particular *Verband* occasionally declared their groups member organizations of that association, but such decisions were generally arbitrary and not necessarily indicative of the composition of the populace. Ancillary organizations in southern Germany were less complex and more inclusive; even their names avoided the title *Verein* and used the word *Volk* (people) instead—Das Landvolk, Das Werkvolk.[13]

Prior to the 1930s, youth work consisted primarily of scattered *Vereine* for the men or, far more commonly, Marian congregations, which existed separately for men and women. The newer forms of youth work—the youth and liturgical movements—generally arrived in the diocese of Würzburg ten to fifteen years later than in the rural regions of the archdiocese of Cologne. As late as 1946 the leader of the Catholic youth work for the diocese, Oskar Neisinger, noted that many remote villages had never seen the youth movement.[14] Decisive in bringing about this transition was not the example of middle-class *bündisch* youth—there were too few bourgeois families throughout the region—but the influence and guidance from the local monasteries, such as Münsterschwarzach, which served as centers for continuing education.

The bishop of Würzburg from 1924 to 1948, Matthias Ehrenfried, was an old-style monarchist with an authoritarian bent.[15] Until the last year of his life, he refused to give any financial or logistical assistance to young men and women who sought to recountenance groups along the lines of the youth and liturgical movements. The diocese of Würzburg nonetheless became a hotbed of resistance by young persons to the National Socialist regime. From this resistance, and not primarily out of the alternative structures for youth work that the national youth leaders developed between 1936 and 1938, the youth work of the postwar years emerged. Youth work in Lower Franconia thus took on a character very different from that in western Germany. Throughout the Nazi years and well into the postwar years, it was oriented around young, charismatic, homegrown lay diocesan leaders who received little support from elsewhere in the church.

The leader of this illegal youth work, Oskar Neisinger, was born in 1919 to a highly devout Catholic family. Neisinger was blessed with a charismatic personality and a dogged spirit of resistance. Because of a severe eye injury, he was exempted from military service and went instead to the university, ostensibly to study theology. In reality he used his time at the university to run a vast network of youth groups and train other youth leaders.[16] Through these programs he assembled a solid cadre of workers who secretly kept one another abreast of the latest plans and operations. Only in the last year of the war did he come under suspicion—he apparently was to receive a death sentence—at which point he fled to a monastery in Holland. After the war, he returned to Lower Franconia, where he steered Catholic youth for the next six to seven years and became a household name for engaged young Catholics.[17]

Neisinger led his followers in acts not just of passive resistance but of active opposition.[18] Catholic groups engaged in fistfights with the Hitler Youth.[19] In the early 1940s, youth leaders reported that more than 2,000 young persons participated in a procession that coincided with their official "obligations" to the Hitler Youth. Instead of singing the usual hymns for this festival, they brazenly sang verses that were demonstrably anti-Nazi. In another instance, youth leaders mobilized the populace to block the planned seizure of Münsterschwarzach by the Gestapo.[20] Other young men and women distributed leaflets in monasteries and other locations in Würzburg and Munich that decried the murder of Jews or reprinted the text of von Galen's sermons against euthanasia.[21]

What made it possible for illegal youth work to thrive in Lower Franconia and to muster such opposition to the National Socialist state? In this solidly and militantly Catholic region, there were few liberals and Protestants, those most likely to support the Nazis. Since most parishes were small, it was easy to keep a circle of friends and acquaintances informed of the major events in the region. The isolation of the diocese, moreover, made it possible to shroud activities in relative secrecy. As late as 1937 and 1938, Neisinger was still running tent camps with 300 to 400 boys in remote parts of the Spessart and the Odenwald, "without anyone following behind."[22] In the 1940s at least 2,000 young men and women remained part of this movement. It was, in short, the persistence of preindustrial traditions—the predominantly rural, strongly religious, and highly sectarian nature of the population—that allowed such organized acts of resistance to take shape and be more successful in this region.

The presence of strong indigenous leadership and significant resistance meant that the end of the war did not appear as a moment of crisis and catastrophe to youth leaders in Lower Franconia, as it did to church officials in the archdiocese of Cologne.[23] Youth leaders such as Neisinger immediately picked up where they had left off when they returned to their hometowns, even though their illegal youth work remained at a standstill during the last year of the war, when most of its leaders and many of the young members were conscripted to the army or as *Flakshelfer*. Some initial difficulties notwithstanding, Neisinger mobilized more than 700 young leaders, male and female, who reconstituted groups with amazing speed.[24]

This strategy produced results almost immediately. The deanery at Waldbüttelbrunn, located just to the west of the city of Würzburg with a total population of slightly more than 24,000 Catholics in fifteen parishes, saw the number of young persons enrolled in youth groups rise by nearly 34 percent between October 1946 and January 1948. In 1946, 208 young men and 463 young women were members of groups there. By 1948 there were 357 young men and 542 young women in the groups, most of whom were enrolled in the organizations for ten- to fourteen-year-olds.[25] Several parishes had added associations in the intervening two years, so that the deanery had a total of fifty-six groups, twenty-four for the men and thirty-two for the women.[26] As was often the case in such a heartland of traditional, rural Catholicism, these groups disproportionately mustered young women rather than young men. Some of the parishes surveyed had as many as eight groups; others had as few as one or, in some cases, none. At least 25 percent of all young Catholics enrolled in parish organizations, a high percentage for a rural region where distances to and from the church could be significant.

According to Neisinger, signs of success were evident in a diocesan youth festival in 1947, the second major gathering he and his colleagues had organized with no assistance from the church hierarchy. Previous reports had indicated that approximately 20,000 young men and women belonged to the Frankenjugend, the Catholic youth group. The turnout for this major festival, which took place in the courtyards and gardens surrounding the *Residenz* in the center of the city of Würzburg, however, exceeded all expectations.[27] For the first time, Bishop Ehrenfried was genuinely moved by the efforts of the young persons. After beholding from a second-floor balcony more than 10,000 young men and women who cheered his entrance and proudly waved flags and banners, he pulled Oskar Neisinger aside the next day and pledged financial and logistical support for diocesan youth work.[28] Ehrenfried's successor, Julius Döpfner, provided even greater financial assistance and a center for operations in the diocesan headquarters. Neisinger himself became a confidant of the new bishop.[29]

Youth work in Lower Franconia after 1945 thus appeared remarkably strong. Many groups had appropriated the traditions of the youth movement. Other *Verbände* such as Neudeutschland, the Catholic Boy Scouts, and Quickborn recruited new members.[30] Kolping claimed to have 37 Young Kolping and 121 Kolping Family groups in the diocese by the mid-1950s.[31] The CAJ also established a toehold in the diocese. But the decision to form Kolping or the CAJ appears to have been arbitrary, for the membership rosters show almost no difference in social, economic, or professional background among members.[32]

By 1949, youth workers pointed out, young persons, particularly boys and girls who had not undergone the same process of socialization in the National Socialist system, had rediscovered the "joy of life" and were increasingly eager to participate in Catholic youth work.[33] Catholic youth work in Lower Franconia had proved remarkably successful. Leaders had mobilized more than 20,000 young persons, a significant number, given the isolation and small size of many parishes in the region.

SIGNS OF TROUBLE

By the mid- to late 1950s, however, the picture of Catholic youth work began to look less rosy to contemporary observers, as industrial growth, economic prosperity, and social changes fundamentally altered the region. In less than twenty years, Lower Franconia was transformed from an agrarian backwater to a bustling center of trade, commerce, and industry with one of the higher rates of economic growth in the Federal Republic—the German version of the new American South or the Flemish areas of Belgium. The industries that came to the region were not the coal and steel producers of the Ruhr but more vibrant sectors of the economy: electronics operations, machine builders, automobile parts manufacturers, and food processors.[34] As these industries established themselves, the share of the population engaged in agriculture fell dramatically, from 20.7 percent in 1950 to 15.3 percent in 1961 and a mere 8.3 percent in 1970.[35] Between 1950 and 1985 the absolute numbers of agricultural workers plummeted from 164,408 to 38,400, of which only 3,743 were running their operations independently.[36]

This steady socioeconomic transformation was under way prior to 1945 but accelerated immediately after the war, when a steady stream of men and women driven from their homes in the east settled in Lower Franconia. In 1950 more than 16 percent of the population of the Federal Republic was made up of these refugees; the percentage of expellees was slightly higher in Lower Franconia at 16.8.[37] These refugees initially bypassed the major cities that were struggling to put themselves back together after Allied air raids—Würzburg, Aschaffenburg, and Schweinfurt —and settled instead in the countryside. In some regions they comprised almost 30 percent of the population. Unlike in most other areas of Germany, however, the influx of refugees did not fundamentally alter the confessional landscape. Protestant parishes grew rapidly in some villages, but as a whole, the Catholic share of the population declined only slightly, from 80.6 percent in 1933 to 78.1 percent in 1961.[38] In some areas where Protestants once enjoyed majority status, Catholics gained the upper hand. Catholics in Kitzingen and Hofheim increased their share of the population from 44 and 47.3 percent, respectively, to 52.6 and 50.0 percent.[39] In other regions, both the Catholic and the Protestant populations grew apace, so that the confessional balance remained unchanged. In 1953 there were 70,085 Catholics and 21,144 Protestants in the city of Würzburg, 76.8 and 23.2 percent, respectively. These figures changed little by 1962, when there were 92,000 Catholics and 28,161 Protestants, 76.7 and 23.3 percent, respectively.[40] By the late 1950s, many refugees were leaving the countryside for greater work opportunities in the cities, and it appears that most chose to reside in regions where their own confession was already in the majority.

The presence of Protestant refugees unsettled church leaders even more significantly in the archdiocese of Cologne, even though this region, like Lower Franconia, absorbed a relatively small percentage of the total number of evacuees. Church leaders feared that interconfessional organizations would attempt to organize all residents in these regions. This indeed proved to be the case. Against the wishes of the church hierarchy, the German Farmers' Organization, a confessionally neutral *Verband* under the leadership of Andreas Hermes, reached out to local farmers and established a daughter organization, the League of German Rural Youth (Bund der Deutschen Landjugend).[41] Confessionally neutral sporting and equestrian organizations also grew rapidly in many villages.

Leaders of the sporting and equestrian organization were hostile to the church and did not cooperate with religious organizations.[42]

Rural regions in Lower Franconia had already shown tremendous economic growth during the last years of the war, when many large factories in Schweinfurt relocated parts of their operations to the countryside to avoid Allied bombs. After 1945 many factories continued to build their plants in smaller cities or once exclusively rural enclaves. Siemens and another electronics firm, Preh, expanded operations in Bad Neustadt; Ebern became the site for a metalworking plant; Karlstadt hosted a cement factory; and the region around Ochsenfurt was home to food-processing and sugar factories. These areas became regional centers of industry and commerce. The major cities also experienced torrid rates of growth. Schweinfurt became the economic powerhouse of the region, producing not just ball bearings but motors, machine parts, and motor vehicles.

Throughout Lower Franconia, the number of industries and factories declined from almost 2,000 in the mid-1950s to fewer than 1,100 by 1987, but their size and number of employees increased substantially.[43] In the 1950s most operations employed fewer than 20 workers; by 1987 many employed more than 100 workers. The percentage of the population that included workers or artisans accordingly increased from 31.5 in 1950 to 41.2 in 1961 and finally leveled off at 37.2 in 1970.[44] Other sectors benefited as well. The percentage of those working in trade and commerce increased from 9.1 in 1950 to 11.7 in 1961. The share of the population employed in the service industry, which included public service, rose from 11.1 percent to 14.2 percent in 1961.[45] Even agriculture benefited from increased prosperity, although the majority of young persons continued to forsake the farm for work in small factories and shops. New tractors and mechanized plows, some of which dated back to the 1920s and 1930s, helped boost earnings. Some farmers profited so much from the food shortages (and attendant rising prices) in the years of military occupation that church leaders accused them of price gouging and falling victim to an ethic of materialism.

While increased prosperity enabled some of the wealthier farmers to expand their holdings, it was not sufficient to stem the continued flight of many younger men and women from the countryside. The system of partible inheritance—dividing farms equally among all sons, a 700-year-old tradition in most parts of Lower Franconia—made many plots of land unworkable and undoubtedly accelerated the departure of many young men and women from the area.[46] Some areas in the region saw the number of farms decline by more than 75 percent between 1949 and 1959. In Alzenau, where many small factories had taken root and where many residents found work in the industries of Aschaffenburg, the number of farms dropped from 2,556 to 807; in the Landkreis of Aschaffenburg, the number plummeted from 2,162 to 594.[47] Bad Neustadt, Lohr, and Hassfurt recorded similar losses.

This decline in the number of farms had mixed effects on the farmers who remained. Farmers with medium-sized plots of land, between ten and fifty hectares, were generally able to increase their holdings; the number of such farms also rose. Farmers with smaller plots, between two and ten hectares, lost out. The size of the holdings actually decreased by 15 to 30 percent; the number of such farms correspondingly shrank by between 18 and 30 percent.[48] Catholic observers noted, as a result, that tensions often rose between poorer and wealthier farmers in some regions, for some of the larger farmers had no doubt increased their holdings at the expense of others.[49] In the 1960s local authorities attempted to consolidate many of the small plots of land made unworkable by the regional system of inheritance, but these measures did not stave off the continued decrease in the number of farmers and agricultural workers.

The growth of industry and the decline of agriculture went hand in hand and had enormous consequences for the region. Many onetime farmers and their children, particularly those who owned fewer than five hectares, went to work in nearby industries instead of struggling to turn a profit from diminishing agricultural holdings. Most did not leave their homes but commuted to work in the cities. The towns surrounding Schweinfurt were transformed from farming villages to bedroom communities for industrial workers and artisans.[50] Every day some commuters traveled more than 25 miles each way to work in regional centers such as Bad Kissingen, Lohr, or Bad Neustadt. The region to the east around Ebern, where the soil was poor and stony, had a particularly high number of commuters who worked in industry. Many were unmarried women under thirty seeking a better life away from the farm, where women were often overburdened with responsibilities for both family and homestead. Others were "reverse commuters" who lived in the cities and traveled to workplaces in the countryside.[51]

These patterns fundamentally changed the structures of everyday village life. In contrast to other regions of Germany, where farms were adjacent to the area under cultivation, most farmers in Lower Franconia lived in the villages and traveled daily to their plots of land in the countryside.[52] With the increase in the number of commuters, the social structures in many villages changed. Instead of housing farmers almost exclusively, villages became home to equal numbers of industrial workers, artisans, refugees, commuters, and white-collar workers, many of whom were young women who worked as secretaries and office assistants in nearby factories and businesses. Villages lost not only their homogeneity but also their sense of community. According to one Catholic observer, the social pecking order in villages was now derived from status at work.[53] Many farmers, envious of the newfound wealth of these upstarts, cut themselves off from outsiders who were bringing new values and ways of life to the villages.

Some church leaders concluded that the village was more dangerous for young people than the city was.[54] Fritz Eink noted in 1947 the mounting interest in sporting life in the archdiocese of Cologne: "It was sucking up all other interests and was taking place without control or decency; even the once-so-well-preserved girls from the countryside appear to have irredeemably fallen victim to it through the formation of hand-ball groups, which carry out competitions in which the girls behave like men."[55] Others noted the increasing incidence of venereal disease, an indication that society had lost its moorings.[56] In 1958 church leaders estimated that 47 percent of all moviegoers in West Germany were from small communities with fewer than 5,000 people and that 32 percent of the youth in these communities went regularly to the cinema.[57] Television only added to the worries of church leaders, as it, too, meant the intrusion of urban customs into village life.[58]

Such changes in the structures of village life had enormous consequences for local parishes. In many villages the older farmers continued to serve as the nucleus, while the newcomers—the refugees, the commuters, and the workers—gradually dropped out or formed distinct subgroups. The increasing numbers of working women also brought about change. Although women remained far more active than men in most churches, many Catholic leaders claimed that family life in the villages increasingly resembled that of the cities: the divorce rate had gone up, and the "disorganization" of city life had thrown families into disarray.[59]

The fragmentation of everyday life, Catholic publicists concluded, eroded the authority of the church and loosened the ties between the individual and the clergy; the system of patriarchy was on the way out.

These changes were already under way in the rural regions of the archdiocese of Cologne in the 1920s and 1930s, but they accelerated in the postwar economic boom.[60] Farmers were changing their daily and weekly routines. Instead of observing Sunday as a day of rest and attending mass, some farmers were often back out in the fields in order to maximize profits.[61] Others were looking to cultivate their holdings in a more efficient and rational way. They began to use heavy machinery, tractors, and reapers and kept abreast of the latest scientific advances to increase yields. To the dismay of church officials, the widespread use of machinery created a work climate that stressed rationality, profit taking, and logical calculations of risk and gain. Farmers ceased to place their trust in the mercy of God and put their faith instead in the wonders of technology. The rationalism of the Enlightenment now extended to that group that had hitherto proven most resistant to its call.[62]

As young persons were often the first to leave the once-sheltered world of the farm for new opportunities in the cities, youth work was disproportionately affected by these changes in culture and society. Many teenagers started working in factories at the age of fourteen or fifteen, at which point they tried to adapt to the ways of their peers, and "the silver cross (of the Bund) disappears."[63] In the 1950s, youth groups suffered a net loss of members in Lower Franconia. By 1960, youth groups had only 11,779 official members, a drop of more than 8,000 from estimates of 20,000 in the late 1940s.[64] These figures represented little more than 15 percent of the total number of young Catholics who officially belonged to parishes.[65] Although the numbers of young women also decreased, their levels of participation, in sharp contrast to those in North Rhine–Westphalia, still remained higher than those for young men. The survey indicated that 7,623 young women and only 4,156 young men officially remained part of Catholic youth groups. The circulation of official newspapers, another valuable indicator of membership trends, also plunged during the late 1950s. The number of boys between ages 10 and 14 who subscribed to Scheideweg declined from 1,396 in 1955 to 834 in 1960; the number of 14- to 18-year-old boys who received Voran went from 871 in 1955 to 629 in 1960. The number of 10- to 14-year-old girls who subscribed to Die Bunte Kette dropped only slightly from 1,575 to 1,454 in this time period; the number of 14- to 18-year-old girls who received *Morgen* fell precipitously from 1,820 to 1,281.[66]

One immediate consequence of this larger decline in the overall membership—and yet another indicator of social transformation—was a sharp fall-off in the number of young persons who entered the priesthood or joined an order. In the interwar years, many candidates for the priesthood had come through the ranks of Bund Neudeutschland. Josef Stangl, the bishop of Würzburg from 1957 to 1979, cited the role this organization had played during his formative years in his decision to become a priest. Church leaders were wont to blame the declining number of seminarians on a decrease in the number of farmers. They argued, not entirely correctly, that agriculture provided the social base for candidates for the priesthood. In 1952 church officials bemoaned a shortage of more than 2,900 priests for all of Germany.[67] In 1956 diocesan officials in Würzburg noted with alarm that they were short 1,500 nuns and that kindergartens, hospitals, kitchens, and church music programs were suffering as a result.[68]

This decline was a sign that young men and women were no longer willing to commit to those religious activities and professions that required the greatest degree of dedication and sacrifice. Youth leaders likewise realized that most young Catholics were no longer participating in "organized" youth activities.[69] Some leaders observed that young men and women who continued to participate did so not out of genuine spiritual fervor but from a mere sense of obligation or a fear of the clergy or, more commonly, because their parents ordered them to attend the youth activities of the church.[70]

A detailed analysis of church attendance and parish life for all congregations in the city of Würzburg bore out this trend. This study surveyed all those who attended mass on 16 September 1960. The result showed that children under 14 had the highest levels of attendance. As many as 70 to 80 percent of boys and girls attended church, a rate far higher than that of their parents, probably because their parents insisted that the children go, even if the parents themselves did not always attend. The attendance rate was typically 20 percent higher for women than for men.[71] After age 14, the picture changed dramatically. The number of young persons attending mass fell (although it still remained higher than that of adult men in most parishes) even as the participation in youth groups remained low. The parish of St. Josef, one of the larger in the city of Würzburg at that time, had 929 young people between ages 14 and 21. Of these, 413, or 44 percent, attended church on that Sunday, and only 77 were members of the organized youth, a paltry 8.2 percent. A smaller parish, St. Alfons, had only 265 young persons, in contrast. Of these, 153 attended mass, or 58 percent, and 64 were members of groups, or 24 percent. St. Alfons had a larger percentage of civil servants and white-collar workers, and St. Josef had a larger share of blue-collar workers. This situation may have affected the degree of participation within these parishes.[72]

In more diverse parishes, however, groups often fragmented along socioeconomic and occupational lines. The leadership in Bad Neustadt observed that many young men had become workers in their city and could no longer be reached by youth work. "There is no longer a proper class of farmers," the report concluded, and young persons who remained in Catholic groups usually joined Kolping.[73] The deanery of Miltenberg reported in 1955 that the parishioners were divided nearly equally between workers and farmers. It was impossible to get these two cohorts to work together, and young persons were leaving the groups as a result.[74] The leadership in Bad Kissingen noted that many of the workers who lived in the Rhön had to travel long distances to the workplace, a situation that posed an additional challenge to youth leaders.[75] In light of the ensuing tensions, church leaders called for tolerance. The village was no longer an island: "We are no longer by ourselves in the village."[76]

By the mid-1950s in Lower Franconia and by the late 1940s in the archdiocese of Cologne, church leaders realized that something had to be done to counter these dangerous declines in membership. Perspicacious church leaders realized that they could no longer simply urge farmers to return to the old way of village life, as had been the case in earlier rural movements.[77] Eink bemoaned the fact that the existing system of youth work in rural regions was inadequate. He noted that many local clerics and villagers, unaware of the transformation in their midst, had simply taken the presence of young persons in the church for granted and had not bothered to form youth groups. Another priest noted that most smaller parishes in the countryside lacked curates, younger priests who could spend time with and better relate to the younger folk. At clergy conferences many priests repeated the refrain, "Something is going on where a curate is."[78] Others insisted that the youth movement itself was outdated, concerned only with liturgical and aesthetic questions, and foreign to those in the countryside.[79] To be successful, youth work had to emphasize practical concerns and address the pressing questions of daily life, such as how to remain anchored in Catholicism in a time when the world was changing by the day.

Gradually church leaders discovered alternatives. Some presented individual lecture series designed to reach the masses of unorganized youth, while others undertook a more bold and coherent initiative, the KLJB. This movement drew on continuing education programs pioneered in the 1920s and 1930s, perhaps originally in Denmark. It is little wonder that the bishops drew parallels between the KLJB and the CAJ. Both were inspired by foreign models; both were movements—not Vereine—in which young men and women were to take the lead in re-Christianizing their environments; and both incurred the opposition of Altenberg and, for that reason, did not take off until the later 1950s.[80]

Church leaders quickly realized that there was no one way to reach all youth in the countryside, for rural life varied significantly from region to region. Some leaders wanted the movement to include only farmers, while others sought to reach all inhabitants of the countryside—workers, artisans, and farmers, both men and women. Advocates of the first approach were often from regions such as the diocese of Münster, where farmers comprised the overwhelming majority of the rural population. In Westphalia, where farms were larger and farther apart, church leaders conceived of the KLJB primarily as an organization for farmers; the artisans and workers who lived in the region could easily be reached by one of the many Vereine there, such as Kolping, the CAJ, or the KAB. Church leaders south of the Main, however, argued that this strategy would not work for southern Germany, where workers, artisans, and farmers lived in the same villages.[81]

Leaders in both Cologne and Lower Franconia brokered a compromise. Frings allowed both organizational methods to take root in the archdiocese, depending on the character of the individual regions. In Würzburg, officials proposed that, for villages with fewer than 1,000 inhabitants and which consisted largely of farmers, the KLJB was to include all young persons in the region—the "milieu" approach, as it came to be known. For villages where a sizable percentage of the population was working in industry (mostly in the lower regions of the Main), the KLJB was to target specific occupational groups—the "professional group" approach (berufsständisch). In the more socioeconomically diverse, larger villages and cities, the CAJ was to minister to the commuters, the KLJB to the farmers.[82] Youth leaders in Aschaffenburg accordingly went out of their way to support the CAJ in regions where workers resided.[83] The KLJB likewise took root where farmers predominated, in regions such as Hammelburg, Gemünden, and Ochsenfurt.[84]

The KLJB adopted several approaches. The episcopate added two newspapers to the repertoire from Altenberg: The Plow (Der Pflug) for southern Germany and The Sower (Der Sämann) for western Germany. It also encouraged young men and women to form their own "working groups," which were to meet every four to six weeks to attend lectures, participate in discussions, and, during the summer, take trips to other rural locations to see how farmers there were living.[85] The leaders of the KLJB also expanded the continuing education centers in the region, investing them with a new sense of purpose. The center in Rhöndorf, for instance, was to become a "school of life," which would underscore "aspects and tasks of life in their order of importance and show how rural life in all of its circles can be countenanced along Christian lines and how it can be filled with a Christian-rural meaning."[86]

Diocesan leaders also gave the KLJB the go-ahead to form its own groups. By 1957 the movement had taken root in more than 128 villages in the archdiocese of Cologne, most of which were still home to large numbers of farmers.[87] These groups, however, were intended to supplement and not to replace preexisting parish associations, and many of the activities were in the form of lectures and informal meetings. For the farmers, many sessions discussed questions of technology, such as how modern machinery could be harnessed to religious purposes. Leaders widely distributed an address by Alois Muench, papal nuncio in Germany who also served as the bishop of Fargo, who showed how farmers in the American Midwest relied almost exclusively on mechanized equipment and still faithfully attended church.[88]

The main staple of the KLJB was what came to be known as "rural seminars." These were lectures and discussions that were sometimes held in continuing education centers explicitly designed for this purpose (Landvolkhochschulen). More commonly, they took place in local restaurants or classrooms, since many small villages lacked adequate facilities.[89] Seminar topics were designed to address pressing questions in the daily lives of young men and women and were followed by open discussions in which the participants could make their voices heard. In 1957, 11.6 percent of the themes dealt with problems of marriage and family; 9.5 percent, with ideologies (*Weltanschauungen*); 9.3 percent, with social questions; 9.1 percent, with religion; 9.0 percent, with how to use leisure time; 7.7 percent, with newspapers, radio, and film; 5.7 percent, with the histories and culture of local villages; 7.7 percent, with questions of culture; and a mere 1.6 percent, with agricultural and farming problems.[90]

Where farmers made up the majority of the rural population, seminar leaders chose themes such as "The Modern Farmer, as God Will Have Him," "Christ and His Body," "Values, the Worth, and Unique Qualities of the Family," "Is It Still Worth It to Become a Farmer?" and "Farmers, Technology, and Faith in God." Where artisans and workers were in the majority, seminar leaders introduced topics such as "Does the Christian Village Still Have a Future?" "We and Our Parish," "From the History of Our Village," "Dream Factories: The Cinema," and "The Rural Village in the Past and Present."[91] Others addressed the problems faced by commuters: were they city or village dwellers?[92] Some topics were intended to foster greater unity in the villages. One session was titled "Workers, Farmers, Sales Persons, and Artisans Build a Better World." Another was called "The Village: Our Home and Our Task." Other panels were designed to clear up the confusion from the workplace (and give the church an opportunity to show its relevance). Some bore such titles as "Politics in the Workplace," "On the Way to Work," and "Work? Why?"[93]

Activities in Lower Franconia also included lectures, slide shows, and formal discussions. One coordinated program for the diocese—the so-called *Aktion-Stadt-Markt*—set out to offer topics of interest to young men and women. One lecture series was titled "Are You Modern?" Another was "Does the Bible Make Mistakes?" One lecture—"Lenin or Brother Klaus?"—was designed to inform the youth of the struggles of fellow Catholics behind the iron curtain. These programs were just as successful. In the village of Amerbach, 70 percent of the young persons who came to hear the lecture "Are You Modern?" were from the ranks of the unorganized youth. Fifty-five percent of those who showed up for a lecture titled "From the Standard of Living to the Fulfillment of Life" were not members of organized groups.[94] The percentage of unorganized youth was admittedly lower in other parishes, in some cases between 10 and 30 percent.[95]

The KLJB had one major goal: to prevent young persons living in the countryside from migrating to the cities. Some of the leaders of this movement harbored a residual "blood and soil" ideology and believed that the health and stability of Western European societies depended on the survival of a strong class of farmers. Most church leaders, however, were more down-to-earth in their aims. They were well aware that many young persons, on leaving their villages for the cities or in commuting from villages to workplaces elsewhere, also left the sphere of influence of the church. Thus these leaders designed their initiatives to instill a sense of loyalty and pride in belonging to one's village and to give a modern face to religious events. Youth leaders, for instance, scripted a play titled "The Village in the Future," which featured a dialogue between a young man and a conservative older farmer. The young man insisted that the village had to take on the modern trappings of city life: "We are no longer the dumb farmers from yesterday. . . . We also want to be modern. As a result, things are now going on by the dance floor." Outraged, the older farmer asserted that city culture would destroy the hallmarks of village life, such as the costumes, the dirndl, and the folk songs. The play urged young persons to steer a course between these two extremes: to maintain what was best of the old traditions, yet to allow for change in a "clean and genuine manner."[96]

These seminars targeted young women who were about to enter the workplace and eschew village life in favor of opportunities in the cities as secretaries or factory workers.[97] Some of these young women intended to settle permanently in urban centers; others opted for short stints in factories, while an increasing number commuted daily to their urban workplaces. It was not difficult for church leaders to discern why young women sought greener pastures in the cities.[98] Officials in Catholic Charities (Caritas) noted that life for women on the farm was anything but bucolic. Many women worked the equivalent of three full-time jobs, as housewives, mothers, and coworkers with their husbands. These jobs required a minimum of twelve hours a day and offered no vacation time, only perpetual exhaustion; Caritas leaders gravely noted that the life expectancy of women was often much shorter than that of their husbands.[99] Until later in the 1960s, moreover, most farmers' wives had little access to newer technologies (such as dishwashers, electrical appliances, and washing machines) that would have eased their duties. Nor could their burdens be lessened by others in the area, since as many as 350,000 agricultural workers were leaving each year, according to some church estimates.[100] As the exodus of young women continued, male farmers were often left holding the fort alone. According to one estimate, 25 percent of young male farmers were single. Some had chosen not to marry because they had yet to inherit the farm from their parents or because there were too few young women in villages and even fewer willing to assume the burdens of becoming a farmer's wife.[101]

What lessons did church leaders impart to young men and women in the countryside? The seminars taught them to examine critically the environment in which they lived but also reinforced traditional agrarian roles for women. Church leaders believed that education could curb the worst abuses. Young farmers, they insisted, would come to appreciate the tremendous sacrifices their wives were making and, in turn, would treat them better. In one case a farmer, after watching his wife fall into depression and nearly succumb to a life-threatening illness, purchased fabric for a new dress, apparently his first gift to her. Young women between ages twenty and thirty-two were encouraged to set aside a year of their lives to become "village helpers" (*Dorfhelferinnen*) who would lessen the burdens on farmers' wives by helping them with cooking, cleaning, and babysitting.[102] These village helpers were to give to others in need, such as shut-ins, the old, and the sick.[103] Women in the "working groups" were to take evening courses in baking, sewing, child care, home economics, and weaving.[104] Through these programs, it was hoped, young men would learn to treat their wives with greater respect and reverence, and young women, in turn, would return to the villages.

Although some priests initially fulminated against this new movement, many came to embrace it fervently once they realized its power to win over young people. Leaders presented glowing reports of success in both dioceses.[105] In one parish, twenty to twenty-five boys were so inspired that they began to attend religious exercises regularly; one entered a monastery, and the pastor, who had been adamantly opposed to the movement, became one of its most ardent supporters.[106] Another leader from Reckendorf reported in 1957 that the groups he had visited were in good health.[107] The following month he declared that "a new, spiritual class is growing in our villages." Regardless of whether the events consisted of large assemblies or intimate evening socials, the result was the same: "Rural youth [is] in movement!"[108]

It seems that church leaders, depending on the geographical contours of individual villages, succeeded in reaching all strata of rural society: farmers, commuters, workers, and secretaries, men and women. In some

The reconstruction of youth work. First major rally for the Catholic youth in the diocese of Würzburg, 1947. This photo was taken from the *Residenz* with a view of the Festung Marienberg and of the destroyed inner city. (Courtesy of Diözesanarchiv Würzburg)

villages, at least 150 young persons, many of whom were not members of an organized youth group, took part. Some seminar leaders elatedly proclaimed that they had discovered the alternative to traditional groups. Diocesan leaders proudly increased the number of seminars from 1 in 1954 to 280 in 1958.[109] With thousands taking part, the movement had exceeded the wildest expectations of its founders.

Why did this movement prove so successful and give rise to a religious upswing in the countryside during the late 1950s and early 1960s? These lectures demanded a lower degree of commitment than membership in a group, which required dues and weekly attendance as well as many symbolic gestures of loyalty, such as oaths and badges. For the first time, moreover, young men and women in rural regions were able to discuss the issues most dear to them in a climate both religious and tolerant. Even though the responses from seminar leaders were often traditional, many young men and women regarded the mere opportunity for open discussion as groundbreaking, for it signaled that their voices were being heard.

More importantly, church leaders were able to provide new forms of youth work that better met the needs of young persons during the "economic miracle." They merged components of "professional organizations" with the traditional offerings of Catholics groups and, as a result, were able to reach individuals who were concerned about their careers and economic futures in a time of rapid societal change. Many young persons were just as unsettled as church leaders by the fast pace of change in their once-agrarian world, and they were concerned with the rise in the number of commuters, the growth of industry in the countryside, and prosperity.

Most significant was the fact that church leaders were able to launch new initiatives at a time when the Catholic milieu in Lower Franconia was only beginning to experience significant socioeconomic change. Young men and women who joined the Catholic youth movement had been raised Catholic and, as we saw for the city of Würzburg, attended mass more frequently than their parents. The seeds of the movement thus fell on fertile ground, for many teenagers were uncertain how to reconcile their Catholic upbringing with the new patterns of work and recreation in "modern" society. Youth leaders anticipated social change, and by moving in at a time when change was only beginning, they were able to stave off greater erosion. Equally significantly, they did not simply condemn the new developments in culture, employment, and housing; they chose a pattern of accommodation whereby they could exert a greater influence over the new patterns of life that were emerging. Youth leaders in Lower Franconia achieved a reconciliation of sorts with modern culture and society, one which, for at least a generation, stabilized the Catholic milieu in a period of immense change.

The message of the KLJB, unlike that of the CAJ, reached a receptive audience. Unlike their comrades in large cities, young people in the countryside had, in spite of the transformation of many villages, not departed far from their religious roots. According to one survey of 100 seventeen- to twenty-eight-year-olds in the archdiocese of Cologne in 1959, 81 attended mass regularly, 15 occasionally, 3 only on major feast days, and only 1 never.[110] A more extensive study from 1954 surveyed 1,498 young persons between ages fifteen and twenty-four in all of Germany and yielded similar results.[111] This survey reported that 70 percent of the children of independent farmers attended mass regularly, whereas only 45 percent of those in large cities went to church regularly. When asked to identify basic tenets of Christian doctrine and faith, the children of farmers consistently scored highest. The study concluded that religious piety in rural Germany had indeed suffered in recent years, but that it remained far higher in the country than in the urban areas.

In sum, the success of Catholic movements and *Verbände* in the archdiocese depended on how much the Catholic milieu was able to influence the youth. In cities where the milieu no longer functioned, young persons did not respond to efforts at re-Christianization or conversion. In the countryside and among artisans, where a traditional Catholic way of life persisted, church leaders had more authority. Such successes underscored the fact that the Catholic milieu was based not only on a common religious heritage but on common patterns of daily life and occupation. At the least, religious obligations were a product of the environment in which young persons grew up. Where these patterns of daily life changed, loyalty to religious organizations dissipated or at least was called into question. The KLJB made these changes in society and culture its focus and reaped a bountiful harvest, although there were indications that these approaches would work only for a generation coming of age during the mid-1950s to mid-1960s.

Modernization did not necessarily lead to an erosion of religious subcultures. Thus one can still speak of a Catholic milieu that, in many rural regions of the Rhineland and Lower Franconia, flourished well into the 1960s. Within the once thoroughly agrarian domain of Lower Franconia, church leaders were able to graft preindustrial traditions onto the changing surface of modern society—and bring about a religious upswing, however short lived, in the countryside.

SIX

A League of
Their Own: The DJK
Civil War and the
Collapse of Catholic
Integralism

ON 19 SEPTEMBER 1949 the Spiel- und Sportgemeinschaft Rhein-Weser, a confederation of Catholic sporting organizations for youth located predominantly in the Ruhr, issued a pronouncement that sent many prominent Catholics into a panic.[1] It declared itself to be a successor to the DJK, a Catholic sporting organization dissolved by the Nazis in 1934. In its heyday during the late 1920s, the DJK had brought more than 500,000 young men into its fold. But in 1946 the Catholic bishops refused to give their blessing to a reconstituted DJK. In spite of the bishops' opposition, small DJK cells sprang up throughout Westphalia. Pressure from activists, most of whom had been ardent supporters of the DJK prior to 1934, soon forced Catholic youth leaders in Altenberg to change their tack. These leaders subsequently gave the go-ahead to the DJK but insisted on affiliating the DJK-Arbeitsgemeinschaft, at least on the administrative level, with other non-Catholic sporting organizations within Germany.

With this unlikely step, the battle lines were drawn for a civil war that lasted more than fifteen years over whether to allow individual Catholic sporting groups to participate in the activities and to use the facilities of non-Catholic sporting organizations. Those who opposed cooperating with non-Catholic organizations seceded from the main DJK based in Altenberg and formed their own rival association, which they claimed embodied the true spirit of the DJK. The DJK thus was divided between the supporters of the secessionist DJK Rhein-Weser Verband (soon to be rechristened the DJK-Zentral Organisation) and the so-called DJK Hauptverband, based in Altenberg. The DJK "fraternal feud," as it came to be known, was reckoned as one of the worst examples of *Vereinsmeierei* in Catholic history. It pitted bishop against bishop in a contest of wills. Archbishop Lorenz Jaeger of Paderborn rose to become the "protector" of the Zentralverband, and found a partner-in-arms in the bishop of Münster, Michael Keller. Tit for tat was to follow. Frings, close in age to Jaeger, was soon anointed as the protector of the Hauptverband. Disgusted by the emerging imbroglio, Albert Stohr of Mainz threatened to abandon his special position among the bishops as the "youth bishop" should the conflict spread from the dioceses of Münster and Paderborn to the rest of Germany.[2]

This struggle also generated a degree of acrimony and rancor unprecedented within Catholic Germany. In one infamous incident, a layman from the Zentralverband sued a priest from the Hauptverband who had accused him of "behaving like a FDJ lad" at a sporting event.[3] By 1960, leading German newspapers were gleefully printing reports of the infighting within Catholic ranks at a time when Catholic leaders prided themselves on maintaining a facade of unity to the German public.[4] The situation proved so embarrassing that these leaders apparently co-opted no less a person than Konrad Adenauer into intervening, in an effort to resolve this conflict once and for all.[5]

Why did such a seemingly innocuous issue—the participation of Catholic sporting organizations in events sponsored by the League of German Sport (Deutscher Sportbund) (DSB)—spark fifteen years of bitter internecine strife? The confrontation raised several sensitive issues: the theology and understanding of the human body, the extent to which women should be allowed to participate in public sporting events, and the relationship between Catholics and liberal, Protestant, and Socialist society. Most fundamentally, it raised questions of how Catholics were to define and position themselves within postwar Germany and modern society. Fractious integralists hoped to seal off young Catholics from the temptations of the modern world, a position that their critics derided as a ghetto stance or a "deep freeze."[6] Moderates were willing to make accommodations to modern society; these were half-steps, in reality, but measures that they considered to be a step forward. The DJK conflict assumed a significance far greater than the immediate issues would suggest. It is no exaggeration to assert that it seemed a life-and-death struggle to the defenders of the integralist vision of Catholicism. It might also be suggested that the DJK conflict aroused such embittered passions because of its location in Westphalia, where the network of Catholics was more dense and all-encompassing than in any other region of Germany and whose inhabitants enjoy a reputation for being stubborn and unyielding.[7] As tempting as this explanation may be, it ultimately does not explain the deeper issues opened by this conflict.

The background of the fraternal feud in the DJK lay in the Weimar Republic.[8] The DJK was a relative latecomer to the German sporting world. Carl Mosterts launched the organization in 1920, as the end of the First World War brought a major wave of youthful enthusiasm for sports; martial energies were, perhaps, translated into competition on the sporting field.[9] Workers' sporting organizations, in contrast, had existed since the 1870s. The newly formed DJK brought together informal sporting clubs for young artisans that were a part of Kolping as well as gymnastics groups that had sprung up within the preceding ten years on the diocesan level.

That Mosterts spearheaded the DJK gives some indication of its overall philosophy. Mosterts was, by all reports, an extraordinarily pious but nonetheless wan and sickly priest. According to one account, he died from complications after he swallowed his dentures.[10] As he was clearly no athlete, it is no surprise that the DJK, under his leadership, made the building of character—and not the quest for glory—its centerpiece.[11] At various points Mosterts criticized a traditional Catholic mindset that had led many clerics to place priority on the salvation of the soul and to dismiss the body as an agent of temptation and corruption. As he put it, "We feel only too strongly that we are not only soul, we know as well, that we are a unity of body and soul, and we must bring both together, in spite of struggles and resistance."[12] He argued that any religion that purports to believe in the resurrection of the body must also "revere" the human body.

But in spite of this new theology of the body, Mosterts retained the traditional mind-body dualism, the Platonic and Augustinian contribution to the early church. It is not surprising that he urged youth to develop an iron discipline and an unyielding will in order to keep the body in check. "Morality is will. In proper exercises, which we cultivate with our youth, lies a great will, and out of it arises a great will, which when analyzed, produces strong moral power in every individual, and through it, into our entire people."[13] Throughout his lectures and sermons as well as in the DJK newspaper *Sturm und Steuer* [Storm and helmsmen], Mosterts cast rhythmic gymnastics (*Leibesübungen*) as an antidote to a decadent, feminized society around him. He asserted that true masculinity could be achieved only through iron discipline: "For manliness entails resolution toward every task, every obligation, every danger; it entails despising every softness and fear, rejection of all subservience; it is hardening the will and sharpening the intellect, is self-assertion and true independence. Manliness leads to inner manliness, grows to true maturity and to leadership."[14] Though such rhetoric might seem to indicate an antidemocratic spirit, Mosterts, in fact, proved to be a stalwart supporter of the Weimar Republic.[15] This stance would have a critical bearing on the conflagrations that erupted within the DJK after 1945.

The DJK underwent a significant transformation after Mosterts's death in 1926. From 120,000 members in 1920 the DJK grew to more than 250,000 by 1932.[16] In the climate of political radicalization during the twilight years of Weimar, many workers, especially unemployed men in the Ruhr, shifted their political allegiances from the Center to the Communist Party. Catholics within the DJK responded to increased Communist militance with a show of force. They strove to increase Catholic strength within the national sporting committee (Reichskuratorium für Leibesübungen), a confederation of German sporting organizations that included the German Gymnasticists, workers' organizations, and Solidarity, the Workers' Cycling League. DJK leaders were well aware that the membership of their rivals was greater than their own; the German Gymnasticists tallied more than 1.6 million enthusiasts, and the so-called red sporting leagues, taken collectively, registered slightly fewer than 1 million members. They undoubtedly padded their membership statistics in response, for the DJK soon numbered more than 700,000, according to some figures.[17] DJK leaders also began to hold festivals where well-built young men dressed in white paraded in columns into the arena to perform gymnastic exercises. The symbolic nature of these festivals—a figurative and literal flexing of muscle—cannot have been lost on rivals as well as on the general public.

More significantly, the DJK began to be infected by the nationalist currents making their way through society at the time. Wolker, who was on the board of directors of the DJK, played a decisive role in the subsequent imbroglios within the organization. At the behest of the Reichskuratorium für Jugendertüchtigung, Wolker introduced a new sporting event into the DJK in 1932, the so-called reconnaissance sport, or *Geländesport*. Participants undertook six hours of reconnaissance in fields, woods, and streams with only the orders of the commander, a compass, a fifty-pound knapsack, and a guide to target shooting—in other words, thinly disguised military training.[18] Wolker also negotiated an agreement between the DJK and the Deutsche-Turnerschaft, the largest neutral sporting organization within Germany. In what was no doubt an attempt to close ranks against the workers' sporting organizations, the partners agreed to allow common sporting events and an exchange of members. As the pact put it, "German will requires and must require that we come together out of divisions to a people's community (*Volksgemeinschaft*)."[19]

Unfortunately for the DJK, even this outpouring of nationalist sentiment was not sufficient to assuage Nazi leaders. By 1934 they had denied the DJK as well as all other independent sporting organizations within Germany the right to carry on any sporting activities, and on the night of 30 June the DJK's new young and dynamic leader, Adalbert Probst, fell victim to Nazi bullets—"shot while fleeing"—as part of the Röhm purge. The Nazis subsequently confiscated many of the DJK's assets.

With the collapse of National Socialist rule in 1945, Catholic leaders had to decide whether to resurrect the DJK.[20] They could not help but notice that many young persons were forming informal sport leagues and were practicing gymnastics on their own.[21] As one lad explained at a meeting of Catholic sport leaders, youth wanted to engage in sports regardless of whether the DJK or any other organization existed.[22] In spite of the mounting enthusiasm for sports by young persons, the Catholic bishops refused to sanction the DJK.[23] Following a conference at Bad Soden in early May 1946, youth leaders issued a proclamation that they hoped would put an end to efforts to rebuild the DJK: "A sporting organization in the style of the previous DJK will not be formed." They nonetheless urged young Germans to carry on sporting events within other Catholic youth groups. This statement, undoubtedly drafted by Wolker, called for "observing and influencing German sport in accordance with Christian educational principles in connection with the neutral sport organizations."[24]

Why did many prominent clerics, in particular, refuse to reestablish the DJK, which had brought so many young persons into the church fold in the past? The bishops hoped to keep ancillary organizations small and directly under their own authority. That Wolker set himself against the organization that he had faithfully served as president, however, requires elucidation. Wolker feared that a revival of Catholic sectarianism would merely encourage renewed Socialist militancy. Even the name Deutsche Jugendkraft, he argued, would lead to a return of other old names, such as Rotsport.[25] Here, too, Wolker remained committed to his rather mystical notion of unity not merely for Catholics but for the fragmented German nation as a whole. It is no accident that Wolker was at this time working frantically behind the scenes with leaders of the former workers' sporting associations and of the neutral sporting organizations to create a single, unified body for all of Germany—"unity in German sport."[26] Indeed, many contemporaries later asserted that without Wolker's tireless efforts, the DSB never would have come into existence in 1950.[27]

Wolker deplored the disorganization within the German sporting world after the war. He saw the dearth of leadership, the undisciplined matches, and the lack of "fair play" as symptomatic of the larger chaos besetting German society in 1946–48.[28] Indeed, the phrases "ecstatic pleasure" and "moral degeneration" appeared more than once in his speeches. He was well aware that many former liberal sporting leaders had been badly compromised during the Nazi years and were being subjected to denazification proceedings by American and British authorities. Wolker believed that unless proper institutional structures were created, the leadership vacuum within German sport would soon be filled by former Socialist leaders. In a phrase that would incite much ridicule from his opponents, he called for Catholic leaders to try to "influence" German sport, to transplant Christian values of fair play to the larger playing field. With the interconfessional CDU and Einheitsgewerkschaft, the DSB was another significant attempt in the immediate postwar years to expand Catholic influence wherever possible in the German public sphere. Men such as Wolker undoubtedly hoped to rise to leadership positions within these new organizations—the definition per se of influence.[29]

In none of these cases, however, was the transition to interconfessionalism smooth. As late as the early 1950s, representatives from the CDU and the Center Party continued to carry on their conflict, even after it had become clear that the Center Party had no realistic chance of reasserting itself.[30] Similar infighting soon erupted around the DJK. By 1946–47, former DJK leaders in the Ruhr had defied the orders of Wolker and had begun to reestablish their old DJK groups. Catholic sporting groups, to be sure, sprang up elsewhere in Germany, but in no other region did the clamor for the DJK reach the same level as in the dioceses of Münster and Paderborn. Caspar Schulte, the leader of the diocesan center for ministry to men in the archdiocese of Paderborn, set the strident tone for the looming conflict. He issued a public challenge to Wolker that was distributed not just to the church hierarchy but throughout individual parishes.[31] Schulte argued that scattered Catholic sporting organizations would never sate the appetite of young persons for sports. These groups needed all the benefits of a league, such as opponents and equipment, if they were to continue to play sports under the aegis of the Catholic church.[32]

Wolker apparently did not answer Schulte's letter publicly.[33] By February 1947, Schulte had mustered enough support to form the Spiel- und Sportgemeinschaft Rhein-Weser, which soon numbered more than 6,000 members. Wolker described the plans for an integralist DJK *Verband* as illusory, incapable of finding support anywhere outside the Ruhr. In one particularly ill-considered utterance, he gave the newly formed organization a mere six months to live. But bowing to the mounting pressure from Schulte's supporters, he finally approved the DJK but refused to give it the status of a full-fledged *Verband* (along the lines of the old DJK), designating it instead an *Arbeitsgemeinschaft* to be integrated within the DSB. He insisted, moreover, on keeping control at Altenberg, a blow to his opponents who hoped to make Dortmund or Herne the home base.

In a move that subsequently caught Wolker completely off guard, the Rhein-Weser declared itself autonomous (*Eigenständigkeit*) in September 1949, at the conclusion of an elaborate ceremony marked by flowers, processions, and grandiose speeches.[34] Wolker, who was recovering from a heart attack, was unable to attend the ceremony, which had been disguised as a normal business meeting. At this point events rapidly veered out of control. Wolker refused to recognize Rhein-Weser's declaration of independence and instead presented it with an ultimatum. The organization could renounce its claim to autonomy or re-form as an entirely new entity, but one devoid of recognition from Altenberg. After consulting with the bishops of Münster and Paderborn, Rhein-Weser opted for the latter and declared itself (once again) independent of Altenberg. Its leaders also notified local newspapers as well as church leaders that they had founded their own DJK organization and accused Wolker of missing a tremendous opportunity. The following passage from a letter addressed to Cardinal Frings, chairman of the Fulda Bishops' Conference, illustrates how acrid the conflict was becoming: "As laity, we accuse the church's youth leadership of forcing out hundreds of thousands of young persons from the educational domain of the church and pushing them away into so-called neutral organizations, by deciding in 1945 not to let the DJK be reconstituted."[35] Wolker responded with an extensive public relations campaign designed to correct the disinformation emanating from Gelsenkirchen, Dortmund, and Herne. In turn, Rhein-Weser appropriated for itself the legacy of Carl Mosterts, declared itself the sole DJK Verband in the tradition of Mosterts, and deliberately questioned the legitimacy of the DJK under Wolker. A priest in Dortmund summed it up in dramatic fashion: "Until today, I have had Wolker's picture hanging on the wall. Now it's coming down."[36]

By 1950 the situation had become a stalemate, which lasted through the decade. The bishops ordered both DJK organizations to reach an agreement that would unite them in one fold, yet emotions had become so charged that any such union was unlikely. As a result, the bishops forbade Rhein-Weser from recruiting members and building Vereine in other dioceses, thereby limiting the conflict to Münster and Paderborn. Within these two dioceses, each DJK Verein was given the choice of joining either the Hauptverband or Rhein-Weser; once it had decided, it was prohibited from moving to its rival (Uebertritte), barring exceptional circumstances. By 1949 the Rhein-Weser included groups in a band stretching from Duisburg in the southwest through the Ruhr—Oberhausen, Gelsenkirchen, Herne, Recklinghausen, Wanne-Eickel, and Haltern—and all the way up to Münster in the north. To the east, it extended as far as Gütersloh and Paderborn and, in turn, included most of the smaller Westphalian cities between Paderborn and Duisburg: Arnsberg, Soest, Iserlohn, Hagen, Witten, Hamm, and Bochum.[37] The DJK (Altenberger Richtung) did find many adherents in the Ruhr, but its major bases were elsewhere in Germany.

The situation became even more wrangled when Kolping entered the fray. In the 1920s and 1930s Kolping had maintained close ties to the DJK—indeed, many of the original DJK Vereine had been offshoots of artisans' groups. In the 1950s, however, Kolping leaders, who disliked Wolker, took the side of Rhein-Weser and went so far as to sign a treaty of friendship with it. To justify this stance, Kolping leaders noted that participating in the activities of neutral sporting organizations "endangered" their own activities and educational agenda.[38] Only Rhein-Weser, they claimed, insisted that its members follow through on their obligations to the church and other Catholic organizations, such as attending mass on Sunday mornings and participating in their own assemblies and rallies. Like Rhein-Weser, they believed that the purpose of sport was to strengthen body and soul, not to set records and win glory. The rhetoric of Kolping leaders became increasingly belligerent. This pattern of behavior—harsh attacks on liberal and neutral organizations—was hardly new. Throughout the 1950s, Kolping remained defiantly insular, refusing to cooperate with the leadership in Altenberg and shaping criticism of neutral "book rings," which in their eyes helped distribute dangerous, "liberal" literature to young Catholic boys and girls.[39] Kolping's pledges of support invariably strengthened Rhein-Weser's policies of intransigence and perpetuated the conflict for years.

Negotiations between the two DJK brothers-in-arms foundered, above all, on the issue of alignment within the DSB. For many Catholics this question opened wounds that had been festering since 1933. Wolker's attempt to push Catholic athletes into the DSB reminded some within Rhein-Weser of comments made in the 1930s by Baldur von Schirach, who had asserted that there was no such thing as Catholic sport or worker sport; there was only German sport.[40] To make matters worse, many of these former "DJKler" felt personally betrayed by the capitulation to the National Socialist regime by leading Catholics in 1933 and 1934.[41] As one priest averred, "The DJK Rhein-Weser may not behave like the Center Party after the Nazi seizure of power." For such men, the interconfessionalism espoused by Wolker portended the repeat of an unwanted past: "Enter the general sporting organizations, so that we can gain influence there. We have already sung a similar tune. Enter the SA, SS, Nazi Party, Hitler Youth, League of German Girls, so that we can make our influence felt there. The burned child is now afraid of fire."[42]

These attitudes were reinforced by the experiences of Catholic workers within the Einheitsgewerkschaft, where they ran up against Socialist opposition.[43] Many of the adamant Rhein-Weser supporters saw sports, as a result, as one of the few domains of public life left where they could retain a strict separation between Catholic institutions and the outside world. The former Socialist sporting organizations were subjected to similar debates within the late 1940s over whether to enter a unified German sporting association.[44]

Yet most of the men associated with Rhein-Weser—quite understandably—did not realize how equally fragile Socialist institutions were. Perhaps in memory of Communist militance prior to 1933, they tended to see leftist threats lurking at every turn. In one instance the *Geistlicher Prälat* of Rhein-Weser, Anton Kiwitt, detailed how members of the Falcons, the Socialist youth organization, were attempting to hold "cultural lectures" in ostensibly neutral sporting organizations. He claimed that eleven of the twelve *Landesvorsitzenden* were either liberals or SPD members.[45] These accusations were subsequently printed in *Sturm und Steuer*, the old DJK newspaper that they had just revived, and in turn passed on to Wolker.[46] When the accusations were later shown to be false, the editors issued a retraction but continued to print accounts of young Socialists distributing tracts and foisting propaganda on unsuspecting youth during sporting matches.[47] Other Rhein-Weser leaders had apparently declared that German sport was "the systematic work of liberal and socialist circles."[48] British military officials likewise maintained that neutral sporting organizations were pursuing policies hostile to the church but insisted that they posed no threat to the church. "There is evidence in certain quarters to suggest that the Sports Clubs may be pursuing an anti-church policy. This does not refer to their time of meeting which is usually on Sunday (and which in some instances may be due to the fact that it is the only time the Army can make playing fields available to them) but to the statements made in some parts that the Sports Clubs were refusing to allow any of their teams to play teams attached to churches."[49]

That the Ruhr itself was confessionally mixed, a seemingly random patchwork of Catholic, liberal, and Socialist enclaves, lent credence to Rhein-Weser's claims. Regions where Protestants were in the majority also recorded the highest levels of support for the Communists and the Socialists. These considerations undoubtedly led Archbishop Jaeger of Paderborn to support Rhein-Weser. As he put it, "In this area, it sets one thinking that the sport organizations pave the way, in many cases, for the SPD. It has recently been reported to me that in a village not far from Paderborn the leader of the sport club instructed his group to vote for the SPD in the last election, a command which also was obeyed."[50] The hostility between these two camps in Westphalia cannot be overemphasized. In one rural village the local priest refused to administer Communion to parishioners who subscribed to the local SPD newspaper. Only when the subscriptions were canceled did the priest apparently allow these members to return to the Communion altar.[51] It is important to remember that such petty conflicts occurred at a time when class tensions throughout Germany remained high and political power was up for grabs. That such political and ideological considerations were decisive in shaping the DJK conflict is well illustrated in a letter from Anton Kiwitt: "I really don't know what will happen if the independent DJK is given up. It remains a bulwark especially now in the spiritual and ideological conflicts of our days."[52]

Yet Bishop Michael Keller of Münster rose to the defense of Rhein-Weser for reasons that had everything to do with his own theology and little to do with politics. Keller was the leading German theoretician of Catholic Action. Though most other clergy had resigned themselves to the fact that this Italian import hardly functioned within the German *Vereinskultur*, Keller nonetheless persisted in trying to push this program through in his diocese and in placing all lay organizations under his control.[53] For Keller, Rhein-Weser, confined as it was to just two dioceses, seemed far more malleable than Altenberg, whose jurisdiction extended to all German dioceses in the west.[54] In a letter to Wolker he claimed that he hoped to give both organizations equal support.[55] In retrospect, these comments were somewhat disingenuous. In a private letter addressed to fellow-travelers within the Münster episcopate, he admitted that he preferred the philosophy of Rhein-Weser.[56]

How did the larger theologies of these two organizations differ? Rhein-Weser repeatedly claimed that its educational philosophy—its purity of doctrine and cleanliness of spirit—set it apart from its rival. It declared itself to be, in other words, more Catholic than the rest, demonstrating integralism par excellence.[57] Here Rhein-Weser's leaders made themselves the heirs of Mosterts's original vision, as the following passage makes clear: "There is truly in God, a Catholic, more Christian soccer; when exercises are not an end in themselves, when strengthening the body leads to power of the spirit and building character, when the body is subordinated to the soul, then we can speak of Catholic soccer. And what the free German soccer organizations carry out is, in general, un-Christian soccer."[58] The so-called Old Gentlemen of Rhein-Weser went so far as to link the neutral sporting organizations to egregious excesses within German sport: increased professionalization, poor behavior by athletes, and attempts to set sporting records.[59]

In reviving the old body-soul dualism, Rhein-Weser set itself—quite deliberately—against a new theology of the body developed by Wolker as early as the late 1920s, but which was now finding its way into the programs of the Hauptverband. Wolker declared the human body to be the "crown of creation, the most beautiful, the greatest of God's creation." The sumptuous nudes of Peter Paul Rubens and the classical sculpture of ancient Greece illustrated Wolker's joyful dictum: "Glorify God in your body!"[60] Christ had become flesh; his resurrection was not just of the soul but of the body. Wolker's opponents interpreted the hardships of the occupation years—the black market, prostitution, and hunger—through the lens of temptation and sin and, for that reason, tried harder than ever to inculcate virtues of discipline, toughness, and moral resolve. With typically melodramatic rhetoric, Wolker argued the reverse. "That the body of the German people was bleeding, hungering, and in misery" meant that the body had to be allowed to bloom and grow, that light had to triumph over darkness.[61] Wolker's organic conception of the body as a fount of growth, beauty, truth, and strength for the larger society could not have contrasted more sharply with Rhein-Weser's fears of the body as a source of corruption, decadence, and sin.

The question of women's sports, however, challenged both sporting philosophies. It resuscitated fears that the emancipation of women would lead to the masculinization of women and the feminization of men. Already in the early 1920s, women were participating in sporting events, thanks, in part, to the proliferation of public swimming pools and athletic facilities throughout Germany. The church took this development as a challenge not just to women's modesty and purity but to its long-standing belief that male and female spheres should remain separate. A papal encyclical from 1930 attempted to restore the lost balance between these two spheres, as symbolized in changing standards of dress: "At every opportunity the pope must condemn indecent dress, which today in many cases Catholic girls and women as well are indulging in. For this way of dressing does not only severely injure the honor of women, but also incurs on them passing harm and suffices, what is still worse, to condemn them eternally."[62] These fears were, if anything, strengthened by the experiences made under National Socialist rule. The BDM, for

A course for young athletic instructors at the Youth Center in Hardehausen, ca. 1965. A decade earlier this photo would have scandalized many youth leaders and clergy.
(Courtesy of Jugendhaus Hardehausen)

instance, had given young girls the chance to participate in sports (albeit to strengthen their bodies for motherhood), an opportunity often sadly absent within Catholic society.

It is not surprising, then, that Rhein-Weser devoted parts of its official platform to the question of women's sports. As it sought to toughen men through discipline, so, too, did it hope to restore femininity to women through sports. One priest drew up a set of guidelines for women's sports that highlighted essential differences between men and women, as he saw them. "The veil is appropriate for women, because they have much to protect; every indecency, exposure, and unmasking injures the essence of women."[63] It developed groups for women to promote "rhythmic gymnastics," which were held to be particularly suited to the "worth of the woman."[64] Here the participants, typically dressed in white skirts that extended to the knees, gathered in circles to jump or to throw large black balls into the air in a prearranged rhythm.[65] According to directives issued by the bishops, "Rhythmic gymnastics should be carried out in such a way that they relax the people and awaken joy at movement and a sense of grace and beauty of the position."[66]

Even as they sang the praises of the gentle rhythmic gymnastics, they excoriated sports that emphasized competition, such as soccer, track and field, and competitive swimming. The leaders of Rhein-Weser also insisted that male and female sporting activities were to be fully segregated, in accordance with guidelines issued by the German bishops. Men were not to attend female sporting events, lest the events devolve into what they mocked as "female gymnastical exhibitionism."[67] Yet Rhein-Weser was not the epitome of backwardness that this rhetoric might suggest. It offered women the opportunity to run their events themselves, at least at the level of the local *Verein*. Perhaps for this very reason, Rhein-Weser soon grew to include a significant number of female chapters, far more than those of the Hauptverband.

As Rhein-Weser became home to a number of women's sporting organizations, the issue of women's sports soon fed into the existing conflagration within the DJK.[68] Because many young women came to resent their second-class status within the DJK—their *Vereine* received less financial support, publicity, and representation in the top ranks of the organization—many young women began to sign up for sporting activities in the DSB.[69] Unwilling to let this exodus of young women continue, DJK leaders in Altenberg created a division of the DJK that was to minister solely to the needs of the young women.[70] They also agreed, in light of the DJK's affiliation with the DSB, to allow female DJK chapters to take part in sporting events sponsored by the DSB. Wolker even encouraged young women to use the opportunities available in the DSB. This position immediately sent Archbishop Jaeger into convulsions.[71] In a particularly vitriolic letter to the head of the DJK organization for women, Bartholomäus Hebel, Jaeger claimed, "That would mean that [the girls of our DJK groups] would appear before great masses of spectators at their meets, and that they would, like the men, carry out their competitions at the sport places, so that they would during general sporting festivals carry out their activities (gymnastics in a gymnastics hall) before spectators."[72] Jaeger ordered Hebel to desist from further activities in the diocese of Paderborn until this question had been resolved once and for all by the bishops. Jaeger's integralism thus extended not only to separating Catholics from Protestant and liberal society, but also to maintaining the division between men and women. It meant keeping what they presumed to be the agents of emancipation—shorter skirts and more "masculine" forms of competitive sports—as far from Catholic girls as possible.[73]

What, then, was "Catholic sport" like for members of Rhein-Weser? Leaders explicitly rejected the principle, articulated first in the German youth movement and later appropriated by the Hitler Youth, that youth was to lead youth. They came up with a strikingly different slogan: "Youth can not be led by youth."[74] They constructed their organization in a way that placed discipline and obedience at the center. They drew up elaborate lists of rules and penalties for sporting violations, and in their normal business meetings they preoccupied themselves with individual cases.[75] The job of officiating at sporting matches was assigned to individual priests, who in any case were supposed to provide the religious backdrop for each Verein. Here Rhein-Weser proved the stricter. No non-Catholics were to be admitted unless no other sporting organization existed within the local community. Children who were products of so-called mixed marriages (in which one parent was Protestant and the other was Catholic) were to be denied entry unless they had been baptized and reared Catholic.[76] Rhein-Weser, it seems, took this policy to extremes. In one instance it denied admission to a Protestant orphan (both parents had died during the war) who was being raised by Catholic foster parents. In ruling against his entry, the board cited his unwillingness to convert to the one true faith.[77] Yet even Rhein-Weser was forced to bend its own rules in particular circumstances. Protestant boys frequently joined when the DJK was short members or when they were particularly good athletes. In one case, in 1951 seven young Protestant coal miners were admitted when local leaders realized that their Catholic friends would leave the group were they denied admission.[78]

Rhein-Weser also insisted on upholding traditional Roman Catholic religious obligations at a time when everyday life was becoming increasingly secular.[79] It refused to hold sporting events on Sunday mornings (a marked contrast to practices elsewhere) and insisted on celebrating mass either prior to or directly after all sporting events. The second Sunday of each month as well as the preceding Saturday was to remain free of all sporting events so that youth could tend to their own family and spiritual life.

Within Rhein-Weser, certain sports received priority. Ping-Pong, gymnastics, and hiking tended to be most represented, but soccer was less so, perhaps because it still bore the stigma of its proletarian origins. Throughout the 1950s, Rhein-Weser held several major sporting festivals that were designed to increase a sense of solidarity among its members. Most typically began with the march of the participants—accompanied by an orchestra—into the stadium. With the rousing cry, "Jugendkraft Heil," banners were unfurled and the trumpets sounded. During the so-called Carl Mosterts Games in 1955, participants wore armbands and lapels that featured a crudely drawn picture of Mosterts's face. These games summed up the goals of the organizers: the creation of a tightly knit, unambiguously sectarian Catholic community.

The Hauptverband, in contrast, offered youth the chance to play sports in a much looser and more relaxed religious context. Priests were far less visible, and entrance requirements were accordingly less stringent.[80] Even some members of the Hauptverband were prepared to admit that the religious influence within their organization was relatively weak, an assertion that Rhein-Weser was only too happy to corroborate. As a result, Rhein-Weser clubs in Wanne-Eickel and Sodingen alleged that "men who stand away from the church attempt to bring their organization over to the Altenberg direction." Yet both DJK organizations contributed to the tearing down of the integralist walls. Rhein-Weser even began to hold competitive swim meets open to spectators of both sexes; to no surprise, the organization drew immediate fire from critics who pointed out that it was failing to practice what it preached.[81]

Over time, however, Rhein-Weser, in particular, was subjected to a steady erosion of its membership base. Reliable membership statistics are almost impossible to obtain, as both organizations took great liberties with the information they passed on to the episcopate. But it seems probable that membership figures never exceeded 50,000 for Rhein-Weser and 95,000 for the Hauptverband.[82] As the confessional nature of the Ruhr changed significantly during the 1950s and the region became an SPD stronghold, both DJK organizations found their membership pool limited.[83] As as early as 1954, Rhein-Weser considered dissolving itself, faced with a shortage of priests and plummeting membership. It was in such dire straits that Jaeger twice forbid the Hauptverband from forming new Vereine in his diocese and from accepting any switchovers from Rhein-Weser.[84] Keller joined Jaeger in pushing through the first of these measures, but by 1958–59 even he had begun to see the futility of propping up a dying *Verband*. Jaeger was forced to go it alone.

What caused the fortunes of Rhein-Weser to decline so rapidly? As tempting as it is to attribute the organization's sagging fortunes to its strict discipline and narrow sectarianism, far more mundane considerations led many young men to join other sporting organizations. Dependent as it was on clergy to officiate at games, Rhein-Weser simply could not persuade enough priests to devote precious hours to sports at a time when clergy were overworked, frequently ignorant of sporting rules, and in short supply. Some youth began to complain that both referees and sporting equipment were of poor quality, several notches below those of the DSB.[85] The latter, moreover, was able to use the largesse of the state to upgrade facilities and equipment. Rhein-Weser's refusal to play against opponents who did not belong to the fold meant that groups often had to travel long distances just to reach the playing field. In one case from 1957, the leader of a group that faced a standing commute of 40 miles decided to switch to the Hauptverband after members voted sixty-four to one in favor. Despite being a member of the DJK since 1930, the leader faced disciplinary proceedings from the Rhein-Weser board of directors. They dredged up an incident from the past where two members of his group, upset at a bad call, had attacked the referee. It is unclear whether the attack was physical or merely verbal, but both were subsequently suspended for six months. On news of his intentions to switch to the Hauptverband, he was removed from his position in the DJK and was accused of not leading his group "in the sense of the founder of the DJK, Carl Mosterts."[86]

Rhein-Weser, moreover, proved unable to form groups for basketball, volleyball, and badminton, sports that were gaining in popularity; solely in Ping-Pong did it find new recruits, for table tennis requires fewer people to form a league. Once Rhein-Weser developed its reputation for inferiority, the number of groups leaving began to snowball.[87] The best athletes often joined the DSB in search of better competition and organization. Where *Kolpingsvereine* remained strong, Rhein-Weser continued to find a steady stream of recruits.[88] Otherwise, Rhein-Weser became an organization of adults, of "old gentlemen" from its glory days prior to 1933, and not an organization of youth.

Rhein-Weser had one trump card left to play, an issue that had long remained taboo within the Hauptverband: the Nazi past of leaders of the

DSB. *Sturm und Steuer* berated the DSB for having unrepentant Nazis within its leadership. It pointed the finger, in particular, at Guido von Mengden and cited explicitly anti-Semitic statements from his speeches from the 1930s.[89] Though this article, "Forgive, but Do Not Forget," earned its authors severe reproaches from the Hauptverband, Rhein-Weser was, in this case, right on target.[90] Well into the 1950s the DSB continued to print articles with titles such as "Civilization: Prison or Living Space? (*Lebensraum*)."[91] Such articles clearly show the lingering cultural pessimism—fears of the degeneration of the German people—of many German liberals.[92] *Rhein-Weser*, on the other hand, could present virtually impeccable anti-Nazi credentials. One of its most prominent leaders, Franz Ballhorn, had fled to Holland in the 1930s. From there he waged a vigorous anti-Nazi campaign before he was arrested and sent to a concentration camp after the German invasion in 1940.[93] Rhein-Weser was led, once again, to claim for itself Mosterts's democratic vision from the 1920s and to disassociate itself from the course steered later by Wolker, who by this time was long dead. The Rhein-Weser leadership was no doubt using this issue somewhat disingenuously to score points against the Hauptverband, but it was correct in asserting that its integralist vision had left its members largely untainted by the demons of Nazism. If Nazism was indeed a product of modernity itself, as some historians have suggested, then Catholic integralists were beneficiaries (or victims) of their own antimodernism.[94]

By 1960 it had become painfully clear, even to the most loyal supporters of Rhein-Weser, that their organization was on its last legs. Over the next two years, therefore, various individuals attempted to engineer a reconciliation. To succeed, the opposition of both Keller and Jaeger first had to be overcome. Keller was the first to yield. He may well have been angered by Rhein-Weser's repeated displays of intransigence; it had proven far less pliant than he had once believed it would be. Rhein-Weser's own precarious situation ultimately proved, however, to be decisive: "But the sober appraisal of the entire situation suggests also to me, in the interest of my diocese and the general Catholicism in Germany, to favor a conception which is, in itself, less good, but thoroughly Catholic and which is moreover regarded as the better one by many conscientious priests and laity."[95]

Jaeger was a tougher nut to crack. In spite of many attempts at mediation launched by Karl Arnold, the *Ministerpräsident* of North Rhine–

Westphalia, Jaeger proved to be as unyielding as the leadership in Rhein-Weser itself.[96] In the fall of 1960, Willy Bokler, Wolker's successor in the Hauptverband, drafted a letter to Adenauer asking him to pressure Jaeger to yield to the voices calling for reconciliation. Bokler asked Willi Daume, president of the DSB, to append his signature and pass the letter on to the chancellor.[97] Although no records of a meeting between Jaeger and Adenauer appear to exist, it seems highly probable that Adenauer did indeed intervene on behalf of the Hauptverband, for one month later, Rhein-Weser was back at the negotiating table and prepared to make significant concessions to the Hauptverband. The final agreement, oddly enough, provided for the very solution that Wolker had proposed in 1950. This solution allowed Rhein-Weser to continue to exist as a DJK-Ringgemeinschaft within the larger DJK, but it would have the option of participating in events sponsored by the DSB as well as selecting its own opponents.[98] In 1961 both sides came together in a major festival to declare the union official. With this step, the curtain was finally lowered on twelve years of bitterness, acrimony, and wasted energy. The DJK subsequently grew to include several hundred thousand, mostly adult, members by the 1980s; ties to the church became significantly looser. The old Rhein-Weser leadership, on the other hand, printed *Sturm und Steuer* for a number of years and occasionally insulted the top leadership of the united *Verband*, perhaps in reminiscence of the conflicts of the 1950s. But by the late 1960s and early 1970s, the old leadership had either retired or died, *Sturm und Steuer* was discontinued, and the *Ringgemeinschaft* itself became little more than a fount of nostalgia for its glory days in the 1920s and found in the Carl-Mosterts-Kreis its final resting place.

That the Hauptverband was able to prevail in this long struggle is symptomatic of the larger transformations taking place within German Catholicism within the postwar years. Catholic integralism proved unable to sustain itself and maintain its hold on the younger generation. Given a free choice, young persons participated in organizations and activities best suited to their needs, which were state-of-the-art equipment, the most elaborate facilities, the shortest commute, and the most fun. Rhein-Weser could respond only by keeping the range of choices as circumscribed as possible. It was ultimately unable to come to terms with a culture of consumption. Rhein-Weser failed to harness modern means—new technologies and newer sports—to promote its antimodern message, and thus much of its potential power to influence youth was lost. Of course, many Catholics in the Ruhr began to shift their loyalties from church institutions to workers' organizations by the late 1950s.[99] Yet at the same time, Rhein-Weser's largely defensive posture was unable to withstand this transformation.

Yet to keep our gaze solely focused on Rhein-Weser is to miss the other half of the picture. Within the Hauptverband, as we have seen, religious ideals no longer occupied center stage. Even defenders of the Hauptverband admitted that Rhein-Weser did a better job of instilling religious values in young people. Religious sectarianism, in other words, placed far greater demands on the individual than ecumenism did. The Hauptverband's more generous and more tolerant religious vision ultimately triumphed, but it helped dilute the religious heritage from which it emerged.

The DJK "fraternal feud" tells the story of two responses to modernity itself: an ill-fated attempt to turn the clock back to a narrow sectarianism, and the more successful attempt to adapt to modernity. But the vision of modernity that many Catholics ultimately embraced proved to be, at best, highly ambiguous. It provided youth with top-of-the-line facilities, and it gave them the freedom to choose and to consume. It allowed former Nazis to return to high positions and dissolved traditional religious structures of obedience and authority. As Theodor Heuss maintained in a widely quoted speech in Hamburg, "There is no such thing as a Christian handstand and a Marxist pull-up."[100] Rhein-Weser understood the implications of this better than most other Catholics at the time and long before Heuss articulated this sentiment. As peculiar as the details of this feud may appear in hindsight, they underscore a dilemma common to all traditional institutions—Socialist and religious—throughout Germany in the twentieth century. Society changed faster than many leaders of these institutions had realized; youth, for obvious reasons, proved particularly receptive to these changes. To make their traditional institutions palatable to the young, religious leaders were forced to dilute their own core of beliefs or risk losing their influence and credibility altogether.

CONCLUSION

∽

WHY DID THE Catholic milieu erode so significantly in the postwar era, when it was built on organizational forms that once bore modern features? Why did the tried-and-true strategy of appropriating the most current forms of organization no longer bear fruit? In other words, why could the Catholic milieu after 1945 no longer adapt as successfully to the changing currents in culture and society as it had in the 1920s and 1930s, when more than 1.5 million young men and women rallied behind throne and altar through the liturgical and youth movements?

Firstly, Catholic youth work was hindered by a generation gap. In light of the unprecedented dislocations brought on by the war, it was only natural that church officials in 1945 would turn to those who had already amassed a vast reservoir of experience in the youth movement of the 1920s and 1930s. As a result, the men of the "last hour," who were none too young, resumed their old positions at the helm of youth work. Wolker was fifty-six, Klens was sixty-seven, and even Rommerskirchen, one of the youngest, was in his late thirties. Other veterans of the Catholic youth movement returned from the front or from POW camps and attempted to resurrect their old groups. Most of these national youth leaders believed that the liturgical and Catholic youth movements would continue to inspire young persons, just as they had done in their heyday. Wolker saw in the postwar era a golden opportunity to realize his unfulfilled dreams from the 1920s and 1930s of uniting all Catholic youth into a giant Bund. His plans found support from church leaders who insisted on maintaining a powerful show of strength in the public arena toward potential enemies, most notably, Communists and, to a lesser extent, Socialists and liberals. They drew on what appeared to be the obvious lesson of the past: only by standing together, united in a common ideology, could German Catholics triumph over what, they argued, were the forces of darkness.

This older generation of youth leaders created the BDKJ, an awkward superstructure that promised hierarchy, unity, diversity, charismatic leadership, and romanticism, qualities emblematic of the mood of 1933, not 1945. Although the youth movement did take root in some remote rural areas in Lower Franconia, where those traditions remained largely unknown, many Catholic commentators, many of whom were ardent supporters of the youth movement, realized by the early 1950s that their time had passed. They could bring back the songs, uniforms, and hikes, but they could not revive the joy and élan of previous generations. The bündisch forms and their romanticism were ill suited to the sobriety of the postwar era. For many young men, the youth movement conjured up dark images of wartime suffering and shattered idealism. Wolker's quest for unity was, at best, irrelevant to their daily concerns. As sociologist Helmut Schelsky noted, young men and women appeared more excited by dancing, jazz festivals, film, vacations at home and abroad, and later, rock 'n' roll—more individualistic forms of expression.

Hence, the growth in Catholic groups often existed only on paper—more than 1 million members by 1954—as reports from many groups revealed a prevailing spirit of indifference. Only in a few instances were youth leaders able to regenerate youth work. The most successful venue was the KLJB, which substituted discussions and seminars for the flags, pennants, and songs of the bündisch youth movement. Otherwise, membership declined in earnest after the mid-1950s. The numbers participating at the large national youth festivals sank from 100,000 in 1954 to 80,000 in 1959 to a paltry 30,000 in 1965.

Secondly, the Catholic strategy of using modern means to fight the modern world was almost entirely defensive in nature. It left Catholics unable to go on the offensive and undertake widespread missionary and apostolic work in regions with large numbers of unchurched men and women. The revival tent was strikingly absent in postwar Germany. Movements for mass revival, such as the Billy Graham crusade in the United States, never took root, in spite of an offensive rhetoric that exhorted German Catholics to "rebuild the Christian west." When Catholic leaders spoke instead of Germany as a "land for missionary work," they admitted that decades of secularization and the dislocations of war and partition had devastated vast areas of what once had been a thriving religious subculture. Contrary to the expectations of church leaders, the end of the Second World War did not usher in a new era of religiosity. The marked absence of religious fervor after 1945 refutes the argument that social upheaval, a mood of apocalypse, and human suffering invariably steer men and women back to the church. Men and women do not always seek meaning through organized religion in times of hardship.

The exception was the KLJB. Throughout the German countryside, church leaders succeeded in giving modern forms to traditional values. They launched rural seminars, open discussions that even allowed young men and women to question traditional teachings. Here the question of timing is paramount. Church leaders intervened *before* youth in the countryside had left the fold, at precisely the point when forces of modernization were only just beginning to transform daily routines and values.

The success of the KLJB, however, underscores the reality that the church was rarely able to bring groups and individuals who had already left the church back to the fold. But even here it would be a mistake to see this process as linear. The Catholic milieu did not break down uniformly; it broke down where the defenses against the modern world could not be maintained. Young workers were among the first to leave the Catholic milieu; many abandoned Catholic institutions for those of their Socialist rivals in the first decades of the twentieth century. This was particularly true in many of the most industrialized regions of the archdiocese of Cologne, the city of Cologne itself, and cities such as Düsseldorf, Mettmann, and Wuppertal. Catholic youth organizations, not surprisingly, scored few successes in their efforts to lead young workers back to the faith through the CAJ in the late 1940s and 1950s. While the failure of this organization stemmed partially from internal strife, those struggling to win back the industrial working classes ran up against a more fundamental difficulty: when male workers left the church, few returned. Yet this process was not universal. In parts of the Ruhr, Catholic institutions retained a foothold well into the 1950s, at which point their influence waned. The collapse of the DJK Rhein-Weser Verband was hastened in the late 1950s and early 1960s by the corresponding growth in the power of Socialist institutions there. In other locations, young Catholic men deserted church organizations while women remained true to the fold.

Young artisans, by contrast, remained insulated from these changes associated with the movement from church to Socialist institutions. These craftsmen comprised a traditional *ständisch* Catholic milieu, with the notable exception of those who worked as electricians, welders, and metalworkers in large factories or manufacturing operations. Catholic groups for young artisans continued through the 1950s to attract large numbers of young men, who were drawn to the opportunities for socializing, career advancement, and community. But even these organizations were attracting ever smaller numbers of recruits by the late 1950s and 1960s.

Young men and women in Lower Franconia likewise remained untouched for many years by ideas, trends, and patterns of life from the cities. Although there were scattered signs of impending conflicts in the 1920s and 1930s, not until the 1940s and 1950s did church leaders realize that the youth in the countryside were equally under siege by modernization—by technological advances, industrialization, growing prosperity, the diminishing relevance of agriculture, and mass entertainment. The same pattern was largely true for youth in the agrarian regions of the archdiocese of Cologne, even though industry had long permeated the economic and social fabric there. In general, one can speak of a time lag of ten to fifteen years between these regions. The fears (of modernity) that appeared in the archdiocese of Cologne resurfaced ten years later south of the Main. Church leaders nonetheless proved adept at reinvigorating the youth work in the countryside in both regions. They were able to adapt old traditions to the new patterns of everyday life in areas on the cusp of fundamental social change.

Gender also determined the extent to which young men and women remained active in Catholic youth groups. Young men were traditionally less likely to take part in youth activities. Some quit youth groups when they entered the labor force at age fourteen. The notable exceptions were those who, in the 1920s and 1930s, were inspired by the youth and liturgical movements, both largely male phenomena. Some women did join during the 1930s and 1940s, but their numbers never came close to those of younger men, in part because the Catholic youth movement retained elements of the *Männerbund*, which characterized the *bündisch* youth movement after the First World War. In spite of this increase in participation by males, in youth groups young women continued to be more active than young men. By the second half of the 1950s, however, this picture had changed in North Rhine–Westphalia. The number of young women active in Catholic youth groups dropped at a rate nearly twice that of young men. Some young women were seeking new career opportunities in nearby cities, but others were put off by the traditional gender stereotypes in church groups. This scenario, it is important to note, was not true for the diocese of Würzburg or for most other Bavarian dioceses, where women continued to be in the majority. In those regions, however, women were not exposed with the same degree of regularity to the changing mores of German society and the new youth culture of the 1950s.

Thirdly, Catholic youth work ultimately had difficulties coming to terms with the fact that that which was "modern" continually changed. In this respect, the forms of organization that provided the basis for Catholic youth work proved to be antiquated. The model of the Verein, which dated back to the nineteenth century, in many respects had outlived its usefulness by the late 1950s and 1960s. The KAB had difficulty recruiting young persons in the late 1940s and 1950s; Kolping, by the 1960s and 1970s. These organizations had a relatively simple structure. Their activities and events were easy to plan and above all, inexpensive to produce.

In contrast, the alternatives to Catholic youth organizations in the 1950s were varied and complex. Teenagers were exposed to a dizzying array of new influences: foreigners, soldiers, and refugees brought new traditions, customs, and not infrequently, a secular and worldly outlook to formerly homogeneous areas. Unlike the 1920s, mass culture and mass entertainment were within the reach of all who desired them, even in the countryside and small villages. Catholic groups were subsequently forced to compete with cinemas, motorcycles, and hobby clubs. They offered their own hobby clubs, vacation tours to the Alps, jazz performances, film screenings, and even fashion shows. Yet these efforts underscored the difficulty of fighting the modern with modern means in the postwar efforts. The church lacked the financial resources and the technical expertise to make their efforts convincing to young persons. Fighting the modern with modern means worked when what was considered to be modern was none too expensive (such as building a network of Vereine). By the postwar era, competing with Hollywood and the growing entertainment industry was beyond the capabilities of German Catholics. They could not duplicate the offerings of the modern media. They could only admonish, censor, and protect, a return to the familiar defensive posture.

Fourthly, and even more significantly, Catholic youth organizations were unable to come to terms with this new culture of consumption. This ethos of consumption, by which young persons enjoyed the freedom to choose the most pleasurable entertainment products, was difficult to reconcile with traditional Catholic values of hierarchy, spirituality, moderation, authority, and obedience. The *Vereine* and the youth movement, organizational forms that at one point were considered modern, had taken root in Catholic Germany in part because both were anchored in authoritarianism. The *Vereine* were run by a board of directors and often powerful leaders; the *bündisch* organizations, by their *Jugendführer(in)*. Although both frequently came into conflict with the church hierarchy, they still fit into the Catholic system because they stressed subordination, tradition, and obedience. In addition, they underscored the importance of *Gemeinschaft* and community. On the other hand, these models could not flourish (at best, they could hold their own) in an era that was witnessing a transition from authoritarianism to an individualistic democracy. To a significant degree, consumption was a vehicle for this transformation— one that undermined the authority on which the power of the church rested. More importantly, appropriating consumption ultimately meant adopting an ethos of individualism, which directly undercut fundamental values of obedience and hierarchy.

Fifthly, Catholic youth work was, ironically, a victim of postwar Catholic political success. In spite of restrictions and arrests, Catholic youth organizations often benefited from the pressures placed on them by the National Socialist regime. Youth work became more tightly bound to the church, being forced indoors, where it continued to flourish in many regions. After the war, such external pressure disappeared. As Catholics gained political power in the CSU and interconfessional CDU, the external constraints that had kept Catholics confined to their ghetto—hostility from liberals, state oppression, social segregation, and their position on the lower rungs of the socioeconomic ladder—began to disappear. Confessionally neutral and liberal organizations were only too happy to accept Catholic laity—and even clerics—on the boards of directors. Wolker, for instance, was regarded as one of the most decisive backers behind the DJK and earned accolades from fellow non-Catholic sports enthusiasts. The leaders of the BDKJ regularly participated in conferences with non-

Catholic youth leaders, where they set joint policies for national German youth organizations. Catholic youth work in the 1950s was characterized by continued—but diminishing—segregation on the local level, but cooperation and ecumenism at the top. One can even argue that the Catholic and Socialist presence in national institutions—and their acceptance by German liberals—paved the way for the social and political stability of the ensuing decades. The intense fragmentation that had tarred the German political system for decades was coming to an end.

Yet the erosion of the milieu took place not in spite of the fact that the Catholics gained political power, but because of it. The welfare state, which Catholics helped create, took over some of the functions that the milieu had once provided. The defensive rationale for the milieu thus disappeared. Because German Catholicism had been so heavily predicated on an oppositional identity since the second half of the nineteenth century, German Catholics were at a loss once they had gained significant political power. Some responded by seizing on other traditional enemies, such as the Communists, Russians, "materialists," and "nihilists," with an even greater fury. By the late 1950s and early 1960s, the diatribes against even some of these bogeymen had become too shrill and too hysterical and quickly vanished.

Sixthly, the late 1950s represented a new era, that of the "end of ideology," to use Daniel Bell's phrase for the United States. Bearing out this dictum was the fact that the Catholic milieu and the Socialist milieu, once the political whipping boys of liberal and conservative Germany in the second half of the nineteenth century, had entered the mainstream of the late 1950s and early 1960s and found themselves transformed by the forces of liberalism that they had sought to overcome. Both the Catholics, in the Second Vatican Council, and the Socialists, in the Godesberger declaration, were distancing themselves from and even renouncing their ideological heritage. This end of ideology signified that many of the dislocations brought on by industrialization, the tremendous class divisions, and the radical ideologies that came in their wake, were being accommodated. In this sense, the erosion of these nineteenth-century ideologies led to what might be termed a normalization of German society—an end to the *Sonderweg* of German Catholicism. Secularization in Western Europe, more broadly conceived, might be seen as the collapse of integralist ideologies from the nineteenth century.

Seventhly, church leaders themselves contributed to this ideological erosion as a vicious dialectical process emerged within the leadership. Moderate reformers attempted to meet the modern world half way, appropriating modern means to fight modernity. Against the attempts of churchmen and youth leaders to integrate themselves within larger society, conservative Catholics sought to keep the walls of their ghetto high. Conservative opposition to reform led to bitter internecine warfare within the church over the Catholic trade unions and youth work. Church leaders squabbled over whether young Catholic women should be allowed to wear makeup or take part in events sponsored by confessionally neutral sporting organizations.

To the laity and clerics who took sides in these disputes, the fight against modernity and the struggle to bring church institutions in line with modern society often took priority over the apostolic mission of the church: the winning of souls and the search for salvation. As became more evident after the Second Vatican Council, reformers often felt that the message of the church would have little appeal on its own. It lacked glamour and glitz and needed to be enhanced through the techniques of the mass culture and entertainment industries. Conservatives, on the other hand, frequently transmuted the "good news" into angry diatribes against mass culture and society, a defensive stance that also all too often lost sight of the fundamental mission of the church. This constant internecine strife contributed to, and even accelerated, the erosion of church authority. Through intransigence, conservatives drove many away from the church, while reformers, on the other hand, failed to provide certainty, the foundation of absolute truth, necessary to win converts. Years of infighting sapped time and energy that might have been used to carry out the apostolic mission of the church; the cost in wasted energy was enormous. Church leaders found themselves in a catch-22: they could remain true to their religious heritage and lose members, or they could adapt to the modern world and find their own identity diluted in the process. These dynamics can be seen among virtually all religious groups today, be they Roman Catholics, Southern Baptists, or Missouri Synod Lutherans.

In this respect, Catholics found themselves in the same predicament as their Socialist comrades in the Federal Republic, who also felt their hold on youth slipping in the postwar years. According to many reports, the Socialist youth organization, the Falcons, encountered many of the same difficulties in retaining members. More broadly, Socialist leaders, like Catholic church authorities, often disagreed among themselves over the degree to which to emphasize their nineteenth-century ideological heritage. Like the Catholics, they were divided between integralists and those who sought to accommodate changing realities.

All of these explanations ultimately point to the final critical ingredient for the erosion of Catholic youth work and the Catholic milieu as a whole: the changing relationship between the individual and authority in German society. Although the 1950s are often portrayed as an era of social conservatism and reaction, the reverse was actually the case: beneath the surface of normality and restored patriarchy, a younger generation was subtly ignoring the dictates of authority. In some cases, young men and women began to question their elders, in particular on questions of morals. They challenged church teachings on topics of deep concern to them and disregarded the directives of conservative clergy. They wore their makeup anyway, went to the movies, pursued careers as secretaries or factory workers, joined non-Catholic sporting organizations, and listened to rock 'n' roll.

The result was not an open, assertive challenge to but a demystification of authority, which was, in any case, a prerequisite to the more direct rebellions of the 1960s. For the first time, many young men and women had the luxury to ignore authority. The workweek was shortened and jobs were plentiful; they had the financial resources and ease of transportation to travel more extensively. As society modernized, it became increasingly difficult for authorities to bind young men and women to the narrow code of behavior that had previously defined many communities. Church leaders in the late 1950s even accelerated this process. They encouraged young persons to pose questions in open forums but reiterated their policies of prohibition, a stance that unleashed expectations that could not be fulfilled.

The areas of control available to the church shrank as a result. The church once held sway—or attempted to hold sway—over almost all domains of life: the family, religion, politics, charity, culture, recreation, and religious belief. Over time, it found its authority relegated to the narrow sphere of charity. It no longer commanded the authority to shape patterns of family life and gradually lost its ability to influence even the political stage decisively, as the CDU distanced itself from the church.

These observations force us to revise the picture of the 1950s described in much of the recent English historical literature. Many of these writings focus on the policies championed by social conservatives on the national and political levels, by Catholics such as Minister of the Family Franz-Joseph Wuermeling. But even this discourse was not uniform. Social conservatives could not always agree on whether women should be given their own special place independent of men within the church, or whether they should be placed under the direct subordination of men. The debates between Klens, Wolker, and the bishops regarding how to position women within the BDKJ is but one example. But even this "consensus" of social conservatives and religious conservatives did not go unchallenged on the lower levels, particularly in youth work. On the contrary, younger women such as Heidi Carl and Ludgera Kerstholt put forward views on mass culture, fashion, and careers that diverged from those of the more conservative leaders—and found significant acceptance from their young followers. While these views initially came under criticism from more conservative members of the church, by the early 1960s they had become the norm, as youth leaders were forced to rethink their positions on mass culture and consumerism.

It is little surprise that these changes took place in the second half of the 1950s, particularly after 1957, years that seem to have more in common with the first half of the 1960s than the early 1950s. For the first time, consumption levels reached prewar levels. The expansion of the welfare state through such measures as the *Rentengesetz* and the *Wiedergutmachungsgesetz* ensured that no group was destined to remain mired in poverty. Adenauer's triumphant reelection in 1957 bolstered domestic stability, both politically and economically. The climate, in short, was ripe for a rethinking of traditional attitudes toward consumption and mass culture.

The 1950s were ultimately characterized by the marriage of cultural conservatism and political and economic modernization—and the latter gradually undid the former by the second half of the decade and the early 1960s. The leading national Catholic politicians attempted to pursue two sets of policies concurrently: the social market economy and family values. As those in the driver's seat, Catholic politicians had the power to put these policies into action or to leave them on the political dust heap. Policies to promote family values, however, were unmistakably Catholic; Wuermeling received strong support from the ecclesiastical hierarchy throughout his tenure as minister of the family. Catholic leaders staked their future on this recipe—and it succeeded too well. This picture of changing cultural and social constellations corresponds to that of recent works on this era by Maria Höhn, Uta Poiger, and Axel Schildt.[1] The influence of religious conservatives who continued to thunder against materialism was replaced by that of economic modernizers and conservative liberals within the CDU, youth work, and, in part, the clergy itself. This helped normalize relations with the West but corroded the Catholic religious subculture.

These observations also force us to modify the positions that have been taken in the debates over secularization. Defenders of secularization theories have correctly pointed out that Protestant and Catholic institutions in Europe have fared dismally since the 1960s. Yet to paint the entire European religious scene with a single brush, as do most of these writings, is not just to compare apples and oranges but to do a grave injustice to the highly diverse religious traditions throughout the continent. While all Western European religious institutions have had to wrestle with the impact of modernization, consumerism, and economic prosperity on religious faith and practice, other factors have influenced the manner in which religious institutions have been transformed in the last fifty years. Put simply: Roman Catholic religious communities, institutions, and subcultures in Europe eroded at different times, in different manners, and for different reasons.

Decisive was whether Catholicism enjoyed a majority or a minority status. In Spain or Italy Catholicism was the dominant national religion. It was also connected to nationalist, conservative, and antileftist movements. Catholicism in France from the French Revolution to the 1950s was closely linked to royalism; telling the story of the erosion of French Catholicism is to analyze French conservatism and its hostility to the French republican tradition in a cultural context of anticlericalism and the separation of church and state.[2] In addition, French Catholicism was decisively shaped by the peculiar relationship between urban and rural; sociocultural transformations within the worlds of rural France since the 1960s sapped the religious heart of France.[3] In Poland and Ireland Catholicism was strongly connected to nationalism and agrarian traditions. Only in the last five to ten years have sociologists of religion detected a decline in attendance at mass and an increased questioning of religious authorities, processes that can be linked to increased prosperity in both nations but also, in the case of Poland, to the end of the Cold War and a diminution of the Russian threat.

In contrast, Catholic subcultures in the Netherlands and Switzerland display a remarkably different pattern of erosion. Drawing on the anti-modernist ideologies emanating from the Vatican, these milieus came into existence, to no small degree, because of the minority status of Roman Catholics. As in Germany, the Swiss Catholic milieu was strengthened by persecution at the hands of liberals following military defeat in the Sonderbundkrieg of the late 1840s; throughout the rest of the century, Catholics remained politically disadvantaged. In Holland Catholics benefited from a process of "pillarization" that extended across the entire Dutch society. Dutch Calvinists, Socialists, and Catholics all formed their own political parties, ancillary institutions that often cooperated on the national level but were completely detached on the local level.

In these three nations, processes of erosion were shaped by the degree to which Catholics, both leaders and the flock, chose to integrate themselves into the mainstream. The Swiss pattern presents many parallels with the German: political integration, the rise of consumerism, and economic prosperity gradually helped Swiss Catholics blend into the cultural and social mainstream throughout the postwar era.[4] In the Netherlands the Catholic subculture, or pillar, collapsed somewhat belatedly but to a much greater degree. Within ten years a "revolution from above" eviscerated the Dutch Catholic pillar. Until the 1960s the Dutch Catholic pillar had remained remarkably cohesive, achieving attendance rates at mass and in youth organizations that surpassed even those of the most Catholic regions of Westphalia. Already in the 1950s, however, there were signs of an ominous decline in the membership in youth organizations and the numbers of seminarians, just as there had been in Germany.[5] To address this growing threat, the Dutch bishops, inspired by the more progressive ideals expressed in the Second Vatican Council, began to speak of a theology of love, relaxed their control over lay organizations, and called for a more open attitude toward non-Catholics.[6] In 1967 one bishop proclaimed that Catholics could vote for any political party. Overcompensating, the Dutch bishops threw out the baby with the bath water. Of nearly one dozen youth organizations from 1970, only three were left by 1978. The percentage of Catholics voting for the Catholic political party dropped in half from the 80 percent that had supported it in the early 1960s; the party eventually merged with the Calvinist Anti-Revolutionary Party to form a Christian Democratic Party. As in Germany, the church hierarchy lost its authority once Catholic identity became indistinguishable from that of the mainstream.

These observations support claims made by advocates of both rational choice theories and more traditional secularization theories. The former have correctly pointed out that religious elites often initiated and accelerated processes of secularization by diluting their own religious content.[7] The actions of the Dutch bishops and Catholic youth leaders illustrate this pattern. Similarly, ecumenical movements that relax ecclesiastical authority, while providing emancipation for those who suffered under the old order, eliminate what makes individual denominations distinctive and lower the bar for entry. The resulting institutions have become self-secularized and indistinguishable from the society around them. In appropriating popular culture and consumption in the late 1950s and early 1960s (even while predicating it on an elitism), youth leaders diluted traditional moral teachings in the process.

This phenomenon—the impact of a culture of consumption—explains why Catholicism in Germany was hit so much harder by the forces of modernity than its counterpart in the United States, whose church leaders also appropriated a culture of consumption. Religious leaders in the United States succeeded more easily, as individualism was part of the founding ethic of the United States (and not as foreign and disruptive a force in the twentieth century). It is true that Catholic immigrant communities were often ethnic islands centering around the neighborhood parish, resembling the Catholic milieu in Germany. Nonetheless, as these immigrant communities began to assimilate into the larger culture after the Second World War, church leaders approached this process of transition with more confidence and verve than their counterparts in Western Europe. There were good reasons why church leaders could be so self-assured. Between 1940 and 1960 the Catholic population of the United States more than doubled; church leaders quickly founded new parochial schools, Catholic Action cells, workers' organizations, student groups, and parishes, particularly in the fast-growing suburbs. Hence, church leaders were less apprehensive of entering a dialogue with the modern world. They possessed a boldness "bred not just of neo-scholasticism and papal directives," as one historian of American Catholicism has summed it up, but born of the postwar "American high."[8] Catholic priests even had their own television shows, and young priests played basketball with the youth.

Although the immigrant subculture collapsed as a result of the process of suburbanization, the larger institutions of Roman Catholicism retained a vital presence well past the Second Vatican Council into the 1970s and 1980s, in part as a result of the adaptation to the modern world. Evangelical Protestant churches have since added movie theaters, rock bands, and even ATMs to their own houses of worship—modern means to fight modernity. The crisis for Catholicism came later, in the 1990s and early 2000s, as a response to the church's dismal handling of accusations of pedophilia.[9]

What has filled the void left by the erosion of the Catholic milieu? The rational choice theorists erroneously insist that the European religious marketplace remains more active than would appear on the surface. They argue that the growth of cults, New Age spirituality, and the spread of Eastern religions indicate that the need for religion has far from vanished. But as a number of commentators have pointed out, such prognostications are wildly optimistic. A more careful examination of the religious world of Western Germany since the 1960s indicates that the predictions of the secularization theorists regarding Christian institutions in Europe have been largely borne out.[10] The demise of these religious subcultures has left only vestigial remains in parts of rural Westphalia and Bavaria and, more to the point, a vacuum filled by consumerism, a welfare state, and an angry church hierarchy that has become increasingly alienated from its ever more secular followers.

This pattern bore itself out in youth work. The membership in the BDKJ continued to drop through the 1960s but stabilized in the mid-1970s. According to Wilhelm Damberg's analysis for the diocese of Mün-ster, 38 percent of Catholic youth between ages ten and twenty-five were organized in youth groups in 1932, 30 percent in 1953, 18 percent in 1963, 11 percent in 1973, and 14 percent in 1992.[11] Even as the membership stabilized by the 1970s, youth work took on an entirely different character. Instead of allying itself with the church, the increasingly professionalized BDKJ adopted policies sharply critical of the church hierarchy on questions of politics, ideology, culture, and gender. As the organization's disdain for the church became so great, the church hierarchy threatened to cut off finances for the BDKJ and created alternative youth organizations for young acolytes (Messdienergruppen) that resembled the parish youth groups created in the late 1930s.

Membership in the BDKJ had stabilized by the 1970s, but the overall membership in the church has continuously dropped. The percentage of Catholics attending mass fell from 50.6 percent in 1950 to 46.3 percent by

1960 to 37.3 percent by 1970 to 27.0 percent by 1980 to 21.9 percent by 1990 and, finally, to 18.0 percent by 1996.[12] Put simply: the erosion of the top of the pyramid of religious behavior (from the start of this study) continued apace further down at the base. In the 1950s many young persons were reluctant to participate in activities that required the greatest effort and dedication; by the 1980s and 1990s, many nominal Catholics were no longer even willing to take part in activities that required the least amount of effort. After a certain point, many Catholics—or, as is probably more likely, their children—ceased to take part in the life of the church at all.

For Catholics who remained in the church, the relationship to the hierarchy was markedly different from that in the 1950s, a cafeteria Catholicism characterized by mutual acrimony and disdain. Since the Second Vatican Council the church in Western Europe has been mired in struggles, over *Humanae Vitae*, in the *Kirchenvolksbegehren* (We are the church movement), and between a hierarchy determined to reassert its authority over doctrine and church practice and an equally dogged laity seeking to "have it their way." Such issues challenge the very identity of the church. Is the Roman Catholic church defined by the laity or the hierarchy? Such cafeteria Catholicism is tantamount to a Protestantization of the church. Individual belief is shaped not by church authority but by the dictates of one's own conscience and social culture.

In sum, the theorists of secularization are correct in seeing the European Christian landscape as barren, but they are not correct in identifying the causes. They postulate an immense conflict between religion (defined extremely broadly) and modernity, in which religion was to lose out. Belying such predictions have been the formation of Islamic and Turkish subcultures in Germany and elsewhere in Europe—"new religious milieus" for alienated groups that also use modern means to fight modern society (this underscores the fact that the erosion has been of Christian institutions).[13] The rational choice theorists correctly identify the roles played by religious elites themselves but overemphasize and exaggerate the scale of the remaining religious marketplace for nonimmigrant Europeans. Those who euphemistically label this erosion as a process of religious transformation similarly minimize the extent to which the authority of the Christian churches in Germany has been destroyed.[14]

This book, in contrast, argues that the erosion of the Catholic milieu in Germany (and the Netherlands and Switzerland) lay in the manner in which these insular subcultures took shape in the second half of the nineteenth century, grounded in an ideology of antimodernism and alienated from the mainstream. Once this hostility dissipated, a welfare state provided material security, and a culture of consumption began to take hold, there was little to replace the confessional identities that by the late 1950s already belonged to a bygone era. In this journey from *The Watch on the Rhine (Die Wacht am Rhein)* to *Baywatch*, it proved impossible to reconcile the imperatives of an oppositional Catholic identity to the demands of a modern culture of consumption.

In addition to the abbreviations that appear in the text,
the following are used in the notes.

AKKZG: Arbeitskreis für kirchliche Zeitgeschichte
BA: Bundesarchiv Koblenz
BAM: Bistumsarchiv Münster
BDKJ-Köln: Bund der Deutschen Katholischen Jugend, Cologne
BDKJ-Würz: Bischöfliches Jugendamt Würzburg
CAJ-Essen: Christliche Arbeiterjugend, Essen, Aktenkeller
CUA: Catholic University Archives
DAW: Diözesanarchiv Würzburg
DJK Archiv: Archiv der Deutschen Jugendkraft, Düsseldorf
HA: Haus Altenberg, Archiv
HAEK: Historisches Archiv des Erzbistums Köln
JHD: Bund der Deutschen Katholischen Jugend, Jugendhaus Düsseldorf
JHH: Dokumentationsstelle des BDKJ im Erzbistum Paderborn im
    Jugendhaus Hardehausen
KAS: Konrad-Adenauer Stiftung, St. Augustin
KFG: Katholische Frauengemeinschaft, Düsseldorf
KJBW: Bischöfliches Jugendamt
Kolping: Kolpingshaus, Cologne
KZG: Kommission für Zeitgeschichte, Bonn
KZK: *Kirchenzeitung für das Erzbistum Köln*

NA: National Archives, Washington, D.C.
NLLW: NL Ludwig Wolker
NLWB: NL Willy Bokler
PRO: Public Records Office, Kew
ZDK: Zentralkomitee der Deutschen Katholiken, Bad Godesberg

INTRODUCTION

1   See Michael Ebertz, *Erosion der Gnadenanstalt? Zum Wandel der Sozialgestalt der Kirche* (Frankfurt, 1999), 114. For a more popular and sensationalized account of the recent changes in the major religious bodies in Germany, see "Liebster Jesu, Wir sind Vier . . . ," *Der Spiegel*, no. 52 (1997), 58–73.

2   See the first issue of *Kirchliche Zeitgeschichte* for 1998 and, in particular, Hartmut Lehmann's contribution, "The Christianization of America and the Dechristianization of Europe in the 19th and 20th Centuries." See also Lehmann, ed., *Säkularisierung, Dechristianisierung, Rechristianisierung im neuzeitlichen Europa: Bilanz und Perspektiven der Forschung* (Göttingen, 1997) and *Religion und Religiosität in der Neuzeit: Historische Beiträge* (Göttingen, 1996).

3   For the most prominent scholarly formulation of this position, see Karl Gabriel, *Christentum zwischen Tradition und Postmoderne* (Freiburg, 1994), esp. 52–59. For accounts by conservative clerics, see esp. Joseph Kardinal Ratzinger, *Aus Meinem Leben: Erinnerungen, 1929–1977* (Stuttgart, 1998). See also Alfred Lorenzer, *Das Konzil der Buchhalter: Die Zerstörung der Sinnlichkeit: Eine Religionskritik* (Frankfurt, 1981).

4   This latter argument dates back even to Ernst Troeltsch in his seminal work from 1912, *Protestantism and Progress: The Significance of Protestantism for the Rise of the Modern World* (Philadelphia, 1986). See also Wilhelm Pauck, *The Heritage of the Reformation* (Chicago, 1950).

5   For Holland, see above all, Paul Luyks, "Versäulung in den Niederlanden: Eine kritische Betrachtung der neueren Historiographie," in *Jahrbuch des Zentrums für Niederlande-Studien* 2 (1991), 39–51; Hans Righart, *De katholieke Zuil in Europa: Het Onstaan van Verzuiling onder Katholieken in Oostenrijk, Zwitserland, België en Nederland* (Amsterdam, 1986). For Switzerland, see Urs Altermatt, *Katholizismus und Moderne: Zur Sozial- und Mentalitätsgeschichte der Schweizer Katholiken im 19. und 20. Jahrhundert* (Zürich, 1989). For further comparisons, see Andreas Holzem, "Dechristianisierung und Rechristianisierung: Der deutsche Katholizismus im europäischen Vergleich," *Kirchliche Zeitgeschichte*, no. 11 (1998), 69–93.

6   See Margaret Lavinia Anderson, "Historiographical Review: The Limits of Secularization: On the Problem of the Catholic Revival in Nineteenth-Century Germany," *Historical Journal* 38, no. 3 (1995): 647–70, and Karl-Egon Lönne, "Literaturbericht: Katholizismusforschung," *Geschichte und Gesellschaft* 26 (2000): 128–70, as well as Otto Weiss, "Religiöse Geschichte oder Kirchengeschichte? Zu neuen Ansätzen in der deutschen Kirchengeschichtsschreibung und Katholizismusforschung—Ein Forschungsbericht," *Rottenburger Jahrbuch*

für Kirchengeschichte 17 (1998): 289–312. For two reports in English, see Jonathan Sperber, "Kirchengeschichte or the Social and Cultural History of Religion?," *Neue Politische Literatur* 43 (1998): 13–35, and Joel Harrington and Helmut Smith, "Confessionalization, Community, and State Building in Germany, 1555– 1870," *Journal of Modern History* 69 (1997): 77–101. Much of this new literature has focused, however, on the formation of the Catholic milieu in the nineteenth century and its trajectory in the first decades of the twentieth century. See, for example, Olaf Blaschke and Frank-Michael Kuhlemann, "Religion in Geschichte und Gesellschaft: Sozialhistorische Perspektiven für die vergleichende Erforschung religiöser Mentalitäten und Milieus," in *Religion im Kaiserreich: Milieus, Mentalitäten, Krisen,* ed. Blaschke and Kuhlemann (Gütersloh, 1996), 7– 57. See also Wolfgang Schieder, ed., *Religion und Gesellschaft im 19. Jahrhundert* (Stuttgart, 1993); Erich Yonke, "The Catholic Subculture in Modern Germany: Recent Work on the Social History of Religion," *Catholic Historical Review* 80 (1994): 534–45. For an extremely controversial work that goes so far as to describe the nineteenth century as a "second confessional age," see Olaf Blaschke, "Das zweite Konfessionelle Zeitalter? Ein Deutungsangebot für Katholizismus- und Sozialhistoriker," *Geschichte und Gesellschaft* 26 (2000): 25–52.

7 See Troeltsch, *Protestantism and Progress,* as well as Bernard Reardon, *Liberal Protestantism* (Stanford, 1968), and John Dillenberger and Claude Welch, *Protestant Christianity Interpreted through Its Development* (New York, 1954).

8 See David Blackbourn, *Marpingen: Apparitions of the Virgin Mary in the Nineteenth Century* (New York, 1994).

9 This is the major argument in Altermatt, *Katholizismus und Moderne.*

10 On the changes in culture, society, and daily life, see the collection of essays in Axel Schildt and Arnold Sywottek, eds., *Modernisierung im Wiederaufbau: Die westdeutsche Gesellschaft der 50er Jahre* (Bonn, 1993). See also Schildt, *Moderne Zeiten: Freizeit, Massenmedien und "Zeitgeist" in der Bundesrepublik der fünfziger Jahre* (Hamburg, 1995). For a longer perspective on the development of mass culture and entertainment, see Kaspar Maase, *Grenzenloses Vergnügen: Der Aufstieg der Massenkultur, 1850–1970* (Frankfurt, 1997).

11 For the best description of the new youth culture, see Kaspar Maase, *Bravo Amerika* (Hamburg, 1992).

12 For a summary of the debates over restoration or new beginnings, see Jürgen Kocka, "1945: Neubeginn oder Restauration?," in *Wendepunkte deutscher Geschichte, 1848–1945,* ed. Carola Stern and Heinrich August Winkler (Frankfurt, 1979), 141–68. For accounts that analyze the conservative restoration, see Eberhard Schmidt, *Die verhinderte Neuordnung, 1945–1952* (Frankfurt, 1970); Theo Pirker, *Die verordnete Demokratie: Grundlagen und Erscheinungen der Restauration, 1945–1949* (Frankfurt, 1972); Ute Schmidt and Tilman Fichter, *Der erzwungene Kapitalismus: Klassenkämpfe in den Westzonen, 1945–1948* (Berlin, 1971).

13 See, for instance, Hans-Peter Schwarz, *Die Ära Adenauer: Gründerjahre der Republik, 1949–1957* (Stuttgart, 1981).

14 German social historian Michael Klöcker likewise depicts the 1950s as a period

when traditional Catholic education (he provides "ideal types" of Catholic values and education) exerted a nearly unrestricted hold over faithful and fearful Catholics throughout Germany. His account, though well written and thorough, remains all too static and does not account for the changes in Catholic doctrine that were beginning at this time. See Michael Klöcker, *Katholisch von der Wiege bis zur Bahre: Eine Lebensmacht im Zerfall?* (Munich, 1991). For the more recent literature in English, see Robert Moeller, *Protecting Motherhood: Women and the Family in the Politics of Postwar West Germany* (Berkeley, 1993); Heide Fehrenbach, *Cinema in Democratizing Germany: Reconstructing National Identity after Hitler* (Chapel Hill, 1995); Elizabeth Heinemann, *What Difference Does a Husband Make? Women and Marital Status in Nazi and Postwar Germany* (Berkeley, 1997). See the collection of essays in Robert Moeller, ed., *West Germany under Construction: Politics, Society, and Culture in the Adenauer Era* (Ann Arbor, 1997), and in Hanna Schissler, ed., *The Miracle Years: A Cultural History of West Germany, 1949–1968* (Princeton, 2001). These collections contain fine essays on returning veterans, gender, race, film, youth culture, consumption, and other topics, but they lack discussion of or chapters specifically on the churches or, more broadly, religious changes. Heide Fehrenbach's article in the Moeller collection, "The Fight for the 'Christian West': German Film Control, the Churches, and the Reconstruction of Civil Society in the Early Bonn Republic," discusses the Catholic reaction to film but is not primarily about the churches, but about the conservative discourse that some members of the churches put forward in this area. Even Michael Geyer and Konrad Jarausch's excellent work, *Shattered Past: Reconstructing German Histories* (Princeton, 2003), does not explicitly deal with religious changes or the churches. This book will attempt to stand as a corrective to this body of literature.

15 See Uta Poiger, *Jazz, Rock, and Rebels: Cold War Politics and American Culture in a Divided Germany* (Berkeley, 2000). For a more comprehensive analysis of her arguments, see Chapter 2. See also Erica Carter, *How German Is She? Postwar West German Reconstruction and the Consuming Woman* (Ann Arbor, 1996). The pioneering works here are Schildt, *Moderne Zeiten*, and the massive collection of essays in Schildt and Sywottek, *Modernisierung im Wiederaufbau*. For an excellent summary of recent accounts of consumption, see the chapter "In Pursuit of Happiness: Consumption, Mass Culture, and Consumerism," in Geyer and Jarausch, *Shattered Past*, 269–316. For another work that fits into this newer literature, see Maria Höhn, *GIs and Fräuleins: The German-American Encounter in 1950s West Germany* (Chapel Hill, 2002).

16 Carl Amery, *Die Kapitulation oder der deutsche Katholizismus heute* (Rheinbek, 1963).

17 M. Rainer Lepsius, "Parteiensystem und Sozialstruktur: Zum Problem der Demokratisierung der deutschen Gesellschaft," in *Wirtschaft, Geschichte und Wirtschaftsgeschichte: Festschrift zum 65. Geburtstag von F. Lütge*, ed. Wilhelm Abel (Stuttgart, 1966), 382.

18 For an excellent compilation of the recent controversies that have arisen over the use of the "milieu" vocabulary, see Christoph Kösters and Antonius Lied-

hegener, "Historische Milieus als Forschungsaufgabe: Zwischenbilanz und Perspektiven," in *Konfession, Milieu, Moderne: Konzeptionelle Positionen und Kontroversen zur Geschichte von Katholizismus und Kirche im 19. und 20. Jahrhundert*, ed. Antonius Liedhegener and Johannes Horstmann (Schwerte, 2001), 15–25. This collection also provides an eleven-page bibliography of regional studies on the Catholic milieu; see "Verzeichnis der ausgewerteten Regionalstudien," in Liedhegener and Horstmann, *Konfession, Milieu, Moderne*, 133–43. For another excellent summary of the literature on milieus, see Klaus Tenfelde, "Historische Milieus—Erblichkeit und Konkurrenz," in *Nation und Gesellschaft in Deutschland*, ed. Paul Nolte and M. Hettling (Munich, 1996), 247–68. Karl Rohe speaks not of milieus but of *Lager* in his analyses of the political structures of German society. Like Lepsius, he emphasizes the need to differentiate and segregate oneself from those in the other camps. Whereas four milieus exist for Lepsius, only three are of significance for Rohe: the Catholic, the Socialist, and the liberals and conservatives, who belonged to the same political constellation. See Karl Rohe, "Parteien und Parteiensysteme in Nordrhein-Westfalen: Traditionen und Mentalitäten nach 1945," in *Nordrhein-Westfalen: Fünfzig Jahre Später*, ed. Wolfram Köhler (Essen, 1996), 8–26. For the most convincing definitional analysis of the term "Catholic milieu," see AKKZG, Münster, "Katholiken zwischen Tradition und Moderne: Das katholische Milieu als Forschungsaufgabe," *Westfälische Forschung* 43 (1993): 588–654. For works that criticize the use of the word "milieu," see Wilfried Loth, "Milieu oder Milieus? Konzeptionelle Überlegungen zur Katholizismusforschung," in *Politische Deutungskulturen: Festschrift für Karl Rohe*, ed. Othmar Habert and Tobis Korenke (Baden Baden, 1999), 123–36, and Loth, *Katholiken im Kaiserreich: Der politische Katholizismus in der Krise des wilhelminischen Deutschlands* (Düsseldorf, 1984). In light of the controversies that have arisen, this book will use the term "Catholic milieu" descriptively, not prescriptively.

19 Detlef Lehnert and Klaus Megerle, "Identitäts- und Konsensprobleme in einer fragmentierten Gesellschaft: Zur politischen Kultur in der Weimarer Republik," in *Politische Kultur in Deutschland: Bilanz und Perspektiven*, ed. Dirk Berg-Schlosser und Jakob Schissler (Opladen, 1987), 80–95. See also Siegfried Weichlein, *Sozialmilieus und politische Kultur in der Weimarer Republik: Lebenswelt, Vereinskultur, Politik in Hessen* (Göttingen, 1996). The primary proponent of this structural argument is Detlev Peukert, *The Weimar Republic: The Crisis of Classical Modernity* (New York, 1991).

20 See Werner Blessing's convincing analysis of the diocese of Bamberg, "'Deutschland in Not, Wir im Glauben . . .' Kirche und Kirchenvolk in einer katholischen Region, 1933–1949," in *Von Stalingrad zur Währungsreform: Zur Sozialgeschichte des Umbruchs in Deutschland*, ed. Martin Broszat (Munich, 1989), 3–111. Christoph Kösters underscores the extent to which the Catholic milieu in Münster was able to resist the encroachments of the National Socialist state in his *Katholische Verbände und moderne Gesellschaft: Organisationsgeschichte und Vereinskultur im Bistum Münster, 1918–1945* (Paderborn, 1995). For an analysis of the

milieus in the Saarland, see Gerhard Paul and Klaus-Michael Mallmann, *Milieus und Widerstand: Eine Verhaltensgeschichte der Gesellschaft im Nationalsozialismus* (Bonn, 1995).

21   On the role of the church after 1945, see Joachim Köhler and Damian van Melis, eds., *Siegerin in Trümmern: Die Rolle der katholischen Kirche in der deutschen Nachkriegsgesellschaft* (Stuttgart, 1998). For one discussion of the function of Catholicism in the Federal Republic, see Detlef Pollack, "Funktionen von Religion und Kirche in den politischen Umbrüchen des 20. Jahrhunderts: Untersucht anhand der politischen Zäsuren von 1945 und 1989 in Deutschland," *Kirchliche Zeitgeschichte*, no. 1 (1999), 64–105. On Catholicism in Germany in the postwar years, see Ulrich von Hehl, "Der deutsche Katholizismus nach 1945 in der zeitgeschichtlichen Forschung," in *Christentum und politische Verantwortung: Kirchen im Nachkriegsdeutschland*, ed. Joachim-Christian Kaiser and Anselm Doering-Manteuffel (Stuttgart, 1990), 146–75; Anselm Doering-Manteuffel, "Deutsche Zeitgeschichte nach 1945: Entwicklungen und Problemlagen der historischen Forschung zur Nachkriegszeit," *Vierteljahresheft für Zeitgeschichte* 4 (1993): 1–29; Thomas M. Gauly, *Kirche und Politik in der Bundesrepublik Deutschland, 1945–1976* (Bonn 1990) and *Katholiken: Machtanspruch, Machtverlust* (Bonn, 1991); Thomas Grossmann, *Zwischen Kirche und Gesellschaft: Das Zentralkomitee der deutschen Katholiken, 1945–1970* (Mainz, 1991); Wolfgang Schroeder, *Der Streit um die Einheitsgewerkschaft und der Niedergang des traditionellen Sozialkatholizismus, 1945–1960* (Frankfurt, 1991). See also the extensive collection of works by the AKKZG, "Deutscher Katholizismus im 19. und 20. Jahrhundert," with the following authors: Anton Rauscher, Albrecht Langner, and Konrad Repgen. Most of these works concentrate on political Catholicism. For significant newer works that explore in depth the social texture of German Catholicism and Catholic *Verbände* during this time, see Wilhelm Damberg's excellent work, *Abschied vom Milieu? Katholizismus im Bistum Münster und in den Niederlanden, 1945–1980* (Paderborn, 1997); Lukas Rölli-Alkemper, *Familie im Wiederaufbau: Katholizismus und bürgerliches Familienideal in der Bundesrepublik Deutschland, 1945–1965* (Paderborn, 2000); Petra von der Osten, *Jugend- und Gefährdetenfürsorge im Sozialstaat: Auf dem Weg zum Sozialdienst katholischer Frauen, 1945–1968* (Paderborn, 2003); Dietmar Grypa, *Die Katholische Arbeiterbewegung in Bayern nach dem zweiten Weltkrieg, 1945–1963* (Paderborn, 2000).

22   Franz Walter, "Milieus und Parteien in der deutschen Gesellschaft," *Geschichte in Wissenschaft und Unterricht* (1995): 479–93; Gabriel, *Christentum zwischen Tradition und Postmoderne*; Herbert Kühr, "Katholische und evangelische Milieus: Vermittlungsinstanzen und Wirkungsmuster," in *Wirtschaftlicher Wandel, religiöser Wandel und Wertwandel: Folgen für das politische Verhalten der Bundesrepublik Deutschland*, ed. Dieter Oberndörfer (Berlin, 1985), 245–61; Cornelia Quink, "Milieubedingungen des politischen Katholizismus in der Bundesrepublik," in Berg-Schlosser and Schissler, *Politische Kultur in Deutschland*, 309–21.

23   For an excellent overview, see Axel Schildt, Detlef Siegfried, and Karl Christian

Lammers, eds., *Dynamische Zeiten: Die 6oer Jahre in den beiden deutschen Gesellschaften* (Hamburg, 2000).

24 For summaries of these positions, see Steve Bruce and Roy Wallis, "Secularization: The Orthodox Model," in *Religion and Modernization: Sociologists and Historians Debate the Secularization Thesis*, ed. Steve Bruce (Oxford, 1992), 8–30; Toby Lester, "Oh, Gods! An Explosion of New Religions Will Shake the 21st Century," *Atlantic Monthly*, February 2002, 37–45; Callum Brown, *The Death of Christian Britain: Understanding Secularization, 1800–2000* (London, 2001); Hugh McLeod, *Secularisation in Western Europe, 1848–1914* (New York, 2000) and *Religion and the People of Western Europe, 1789–1989* (Oxford, 1997); Sharon Hanson, "The Secularization Thesis: Talking at Cross Purposes," *Journal of Contemporary Religion* 12, no. 2 (1997): 159–79; William H. Swatos Jr. and Kevin J. Christiano, "Secularization Theory: The Course of a Concept," in William H. Swatos Jr. and Daniel V. A. Olson, *The Secularization Debate* (Oxford, 2000), 1–20. For the rational choice positions and criticisms of traditional secularization theories, see Rodney Stark and Laurence Iannaccone, "A Supply-Side Reinterpretation of the 'Secularization' of Europe," *Journal for the Scientific Study of Religion*, September 1994, 230–53; Rodney Stark and Roger Finke, *Acts of Faith: Explaining the Human Side of Religion* (Berkeley, 2000); Peter Berger, ed., *The Desecularization of the World: Resurgent Religion and World Politics* (Grand Rapids, 1999). For older works, see B. R. Wilson, *Religion in Secular Society* (London, 1966) and *Religion in Sociological Perspective* (Oxford, 1982); P. L. Berger, *Facing up to Modernity* (Harmondsworth, 1979) and *The Social Reality of Religion* (London, 1969); David Martin, *A General Theory of Secularization* (Oxford, 1978). For a recent defense of the secularization paradigm, see Steve Bruce, *Religion in the Modern World* (Oxford, 1996) and *God Is Dead: Secularization in the West* (Oxford, 2002).

25 For the best account of the changes within Catholicism in Switzerland, see Altermatt, *Katholizismus und Moderne*. For the Netherlands, the literature on pillarization (*Verzuiling*) is extensive. Like the phrase "Catholic milieu" in Germany, the term was at first used rather polemically to describe a system of social control. See J. C. Blom, *Verzuiling in Nederland, 1850–1925* (Amsterdam, 1981); Erik Bax, *Modernization and Cleavage in Dutch Society: A Study of Long Term Economic and Social Change* (Brookfield, 1990); A. Lijphart, *The Politics of Accommodation: Pluralism and Democracy in the Netherlands* (Berkeley, 1975) and *Verzuiling, Pacificate en Kentering in de Nederlandse Politiek* (Amsterdam, 1982); Righart, *De katholieke Zuil in Europa*; J. H. C. Blum and J. Talsma, *De Verzuiling Voorbij: Godsdienst, Stand en Natie in de lange Negentiende Eeuw* (Amsterdam, 2000). The latter is a revisionist work that fundamentally criticizes the notion of pillarization.

26 For statistics for the diocese of Münster, for instance, see Damberg, *Abschied vom Milieu?*, 419.

27 As I was in the final stages of editing, it was brought to my attention that many of the box numbers and file numbers that I have provided for the Diözes-

anarchiv Würzburg are no longer valid. In the intervening years, some of the materials were transferred to other collections, were lent to users outside the immediate archival facilities, or simply vanished. Other materials were held in collections that had not yet been cataloged and were also transferred elsewhere. I am continuing to use the original locations, since the new diocesan archivist himself could not with certainty indicate where the materials are now located.

28 See the often conflicting and contradictory statistics, for instance, in the handbooks of the archdiocese of Cologne, which are available only for 1933, 1954, 1958, and 1966. See Erzbischöfliches Generalvikariat Köln, ed., *Handbuch des Erzbistums Köln*, Köln 23/1933; *Handbuch des Erzbistums Köln* 24/1954; *Handbuch des Erzbistums Köln*, Köln 25/1958; and *Handbuch des Erzbistums Köln*, vol. 1, *Geschichtlicher Teil*, and vol. 2, *Realer und Personaler Teil*, Köln 26/1966. There is no publisher's information for these volumes, which are in HAEK.

29 See JHD, A526, Hauptversammlung 1953, Drucksache 21, and JHD, Statistische Sammlung, Jahresstatistik der Gliedgemeinschaften 1964, Stichtag 31.12.1964. Martin Schwab has provided a different set of statistics that estimated the *Bund's* memberships in the 1950s at approximately 1 million. By 1964 this number had fallen to 830,000, and by 1965, to 772,000. These statistics were taken from the Informationsdienst des BDKJ. See Schwab, *Kirche Leben und Gesellschaft Gestalten: Der Bund der Deutschen Katholischen Jugend (BDKJ) in der Bundesrepublik Deutschland und der Diözese Würzburg, 1947–1989* (Würzburg, 1997), 45.

CHAPTER I

1 This theme has provided the basis for numerous works on German Catholicism. For the postwar period, see Thomas Grossmann, *Zwischen Kirche und Gesellschaft: Das Zentralkomitee der deutschen Katholiken, 1945–1970* (Mainz, 1991).

2 AKKZG, Münster, "Katholiken zwischen Tradition und Moderne: Das katholische Milieu als Forschungsaufgabe," *Westfälische Forschung* 43 (1993): 632.

3 Josef Mooser, "Das katholische Milieu in der bürgerlichen Gesellschaft: Zum Vereinswesen des Katholizismus im späten Deutschen Kaiserreich," in *Religion im Kaiserreich: Milieus, Mentalitäten, Krisen*, ed. Olaf Blaschke and Frank-Michael Kuhlemann (Gütersloh, 1996), 59–92.

4 See Paul Hastenteufel, *Katholische Jugend in ihrer Zeit*, vol. 1, 1900–1918 (Bamberg, 1988). For another overview, see Georg Pahlke, *Trotz Verbot nicht Tot: Katholische Jugend in ihrer Zeit*, vol. 3, 1933–1945 (Paderborn, 1995).

5 Detlev Peukert, *Grenzen der Sozialdisziplinierung: Aufstieg und Krise der deutschen Jugendfürsorge, 1878–1932* (Cologne, 1986); John Gillis, *Youth and History: Tradition and Change in European Age Relations, 1770–Present* (London, 1981).

6 Elizabeth Harvey, *Youth and the Welfare State in the Weimar Republic* (Oxford, 1993); Derek S. Linton, *Who Has the Youth, Has the Future: The Campaign to Save Young Workers in Imperial Germany* (Cambridge, 1991).

7   In practice, however, the lines between the various *Vereine* were often fluid. A dynamic group of young workers often flourished behind the stern face of a Marian congregation, and vice versa. For an excellent overview of Kolping, see Heiner J. Wirtz, *Katholische Gesellenvereine und Kolpingsfamilien im Bistum Münster, 1852–1960, "Gott zur Ehre und den Gesellen zum Vorteil"* (Münster, 1999).

8   Grossman, *Zwischen Kirche und Gesellschaft*, 18.

9   Heinz Hürten, *Deutsche Katholiken, 1918–1945* (Paderborn, 1992), 131.

10   This criticism remained in place even after 1945. See the comments of the diocesan youth minister (*Diözesanjugendseelsorger*) for the archdiocese of Cologne, Fritz Eink, who maintained that the *Vereine* were often little more than a front for a good time. See KZG, NLWB, D II, 5. For descriptions from the 1920s, see Christoph Kösters, *Katholische Verbände und moderne Gesellschaft: Organisationsgeschichte und Vereinskultur im Bistum Münster, 1918–1945* (Paderborn, 1995), 111, and for descriptions from the 1940s, see Wirtz, *Katholische Gesellenvereine*, 203.

11   For one example, see HAEK, Gen 23.2 (I), Paderborn, 20 August 1918.

12   Detlev Peukert, *The Weimar Republic: The Crisis of Classical Modernity* (New York, 1991); Hürten, *Deutsche Katholiken*. Antonius Liedhegener has spoken of the crisis of the Catholic milieu. For a description of this crisis in Münster, see Liedhegener, *Christentum und Urbanisierung: Katholiken und Protestanten in Münster und Bochum, 1830–1933* (Paderborn, 1997), 227–39; for Bochum, see 466–69, 574.

13   HAEK, Gen 23.11, 1a, "Anlage I. Die Organisation der heranwachsenden Jünglinge oder jungen Männer. (Richtlinien von Generalpräses Mosterts)" (n.d., but probably 1916).

14   AKKZG, Münster, "Katholiken zwischen Tradition und Moderne," 650.

15   Peukert, *Weimar Republic*, 154–55.

16   Christoph Kösters, "Carl Mosterts, 1874–1926," in *Zeitgeschichte in Lebensbildern: Aus dem deutschen Katholizismus des 19. und 20. Jahrhunderts*, ed. Rudolf Morsey, Jürgen Aretz, and Anton Rauscher (Mainz, 1997), 8:9–25.

17   See Chapter 6 for a fuller description of the DJK.

18   The literature on the youth movement is enormous. For two works, see Walter Lacquer, *Die Deutsche Jugendbewegung* (Cologne, 1962), and Peter Stachura, *The German Youth Movement, 1900–1945: An Interpretation and Documentary History* (London, 1981). See also Elisabeth Korn, Otto Suppert, and Karl Vogt, eds., *Die Jugendbewegung: Welt und Wirkung* (Düsseldorf, 1963); Werner Kindt, ed., *Dokumentation der Jugendbewegung*, 3 vols. (Düsseldorf, 1963–74); Jürgen Reulecke, "Jugendbewegung als Objekt der Geschichtswissenschaft," *Ludwigsteiner Blätter* 187 (1995): 6–23.

19   Hürten, *Deutsche Katholiken*, 41–44, 46–48, 63–65.

20   See Alois Baumgartner, *Sehnsucht nach Gemeinschaft: Ideen und Strömungen im Sozialkatholizismus der Weimarer Republik* (Paderborn, 1977); Ferdinand Tönnies, *Gemeinschaft und Gesellschaft: Grundbegriffe der reinen Soziologie* (Berlin, 1920).

21   On this movement, see Kösters, *Katholische Verbände und moderne Gesellschaft*, 159;

Erwin Iserloh, "Die Geschichte der Liturgischen Bewegung: Der Beitrag des Bundes Neudeutschland," in *Kirche—Ereignis und Institution: Aufsätze und Vorträge*, vol. 1, *Kirchengeschichte als Theologie* (Münster, 1985), 436–51; Alois Baumgartner, "Die Auswirkungen der Liturgischen Bewegung auf Kirche und Katholizismus," in *Religiös-kulturelle Bewegungen im deutschen Katholizismus seit 1800*, ed. Anton Rauscher (Paderborn, 1986), 121–36.

22 Kösters, *Katholische Verbände und moderne Gesellschaft*, 190–91.

23 Barbara Schellenberger, "Ludwig Wolker, 1887–1955," in *Zeitgeschichte in Lebensbildern: Aus dem deutschen Katholizismus des 19. und 20. Jahrhunderts*, ed. Rudolf Morsey, Jürgen Aretz, and Anton Rauscher (Mainz, 1982), 5:134–46. His sympathies and later support for interconfessionalism at the highest realms of youth work may have stemmed from his interconfessional upbringing.

24 An early account from a member of this group shows Wolker surrounded by a group of city boys from Munich on their first excursion away from home in the mountains just south of the city. A local farmer provided food, while they slept on haystacks in his barn. Some of the boys were captivated by the accordions and guitars Wolker had brought with him, instruments completely new to most of them. See, DAW, NL Max Rößler, Kasten, Ludwig Wolker, Begegnungen mit General Präses Ludwig Wolker (this is commonly known as the Geburtstagsalbum).

25 Georg Thurmair, *Ein Priester der Freude: Das Leben des Prälaten Ludwig Wolker* (Buxheim, 1957). For another description, see Hans Schroer, "Ludwig Wolker," in *Sie hielten Stand: Sturmschar im Katholischen Jungmännerverband Deutschlands*, ed. Bernd Börger (Düsseldorf, 1989), 215–20.

26 HAEK, Schallplattensammlung, Wolker.

27 DAW, NL Max Rößler, Wolker, Geburtstagsalbum.

28 Barbara Schellenberger, *Katholische Jugend und Drittes Reich: Eine Geschichte des Katholischen Jungmännerverbandes 1933–1939 unter besonderer Berücksichtigung der Rheinprovinz* (Mainz, 1975).

29 This phrase does not translate well. The term "Reich" here represents a *ständisch* conception of dominion or realm with a mythological origin in the Middle Ages. See Irmtraud Götz von Olenhusen, *Jugendreich, Gottesreich, Deutsches Reich: Junge Generation, Religion und Politik, 1928–1933* (Cologne, 1987).

30 Eric Hobsbawm has spoken of the "invention of tradition." See Hobsbawm and Terence Ranger, eds., *The Invention of Tradition* (New York, 1983).

31 For examples of the new emphasis on St. Michael, see Börger, *Sie hielten Stand*, 52–54.

32 Pahlke, *Trotz Verbot nicht Tot*, 318–75.

33 Wilfried Loth, "Integration und Erosion: Wandlungen des katholischen Milieus in Deutschland," in *Deutscher Katholizismus im Umbruch zur Moderne*, ed. Loth (Stuttgart, 1991), 266–81. See Rudolf Morsey and Erich Matthias, *Das Ende der Parteien, 1933* (Düsseldorf, 1961), for a discussion of the need for unity.

34 This was the slogan unveiled by Wolker at the annual meeting of the Katholischer Jungmännerverband in Neisse in 1928. See KZG, NLLW, II, I d-c, 5, Ver-

bandstag in Neisse von Generalsekretär Clemens (entnommen der Zeitschrift *Jungführer*, no. 9/10 1928, 258). See also Pahlke, *Trotz Verbot nicht Tot*, 350.

35 Karl Hofmann, *Eine Katholische Generation zwischen Kirche und Welt: Studien zur Sturmschar des Katholischen Jungmännerverbandes Deutschlands* (Augsburg, 1992); Börger, *Sie hielten Stand.*

36 Kösters, *Katholische Verbände und moderne Gesellschaft*, 206.

37 See text of Chapter 6 at n. 42.

38 AKKZG, Münster, "Katholiken zwischen Tradition und Moderne," 650.

39 Schellenberger, "Ludwig Wolker."

40 HAEK, CR II, 22.37, "Bericht über die KA. im Ganzen," aus 1935, and 22.37.5, "Die Katholische Aktion."

41 For the best account of Catholic Action in Germany, see Doris Kaufmann, *Katholisches Milieu in Münster, 1928–1933: Politische Aktionsformen und geschlechtsspezifische Verhaltensräume* (Düsseldorf, 1984). See also Angelika Steinmaus-Pollak, *Das als Katholische Aktion organisierte Laienapostolat: Geschichte seiner Theorie und seiner kirchenrechtlichen Praxis in Deutschland* (Würzburg, 1988).

42 See Gianfranco Poggi, *Catholic Action in Italy: The Sociology of a Sponsored Organization* (Stanford, 1987).

43 See Kösters, *Katholische Verbände und moderne Gesellschaft*, 156.

44 "Bis an die Hecken und Zäune," interview mit Theresia Hauser über die Anfangsjahre des Bundes der Deutschen Katholischen Jugend, in *Katechetische Blätter*, November 1987, 861.

45 Oskar Neisinger, the leader of the Catholic youth work in Unterfranken after 1945, continued to voice this criticism after the war.

46 For descriptions of this process, see Pahlke, *Trotz Verbot nicht Tot*, 199–240; Kösters, *Katholische Verbände und moderne Gesellschaft*, 487–500.

47 See the collection of documents in *Katholische Jugend in der NS-Zeit, unter besonderer Berücksichtigung des Katholischen Jungmännerverbandes, Daten und Dokumente*, ed. Heinrich Roth (Düsseldorf, 1959); "Richtlinien für die katholische Jugendseelsorge 1936," in *Grundlagentexte zur katholischen Jugendarbeit* (Handbuch kirchlicher Jugendarbeit, vol. 3), ed. Franz Schmid (Freiburg, 1986), 105–8. Representatives of the *Kolpingsverband*, on the other hand, saw in these statutes their death knell.

48 Kösters, *Katholische Verbände und moderne Gesellschaft*, 438.

49 A conservative monarchist to his death in 1946, von Galen had an ambivalent relationship to the youth movement. He, on one hand, enjoyed the reputation of being a foe of both the liturgical and the youth movements. On the other hand, he seemed to have sensed how powerfully these movements were inspiring youth and lent them a cautious support. See Wilhelm Damberg, "Bischof von Galen, die münsterische Synode von 1936 und der Wandel pastoraler Planung im 20. Jahrhundert," in *Neue Forschungen zum Leben und Wirken des Bischofs von Münster*, ed. Joachim Kuropka (Münster, 1993). For a recent and highly critical work on von Galen, see Beth A. Griech-Polelle, *Bishop von Galen: German Catholicism and National Socialism* (New Haven, 2002).

50 Pahlke, *Trotz Verbot nicht Tot*, 189–90.

51 Augustinus Reineke, *Jugend zwischen Kreuz und Hakenkreuz: Erinnerungen und Erblebnisse: Ereignisse und Dokumente* (Paderborn, 1987), 69.

52 On Gröber, see Erwin Keller, *Conrad Gröber, 1872–1948: Erzbischof in schwerer Zeit* (Freiburg, 1981); Bruno Schwalbach, *Erzbischof Conrad Gröber und die deutsche Katastrophe: Sein Ringen um eine menschliche Neuordnung* (Karlsruhe, 1994).

53 HAEK, Gen 32.30, II, "Gedanken zur Kleruspredigt am 9. Februar 1943."

54 Reineke, *Jugend zwischen Kreuz und Hakenkreuz*.

55 Ibid., 188.

56 *Ewige Gestrigen*—those who dwell in the past.

57 For a fine summary of these trends, see Kösters, *Katholische Verbände und moderne Gesellschaft*, 576–78.

58 KZG, NLLW, I a 1, "Zur Jugendseelsorge (männliche Jugend) 1942."

59 A collection of instructional material from the Pfarrarchiv in the Rhenish town of Walberberg provides one example of this new current within Catholic youth work.

60 "Bis an die Hecken and Zäune."

61 DAW, Klinkhammer Sammlung, K1, interview, 22 November 1984, Gesprächspartner Oskar Neisinger, Monika Klinkhammer; Oskar Neisinger, *Flugblätter: Katholische Jugend im Widerstand gegen den Nationalsozialismus* (Würzburg, 1982).

62 Christel Beilmann, *Eine katholische Jugend in Gottes und dem Dritten Reich: Briefe, Berichte, Gedrucktes, 1930–1945* (Wuppertal, 1989).

63 This corresponds to the picture painted by officials in the archdiocese of Cologne after the war. See HAEK, Gen 23.30, Bericht über die Seelsorge in Köln, 1936–46.

64 Kösters, *Katholische Verbande und moderne Gesellschaft*, 576–78.

65 Werner Blessing, " 'Deutschland in Not, Wir im Glauben . . .' Kirche und Kirchenvolk in einer katholischen Region, 1933–1949," in *Von Stalingrad zur Währungsreform: Zur Sozialgeschichte des Umbruchs in Deutschland*, 3d ed., ed. Martin Broszat (Munich, 1990), 3–111.

66 KZG, NLLW, I a 1, "Über Lage und Aufgabe der Jugendseelsorge, zum August 1944."

67 Ibid., "Zur Jugendseelsorge, 1941."

68 Ibid., "Über Lage und Aufgabe der Jugendseelsorge."

69 Ibid.

70 These figures are based on my own rough calculations of data compiled from approximately 200 parishes from four statistical handbooks from the archdiocese of Cologne from 1933, 1954, 1958, and 1966. For each parish, the number of members for male and female youth groups are listed. This information, however, is extremely unreliable; wild fluctuations appear throughout, and pastors submitted dubious statistics or (in many cases) none at all. One can still grasp general trends from this data. See Introduction, n. 28.

71 Up to 80 percent of the young people had vanished from the ranks of the

Catholic youth. See JHH, 1.2201.3, Katholische Jugendführung: Überlegungen und Vorschläge für das katholische Jugendwerk, Referat ca. 1945.

72 Wolfgang Löhr, ed., *Hirtenbriefe und Ansprachen zu Gesellschaft und Politik, 1945–1949* (Würzburg, 1985), 125. Once Frings became chairman of the Fulda Bishops' Conference, he was forced to intervene on many critical issues concerning youth work. In many cases, he left decisions to Stohr or to Wolker.

73 For an early summary of this debate, see Jürgen Kocka, "1945: Neubeginn oder Restauration?," in *Wendepunkte deutscher Geschichte, 1848–1945*, ed. Carola Stern and Heinrich August Winkler (Frankfurt, 1986), 141–68.

74 Many of the bishops who had been appointed prior to 1934 remained on their thrones in 1945. The most influential of these were Clemens August von Galen, the so-called Lion of Münster; Michael Faulhaber of Munich; and Konrad Graf von Preysing of Berlin. Even the "newcomers" during this time— Joseph Frings of Cologne, Albert Stohr of Mainz, and Lorenz Jaeger of Paderborn—were in their forties or fifties when appointed to the bishop's throne. In sharp contrast to German Protestants, very few clergy had been compromised by pro-Nazi behavior between 1933 and 1945.

75 There was one caveat: Frings, obviously astute enough to recognize the potential for a power struggle between the bishops and a figure as powerful as Wolker, informed Wolker in no uncertain terms that this post was subject to his authority, that of the archbishop of Cologne. See HAEK, Gen 23.11.3, Frings an Wolker, 23 August 1945.

76 Ingeborg Rocholl-Gärtner, *Anwalt der Frauen: Hermann Klens: Leben und Werk* (Düsseldorf, 1978).

77 "Wir bauen die Arbeit nicht auf dem Boden von Verbänden, sondern auf die im Wesen der Kirche gelegene Ordnung (Diözese, Dekanat, Pfarrei), das entspricht dem neu erwachsenen Kirchenbewußtsein und gewährleistet die Einheit der ganzen Katholischen Jugend." Frings even intervened at one point to insist that plans being considered by unidentified youth leaders in the summer of 1945 went well beyond the guidelines of 1936. See HAEK, Gen 23.11.3, Frings an Stohr, 29 August, 1945.

78 KZG, NLLW, III, 4a, "Beschluß der Westdeutschen Bischöfe in Werl am 4.–6. Juni 1945."

79 See Matthias Schulze, *Bund oder Schar—Verband oder Pfarrjugend? Katholische Jugendarbeit im Erzbistum Paderborn nach 1945* (Paderborn, 2001), 98–114.

80 Ludwig Volk, *Akten deutscher Bischöfe über die Lage der Kirche, 1933–1945* (Mainz, 1985), 6:662.

81 Wilhelm Damberg has described the *Jugendreich* as a central motif of the immediate postwar era in regard to youth work; see *Abschied vom Milieu? Katholizismus im Bistum Münster und in den Niederlanden, 1945–1989* (Paderborn, 1997), 307–83.

82 JHH, 1.22012.3, Ludwig Wolker, "Rede an die Jugend," 24 February 1946, 6.

83 JHD, "Die erste Hauptkonferenz der katholischen Jugendseelsorge und Jugend-

organisationen in den Deutschen Diözesen, 29.4. bis 3.5.1946 in Bad-Soden-Salmünster, Bericht an die Diözesen": "Die Uebersteigerung des geistigen Prinzips der Jugendseelsorge, nach einem zu eng gefaßten Begriff relgiöser [sic] Jugendführung, in einem gewissen Spiritualismus. Es kann katholisches Jugendleben und darum katholische Jugendführung nicht auf den sogenannten rein religiösen Raum beschränkt werden. . . . Katholische Jugendarbeit ist mit dem Priestertum der Kirche eng verbunden und will in seelsorglicher Verantwortung von da geführt sein. Ein Klerikalismus der Jugendführung aber muß als ebenso abwegig gesehen werden wie ein Laizismus."

84 Ibid.

85 HAEK, NL Heinen, #33, Klaus Koch an die Jungmannschaft, Köln, in der Fastenzeit 1947, 2.

86 KZG, NLLW, I 3b, II 1a, Hans Fischer, "Zum Entwurf einer Ordnung der 'Katholischen Jugend' " (n.d.).

87 See Arno Klönne, "Blaue Blumen in Trümmerlandschaften: Bündische Jugendgruppen in den Jahren nach 1945," Puls 18: Dokumentationsschrift der Jugendbewegung, 18 October 1990. Norbert Schwarte and Jürgen Reulecke argue that the romantic traditions of the youth movement did not die out after 1945. They also point out that the bündisch forms always made up only a small percentage of the youth movement. I would, nonetheless, maintain that the youth movement was largely over after 1945, even if the forms of the movement were adapted to the new era and if small groups did persist in carrying out these traditions. See Schwarte and Reulecke, "Fernweh und Grossfahrten in der bündischen Jugend der Nachkriegszeit," in Rückkehr in die Ferne: Die deutsche Jugend in der Nachkriegszeit und das Ausland, ed. Jürgen Reulecke (Weinheim, 1997), 151–67.

88 To be fair, the first German youth movement at the turn of the century was, to a significant degree, inspired by adults.

89 As Maria Mitchell has noted, the church's critique of materialism allowed Catholics to broaden their base politically and attract Protestant recruits. See Mitchell, "Materialism and Secularism: CDU Politicians and National Socialism, 1945–1949," Journal of Modern History 67 (1995): 278–308; Noel Cary, The Path to Christian Democracy: German Catholics and the Party System from Windthorst to Adenauer (Cambridge, 1996).

90 See quotes by Joseph Godehard Machens, bishop of Hildesheim, in Löhr, Hirtenbriefe und Ansprachen zu Gesellschaft und Politik, 137–38. Michael Buchberger, the bishop of Regensburg, to some extent put forward a contrary interpretation: "Hat nicht der Kampf gegen Christus, den der Unglaube und der Kirchenhaß, den der Unglaube und der Kirchenhaß in unserem deutschen Vaterland seit langer Zeit führte und den der Nationalsozialismus auf die Spitze trieb, weite Kreise unseres Volkes entchristlicht?" (ibid., 135).

91 JHD, Bokler, Referat zum Jahreskonferenz der Führerschaft, April 1954, 20.

92 KZG, NLWB, D II, 2, Wolker an alle, Freiburg, 19 July 1945, Dr. A. Stiefvater an

Wolker, Freiburg, 30 July 1945. Other *Verbände* complained in the years to come, often bitterly, that Wolker was shortchanging them.

93 The conflicts with Kolping proved to be particularly acrimonious. See KZG, NLWB, D II, 2, "Kolpingsfamilie und Katholische Jugend" and Wolker an die Hochwürdigen Herren Diözesan-Jugendseelsorger, Schondorf, 22 October 1945. The bishops were eventually forced to put a halt to misconceptions that had arisen from their conference at Salmünster in 1945. "Durch irrtümliche Berichterstattung über die Stellungnahme der Salmünster-Konferenz zum Kolpingswerk war eine Mißtimmung eingetreten, die wir gerade im Zeitpunkt des neuen anfangs besonders bedauerten. . . . Die jugendlichen Mitglieder des katholischen Gesellenvereins zwischen 18 und 25 Jahren gehören als Kolpingsgruppen zum Ganzen 'katholische Jugend' in Pfarrei bzw Dekanat und Diözese. Für junge Handwerker aus pfarrlichen Jungmännergruppen soll es auch eine Verbandsmitgliedschaft zum Kolpingswerk geben" (JHD, Haus Altenberg, "Dezember-Bericht, 1945, an die Diözesen").

94 Guardini an Stohr, Mooshausen, 14 August 1945, in Volk, *Akten deutscher Bischöfe*, 6:646–49.

95 Ibid., 649.

96 The literature on this subject, both primary and secondary, is voluminous and, of course, often controversial. See CUA, NL Muench, HM 37/138/1, Katholischer Volksbund im Bistum Limburg, Rundbrief no. 11: Die Kirche und der Nationalsozialismus (n.d.); the sermons and pastoral statements in Löhr, *Hirtenbriefe und Ansprachen zu Gesellschaft und Politik*; Karl-Egon Lönne, "Katholizismus 1945: Zwischen gequälter Selbstbehauptung gegenüber dem Nationalsozialismus und Öffnung zur pluralistischen Gesellschaft," in *Ende des Dritten Reiches—Ende des Zweiten Weltkriegs: Eine perspektivische Rückschau*, ed. Hans-Erich Volkmann (Munich, 1995), 745–69; Karen Riechert, "Der Umgang der katholischen Kirche mit historischer und juristischer Schuld anlässlich der Nürnberger Hauptkriegsverbrecherprozesse," in *Siegerin in Trümmern: Die Rolle der katholischen Kirche in der deutschen Nachkriegsgesellschaft*, ed. Joachim Köhler and Damian van Melis (Stuttgart, 1998), 18–41; Frederic Spotts, *The Churches and Politics in Germany* (Middletown, 1973).

97 HAEK, Gen 23.11.1, Köln, Esch an Frings, 21 July 1946.

98 HAEK, Gen 23.24.1, "Entwurf" (n.d., but undoubtedly 1945).

99 Ibid., Esch an Frings, 18 January 1948.

100 Ibid., Joseph Stoffes, Organist, Köln-Buchforst an Pater Rommerskirch, 10 May 1951.

101 Ibid., Frings an Esch, 14 December 1946, and Esch an Frings, 26 November 1946.

102 KAS, NL Rommerskirchen, I 234-34, Rommerskirchen an Georg, Kettwig, 20 August 1947.

103 PRO, FO 1050/1251, pt. 2, "The Falcons—German Socialist Youth Movement— Report concerning the First annual Central Conference, 6th and 7th April,

1947 in Bad Homburg, v.D.H." For fuller histories of the Socialist youth movement in Germany, see Bodo Brücher, *Die Sozialistische Jugendbewegung Deutschlands: Politisch-pädagogisches Konzept und Realität sozialistischer Jugend- und Erziehungsarbeit in den Nachkriegsjahren* (Werther, 1995) and *Bibliographie zur Geschichte
der Geschichte der deutschen Arbeiterjugendbewegung von den Anfängen bis 1945*, zusam-
mengestellt von einer Kollektiv unter Leitung von Bodo Brücher und Karl Heinz Jahnke
unter Mitarbeit von Beate Behrens (Rostock, 1989).

104 PRO, FO 1050/1536, copy, "Jugend in Deutschland," 13 July 1947.

105 For the best overview of the FDJ, see Alan Nothnagle, *Building the East German
Myth: Historical Mythology and Youth Propaganda in the German Democratic Republic,
1945–1989* (Ann Arbor, 1999).

106 On the relationship between the Catholic youth and the FDJ, see Wolfgang
Tischner, *Katholische Kirche in der SBZ/DDR, 1945–1951* (Paderborn, 2001), 323–
49.

107 HAEK, Gen 23.11.3, Wolker an Frings, am Lichtmeßtag 1946.

108 See the following quote by Wolker: "Was eine ganze Jugendzeit hindurch als
neues Evangelium gepredigt ward, das ist nun als bodenlose dämonische Lüge
erwiesen . . ." (ibid.).

109 Helmut Schelsky, *Die skeptische Generation: Eine Soziologie der deutschen Jugend* (Düsseldorf, 1957).

110 Enormous debates have raged among historians concerning the Edelweiss
Pirates. To some, they exemplified a heroic resistance against the Nazi system.
To others, including officials within the American military government, they
were little more than delinquents and hooligans who attacked and often severely injured former Polish slave laborers and concentration camp inmates
throughout Germany. See Detlev Peukert, *Die Edelweißpiraten: Protestbewegungen
jugendlicher Arbeiter im Dritten Reich* (Cologne, 1980); Arno Klönne, *Jugend im
Dritten Reich: Die Hitlerjugend und ihre Gegner* (Munich, 1995); "German Youth
Activities of the United States Army," Office of the Chief Historian, Frankfurt,
1949, Dept. of the Army, U.S. Army Military History Institute, Carlisle Barracks, Carlisle, Pa. See also Alfons Kenkmann, *Wilde Jugend: Lebenswelt großstädtischer Jugendlicher zwischen Weltwirtschaftskrise, Nationalsozialismus und Währungsreform* (Essen, 1996).

111 Volk, *Akten deutscher Bischöfe*, 6:701.

112 Löhr, *Hirtenbriefe und Ansprachen zu Gesellschaft und Politik*, 100.

113 HAEK, Gen 23.11.3, Wolker an Frings, am Lichtmeßtag 1946.

114 Löhr, *Hirtenbriefe und Ansprachen zu Gesellschaft und Politik*, 38.

115 See the following quote from Rommerskirchen: "Freiheit ohne Bindung, Freiheit von der Gemeinschaft endet im Chaos—die sie wollen, sind Handleger
der Zerstörung" (KAS, NL Rommerskirchen, I 234, 022, Rede, 1957).

116 KZG, NLWB, D II, 1, Ludwig Wolker, "Rede an die Jugend."

117 CAJ-Essen, CAJ-M 1947, Deutsche Kolpingsfamilie, "Tagungsbericht von der
Hauptkonferenz der Führerschaft der kath. Jugend in Hardehausen vom
24.3.–28.3. 1947." This is the only surviving account of the conference at

Hardehausen that I have been able to locate. For an account written much later, see Reineke, *Jugend zwischen Kreuz und Hakenkreuz*, 238–41. For another very detailed account of the struggles to shape youth work after 1945, see Schulze, *Bund oder Schar—Verband oder Pfarrjugend?*; on the conference in Hardehausen, see 227–37.

118 Reineke, *Jugend zwischen Kreuz und Hakenkreuz*.

119 CAJ-Essen, CAJ-M 1947, Deutsche Kolpingsfamilie, "Tagungsbericht von der Hauptkonferenz der Führerschaft der kath. Jugend in Hardehausen vom 24.3.–28.3. 1947," 5.

120 Reineke, *Jugend zwischen Kreuz und Hakenkreuz*, 240.

121 Wolfgang Tischner, *Katholische Kirche in der SBZ/DDR*, 346.

122 For Gröber and others of like mind, an emphasis on the *Pfarrprinzip* represented a continuation of their war against the secularizing tendencies they believed to be present within the church itself—secularization from within.

123 A parallel might be drawn to the CDU, an organization that was officially interconfessional but in reality relied heavily on the sectarian base of support of the Center Party. See Markus Köster, *Katholizismus und Parteien in Münster 1945–1953: Kontinuität und Wandel eines politischen Milieus* (Münster, 1993).

124 KZG, NLLW, I 3b–II 1a, "Besondere Aufgaben der Jugendseelsorge in der Gegenwart."

125 Interview with Josef Rommerskirchen, Bonn, November 1995.

126 Kolping, in particular, led an acrid campaign against the BDKJ in the 1950s, but other organizations, such as Die Schar, a small *bündisch* organization from Westphalia, and the CAJ, had their own grievances against Altenberg. For a detailed description of the conflicts involving Die Schar, see Schulze, *Bund oder Schar—Verband oder Pfarrjugend?*

127 For accounts of the BDKJ, see Martin Schwab, *Kirchlich, Kritisch, Kämpferisch: Der Bund der Deutschen Katholischen Jugend (BDKJ), 1947–1989* (Würzburg, 1994) and *Kirche Leben und Gesellschaft Gestalten: Der Bund der Deutschen Katholischen Jugend (BDKJ) in der Bundesrepublik Deutschland und der Diözese Würzburg, 1947–1989* (Würzburg, 1997); Bernd Börger and Karin Kortmann, eds., *Ein Haus für Junge Menschen: Jugendhaus Düsseldorf, 1954–1994: Beiträge zur Geschichte der katholischen Jugendarbeit in Deutschland* (Düsseldorf, 1994).

CHAPTER 2

1 On marching, see a photo spread in Georg Pahlke and Wilhelm Pohlmann, eds., *Jugendhaus Hardehausen: 40 Jahre, 1945–1985* (Paderborn, 1985), 19–26.

2 JHH, 1.2201.3, Ludwig Wolker, "Rede an die Jugend," 24 February 1946.

3 HAEK, NL Heinen, #35, Aufnahme der Schulentlassenen Jugend in die Jugendgemeinschaft des Bundes: Ein Vorschlag für alle Pfarrgemeinden, von Fritz Eink, Diözesanjugendseelsorger (probably late 1940s or early 1950s).

4 This financial crisis was the subject of much attention between 1948 and 1952. Some described the financial state of Haus Altenberg as "miserable" and

pointed the finger at Wolker's inability to manage the affairs properly; see HAEK, Gen 23.11.6, Hermann Freiherr von Böselager an Generalvikar David, 4 January 1951. Others spoke of a debt of more than 250,000 deutsche marks, a figure I have not able to corroborate; see HAEK, Gen 23.11.6, Seelsorge und Jugendamt w.J. der Erz. Köln, Bonn-Venusberg-Liebfrauenhaus an Frings, 29 January 1951. The bishops, moreover, were forced to ask individual dioceses for greater financial assistance. See HAEK, Gen 23.11.4, Frings und Stohr an Hochwürdigste Eminenz/Exzellenz, 13 December 1948. In this letter they claimed that the money they needed was far less than what the Communist youth were spending for their organizations.

5   CUA, NL Muench, HM 149/7, "Jugend in Dortmund: Erlebnisbericht unserer nach Dortmund entsandten Mitarbeiterin, Angelika Merkelbach-Pinck."

6   JHD, A527–537, Ziel und Aufgabe Katholischer Jugend (n.d., but late 1940s). Only within two areas did these guidelines depart from previous practice. Youth leaders explicitly rejected military models. They urged young persons to engage in sporting events and gymnastics but took pains to disassociate themselves from the military trappings these activities had had in the past. They no doubt remembered all too well the paramilitary training of the last years of the Weimar Republic—the so-called *Geländesport*—and were mindful of the restrictions imposed by the Allied governments that forbade such activities. Youth leaders likewise exhorted young Catholics to develop a sense of what it meant to be part of the national community of Germans, but without indulging in a belligerent nationalism. ("Hinführung zu einem echten Volkstum ohne übersteigerten Nationalismus.") They ultimately saw their task as engineering the national recovery in a time of scarcity, hunger, and psychological despair.

7   See, for instance, HAEK, Gen 23.11c, Übersicht über das katholische Jugendamt (in der Stadt Köln) (n.d., possibly 1959); HAEK, NL Heinen, #96, Diözesan-Synode 1950, Das Seelsorgeamt.

8   HAEK, NL Heinen, #33, Jungschar und Jungenschaft, P. Eucharius Zenzen OSB, Anlage 3 (n.d.).

9   Jürgen Reulecke, "Männerbund versus Familie: Bürgerliche Jugendbewegung und Familie in Deutschland im ersten Drittel des 20. Jahrhundertes," in *Mit uns zieht die neue Zeit: Der Mythus Jugend*, ed. Frank Trommler, Thomas Kochner, and Rolf-Peter Janz (Frankfurt, 1985), 199–223.

10 For a strong criticism of this practice, see DAW, NL Neisinger, Karl Heinrich an Döpfner, 17 February 1950, file: Korrespondenz 1950.

11 For one example of a social evening in 1960, see DAW, KJBW, BJ, K2, Klinkhammer Sammlung, folder Chronik der Jungschargruppe, St. Michael, Dekanat Klingenberg, Heimabend am 4 April 1960.

12 BDKJ-Köln, "Unsere Zelte standen über dem See," *Unser Weg*, July 1955.

13 BDKJ-Köln, "Eine Gruppe feiert Jubiläum," *Unser Weg*, 1960.

14 BA, B268/79, Bundesjugendring, Abteilung, Jugendfunk, "Restauration oder Evolution: Eine kritische Betrachtung der Arbeit in den Jugendverbänden, von

Willi Weiskirch," 5. This fictitious dialogue among five persons was produced for radio in 1958.

15 BDKJ-Würz, vol. 4, Dekanatsführerkonferenz, Dekanat Hammelburg, January 1955.

16 Interview with Heidi Carl-Neisinger, Würzburg, June 1996.

17 Haus Altenberg, for instance, sponsored 1,884 courses and conferences with 73,103 participants between 1945 and 1959. See Archiv Haus Altenberg, "Vierzehn Jahre Schulungsstätte Altenberg," taken from *Die Katechetische Blätter*, June 1960.

18 I reached this conclusion after examining dozens of pedagogical tracts and training materials in the NL Wolker, Jugendhaus Düsseldorf, and Jugendhaus Hardehausen. For several examples, see KZG, NLLW, II 1e, Jungmannschaftsabend, NLLW, II 1d–e, folder, Jugendseelsorge, "Referat vom P. Wulf, Gelegentlich der Tagung der Arbeitsgemeinschaft bayerischer Klöster in München am 22.5.49." Some young persons, however, voiced similar complaints. Martin Schwab likewise argues that youth leaders were often overwhelmed by the demands placed on them; see Schwab, *Kirchlich, Kritisch, Kämpferisch: Der Bund der Deutschen Katholischen Jugend (BDKJ), 1947–1989* (Würzburg, 1994), 44.

19 KZG, NLLW, III 1a, Miteindander, Gegeneinander oder Nebeneinander? Priester und Jugend—ein heikles Kapitel (no author, n.d.).

20 BDKJ-Würz, vol. 3, newspaper article, Schweinfurt, "Die Verwandlung der drei Kapläne" (n.d.).

21 BDKJ-Köln, *Unser Weg*, "Jungscharleben: Ein Jungführer erzählt," March 1953.

22 BDKJ-Würz, Dekanatsführerkonferenz, Dekanat Hassfurt, January 1955.

23 JHH, Ausstellung, open display at the front of the document center.

24 HAEK, NL Heinen, #33, Bericht über die Herbsttagung der Dekanatsführer vom 22–25 Oktober 1948 in Altenberg, 5. This conference focused, in part, on the many-faceted relationships between priests and their groups.

25 DAW, Kasten, BDKJ, Jubiläumsausstellung, 1987, Bisch. Dekanat Würzburg I.D.M., in Zell am Main, an das Hochwürdigste Bischöfliche Ordinariat, Würzburg, 13 July 1959, and an die Diözesanjugendstelle des BDKJ-Würz, 9 July 1959.

26 DAW, KJBW, BJ, K1, Otto Slong, Kaplan, letter written to the youth leader and forwarded on to Oskar Neisinger, the youth leader for Würzburg, 23 May 1947.

27 BDKJ-Köln, "Jungscharleben," in *Unser Weg*, March 1953.

28 Ibid.

29 NA, RG 260, Religious Affairs, box 164, L. D. Gresh to the Director, Office of Military Government for Hesse, Subject: Use of Emblems and Banners by Church Youth Groups, 9 September 1947. In this document, the American military government acquiesced in the use of uniforms by church groups, so long as they were not of a specifically military nature. Any group that wore uniforms, however, had to be licensed, and any new "distinctive garb, em-

blems, banners or flags introduced after the time of licensing would require specific approval."

30 DAW, KJBW, BJ, K1, Pfarrer von Weilbach über Miltenberg an Oskar Neisinger, 28 August 1947. This letter described the growing opposition to the spirit of the Catholic youth: "Was der macht, das ist genau dasselbe wieder wie die Hitlerjugend." In this letter the writer noted that others accused the Catholic youth of proceeding as though there had never been a Hitler Youth.

31 "Die neue Jungscharkluft," Der Jungführer, 1952, 75. This article actively came out in favor of the new uniforms but nonetheless cited the contrary arguments, such as "Wenn alle Jugendbünde sich wieder uniformieren, dann werden Kluften in der Jugend aufgerissen, die unheilsame Fronten in unserem Volke schaffen."

32 These assertions were, in fact, true. The Hitler Youth deliberately appropriated ideas and approaches from the youth movement, having recognized their power to inspire and move young men. See JHD, A527–537, "Zur Beanstandung des Artikels 'Jungführertum' im Konferenzbericht der Katholischen Jugend erlauben wir uns, folgendes zu bemerken . . ." (no author, n.d.). The youth center in Altenberg also sent similar letters to the American military government, justifying their continued use of certain terms without which, they asserted, Catholic youth work could not function.

33 "Die neue Jungscharkluft," Der Jungführer, 1952, 74–78.

34 Ibid.

35 NA, RG 260, Religious Affairs, box 166, "Semi-Annual Report, Religious Affairs Branch, 1 July–31 October 1949," 39–42.

36 HAEK, CR II, 22.37, 2, K.A., Urban Fleege, Acting Chief, Religious Affairs Branch an sehr geehrte Gäste, 22 May 1951. Of the leaders in the Religious Affairs Branch of the Office of the Military Governor (OMGUS) and, after 1949, the High Commissioner for Germany, Fleege, formerly of Marquette University, took the greatest interest in Catholic youth work. To quote from this document further: "Auf der anderen Seite habe ich von Geistlichen wie auch von Laien oft gehört, daß die Führer in zu vielen Fällen es daran fehlen lassen, wirkliche Autorität und wirkliche Verantwortung denen zu geben, deren Mitarbeit sie zu erhalten hoffen. Einige beklagen sich darüber, daß die Führer —und nicht nur die Geistlichkeit—dazu neigen, in Bezug auf organisatorische Ausrichtung und Entwicklung von Programmen in gewissen Sinne autoritär und diktatorisch zu verfahren." He was of the opinion that more young persons would participate if they were given greater responsibility and authority.

37 NA, RG 260, Religious Affairs, box 166, Semi-Annual Report, Religious Affairs Branch, 1 July–31 December 1949, 39–42.

38 On the GYA, see Hermann-Josef Rupieper, Die Wurzeln der westdeutschen Nachkriegsdemokratie: Der amerikanische Beitrag, 1945–1952 (Opladen, 1993).

39 CUA, National Catholic Welfare Conference, box 29, Education: Educational Institutions, "German Catholics See America: An evaluation of the experiences of 82 Germans who visited the United States at the invitation of the Depart-

ment of State during the years 1949–51, and who were sponsored during their stay in America by the National Catholic Welfare Conference." This was an extensive survey carried out by the National Catholic Welfare Conference.

40 See the following, somewhat embittered, quote by Oskar Neisinger, who also clearly resented the paperwork he was required to fill out: "Und trotzdem fragt man heute nicht uns nach dem Wesen der Schwierigkeit und der besten Lösung, sondern propagiert Ideologien, die vielleicht der amerikanischen Jugend ganz hilfreich sind, bei uns aber der Faustaufsauge entsprechen" (DAW, BDKJ, Ausstellungsmaterial, 1989, Würzburg, Oskar Neisinger an den Bayr. Landesjugendausschuß z.h. Herrn Präsidenten A. J. Lippl, 7 November 1946).

41 On the American support, see DAW, Ausstellungsmaterial (1987), Oskar Neisinger, Einzelbericht über die Jugendarbeit in Unterfranken, 10 January 1947, and NA, RG 260, Religious Affairs, box 183, "Part 7: Youth and recreational activities, Section B, Youth Activities" (n.d., but probably 1948).

42 DAW, BDKJ, Ausstellungsmaterial (1987), Kath. Jugendstelle am Dom, Würzburg, an die Leitung des Amer. Rotkreuzklubs, Würzburg, gez. Leiterin der K. J. Würzburg.

43 Rupieper, Wurzeln der westdeutschen Nachkriegsdemokratie, 156–62. See the quote by a pastor in Würtingen: "My business is dealing with German youth. I look upon anyone else who has anything to do with the loyal youth as a competitor and I shall fight him" (NA, RG 466, Office of the Land Commissioner for Bavaria, Central Files, box 28, Eric W. Isenstead, Innis D. Harris, Office of Intelligence, 25 May 1950).

44 NA, RG 287, Publications of the United States Government, National Military Establishment, 1947–1949, OMGUS, Education and Cultural Relations Division, Berlin, "German Youth between Yesterday and Tomorrow," 30 April 1948.

45 For the response to the waning of the youth movement, see Peter Bevelius, "Deutsche Jugendbewegung heute? An die 'dritte Generation,'" Rheinische Merkur, 19 April 1947; "Ende der Jugendbewegung?," Rheinische Merkur, 31 May 1947; Otto Roegele, "Erbe der Jugendbewegung," Rheinische Merkur, 30 July 1949. This criticism mounted well into the late 1950s. For one example, see "Ist die Jugendarbeit noch zeitgemäß?," Der Jungführer, 1958–59, 3–4.

46 KAS, NL Rommerskirchen, Rommerskirchen an Georg, Kettwig, 20 April 1947.

47 Helmut Schelsky, Die skeptische Generation: Eine Soziologie der deutschen Jugend (Düsseldorf, 1957).

48 "Katholische Jugendarbeit in der Krise?," Der Jungführer, 1959–60, 4; "Zur Lage der deutschen Katholischen Jugend," Deutsche Volksschaft, May 1951, 3–4; BA, B268/79, Ernst E. Timke, "Elite—vielleicht bei den Nichtorganisierten, Der kritische Zeitbeitrag eines rheinischen Jugendringes" Zeitungsausschnitt, 10 January 1960.

49 See, for instance, Friedhelm Böll, Auf der Suche nach Demokratie: Britische und Deutsche Jugendinitiativen in Niedersachsen nach 1945 (Bonn, 1995).

50 Catholic leaders were all too aware of this growing generation gap and frequently expressed feelings of guilt and shame about their inability to bridge it. See "Zwischen den Generationen," *Der Fährmann*, April 1947, 10; "Nochmals: Zwischen den Generationen," *Der Fährmann*, September 1947, 7; "Haben wir die Gelegenheit verpasst? Brief an die Deutsche Katholische Jugend von 1939, Von einem, der dazu gehört, und der nach Gründen sucht," *Michael*, September 1951, 47; "Zwischen Restauration und neuer Jugendbewegung? Das Fürstenecker Gespräch des Deutschen Bundesjugendringes," *Deutsche Jugend*, 1954, 491–508.

51 *KZK*, 20 February 1949, 56, and 3 April 1949, 80 (no headline).

52 See George Mosse, *Fallen Soldiers: Reshaping the Memory of the World Wars* (Oxford, 1990).

53 See Norbert Schwarte and Jürgen Reulecke, "Fernweh und Grossfahrten in der bündischen Jugend der Nachkriegszeit," in *Rückkehr in die Ferne: Die deutsche Jugend in der Nachkriegszeit und das Ausland*, ed. Jürgen Reulecke (Weinheim, 1997), 151–68.

54 The inscription "Jawohl, Entartung der Fahrt weithin" was placed in the middle of an article that examined the role of hitchhiking. See "Kalte Dusche ins Fernwehfeuer: Fahrten so oder so," *Die Wacht*, 1 June 1948.

55 Arno Klönne has argued, however, that hitchhiking embodied the spirit of a new wave to the youth movement, one that lasted only several years after 1945. See Klönne, "Blaue Blumen in Trümmerlandschaften: Bündische Jugendgruppen in den Jahren nach 1945," *Puls 18: Dokumentationsschrift der Jugendbewegung*, 18 October 1990.

56 The Monika Klinkhammer collection in the diocesan archive in Würzburg contains many photos of group activities. This collection features photos of a group who went on a hike in the attire mentioned above. These photos were not dated but were undoubtedly from the late 1950s or early 1960s. See DAW, KJBW, BJ, K2, Klinkhammer Sammlung.

57 Some youth leaders gently criticized youth who participated in these trips simply because they were considered "modern": "Weil es offensichtlich modern ist, in kurzer Zeit große Strecke zurückzulegen, weil man mal 'da' gewesen sein muß, weil es zur Allgemeinbildung gehört durch fremde Länder zu fahren—kurzum, ist unsere Reise eine Sache der Mode, entspricht sie einer Laune, genügt sie zur Befriedigung der Neugierde?" (BDKJ-Köln, *Unser Weg*, May 1955). Along these lines, another youth worker rejected new trends in camping and their excesses: "Eine Katholische Jugendgruppe darf nicht die Auswüchse des Camping und anderer Fahrt und Zeltmoden mitmachen. . . . Wir mußten mehr und mehr das Wandern wieder erlernen" (*Unser Weg*, June 1955).

58 HAEK, Gen 23.11.11, Seine Heiligkeit, Papst Pius XII, über "DEN CHRISTLICHEN BEGRIFF DES REISENS," handwritten inscription, 1959.

59 Axel Schildt has reported on the results of these surveys, one taken in Hesse in 1950, another by a joint Finnish–West German group of sociologists. See

Schildt, *Moderne Zeiten: Freizeit, Massenmedien und "Zeitgeist" in der Bundesrepublik der fünfziger Jahre* (Hamburg, 1995), 163.

60   For a more extended bibliography, see ibid., 152–79, and Axel Schildt, "Von der Not der Jugend zur Teenager-Kultur: Aufwachsen in den 50er Jahren," in *Modernisierung im Wiederaufbau: Die westdeutsche Gesellschaft der 50er Jahre*, ed. Axel Schildt and Arnold Sywottek (Bonn, 1993), 335–48.

61   "Freizeit ist Not," in *Der Jungführer*, 1953, 262.

62   This data is based on official statistics from the BDKJ in Düsseldorf. See JHD, A526, HV 1956, Hauptversammlung 1956, Bezieherstand am 1.10.1956 mit Vergleichszahlen vom 1.10.1955, and HV 1960. Hauptversammlung 1960, Verkaufsauflagen der Zeitschriften aus dem Verlag Haus Altenberg per 1.9.1960 mit Vergleichszahlen vom 1.9.1959.

63   These publications actually combined to form *Mann in der Zeit*, a weekly newspaper aimed at a better-educated and older audience.

64   Martin Schwab makes many of the same points in his survey of the BDKJ from 1947 to 1989. See Schwab, *Kirchlich, Kritisch, Kämpferisch*, 56–58.

65   Willy Bokler, "Die Mindestforderungen," *Der Jungführer*, 1955, 1–5. Bokler was the *Bundespräses* of the BDKJ, Wolker's successor who saw himself as the defender of Wolker's legacy. The tone of this article was one of grave concern for the future of the *Bund*. This complaint, however, had been voiced much earlier. See DAW, NL Neisinger, Karl Heinrich an Döpfner, 17 February 1950, file: Korrespondenz 1950.

66   BDKJ-Köln, "Was schreiben unsere Jungscharführer, wenn sie unvorbereitet einige Fragen über den Bund beantworten sollen?," *Unser Weg*, January 1958–59. The participants in this informal study were asked ten questions about the *Bund* regarding the names of the leaders, the names of the member organizations, and the basic obligations that they were to fulfill. Those analyzing the results regarded the results as a wake-up call.

67   BDKJ-Köln, "Da ist eine Gruppe," *Unser Weg*, January 1953. This article is also in HAEK, Gen 23.11.7.

68   Schildt, *Moderne Zeiten*, 154. In this vein, Schildt has spoken of the transition from conceptions of *Jugendnot* to *Jugendschutz*. According to Schildt, this transition mirrored the rapid pace of societal change in the 1950s. The church also established sites to coordinate their efforts at "protecting" youth, the so-called Bundesarbeitsstelle Jugendschutz. These sites were concerned with immoral behavior at major festivals celebrating Carnival, Christmas, and New Year and in the workplace, camping, film, games (*Spielautomaten*), kiosks, and pubs. See HAEK, Gen 23.42, Jahresbericht über die Arbeiten der Katholischen Bundesarbeitsstelle Jugendschutz in der Bundesrepublik Deutschland, 18 October 1956. This collection contains annual reports from 1957 and 1958 as well. Although these reports document immoral behavior by teenagers, they also focus on crimes against children by adults and teenagers. See HAEK, Gen 23.42, "Zur Situation der Jugendgefährdung," 7 July 1958, "Wachsende Zahl der Sittlichkeitsverbrechen an Kindern und von Jugendlichen."

69   "Mut zum Neuen: Von Abteilungen und Arbeitskreisen," *Der Jungführer*, 1954, 342–44.

70   "Auf ins Lager," *Der Jungführer*, 1955–56, 6–9.

71   See Horst W. Opaschowski, *Jugendauslandsreisen: Geschichtliche, soziale und pädagogische Aspekte* (Darmstadt, 1970), 112–54; Franz Pöggeler, ed., *Jugendtourismus zwischen Erziehung und Kommerz* (Detmold, 1986).

72   BDKJ-Köln, "Katholisches Jugendferienwerk im Erzbistum Köln," *Unser Weg*, 1960.

73   According to one newspaper article, youth hostels were becoming increasingly unpopular because of the restrictions they imposed, such as banning smoking and imposing early curfews. See BDKJ-Würz, vol. 3, newspaper article, "Jugend wünscht mehr Komfort: Wanderromantik stirbt aus, Auch Jugendherbergen werden unpopulär," *Main Post*, 15 October 1959.

74   "Wir Diskutieren: Noch einmal: Gemeinsam in Urlaub?" *Mann in der Zeit*, 10 October 1957, in HAEK, NL Böhler, Zeitschriftensammlung.

75   HAEK, Gen 23.11.11, Betreffend gemeinsame Reisen der männlichen und weiblichen Jugend, gez. Das Erzbischöfliche Generalvikariat in Durchschrift an Herrn Hochwürden Direktor Fillbrandt, 22 January 1960. For examples of other trips available, see BDKJ-Köln, "Romfahrt der KJG," *Unser Weg*, April 1959.

76   For one example, see DAW, KLV, KLJB, K3, Freizeit—Freie Zeit in Landfamilien, Unser Jahresthema, 27 June 1963.

77   HAEK, Gen 23.2.10, Richtlinien zur Erholung, Herausgegeben vom Fachausschuß der Kath. Arbeitsgemeinschaft für Volksgesundung.

78   HAEK, Gen 23.11c, Katholisches Jugendamt M.J. in der Stadt Köln, Denkschrift über den Jugendfreizeitheimbau der Katholischen Jugend in der Stadt Köln.

79   "Tischtennis und Federball in der KJG," *Der Jungführer*, 1958–59.

80   "Freizeit ist Not."

81   BDKJ-Köln, "Das ist eine Gruppe: Eine Antwort auf den Artikel von H. Bielefeld im Februar, die wir ernst negmen müssen," *Unser Weg*, March 1953. This excerpt is also in HAEK, Gen 23.11.7.

82   "Austritt aus der Gruppe—Warum?," *Die Jungführerin*, 1955, 140–41.

83   These statistics are undoubtedly of dubious accuracy, but more important than the precise number of moviegoers is the perception that church leaders had of this new and influential form of communication. See HAEK, Gen 23.33.6, Materialmappe "Filmarbeit, Nummer 7, Material für Predigten, Vorträge und Diskussion." According to these statistics, there were almost 5,000 theaters in West Germany. Americans went, on average, thirty times a year to the movies; the English, twenty times.

84   KZG, NLLW, II 1d–e, Film und Kino: Ein paar Grundsätze für Buben und Mädchen unserer Gruppen (n.d., no author).

85   HAEK, Gen 23.33.8, Pius XII quoted in "Pontificia Commissione per la Cinematografia," Martin O'Connor, Präsident der Päpstlichen Filmkommission an Hochwürdigste Exzellenz, 1 June 1953, 5.

86 HAEK, Gen 23.33.6, Materialmappe "Filmarbeit," Material für Predigten, Vorträge und Diskussion (n.d., but probably 1951).

87 KZG, NLLW, II 1d–e, Film und Kino: Ein paar Grundsätze für Buben und Mädchen unserer Gruppen (n.d., no author).

88 Heide Fehrenbach has extensively analyzed the often violent reaction to this film and has concluded that because it depicted a weak, infirm man and a much stronger woman, it challenged gender norms that many conservatives were trying to restore after the upheavals of the war. She cites the account of a Düsseldorf priest, Dr. Carl Klinkhammer, who was arrested after a protest against the film in 1951 got out of hand. In an interview filmed decades later, however, Klinkhammer maintained that his objections to the film were based not on the nude scene but, rather, on the final act of euthanasia. In this last scene, the woman, played by Hildegard Knef, administered a mercy killing to her terminally ill husband and then killed herself. Klinkhammer asserted that this scene was all too reminiscent of the Nazi propaganda film *Ich klage an*, which was used to sway popular opinion toward and justify the Nazi euthanasia program, against which church leaders actively crusaded. Klinkhammer, moreover, was not conservative but was widely regarded as a "red priest," one with an activist social agenda. Most of the objections recorded in the Klinkhammer files were vague references to moral indecency, euthanasia, adultery, and fears that love justifies all. (See HAEK, Gen 23.22.8, Nach Auskunftserteilung des Historischen Archivs des Erzbistums Köln.) This is not to invalidate Fehrenbach's argument that gender played a central role in the reaction to this film. The Klinkhammer affair was but one isolated case. Klinkhammer may not have been aware of a visceral, subconscious reaction in which questions of gender were central. But it does underscore the dangers of applying a discourse to individual situations. See Klinkhammer, Video-Bibliographie Projekt, Dr. Carl Klinkhammer, Stadt Düsseldorf, 1993, in author's possession; Fehrenbach, *Cinema in Democratizing Germany: Reconstructing National Identity after Hitler* (Chapel Hill, 1995), 92–117. For an extensive list of interviews with Klinkhammer that were recorded on video and where he discusses the reasons for his involvement in the protests against *Die Sünderin*, see Bruno Kammann, *Carl Klinkhammer: Ruhrkaplan, Sanitätssoldat, und Bunkerpastor, 1903–1997* (Essen, 2001), 329. See also Kammann, *Klinkhammer*, 193–225.

89 HAEK, Gen 23.33.9, Frings an Herrn Minister des Inneren, Dr. Adolf Flecken, 5 March 1051, Nach Auskunftserteilung des Historischen Archivs des Erzbistums Köln.

90 HAEK, Gen 23.22.1, Frings an Barraclough, 7 June, 31 July 1946; Barraclough an Frings, 17 July 1946.

91 "Blick hinter die Kulissen," *Der Jungführer*, 1954, 352.

92 HAEK, Gen 23.33.2, Vorschläge zu einem Neuaufbau des deutschen Filmes auf katholischer Grundlage, stamped, General Vikariat, 14 November 1946.

93 HAEK, Gen 23.33.6, Materialmappe, "Filmarbeit," Material für Predigten, Vorträge und Diskussion.

94 On the national Legion of Decency, see James M. Skinner, *The Cross and the Cinema: The Legion of Decency and the National Catholic Office for Motion Pictures, 1933–1970* (Westport, 1993); Gregory Blake, *The Catholic Crusades against the Movies, 1940–1975* (Cambridge, 1998).

95 HAEK, Gen 23.33.6, Materialmappe, "Filmarbeit," 5.

96 DAW, NL Max Rössler, Kasten, Jugendarbeit, Filmarbeit (no author), 22 September 1951.

97 The legal proceedings against Klinkhammer provide one account of what transpired in all of these events. See HAEK, Gen 23.33.8, Abschrift, Der Oberstaatsanwalt bei dem Landgericht, Düsseldorf, an das Landgericht, Strafkammer, Düsseldorf, 15 November 1951, Nach Auskunftserteilung des Historischen Archives des Erzbistums Köln. For a fuller description of other youth protests against this film, see Heide Fehrenbach, "The Fight for the 'Christian West': German Film Control, the Churches, and the Reconstruction of Civil Society in the Early Bonn Republic," in *West Germany under Construction: Politics, Society, and Culture in the Adenauer Era*, ed. Robert Moeller (Ann Arbor, 1997), 321–46. Fehrenbach provides a fine description of Catholic attitudes toward film in the late 1940s and early 1950s.

98 "Der Filmklub," *Der Jungführer* 1959–60, 56–57.

99 "Deine Jungmänner und der Film . . . und abends ins Kino," *Der Jungführer*, 11–14.

100 "Der Filmklub."

101 For an excellent, larger account of the reevaluation of popular music among West German liberals in particular, see Uta Poiger, *Jazz, Rock, and Rebels: Cold War Politics and American Culture in a Divided Germany* (Berkeley, 2000), 177–267.

102 Michael Kater, *Different Drummers: Jazz in the Culture of Nazi Germany* (New York, 1992); Arno Klönne, *Jugend im Dritten Reich: Die Hitlerjugend und ihre Gegner* (Munich, 1990).

103 See a quote by Frings, "die Verwerflichkeit gewisser Arten des Tanzes, die als Negertänze bezeichnet werden und von denen urteilsfähige Augenzeugen sagen, dass sie unsittlich 'seien' und nur zum sittlichen Verderb der Jugend beitragen" (qtd. in Dan Diner, *Verkehrte Welten, Antiamerikanismus in Deutschland* [Frankfurt, 1993], 83). See also Alfons Kenkmann, *Wilde Jugend: Lebenswelt großstädtischer Jugendlicher zwischen Weltwirtschaftskrise: Nationalsozialismus und Währungsreform* (Essen, 1996), 281–87, for an account of the German response to American popular culture.

104 A parallel can be made to the problem of juvenile delinquency and the so-called *Halbstarken*. The attention that many Germans in positions of authority and influence devoted to these youth was far out of proportion to the relatively small number of teenagers who skirmished with the police. On the *Halbstarken*, see Poiger, *Jazz, Rock, and Rebels*, 71–105.

105 Some church leaders did condemn the excesses of Carnival; see Chapter 5. They also forbade young women from dancing modern dances during Carnival or Fasching. One set of advisories for Lower Franconia stated, "Ka-

tholische Jugend tanzt nicht Tänze, die in ihrer Grundanlage unsittlich, meist mit fränkischer Sitte unvereinbar sind oder doch zuchtlos getanzt werden. Wie nennen hier diese Tänze: Zitterfox—Jitterbug—Rumba—Samba—Boogie —Woogie" (DAW, B.J.A, Drucksachen, 1950–9, Diözesanrundbrief 1950, 10 January 1950).

106 Ottilie Mosshammer, *Werkbuch der katholischen Mädchenbildung*, vol. 1, *Leben in der Zeit, Zweiter Teil, Wege der Frau* (Freiburg, 1951), 210.

107 CAJ-Essen, Korrespondenz 1947–8, Fritz Eink, Neue Ausrichtung und Aufgaben in der Landjugend, "Dorfapostolat," 1 February 1947.

108 The quote in German reads, "Die Jugend ist von einer Tanzwut bessessen" (ibid.). This word, however, dated back to the 1920s.

109 The phrase in the document reads, "sie köderten sich damit die Mädchen zum Poussieren" (DAW, KJBW, BJ, K1, folder 1, Franz Mahr an Oskar Neisinger, 17 August 1947). This was a report on groups and tent camps in Bad Kissingen from 23 July to 10 August 1947. The author was careful to emphasize that his parish groups were not the culprits in this case.

110 JHD, *Michael*, 9 December 1951.

111 JHD, "Porträt der Woche: Adolf vom Jahrgang 33," *Michael*, 24 February 1952.

112 See Poiger, *Jazz, Rock, and Rebels*, 66.

113 HAEK, Gen 23.6.1, Verband der Jungmädchen und Jungfrauenvereine der Erzdiözese Köln, Anweisungen für die Tanz-Singe und Lautengruppen am 11. Juni 1933.

114 "Über den Tanz und das Tanzen," *Die Jungführerin*, 1954, 27–29.

115 "Boogie Woogie, Was soll man denn bloss davon halten?," *Die Wacht*, 2 January 1953.

116 HAEK, Gen 23.11.10, enclosed newspaper article, "Rock n' roll ist prima, sagte der Kaplan."

117 "Boogie Woogie, Was soll man denn bloss davon halten?," *Die Wacht*, 2 January 1953.

118 See, for example, BDKJ-Köln, "Kursus für Tanz und Geselligkeit," *Unser Weg*, 1956. For a still earlier example, see "Tanzkursus der Jungenschaft?," *Unser Weg*, November 1953.

119 BDKJ-Köln, "Zum Tanzen geboren: Kursus für modernen Tanz und Geselligkeit in Altenberg vom 31.1.–1.2. 1959," *Unser Weg*, March 1959.

120 For a criticism of these masses, see DAW, NL Neisinger, A.I.3.3, Alois Pottler an Neisinger, 28 May 1965.

121 HAEK, Gen 23.11.10, enclosed newspaper article, " 'Rock 'n 'Roll ist prima,' sagte der Kaplan: Experiment in der Offenen Tür an der Machabäerstrasse— Nicht entmutigt" (n.d., but 1957). For another, distinctly more positive account, see "Wohin der tanz führen soll, wissen sie nicht zu sagen: Rock 'n' Roll in der 'Offenen Tür'—Idol: Heiß Rhythmen—Jugendleiter suchen Kontake," *Neue Rhein-Zeitung*, 9 March 1957.

122 DAW, Jugendarbeit/BDKJ, 1960–4, Der Plattenteller—genau besehen, Vom Umgang mit Schlagertexten.

123 HAEK, Gen 23.11.10, newspaper article, " 'Rock 'n 'Roll ist prima' sagte der Kaplan." For another example, see DAW, Jugendarbeit/BDKJ, 1960–4, Leitfaden für das ganze Leben? Gemeinschaftstage 1959, Der Schlager in unserer Zeit. For another article critical of the new dances in youth centers, see "Kein Tanz in Juendheimen," Die Befreiung, January 1959.

124 Interview with Paul Gail, Euskirchen, November 1995.

125 Poiger, Jazz, Rock, and Rebels, 162–67, 205.

126 Schwab, Kirchlich, Kritisch, Kämpferisch, 61–64.

127 On the changes in the BDKJ, see ibid., 74–87, and more extensively, Martin Schwab, Kirche Leben und Gesellschaft Gestalten: Der Bund der Deutschen Katholischen Jugend (BDKJ) in der Bundesrepublik Deutschland und der Diözese Würzburg, 1947–1989 (Würzburg, 1997).

CHAPTER 3

1 These figures were used to determine the level of state funding. See KAS, NL Rommerskirchen, I 234 024, Mitteilungsblatt Landesjugendring Nordrhein-Westfalen, no. 18, February–March 1960, 18–19. It is possible that these figures reflect administrative changes in who was considered to be a member of the BDKJ. However, the circulation figures for the newspapers of the BDKJ mirror this decline almost perfectly for the archdiocese of Cologne. See JHD, A526, HV 55–58.

2 These losses outstripped those registered by all other non-Catholic organizations. The Protestant youth organizations, the Socialist Red Falcons, and the bündisch groups did see their membership decline during this period, but only between ten and fifteen percent. See KAS, NL Rommerskirchen, I 234 024. The membership of the Falcons actually remained at the same level, but once again, if one considers the increase in population, it becomes clear that the membership of the Falcons did not keep pace with the overall increase in population. In 1953 the Falcons had 58,000 members; by 1959 this figure had increased slightly to 61,419. The percentage decline in the Falcons' membership took place, moreover, at a time when many Catholic workers in the Ruhr were shifting their political allegiances from the Christian Democratic Party to the Social Democrats, a development that should have led to a corresponding increase within the ranks of the Falcons.

3 In 1933, the last year before the war for which statistical information is available for the archdiocese of Cologne, most parish groups contained twice as many young women as young men. Women outnumbered men in spite of the fact that men had an array of smaller, more specialized organizations at their disposal, such as Kolping, which together made up almost 30 percent of the entire male membership of the BDKJ. By contrast, the few specialized organizations for women, such as Heliand (the female counterpart to Bund Neudeutschland), were insignificant, never numbering more than several thousand.

4   Eva Kolinsky, *Women in West Germany: Life, Work, and Politics* (Oxford, 1989); Klaus-Jörg Ruhl, *Frauen in der Nachkriegszeit* (Munich, 1988), 205–6. Between 1952 and 1959, working women as a percentage of the total labor force rose from 30.9 to 33.9. Some women, particularly those who were single or badly off financially, went back to work for economic reasons. Others entered the labor force for social reasons—for a change of pace from life in the home or on the farm.

5   In such cases many young women in their mid- to late teenage years and early twenties were understandably reluctant to commit to the life of a group in a foreign parish where friendships often dated back a dozen or more years.

6   "Warum ich nicht vorzeitig mit Mädchen laufe," *Der Jungführer*, 1952, 200–201; "Es gibt keine anständigen Mädchen mehr!," *Die Befreiung.*

7   Robert Moeller concentrates almost exclusively on the political impact of religious conservatives. According to Moeller, "On questions of economic policy or foreign relations, Adenauer turned elsewhere for advice. But on questions of the family and women's status, Christian Democracy was particularly susceptible to conservative Catholic influence" (*Protecting Motherhood: Women and the Family in the Politics of Postwar West Germany* [Berkeley, 1993], 105). Heide Fehrenbach likewise focuses on the discourse of conservatives; see Fehrenbach, *Cinema in Democratizing Germany: Reconstructing National Identity after Hitler* (Chapel Hill, 1995).

8   As we will see in Chapter 5, one can point to a "time lag" between the western and the southern agrarian regions of Germany. Questions of makeup continued to dominate discussions within the mid- to late 1950s, whereas this issue had largely exhausted itself by this point in the newspapers in the western Catholic dioceses.

9   See Hugh McLeod, *Religion and the People of Western Europe, 1789–1970* (Oxford, 1981), 28–35; David Blackbourn, *Marpingen: Apparitions of the Virgin Mary in Nineteenth-Century Germany* (New York, 1994), 30–31.

10   Ingeborg Rocholl-Gärtner, *Anwalt der Frauen: Hermann Klens: Leben und Werk* (Düsseldorf, 1978), 101–2.

11   I use the phrase "separate but equal" ironically, in full light of the inequalities that this doctrine presupposes.

12   See the collection of materials at BA, B153, 001127 AZ: 9699 Bundesausstellung 1959: Die Familie.

13   Many historians have detailed in great depth the rise of an ideology of domesticity in the nineteenth century. See Joan Scott, *Gender and the Politics of History* (New York, 1988); Leonore Davidoff and Catherine Hall, *Family Fortunes: Men and Women of the English Middle Class, 1780–1850* (London, 1987); Catherine Hall, *White, Male, and Middle Class: Explorations in Feminism and History* (New York, 1992); Bonnie Smith, *Ladies of the Leisure Class: The Bourgeoisie of Northern France in the Nineteenth Century* (Princeton, 1981), among many others. For Germany, see Rebekka Habermas, *Frauen und Männer des Bürgertums: Eine Familiengeschichte, 1750–1850* (Göttingen, 2000); Heinz Reif, *Westfälischer Adel: Von Herrschaftsstand*

zur regionaler Elite (Göttingen, 1979). See also Isabel Hull, *Sexuality, State, and Civil Society in Germany, 1700–1815* (Ithaca, N.Y., 1996); Dagmar Herzog, *Intimacy and Exclusion: Religious Politics in Pre-Revolutionary Baden* (Princeton, 1996); Lynn Abrams, "The Personification of Inequality: Challenges to Gendered Power Relations in the Nineteenth Century Divorce Court," *Archiv für Sozialgeschichte* 38 (1998): 41–56.

14 DAW, Bestand: Dokumentation, K3, Die Entwicklung der Frauenerwerbstätigkeit von 1895–1950; Klaus-Jörg Ruhl, *Verordnete Unterordnung: Berufstätige Frauen zwischen Wirtschaftswachstum und konservativer Ideologie in der Nachkriegszeit, 1945–1963* (Munich, 1994).

15 Ottilie Mosshammer, *Werkbuch der katholischen Mädchenbildung*, pt. 1, *Leben in der Zeit, Zweiter Teil, Wege der Frau* (Freiburg, 1951), 174.

16 In one example of this, a young woman in Würzburg compiled a booklet of sayings given to her by leaders in her parish who sought to mold her behavior after that of Mary. See DAW, KJBW, BJ, K1, Sammlung, Frl. Linda Fischer, booklet, Ein Wort auf den Weg: Maiandachten zu Neumünster, 1951, von Dr. Regens A. Schäfer. Other aphorisms included "Gott hat seine Gnade nicht an die Sterne geknüpft, sondern an ein liebendes Mutterherz" or "Es ist gleichwertvoll, ob man für Gott Kartoffel schält oder Dome baut" and "Ich bin nur ein durchschnittlicher Mensch, aber an diesem durchschnittlichen Menschen arbeite ich härter als der durchschnittliche Mensch."

17 "Marianische Kongregationen einst und jetzt," *Die Jungführerin*, 1954, 143–45.

18 KFG, NL Klens, #570, Die gemeinsamen Übungen der Marianischen Kongregationen (n.d.); HAEK, Gen 23.6.2, Normalsatzungen für die Marianischen Kongregationen in der Erzdiözese Köln, 1957.

19 HAEK, Gen 23.6.1, "Apostolische Konstitution über die Marianischen Kongregationen, Pius Bischof, Diener der Diener Gottes zu immerwährendem Gedenken Übersetzung des lateinischen Textes A.A.S. 27 September 1948, Heilige Apostolische Poenentiarie: Offizium der Ablässe, Zusammenfassung der Ablässe und Priviligen, die der Prima Primaria mit dem Titel von der Verkündigung unserer lieben Frau und den Heiligen Aposteln Petrus und Paulus, welche im Römischen Kolleg der Gesellschaft Jesu errichtet ist, bewilligt worden sind."

20 DAW, KJBW, BJ, K1, Sammlung, Frl. Linda Fischer, JHS.

21 Willy Bokler, "Vorgeschichte und Entstehung der sexualpädagogischen Richtlinien für die Jugendseelsorge," in *Die sexualpädagogischen Richtlinien: Probleme der praktischen Theologie*, ed. Willy Bokler and Heinz Fleckenstein (Mainz, 1967), 22.

22 For one example, see KZG, NLLW, II I b–c, Informationsdienst, Nummer 2, 15 November 1947, which states, "Die zu frühe häufige Begegnung mit dem anderen Geschlecht schwächt das gesunde kritische Urteil, macht platt und fördert den häufig verfrühten Entschluss der völligen Bindung an den anderen Partner, sie denn so oft und so leicht bricht." See also Zur mündlichen Verwendung innerhalb des Bundes . . . "Bei der häufig verfrühten Begegnung

verweichen die Jungen, derweil die Mädchen allzusehr jungenhafte Züge an-
nehmen."

23 "Warum ich nicht vorzeitig mit Mädchen laufe," 200–201.

24 LeFort quotation in "Polarität der Geschlechter," *Der Jungführer*, 1954, 365–70.

25 Rocholl-Gärtner, *Anwalt der Frauen*, 19. See also "Prälat Klens: Wegbereiter für
die Frauenjugend," *Die Wacht*, 2 January 1953.

26 Rocholl-Gärtner, *Anwalt der Frauen*, 22–29.

27 Interview with Josef Rommerskirchen, Bonn, November 1995. Rommerskirchen, who worked with Klens between 1948 and 1951, described him as
pious and gentle but somewhat out of touch with reality (*realitätsentfernt*).

28 Irmtraud Götz von Olenhusen, *Gottesreich, Jugendreich, Deutsches Reich: Junge Generation, Religion und Politik, 1928–1933* (Cologne, 1997), 82.

29 Christel Beilmann, *Eine katholische Jugend in Gottes und dem Dritten Reich: Briefe,
Berichte, Gedrucktes, 1930–1945, Kommentare 1988/89* (Wuppertal, 1989). Beilmann, who later moved to the left politically, provides a critical, firsthand
account of her experiences within the Catholic youth at this time.

30 KFG, NL Klens, #570, Schneider an Vikar Stockman, 21 July 1948.

31 HAEK, NL Heinen, #33, Sommerlager der Jugend, 1948.

32 Martin Klaus, *Mädchen im Dritten Reich: Der Bund Deutscher Mädel* (Cologne, 1983);
Jost Hermand, "All Power to the Women: Nazi Concepts of Matriarchy," in
Journal of Contemporary History 19 (1984): 649–67; Gabriele Kinz, *Der Bund
deutscher Mädel: Ein Beitrag zur Außerschulischen Mädchenerziehung im National-
sozialismus* (Frankfurt, 1990); Dagmar Reese, *Straff aber nicht Stramm: Herb aber
nicht Derb: Zur Vergesellschaftung von Mädchen durch den Bund Deutscher Mädel im
Sozialkulturellen Vergleich Zweier Milieus* (Weinheim, 1989); Birgit Jurgens, *Zur
Geschichte des BDM von 1923 bis 1939* (Frankfurt, 1994).

33 KZG, NLLW, II 1e, Ehe und Familie (n.d., but probably immediately after the
war).

34 KFG, NL Klens, #570, Dr. Schuldis an die Schriftleitung der Zeitschrift "Der
Fährmann," 13 August 1947.

35 Interview with Felix Raabe, Bad Godesberg, November 1995.

36 KFG, NL Klens, #570, Klens an Schneider, 17 August 1946.

37 Mosshammer, *Werkbuch der katholischen Mädchenbildung*, 147; Claudia Koonz,
Mothers in the Fatherland: Women, the Family, and Nazi Politics (New York, 1987).
Koonz's arguments came under widespread attack, particularly from Gisela
Bock.

38 KZG, NLWB, D II, 1, Referat Msgr. Klens zur Lage der Frauenjugendseelsorge,
Die Erste Hauptkonferenz der Katholischen Jugendseelsorge und Jugendor-
ganisationen in den deutschen Diözesen, Bericht an die Diözesen, 29 April–3
May 1946.

39 See Petra Goedde, *GIs and Germans: Culture, Gender, and Foreign Relations, 1945–
1949* (New Haven, 2003), and Maria Höhn, *GIs and Fräuleins: The German-
American Encounter in 1950s West Germany* (Chapel Hill, 2002).

40 HAEK, Gen 23.30.6, Clemens Busch, "Reklameauswüsche—Bekämpfung dieser

Jugendgefährdung," stamped, 15 March 1955, NL Böhler, Zeitschriftensammlung, "Unheil über Schönheitsköniginnen?," Katholische Nachrichten-Agentur, no. 48, 17 April 1956; Joseph Frings, "Kirmesfeiern," *Kirchlicher Anzeiger*, August 12, 1947, 202–4. See Fehrenbach, *Cinema in Democratizing Germany*, on this point as well.

41 CAJ-Essen, CAJ-M 1947, Deutsche Kolpingsfamilie, "Tagungsbericht von der Hauptkonferenz der Führerschaft der kath. Jugend in Hardehausen vom 24.3–28.2," 1947.

42 HAEK, Gen 23.6.1, Erzbischöfliches Seelsorgeamt, "Ist der Standort der älteren weiblichen Unverheirateten in der Jungfrauen oder Frauenseelsorge?," 26 July 1946.

43 "Nochmals: Die Unverheiratete," KZK, 1954, 696.

44 Ibid.

45 HAEK, Gen 23.6.1, Hermann Klens, "Schicksal oder Berufung? Gedanken und Wege zur Seelsorgerlichen Führung der 'Älteren Jungfrauen,'" 28 February 1948. For a larger examination of this theme, see Elizabeth Heinemann, *What Difference Does a Husband Make? Women and Marital Status in Nazi and Postwar Germany* (Berkeley, 1997), 162–75.

46 Mosshammer, *Werkbuch der katholischen Mädchenerziehung*, 86–87.

47 For an excellent discussion of the Catholic ideals for women from the 1930s, see Georg Pahlke, *Trotz Verbot nicht Tot: Katholische Jugend in ihrer Zeit*, vol. 3, 1933–1945 (Paderborn, 1995), 384–87.

48 Klens, in turn, accused Wolker of overdoing the "romantic" aspects of the youth movement: "auch ein Weg, die Gefahr einer romantischen lebensfremden Überbetonung des Jungseins zu überwinden" (HAEK, Gen 23.6.1, Hermann Klens, "Schicksal oder Berufung," 6).

49 Bokler, "Vorgeschichte und Entstehung," 22–23. Wolker was not the only youth leader who strove to revise the church's condemnations of masturbation. In 1941–42 Augustinus Reineke also put together new guidelines, which were likewise put back in the closet by church leaders who regarded this issue as too touchy to be dealt with publicly. See Georg Pahlke and Wilhelm Pohlmann, eds., *Jugendhaus Hardehausen: 40 Jahre, 1945–1985* (Paderborn, 1985), 52.

50 Rocholl-Gärtner, *Anwalt der Frauen*, 74–77.

51 Interview with Rommerskirchen; interview with Bernd Börger, Düsseldorf, 1995.

52 JHH, 1.2201.3, München-Fürstenriedkonferenz, 26 April 1947. See Klens's comments: "Es ist die Sorge, dass die Anliegen der Mädchenseelsorge nicht genügend zu ihrem Recht kommt. Die Gründe liegen vielleicht darin, dass man die Anliegen der Mädchenseelsorge nicht ernst genug nimmt. Ein zweiter Grund ist, dass verschiedene Schwierigkeiten entstanden sind durch Übergriffe der Mannesjugend in die Frauenjugendarbeit."

53 HAEK, Gen 23.11.2, Ausgaben—Etat Hauptstelle. According to these figures, the male organizations—*Mannesjugend*—although they were in the minority, were to receive 100,000 reichsmarks; the female organizations, 84,000. This

document has no date but probably stems from 1948. Others noted that male youth organizations received special subsidies from the bishops—perks that the female youth organizations, as of 1952, had apparently not received. See HAEK, Gen 23.6.2, Seelsorge- und Jugendamt der Erzdiözese Köln, Josef Querbach, an das Generalvikariat, Köln, 25 January 1952.

54 HAEK, Gen 23.6.1, Schneider (Seelsorgeamt für Jungmädchen und Jungfrauen) an Stohr, 16 February 1950.

55 JHD, 10, "Mädchen und Frauen im BDKJ: Gesichtspunkte aus einem Treffen mit Ehemaligen, 1984, Frauenforum." Within the BDKJ, each of the two female leaders, the two male lay leaders, and the two clerics (one for the male youth, one for the female youth) had one vote.

56 Ibid.

57 CAJ-Essen, CAJ-FJ 1949, Bericht über den Schulungstag der CAJ-Frauenjugend, am 10.7.1948. This group evinced a mixture of conservatism and radicalism. "Die Art der Frau ist immer irgendwie mütterlich. Allerdings dürfen wir uns unter einer Mutter nicht allein die Sanftmütige, Stille und Zärtliche vorstellen. Auch die Mutter muss zuweilen hart zufassen, muss auch einmal Schläge ausstellen, und wenn es sein muss, kämpfen für Kinder. Auch der 'männliche Mut' der makabäischen Mutter ist nicht männlich in dem oben genannten Sinne, sondern entspricht dem Bilde der Mutter, die zur gegebenen Zeit auch heroischen Mut im Kampfe, nicht nur im Leiden, beweisen muss, im Interesse des Lebens, das ihrem Schutze anvertraut ist."

58 CAJ-Essen, CAJ M-F 1948, an Karl, 5 October 1948.

59 HAEK, Gen 23.2.3, Toni Vogelwiesche an Frings, 17 September 1948, and Vogelwiesche an Frings, 1 May 1948.

60 This issue gave rise to prolonged struggles in the late 1940s, as the male CAJ repeatedly denied the women's request for a workers' organizations solely for women.

61 CAJ-Essen, CAJ-FJ 1948, letter marked "Essen, den 19.5.1951., Liebe Lina!"

62 CAJ-Essen, CAJ-F 1959–61, 1950, Ortsausschuss-Sitzung der CAJ-Frauenjugend Essen am 2. März im Stadtsekretariat. The women also adamantly rejected calls for coed swimming. See CAJ-FJ 1948, "2. Teil des Schulungstages am 16.7.49 in St. Ignatius."

63 CAJ-Essen, CAJ-F 1959–61, Ortsausschuss-Sitzung der CAJ-Frauenjugend Essen am 2. März 1949 im Stadtsekretariat.

64 CAJ-Essen, CAJ-F 1959–61, 1950, Ortsausschuss-Sitzung am 6.7.1949.

65 Ibid., Ortsausschuss-Sitzung am 2. November 1949 im Stadtsekretariat.

66 Interview with Christel Beilmann, Witten, 19 December 1995.

67 Letter, Christel Beilmann to Mark Ruff, 18 August 1996. Beilmann also mentioned that other marriages were successful.

68 JHD, 10.4, "Warum haben die sozialen Frauenberufe keinen Nachwuchs?," 1954.

69 Ibid., 457.

70 Ibid., 484.

71 Ibid., 520.

72 Ibid., 484, 520.

73 Ibid., 484.

74 Ibid., 568.

75 These figures are all the more remarkable in light of the fact that life expectancy for women over age sixty-five is typically seven to eight years longer than for men. See Archiv des Deutschen Caritasverbandes, Zentralrat des DCV, October 1953, Sonderbericht betr. Dorfcaritas, Die Landfamilie in ihrer helfenden Kraft in der Sorge der Caritas.

76 See the reprint of this speech in "Jahresthema: Das christliche Menschenbild," Der junge Katholik: Die Jugendbeilage des "Christlicher Beobachter," January 1955.

77 HAEK, Gen 23.6.2, Secretary for Cardinal Frings an Studienrätin Baumhauer, 30 December 1954.

78 "Jahresthema."

79 Erich Fromm, Arbeiter und Angestellte am Vorabend des Dritten Reiches: Eine sozial-psychologische Untersuchung (Stuttgart, 1967).

80 DAW, JA-Kirchliche—K1; P. Saturnin Pauleser, O.F.M., Schönheit, Liebe und Glück (Würzburg, 1955).

81 "Krach mit Lieselotte," KZK, 1952, 648.

82 Ibid.

83 Ibid.

84 "Um Lieselotte und Peter, Discussion III," KZK, 1952, 711.

85 Ibid.

86 "Um Lieselotte und Peter, Diskussion IV," KZK, 1952, 725.

87 "Um Lieselotte und Peter, Diskussion V," KZK, 1952, 740.

88 Ibid.

89 "Strich Darunter! Ein Schlußwort der Schriftleitung zu unserer Diskussion um Peter und Lieselotte," KZK, 1953, 37.

90 "Um Lieselotte und Peter, Diskussion VIII (VII)," KZK, 1953, 9.

91 "Um Lieselotte und Peter, Diskussion IV," KZK, 1952, 725.

92 The editors also admitted that they had taken some liberties with the original letters printed—the letter from Uncle Wilhelm came from another debate—but had not hesitated to print letters critical of church positions.

93 "Strich Darunter," 37.

94 "Um Lieselotte und Peter, Diskussion VIII (VII)," KZK, 1953, 9.

95 See the discussion between August and October 1960 in Der Pflug, a newspaper for the KLJB in southern Germany. See an article in October 1960 titled, "Sind Mädchen schlechter?," 20.

96 DAW, Kasten, BDKJ, Jubiläumsausstellung (1987), Burg Rothenfels, 1954, 1964.

97 Ibid.

98 See DAW, Kasten Jugendarbeit, 1960–4, BDKJ, Liebe will gelernt sein (no author, n.d.).

99 BDKJ-Würz, folder 5, "Autorität der Liebe erforderlich," *Allgemeines Volksblatt*, 8 May 1962.

100 DAW, LV/LB, LVHS, K3, "Themenvorschläge für die Familienarbeit—Diözese Würzburg."

101 Interview with Frau Börger, Jugendhaus Düsseldorf, November 1995.

102 KFG, NL Klens, #570, P. Deitmar, "Die Bedeutung der M.K. für die Jetztzeit" (n.d., probably 1947).

103 "MC oder Bund?—MC im Bund," *Die Jungführerin*, 1954, 208–9.

104 KFG, NL Klens, #570, Christian Siepchen an Schneider, 7 July 1947. Schneider confirmed the existence of this situation for the archdiocese of Cologne, although he admitted that conditions had not deteriorated as much as they had in Mainz. See ibid., Schneider an Siepchen, 19 July 1949.

105 Ibid., Auf alten Wegen in neuer Zeit: Referat von P. Dietz, S.J., am Feste Lichtmeaß, 1944, 9.

106 For the criticism of this approach, see JHD, A526, HV, 55–58, Neuaufbau beziehungsweise Umbau der Mcen: Ein Tagungsbericht, 10 (undoubtedly from late 1954).

107 KFG, NL Klens, #570, Auf alten Wegen in neuer Zeit: Die Marianische Pfarr-Kongregation (MC); HAEK, Gen 23.6.2, Leitsätze für die MC der Frauen-jugend in der Erzdiözese Köln, 16 December 1955.

108 HAEK, Gen 23.6.2, Leitsätze.

109 Ibid., Joseph Querbach an Frings, 16 December 1955. See also "MC oder Bund? MC im Bund!," 208–9.

110 KFG, NL Klens, #570, Schneider an das Kongregations-Sekretariat Zürich, 28 February 1948. Wolker himself was personally devoted to Marian traditions and devotions but separated his own spirituality from his work. See also a quotation from a letter from 3 March 1949: "Aus unserer Arbeitsgemeinschaft ist nicht das geworden, was wir wollten, und es wird auch nicht das, was wir erhofften."

111 HAEK, Gen 23.6.2, Normalsatzungen für die marianischen Kongregationen im Erzdiözese Köln und dazu betreffend Zusatzbemerkung zu den Kongrega-tionen der Frauenjugend und der Frauen, gez., Josef Querbach, G. Alfes and J. Hanrath, 16 September 1957.

112 Ibid., Querbach an Frings, 12 November 1954. "Die noch bestehenden Mar-ianischen Kongregationen sind praktisch mit ihren Jugendgruppen im BDKJ. . . . In Gemeinschaftsleben ist kaum ein Unterschied zu den anderen Stamm-gruppen, die nicht MC sind, vielleicht nur, daß die Aufnahme in den Bund in der Form der Aufnahme in die MC geschieht, daß die monatliche Glaubens-stunde in der Form der MC-Versammlung gehalten wird, daß das Titelfest der MC als das jährliche Fest der weiblichen Jugend gilt."

113 HAEK, Gen 23.4.1, P. O. Semmelroth, "Theologische Begründung und prak-tische Gestaltung des marianischen Gedankens in der Führung der Jugend," *Korrespondenz der Präsides und Theologen Marianischer Kongregationen*, December 1952, 2–9.

114 HAEK, NL Heinen #33.

115 JHD, A526, HV, 55–58, "Neuaufbau beziehungsweise Umbau der Mcen: Ein Tagungsbericht," 4.

116 In another example, a young youth worker wrote to Frings bemoaning the fact that her Marian week was poorly attended. See HAEK, Gen 23.6.2, Trude Pfeiffer an Frings, 22 April 1958.

117 "Austritt aus der Gruppe? Warum?," *Die Jungführerin*, 1955, 140–41.

118 ZDK, "Frauenjugendfragen," in *Der Christ in der Zeit—72. Deutscher Katholikentag, 1948, Herausgegeben vom Generalsekretariat des Zentralkomitee der Katholiken*, 1949, 123.

119 "Moderne Frömmigkeit: Ein Gespräch," *Die Jungführerin*, 1955–56, 260–61.

120 HAEK, Gen 23.6.2, Christa Vollbach an Frings, Langenfeld, 2 January 1958.

121 Ibid., L. Schöller an Vollbach, 10 January 1958.

122 As quoted in *Die Wacht*, 19 November 1951.

123 ZDK, "Frauenjugendfragen," 125.

CHAPTER 4

1 For one overview of the CAJ, see Dietmar Grypa, *Die Katholische Arbeiterbewegung in Bayern nach dem Zweiten Weltkrieg, 1945–1960* (Paderborn, 2000), 244–59, and Mark Edward Ruff, "Die CAJ in Deutschland: Vom adoptierten Kind zum Sorgenkind," in *Christliche Arbeiterbewegung in Europa*, ed. Claudia Hiepel and Mark Edward Ruff (Stuttgart, 2003), 64–82.

2 Kolping, Schriftverkehr A-K, 1, Rempe an Baur, 5 October 1951. Many parish associations were, in fact, groups of young artisans, or Kolping groups. Few records for ordinary parish groups have been preserved by diocesan officials, aside from general reports issued by the leaders of the BDKJ in the late 1940s and early 1950s.

3 The arrival of refugees from the east scarcely altered the confessional landscape. North Rhine–Westphalia received one of the smallest percentages of refugees anywhere in South and West Germany. Only 7.4 percent of the population consisted of refugees in the mid-1950s, compared with 37.8 percent in Schleswig-Holstein. Of these 1.4 million refugees who found themselves in the region, nearly two-thirds settled in Westphalia, and only 470,000 chose to resettle in the Rhineland. See Jörg Engelbrecht, *Landesgeschichte Nordrhein-Westfalen* (Stuttgart, 1994), 321. In some cities, however, refugees made up a sizable share of the population. In Euskirchen, refugees comprised nearly 13 percent of the population in 1955. See Detlef Briesen, "Vom Durchbruch der Wohlstandsgesellschaft und vom Ende des Wachstums, 1955–1995," in *Gesellschafts- und Wirtschaftsgeschichte Rheinlands und Westfalens*, ed. Detlef Briesen, Gerhard Brunn, Rainer Elkar, and Jürgen Reulecke (Cologne, 1995), 202–68.

4 HAEK, Bestand Z50, Handbuch 1954, Statistik über die Seelsorgebezirke, die Geistliche und die Bevölkerung der Erzdiözese für die Jahre 1915–1952.

5   Friedrich-Wilhelm Henning, *Düsseldorf und seine Wirtschaft: Zur Geschichte einer Region*, vol. 2, *Von 1860 bis zur Gegenwart* (Düsseldorf, 1981).

6   Wolfgang Zorn, "Die Struktur der Rheinischen Wirtschaft in der Neuzeit," *Rheinische Vierteljahrsblätter* (1963): 37–62.

7   Kardorf, in the deanery of Alfter, a rural region in the Vorgebirge, totaled 755 members, according to official statistics from 1958. See HAEK, Bestand Z50, Handbuch 1958, Alfter-Kardorf.

8   Ibid.

9   Ibid., Handbuch 1954, Leverkusen-Wiesdorf.

10 Werner Abelshauser und Ralf Himmelmann, *Revolution in Rheinland und Westfalen: Quellen zu Wirtschaft, Gesellschaft und Politik, 1918–1923* (Essen, 1988).

11 Siegfried Gehrmann, *Fußball—Vereine—Politik: Zur Sportgeschichte des Reviers, 1900–1940* (Essen, 1988), 160.

12 Hans-Werner Frohn, *Arbeiterbewegungskulturen in Köln, 1880–1933* (Essen, 1997), 309.

13 Karl Rohe, "Politische Traditionen im Rheinland, in Westfalen und Lippe: Zur politischen Kultur Nordrhein-Westfalen," in *Nordrhein-Westfalen: Eine politische Landeskunde*, ed. Die Landeszentrale für politische Bildung Nordrhein-Westfalen (Cologne, 1984), 14–34.

14 Ulrich von Hehl, *Priester unter Hitlers Terror: Eine Biographische und statische Erhebung* (Paderborn, 1996).

15 Wilfried Evertz, "Im Spannungsfeld zwischen Staat und Kirche," in *Studien zur Kölner Kirchengeschichte*, ed. Historisches Archiv des Erzbistums Köln (Siegburg, 1992), 336–37.

16 For a full account of the effect of the war on the archdiocese, see HAEK, Gen 32.30, Bericht über die Seelsorge in der Erzdiözese Köln in den Jahren 1939–1946. The account presented above is partially drawn from this report, but it should be pointed out that the tone of this report, as it pertained to youth work, remained optimistic. See also Otto Roegele, "Der Deutsche Katholizismus im sozialen Chaos: Eine nüchterne Bestandsaufnahme, *Hochland*, 1948–49, 205–33.

17 HAEK, Gen 23.11.4, Bericht des Erzbischöflichen Jugendamtes m.J. Köln über seine arbeit im Jahre 1947, Köln im Januar 1948, Fritz Eink.

18 HAEK, Gen 23.11.5, Bericht des Erzbischöflichen Jugendamtes m.J. Köln über seine Arbeit im Jahre 1948, Fritz Eink, Diözesanjugendseelsorger. This number was based on those who belonged to parishes.

19 These figures are based on numbers provided by handbooks for the archdiocese of Cologne for 1933 and 1954. As discussed in the introduction, the accuracy of these figures is highly questionable and, at most, general trends can be discerned.

20 KZG, NLLW, II 1 a, Fritz Eink, Einrichtung von Aktivgruppen in Werken und Betrieben, die "Werkaktivs," Cologne, 10 September 1946.

21 HAEK, Gen 23.3.2, Leppich an Pater Schmitz (26 October, no year).

22   Ibid., Wolker and Klens an Frings, 14 March 1947.

23   The JOC was an organization with a hierarchy, of larger groups at deanery and diocesan levels. For these reasons, church leaders considered it to be in the tradition of Catholic Action. It embodied militancy but was clearly organized along diocesan lines.

24   HAEK, Gen 23.2.3, Wolker an Berning, 28 February 1948. Wolker noted that it was the intent of the pontiff to bring the JOC to Germany, a statement that might be interpreted to mean that Pius XII had pressured the German bishops.

25   CAJ-Essen, CAJ M-F 1948, Rom oder Moskau, P. Leppich am 4.9.48 auf dem Burgplatz in Essen. For another account of his tour, see Bericht über die 2, Großkundgebung der C.A.J. Düsseldorf am 21.2.48.

26   Some members of the CAJ maintained that their organization was actually born years earlier out of contacts between French and Belgian forced labor and German workers in German factories during the war, for which several of the young Catholic fighters had died martyrs' deaths. See interview with Erika Köster, Essen, November 1995; "Sie steckten auch die Deutschen an," KZK, 7 June 1985.

27   CAJ-Essen, CAJ M-F 1948, CAJ, Hauptsekretariat, Die Arbeitsgemeinschaft der CAJ, Schulung Blatt 2 (n.d.).

28   Ibid., Jahreskonferenz der Diözesanjugendseelsorger in Limburg vom 16. bis 21. Juli 1948, 7, Drucksache.

29   JHH, 1.2201.3, München-Fürstenried Konferenz, 1949, P. Johannes Leppich, Erfahrungen und Aufgabe der Christlichen Arbeiterjugend, Fürstenried, 27 April 1947.

30   CAJ-Essen, CAJ M-F 1953, 4, 5, Die CAJ-Freundschaft (n.d., no author).

31   CAJ-Essen, CAJ M-F 1949, Alfred Kaiser an Sroka, 2 March 1949.

32   CAJ-Essen, CAJ-M 1949, Tagung von 24.4.49 bis 24.4.49 in Wiesbaden, 41, Protokoll des Zentralausschusses, 5, 6 September 1949, Essen, 9. See also CAJ-Essen, CAJ-M 1947, Fuer oder wider die Romantik in der Junge-CAJ (n.d.).

33   CAJ-Essen, Mitteilungen des Gebietssekretariates Köln, August/September 1957, no. 8/9, Jungarbeiter aller Länder in Rom.

34   CAJ-Essen, CAJ M-F 1951–52, Protokoll zur Westdeutschen Studientagung der CAJ, K. Vallot, Aachen, 20 January 1951, and Die CAJ als Nationale Bewegung, 3 N. St.W., 17–28 November 1952.

35   CAJ-Essen, Mitgliederstatistik, 1956–63, #2, 1 January 1956.

36   Ibid., 10 March 1959, Christliche Arbeiter-Jugend, Nationalleitung.

37   Wilhelm Damberg, Abschied vom Milieu? Katholizismus im Bistum Münster und in den Niederlanden, 1945–1980 (Paderborn, 1997), 217. Diocesan leaders were also motivated by the failure of Christian trade unions, a development that was linked to the difficulties in the CAJ and the KAB.

38   CAJ-Essen, CAJ M-F 1948, Sroka an Wolker, 10 November 1948.

39   Ibid., Sroka an Deschuyffeleer, 1 October 1948.

40   Ibid., Karl Sroka an Diözesanseelsroger, Osnabrück, 29 June 1948.

41   JHD, CAJ, Paul Gail an die Bundesführung des Bundes der Deutschen Kathol-

ischen Jugend, 1 November 1952. Gail complained of having been abandoned and even "stabbed in the back" by the *Bund* during its ongoing war with the KAB.

42   On the rivalries that emerged in Düsseldorf between the KAB and the CAJ, see HAEK, Gen 23.3, Anlage zum Schreiben der CAJ-Düsseldorf vom 13.9.1948 an Seine Eminenz. On the KAB and its difficulties, see HAEK, Gen 23.2.13, Rolf Diekamp an Frings, 12 November 1959.

43   HAEK, Gen 23.2.8, Schmitt an Generalvikar Teusch, 12 August 1954.

44   JHD, CAJ4, 1953–55, Frings an die Verbandsleitung der KAB, Verbandsleitung der CAJ, Verbandsleitung des Kolpingwerkes und die Bundesführung des Bundes der Deutschen Katholischen Jugend, 4 April 1955.

45   HAEK, Gen 23.2.10, Schmitt an Frings, 28 October 1957; Kolping, Jugendreferat, Bundesführungsamt, BDKJ, 1953–9, 1957; Kolping, BDKJ und Jungkolping, 4–7 (n.d., but probably 1957).

46   HAEK, Gen 23.2.2, Cardijn, Visite en Allemagne, 2 April 1947.

47   Ibid., Cardijn an Frings, 31 March 1948. See also Gen 23.2.3, Voyage de Jef Deschuyffeleer en Allemagne, Conclusions, 25 February 1948.

48   CAJ-Essen, CAJ-M 1947, Kaplan Reintges, Denkschrift zur Entwicklung der "Christlichen Arbeiterjugend (CAJ) in Deutschland" (n.d., but 1947).

49   HAEK, Gen 23.3.2, Jef Deschuyffeleer and Patrick Keegan aux membres du Comite Central de la C.A.J., Essen, 18 November 1947; HAEK, Gen 23.2.8, Paul Gail, Die CAJ in der Erzdiözese Köln (Bericht des Gebietskaplans), 14 December 1953.

50   CAJ-Essen, CAJ-M 1947, Kaplan Reintges, Denkschrift zur Entwicklung der "Christlichen Arbeiterjugend (CAJ) in Deutschland" (n.d., but 1947).

51   HAEK, Gen 23.2.8, Paul Gail, Die CAJ in der Erzdiözese Köln (Bericht des Gebietskaplans), 14 December 1953.

52   CAJ-Essen, CAJ-M 1947, an Eugen (Kurz), 1 October 1947.

53   HAEK, Gen 23.2.3, Werner Ott an Frings, 16 August 1948, 2; CAJ-Essen, CAJ-M 1947, Tagung der West-Sekretariate, 1 August 1947, and Koch an Wolker, 3 March 1947.

54   HAEK, Gen 23.2.8, Paul Gail, Die CAJ in der Erzdiözese Köln (Bericht des Gebietskaplans), 14 December 1953.

55   Interview with Paul Gail, Euskirchen, November 1995.

56   CAJ-Essen, CAJ-M 1947, Mitteilungen aus dem Leben katholischer Mannes-Jugend im Erzbistum Köln, September 1947, 11.

57   See *Die Befreiung*, December 1952.

58   HAEK, Gen 23.2.7, Die Kath. Arbeiterbewegung im westdeutschen Braunkohlengebiet, 2 February 1953.

59   CAJ-Essen, CAJ M-F 1949, Sroka an Eink, 16 February 1949.

60   HAEK, Gen 23.2.7, Entwicklung und Stand der CAJ in Deutschland (no author, n.d., but probably the early 1950s).

61   HAEK, Gen 23.2.5, Sroka an Frings, 11 March 1951.

62   HAEK, Gen 23.2.8, Fruchtbares Experiment: Zur Diskussion um die Frage der französischen Arbeiterpriester, taken from KNA—Nr. 70, 23, March 1954/B.

63 HAEK, Gen 23.2.4, Eine Jugendgruppe aus Essen an das Generalvikariat, 31 January 1950. It must be pointed out, however, that this was not a CAJ group; it nonetheless underscored the criticisms of the church that were widespread among many working youths.

64 HAEK, Gen 23.2.13, Wissenschaftlicher Ausschuß zur Erarbeitung eines Schwerpunktsprogramms für die Arbeiterseelsorge, Protokoll der Sitzung vom 7. Nov. 1959 im Kettelerhaus, Köln, "Viele sind der Auffassung, daß die Kirche das 'Ueberholte', 'Gestrige', 'Vergangene' vertrete und hinter dem 'Fortschritt' nachhinke. Zur Begründung verweist man etwa auf die aus dem vorindustriellen Zeitalter stammende Kleidung der Ordensleute und des Klerus."

65 Ibid.

66 *Die Befreiung*, 1958.

67 HAEK, Gen 23.2.8, Paul Gail, Die CAJ in der Erzdiözese Köln (Bericht des Gebietskaplans), 14 December 1953, 1.

68 Ibid.

69 HAEK, Gen 23.2.13, Wissenschaftlicher Ausschuß zur Erarbeitung eines Schwerpunktsprogramms für die Arbeiterseelsorge, Protokoll der Sitzung vom 4.9.1959 in Bad Godesberg.

70 CAJ-Essen, CAJ M-F 1948, Adele Caspari an Sroka, Köln-Mülheim, 8 August 1948, and Sroka an Caspari, 20 August 1948.

71 Martin Rüther, *Zwischen Zusammenbruch und Wirtschaftswunder: Betriebsratstätigkeit und Arbeiterverhalten in Köln, 1945 bis 1962* (Bonn, 1991), 573.

72 Josef Mooser, *Arbeiterleben in Deutschland, 1900–1970: Klassenlage, Kultur und Politik* (Frankfurt, 1984).

73 Ibid., 228.

74 HAEK, Gen 23.2.12, Paul Gail, Willi Fassbender, und Alfred Becker an Frings, Jahresbericht der Gebietsleitung der CAJ im Gebiet Köln über das Jahr 1958, 8.

75 Ibid., 7.

76 CAJ-Essen, Rechenschaft des Nationalkaplans J. Ascherl an den NA vom C./7. Mai 1959, quoted in Christliche Arbeiterjugend (CAJ): Von der Romwallfahrt bis zum Ersten Kongress in Essen: 1955 bis 1966, Theologische Diplomarbeit von Reiner Bleil, Philosophisch—Theologische Hochschule Sankt Georgen, Frankfurt am Main, 23.

77 CAJ-Essen, "Die deutsche CAJ in der deutschen Arbeiterjugend: Ein Bericht des Nationalleiters des deutschen CAJ, Horst Roos, für den Internationalen Rat der CAJ, Nach Unterlagen aus der Untersuchung der deutschen CAJ über die Lehrlingsfrage aus dem Jahre 1955 und über die religiöse Lage der Jungarbeiter aus dem Jahre 1956, angefertigt im März 1957," 10.

78 See also Uta Poiger, *Jazz, Rock, and Rebels: Cold War Politics and American Culture in a Divided Germany* (Berkeley, 2000).

79 HAEK, Gen 23.2.12, Julius Angerhausen, Jahresbericht des Christlichen Arbeiter-Jugend, 11 March 1958.

80 Interview with Gail.

81 For an excellent overview, see Heiner J. Wirtz, *Katholische Gesellenvereine und*

Kolpingsfamilien im Bistum Münster, 1852–1960, "Gott zur Ehre und den Gesellen zum Vorteil" (Münster, 1999).

82 Kolping, Diözese Köln (from a Schematismus, n.d.). This set of data listed all of the Kolping organizations and their founding year.

83 This setup may also have been a response to attacks by the Nazi regime in the 1930s.

84 For a critical summary of this philosophy, see CAJ-Essen, CAJ-M 1947, "Wie stehen wir zur Kolpingsfamilie?," 13 June 1947.

85 AKKZG, Kolping, "Die Krisis im katholischen Organisationswesen," in *Korrespondenz-Blatt für katholische Jugendpräsides*, 1. Vierteljahrheft 1923.

86 Kolping, vol. 72, Mitgliederbewegung seit 1865.

87 Kolping, Zentralversammlung der Deutschen Kolpingsfamilie vom 12.–14. Okt. 1956 im Adam Stegerwald-Haus in Königswinter, "Das Kolpingwerk an der Schwelle der neuen Zeit," Referent: Dr. Johannes Nattermann, 4–5. These arguments were summarized by Nattermann, one of the leaders of Kolping, in his brief account of the history of the organization. Many members in the youth and liturgical movements, especially those in Quickborn, objected to alcohol and nicotine as "impure."

88 Kolping, vol. 72, Mitgliederbewegung seit 1865.

89 For a solid but cautious account of Kolping during the Third Reich, see Heinz-Albert Raem, *Katholischer Gesellenverein und Deutsche Kolpingsfamilie in der Ära des Nationalsozialismus* (Mainz, 1982).

90 Kolping, Kölner Werkbrief für die Diözesanleitungen der Kolpingsfamilie, no. 1, March 1947, 7.

91 Kolping, Diözese Köln, 12. This book listed the Kolpingsfamilien and their founding dates.

92 Kolping, Kölner Werkbrief für die Diözesanleitungen der Kolpingsfamilie, no. 1, March 1947, 7.

93 Jürgen Aretz, *Katholische Arbeiterbewegung und Nationalsozialismus: Der Verband katholischer Arbeiter- und Knappenvereine Westdeutschlands, 1923–1945* (Mainz, 1978).

94 Kolping, vol. 80b, Statistik II, Gliederung der Deutschen Kolpingsfamilie nach der Grössenordnung der Gemeinden, Ergebnis einer statistischen Auswertung des Stammbuches Mitte 1955, verglichen mit den Einwohnerzahlen von 1949.

95 Kolping, vol. 80b, Statistik II, Berufszugehörigkeit der Mitglieder der Gruppe Kolping in der Deutschen Kolpingsfamilie auf Grund einer Auszählung des Stammbuches im Sommer 1955.

96 Kolping, vol. 50, Rempe an Arnold, 26 May 1955.

97 Kolping, vol. 80a, b, Statistik, Statistische Erhebung, "Warum bist Du Mitglied der Kolpingsfamilie geworden?"

98 Kolping, Rundschreiben no. 2/47, Essen, 15 January 1947.

99 Kolping, vol. 75, Fernunterricht notwendig und gefragt, von Berufsschuldirektor Jakob Dams (n.d., but probably from the 1930s).

100 Kolping, Heribert Bick, Die Umschulung von Kriegsversehrten und ihr Einsatz in Handwerksbetrieben (n.d.).

101 Kolping, vol. 75, Der Stand der beruflichen Bildungsarbeit (n.d.).

102 Ibid., An die Kolpingsfamilie, betrf. AFAG-Fernunterricht /M (n.d., but probably late 1950s).

103 Kolping, vol. 80, Statistik I, Ergebnisenbogen der statistischen Erhebung, "Weshalb bis Du Mitglied der Kolpingsfamilie geworden?," Ergebnisbogen von insgesamt 280 Fragebogen (n.d.).

104 Kolping, vol. 50, Rempe an den Vorstand der Kolpingsfamilie Steinfeld i.O, 9 April 1954. This memorandum laid out Kolping's policy toward drinking and festivals, itself a sign that many groups had enjoyed raucous festivals and parties. It is doubtful, however, whether church leaders succeeded in enforcing these directives.

105 Wirtz, *Katholische Gesellenvereine und Kolpingsvereine im Bistum Münster*, 203.

106 Kolping, vol. 72, Zahl der Kolpingsfamilien, DV Köln.

107 Ibid., Mitgliederzahl, DV Köln. This picture was very similar to that in the diocese of Münster. Heiner Wirtz sees the turning point as taking place in 1960, when the number of new recruits began to decline. See Wirtz, *Katholische Gesellenvereine und Kolpingsvereine im Bistum Münster*, 203–10.

108 Kolping, vol. 72, Zahl der Neuaufnahmen, DV Köln.

109 Kolping, vol. 80b, Statistik II, Altersaufbau der Deutschen Kolpingsfamilie, 1 July 1954.

110 Kolping, vol. 42, Die Bildungsaufgabe der Wanderschaft in unserer Zeit (n.d.).

111 Ibid., Rempe an Otto Schmitt, 10 October 1963.

112 Ibid., Wandernde Handwerksburschen sterben aus, excerpt from *Neuer Landes-Deinst Düsseldorf*, 24 August 1960.

113 Ibid., Rempe, Märzenluft und Wandersehnsucht (n.d., but possibly 1950).

114 Ibid., Wanderbücher, ausgestellt ab 3.8. 1951 (n.d., but probably 1968).

115 Ibid., Übersicht über die berufliche Wanderschaft, 4 January 1952, and Überschrift nach Diözesangangehörigkeit, 20 March 1958.

116 Ibid., Lorenz Bauseweinan das Berufsbildungswerk, 17 July 1952. The leader of the program disputed these allegations, noting that free breakfasts and dinners were offered in the Kolping houses. See ibid., Rempe an Bausewein, 19 August 1952, Rempe an Berthold Haas, 9 October 1952.

117 Ibid., Wanderordnung (n.d.).

118 Ibid., Mayr an Rempe, 31 May, 10 June 1956; Rempe an Kolpingsbruder, 25 April 1952.

119 Kolping, vol. 75, Zur Geschichte des Fernunterrichtes der Deutschen Kolpingsfamilie, Überblick über den Fernunterricht seit 1947, 19 March 1964.

120 Kolping, Roland Neuner, "Die Entstehung der Kolpingjugend nach dem Zweiten Weltkrieg," February 1993.

121 HAEK, CR II, 22.17.5, Ridder an Frings, 19 March 1952.

122 Kolping, Jugendreferat, Bunderführungsrat, BDKJ, 1953–9, Memorandum der Deutschen Kolpingsfamilie zum Verhältnis "Bund Deutscher Katholischer Jugend" und "Deutsche Kolpingsfamilie" (n.d.), Ergebnisbericht der Bacharacher Konferenz (n.d.).

123 Kolping, vol. "Verbände," Aktennotiz über das Koordinierungsgespräch zwischen Deutscher Kolpingsfamilie und Bund der Deutschen Katholischen Jugend bzw. Kath. Jungmänner-Gemeinschaft unter Leitung von Sr. Exzellenz Dr. Albert Stohr, 22 May 1958. This pattern was hardly new. In the 1910s and 1920s, tensions had arisen between Kolping and the Katholischer Jungmännerverband over the same questions of how to unify Catholic youth and maintain the independence of individual *Verbände*. See Kolping, Bezüglich des Verhältnisses der kathol. Gesellenvereine zu den Jünglingsvereinigungen, 14 August 1915.

124 Kolping, vol. "Verbände," Bericht über das Treffen der Gliedgemeinschaften des B.D.K.J. in Altenberg am 11.9.1958, 2, and Jugendreferat, Bundesführungsrat, BDKJ, 1953–9, BDKJ und Jungkolping, 195, vol. 50, Rempe an Josef Karsch, 27 February 1953.

125 Kolping, vol. 42, Mayr an Rempe, 10 June 1956.

CHAPTER 5

1 For examples of the romanticism of the countryside, see HAEK, Gen 23.58.3, Protokoll der Plenarkonferenz der Bischöfe der Diözesen Deutschlands in Fulda vom 18. bis 20. August 1953, and Gen 23.69.1, Cardinal Josef Frings, Denkschrift über Fragen der Landjugenderziehung, 15 December 1949.

2 The territorial boundaries of the diocese of Würzburg were nearly identical with those of the region of Lower Franconia, as defined by the state.

3 "Land ohne Seele," KZK, 1951, 664–65.

4 HAEK, Gen 23.68.5, Köln und seine täglichen Ein-Pendler, Statistische Untersuchungen nach der Volkszählung von 1950.

5 "Land ohne Seele," 664–65.

6 "Wandlung eines Dorfes," KZK, 1956, 85A.

7 "Land ohne Seele," 664–65.

8 "Landwirtschaft will am 'Wirtschaftswunder' teilhaben," Volksblatt, 6 February 1956.

9 Ibid.; Peter Spitznagel, *Wähler und Wahlen in Unterfranken, 1919–1969: Versuch einer Analyse der Wählerstruktur eines Regierungberzirkers auf statistischer Grundlage nach den Erhebungen der Volkszählungen 1925, 1950, 1961 und 1970* (Paderborn: Schöningh, 1979), table F, Berufliche Gliederung. This estimate places the portion of the population in Lower Franconia engaged in agriculture at 30.7 percent, 24.7 percent for all of Bavaria, and 18.4 percent for the Federal Republic as a whole.

10 Hans Hubert Hofmann and Hermann Hemmerich, *Unterfranken: Geschichte seiner Verwaltungsstrukturen set dem Ende des alten Reiches, 1814 bis 1980* (Würzburg, 1981), 254–58. These figures were tabulated from a list of the *Gymnasien* and their dates of origins.

11 Statistical information from DAW, Schematismus der Diözese Würzburg, 1948, Stand vom 15. Mai 1948. This figure was only 57 percent if one includes the regions of Meiningen in Thuringia, which were part of the Soviet zone of occupation.

12 Hofmann and Hemmerich, *Unterfranken*, 278–80. The total number of parishes listed for 1955 was 503. This figure included, however, what were called Lokalkaplanien, Expositorkaplanien, Schlosskuratien, and Provisatorische Kuratien. Some of the Lokalkaplanien were elevated to full parish status during the late 1940s and early 1950s, so an exact tabulation is difficult.

13 The organizations for young artisans tellingly disavowed the name Kolping and simply called themselves "journeyman's organizations" (*Gesellenvereine*); see DAW, Bestand, Dokumentation, Werkvolk/CAJ, K3, "Freiheit fordert Verantwortung: Eine Darstellung aus der Arbeit der Verbandszentrale des Werkvolk Süddeutschen Verband Katholischer Arbeitnehmer" (n.d., but probably 1962). This report noted, "Nach 1945 war eine Antipathie gegen alle Vereine. Wir wollten nicht am Ort, im Raum einer Diözese, in einem Land, in einem größeren Raum wieder Vereine, sondern Volk, Werkvolk."

14 DAW, BDKJ, Ausstellungsmaterial, 1987, Oskar Neisinger an den Bayr. Landesjugendausschuß, 7 November 1946.

15 For biographical sketches of Ehrenfried, see Klaus Wittstadt, *Würzburger Bischöfe, 742–1979* (Würzburg, 1979), 85–88, and "Ein Bischof in schwerer Zeit: Das Wirken Bischof Matthias Ehrenfried im Dritten Reich," *Würzburger Diözesangeschichtsblätter* (1995): 407–20.

16 DAW, Klinkhammer Sammlung, K1, interview, 22 November 1984, Gesprächspartner Oskar Neisinger, Monika Klinkhammer.

17 Interview with Elfriede Bonnländer, Weyersfeld, June 1996.

18 For a fuller account of resistance activities, see Karl-Werner Goldhammer, *Katholische Jugend Frankens im Dritten Reich: Die Situation der katholischen Jugendarbeit unter besonderer Berücksichtigung Unterfrankens und seiner Hauptstadt Würzburg* (Frankfurt, 1987) and "Der Kampf der NSDAP gegen die Katholische Jugendarbeit in Unterfranken," *Würzburger Diözesangeschichtsblätter* (1975): 657–84.

19 Neisinger interview. See also DAW, Klinkhammer Sammlung, K1, interview with Herrn Studiendirektor Karl Heinrich, 27 March 1985.

20 For both cases, see DAW, Klinkhammer Sammlung, interview with Franziska Kimpller, Stadträtin der CSU in Würzburg, 7 March 1985.

21 Goldhammer, *Katholische Jugend Frankens im Dritten Reich*, 374.

22 Neisinger interview.

23 Martin Schwab makes the same point in *Kirche Leben und Gesellschaft Gestalten: Der Bund der Deutschen Katholischen Jugend (BDKJ) in der Bundesrepublik Deutschland und der Diözese Würzburg, 1947–1989* (Würzburg, 1997).

24 DAW, BDKJ, Ausstellungsmaterial, 1989, Neisinger an den Bayr. Landesjugendausschuß, Z.H., Herrn Präsidenten, A. J. Lippl, 7 November 1946.

25 DAW, BDKJ, Jubiläumsausstellung, 1987, Dekanatsjugendseelsorger, Karl Lott, Pfarrer, Waldbüttelbrunn, 7 October 1946, and Waldbüttelbrunn, 23 January 1948.

26 These statistics were probably put together at the behest of American occupation authorities. The deanery of Waldbüttelbrunn was referred to elsewhere as the deanery of Würzburg (left of the Main). The modern-day deanery has

twenty parishes, not the seventeen referred to in the statistical information presumably forwarded to the Americans. It is possible that this set of statistics did not take into account all of the parishes within the region. See DAW, Waldbüttelbrunn, den 23. I. 1948.

27 "Diözesantreffen der Katholischen Jugend in Würzburg, 13 July 1947," *Würzburger Bistumsblatt*, 3 August 1947.

28 It is uncertain how many youth showed up for this festival. Neisinger placed the number at 25,000, but a newspaper account was more conservative and estimated that more than 10,000 attended. See Neisinger interview; "Diözesantreffen der Katholischen Jugend in Würzburg, 13 July 1947."

29 DAW, NL Neisinger, K6, Neisinger an Bokler, 27 September 1953.

30 Neudeutschland never had more than 400 members at this time, for it remained confined to those cities that had *Gymnasien* and higher schools, in this case, Würzburg, Aschaffenburg, Bad Neustadt, and Hassfurt. See BDKJ-Würz, vol. 4, Dekanatsführerkonferenz, Januar 1954, Bericht: Neudeutschland.

31 DAW, KJBW, BJ, K1, folder Drucksachen, Kurzprotokoll über die Jahreskonferenz der Jugendseelsorge, 21, 22 February 1956; BDKJ-Würz, vol. 4, Kurzprotokoll über die Jahreskonferenz der Jugendseelsorger in Würzburg, 13, 14 February 1957.

32 DAW, KJBW, K2, BJ, folder KLJB-Seminare, 1960–2. These documents listed the participants in the social seminars in the deanery of Würzburg. Members of the CAJ included bank apprentices, electricians, and hairdressers. The KLJB included, for instance, white-collar and blue-collar workers and auto repairmen.

33 DAW, Kriten, Jugendarbeit, Zur Situation der kirchlichen Jugendarbeit 1949.

34 Klaus Schmidt, *Wirtschaftsraum Mainfranken: Monographien Deutscher Wirtschaftsgebiete* (Oldenbourg, 1988).

35 Spitznagel, *Wähler und Wahlen in Unterfranken*, table F.

36 Klaus Schmidt, *Wirtschaftsraum Mainfranken*, 76.

37 Spitznagel, *Wähler und Wahlen in Unterfranken*, 54–57.

38 Ibid., 56.

39 Ibid. This statistic refers to the *Landkreise*, not the cities, however.

40 DAW, Schematismus der Diözese Würzburg, Diözesan-Statistik, 1953, 92; Schematismus der Diözese Würzburg, 1962, Übersicht über die Dekanate, 184.

41 HAEK, Gen 23.68.1, Frings an Hermes, 24 April 1950, and Gen 23.68.2, Fillbrandt an Hengsbach, 23 March 1954. Frings and Hermes carried on an extensive correspondence at this time regarding the relationship between the church and the German Farmers' Organization. On these discussions, see Wilhelm Damberg, *Abschied vom Milieu? Katholizismus im Bistum Münster und in den Niederlanden, 1945–1980* (Paderborn, 1997) 392–96. Hermes had been active in the pre-1933 Center Party as well as in the post-1945 CDU.

42 HAEK, Gen 23.68.1, Kulturelle Fragen und Aufgaben der Landseelsorge, Mitte 1950 (no author).

43   Klaus Schmidt, *Wirtschaftsraum Mainfranken*, 76.

44   Spitznagel, *Wähler und Wahlen in Unterfranken*, table G.

45   Ibid.

46   "Realteilung oder geschlossene Hofübergabe? Die besondere Situation in Unterfranken—Bundesgesetz wird erwartet," *Volksblatt*, 16 November 1955.

47   DAW, KLV, KJB, K3, Zusammenfassung landwirtschaftlicher Berufsgenossenschaften, Hauptberufliche land- und forstwirtschaftliche Unternehmer in Unterfranken.

48   DAW, KLV, KJB, K3, Veränkerung der Strukturverhältnisse in Unterfranken zwischen 1949 und 1960, Zusammenstellung Dr. Scheuerpflug (Regierung).

49   DAW, Dokumentation: Landvolk/LJ Kathol., K2, Saat und Sendung: Idee, Entstehung, Aufgabe und Arbeitsweise der KLJB, 3; Heft (Sonderheft), Hg, Landesstelle der Katholischen Jugend, Bayerns- Landjugend, 5.

50   Josef Ryba, *Schonungen: Geschichte eines fränkischen Dorfes* (Würzburg, 1966), 146–47.

51   In 1950 nearly 15 percent of workers continued to live in their own villages and commute to work instead of simply moving to the cities and areas where they worked. According to one study, many commuters continued to till small plots of soil in addition to performing their new work in factories. Others found housing costs in the cities to be prohibitive, while many complained about the lack of open space and poor living conditions. Others did not wish to leave family and friends. Above all, the widespread use of the automobile, moped, and motorcycle made commuting longer distances possible, whereas most workers a generation earlier would have been forced to move to the cities, since the road and rail network was too limited in these rural regions to allow for commuting. See DAW, LV/LJ, K2, Katholische Landvolkbewegung Deutschlands, Zum Thema: Der Pendler im heutigen Dorf, Statistische Mitteilungen über den Umfang der Pendlerbewegung in der Bundesrepublik (nach dem Stand der Volkszählung von 1950, seitdem ist nur ein langsamer Anstieg festzustellen).

52   Wolfgang Weiss, "Forschungsperspektiven zum Problemkreis 'Kirche und ländliche Gesellschaft in Mainfranken,'" *Würzburger Diözesangeschichtsblätter* (1990): 305.

53   DAW, KLV, KJB, K3, summary of a speech, "Soziale Wandlungen und ihre Bedeutung für das religiöse Leben," by Dr. W. Menges, Leiter des Kath. Instituts für Sozialforschung (n.d.).

54   CAJ-Essen, Korrespondenz 1947–8, Neue Ausrichtung und Aufgabenstellung in der Landjugend.

55   CAJ-Essen, Korrespondenz 1947–8, Fritz Eink, Neue Ausrichtung und Aufgabenstellung in der Landjugend, "Dorfapostolat," 1 February 1947.

56   JHH, 1.220103, Die 3 Hauptkongerenzen der katholischen Jugendseelsorge und Jugendorganisationen, München-Fürstenriedkonferenz, 1947, Landjugendseelsorge.

57   "Der Film auf dem Lande," KZK, 21 September 1958, 16A.

58 "Ein Fenster zur Welt tut sich auf," KZK, 1956, 353A.

59 "Soziale Wandlungen und ihre Bedeutung für das religiöse Leben."

60 HAEK, Seelsorgeamt Heinen #49, Egidius Schneider, Die Katholische Kand-volkbewegung im Erzbistum Köln, Votrage, gehalten auf der ersten Tagung des Aktionsausschusses der Katholischen Landvolkbewegung im Erzbistum Köln (Sachausschuß für Landvolkfragen im Diözesankomitee der Katholiken-ausschüsse) am 3. Juni 1954 in der Thomas-Morus-Akademie in Honnef.

61 DAW, LV/LJ, K2, Katholische Landvolkbewegung Deutschlands an die Mit-glieder des Aktionsausschusses der KLB, an die Landes- und Diözesanvor-sitzenden, an die Diözesanstellen der KLB, Gründonnerstag 1959, "Der Sonn-tag auf dem Land."

62 "Fluch oder Segen der Technisierung?," KZK, 1954, 365A.

63 DAW, LV/LJ, 1960–5, K1, Das Dorf in der Zukunft (n.d.).

64 BDKJ-Würz, Diözese Würzburg, vol. 4, Mitgliederstand laut Meldekarten vom 22.2.1960, sowie Schuldenstand per 22.2. 1960. The number of members was undoubtedly somewhat higher, as many groups often failed to report their membership or fill their forms out on time.

65 This calculation is based on official figures provided by the diocese. See BDKJ-Würz, vol. 4, Seelenzahl, Schematismus: 910.308.

66 JHH, A 526, HV 55–58, Bezieherstand am 10.10 1955, Verkaufsauflagen der Zeitschiften aus dem Verlag Haus Altenberg per 1.9.1960 mit Vergleichszahlen vom 1.9.1959.

67 DAW, Saat und Sendung: Idee, Entstehung, Aufgabe und Arbeitsweise der KLJB, 1952, Wie steht es unter Landvolk?

68 "Eine alarmiende Feststellung: Unserer Diözese fehlen 1500 Schwestern!," Volksblatt, 30 June 1956.

69 One word of caution must be added here. Youth organizations generally served, even during the best of times, 30 percent of young persons; the share of those reached thus dropped from 30 to 15 percent in most areas.

70 DAW, NL Neisinger, K6, Karl Heinrich, Jugendseelsorger und Zahn, Jugend-seelsorger an Döpfner, Bad Neustadt, 17 February 1950; DAW, KJBW, BJ, K1, Heini an Neisinger, Hain, 26 May 1947. The author wrote, "But what lacks is the enthusiasm and full readiness to sacrifice oneself for Christ."

71 DAW, KLV, KJB, K3, Gebietsmission Würzburg: Ergebnisse der differenzierten Kirchenbesucherzählung vom 16.9.1960. This study, however, has its limits. It was a survey of church attendance for the individual parishes in the city for only one Sunday. This Sunday, however, may have been more representative; it was not a major festival day or a day of obligation (such as Easter), where attendance would have been higher.

72 BDKJ-Würz, vol. 4, Dekanatsführerkonferenz Januar 1955, Bericht: Dekanat Würzburg- Stadt. The city of Würzburg was undoubtedly not representative of the rest of Lower Franconia. As an administrative center, it had far larger numbers of businesspersons, civil servants, and white-collar workers than the more rural parts of the diocese. The expression used here was "Würzburg ist

eine Stadt der Beamten und Angestellten daher gemütlich und bequem, auch in der Jugendarbeit."

73 BDKJ-Würz, vol. 4, Dekanatsführerkonferenz Januar 1955, Bericht: Dekanat Bad Neustadt/Saale.

74 Ibid., Dekanat Miltenberg.

75 Ibid., Dekanat Bad Kissingen.

76 DAW, LJ, K1, Das Dorf im Wandel unserer Zeit, Skizze von Kpl. Bocklet (n.d.).

77 Ibid.

78 HAEK, Gen 23.68.1, Hans Heinrichs an Frings, 23 February 1949. Others, however, claimed that even some curates took little interest in youth work: "The young people in the villages and the renewal of Christian life in the villages rises and falls with the curate in the village."

79 Saat und Sendung, 5.

80 Damberg, Abschied vom Milieu?, 389–91.

81 HAEK, Gen 23.68.4, Scharl an Frings, 8 June 1954.

82 DAW, LJ, K1, Katholische Landjugendbewegung—Diözese Würzburg an die Gebietsleitung der CAJ im Bistum Würzburg, 8 January 1958.

83 BDKJ-Würz, vol. 4, Dekanatsführerkonferenz Januar 1955, Bericht: Dekanat Aschaffenburg-Ost.

84 Ibid., Dekanat Bütthard.

85 "Was bedeutet die Katholische Landjugendbewegung für uns Landmädchen?," Die Jungführerin, 1951, 233–35.

86 HAEK, Gen 23.68.4, "Die Katholische Landvolksschule Rhöndorf/Rhein," December 1954.

87 DAW, LV/LJ, K1, Vorschlag zur Dekanatenkonferenz, 1957, Gefahr für unsere Dörfer durch die interkonfessionelle LJ (Bayerische Jungbauernschaft). This was out of a total of 300 to 400 parishes in the region that were not in the major cities; probably 1 of 3 parishes became a center for the movement. It must also be pointed out that not all parishes had youth groups.

88 Alois Muench, Theologische Grundgedanken zur Katholischen Landvolk-Bewegung: Akademische Ansprache anläßlich der Verliehung des Ehrendoktorates der Kath.—Theo. Fakultät der Universität Münster (Regensburg, 1948).

89 HAEK, Gen 23.68.7, Würmerling an den BDKJ.

90 HAEK, Gen 23.68.6, Anteil der einzelnen Themenkreisen am Gesamtprogramm der Seminare entsprechend der Häufigkeit der Behandlung, KLB und KLJB der Erzdiözese Köln, 28 August 1957.

91 Ibid.

92 HAEK, Gen 23.68.5, Protokoll über die Tagung des Aktionsausschusses der kath. Landvolkbewegung im Erzbistum Köln—Sachausschuß für Landvolkfragen im Diözesankomitee vom 27. Juni bis 28 Juni 1955.

93 DAW, KJBW, K2, BJ, folder KLJB—Seminare 1960–2.

94 BDKJ-Würz, vol. 4, BDKJ, Dekanat Miltenberg, Bericht an die Diözesanführung über die Zeit vom Monat Mai 1956 bis April 1957.

95 BDKJ-Würz, vol. 4, Bad Kissingen, Mai 1956–April 1957, Bericht über die Zeit

von Mai 1956–April 1957, Dekanats Schweinfurt–Land and Dekanat Lohr Main, Mannesjugend.

96 DAW, LJ, K1, Das Dorf in der Zukunft: Entwurf zu einer Art Hörspiel (n.d.).

97 BDKJ-Würz, vol. 33, Stellungnahme des Bischöflichen Jugendamtes Würzburg/Frauenjugend zur Durchführung der Berufsvorbereitenden Seminare für Mädchen des 8. Schülerjahrganges, 3 April 1964.

98 "Landflucht der Frauen," KZK, 29 June 1958, 16A.

99 Archiv des Deutschen Caritasverbandes, Zentralrat des DCV, October 1953, Sonderbericht betr. Dorfcaritas, Die Landfamilie in ihrer helfended Kraft u. in der Sorge der Caritas, 2.

100 "Weiterer Rückgang der Arbeitskräfte auf dem Lande," KZK, 1 February 1959, 16A.

101 "Landflucht der Frauen," KZK, 28 June 1958, 16A. See excerpts from a Caritas report that estimated that 350,000 young people were leaving the land annually: HAEK, Gen 23.69.3, "Von ländlichen Jugendnot–Unsere Leitsätze," October 1953.

102 "Die Dorfhelferinnen," KZK, 1956, 717A.

103 DAW, KLV/LJ, K2, Die Dorfhelferin, Katholische Landvolkbewegung Deutschlands, Munich, 16 May 1956.

104 "Was bedeutet die Katholische Landjugendbewegung für uns Landmädchen?"

105 These were the conclusions from evaluations of the seminars from 1957–58. See HAEK, Hen 23.68, Die Ländlichen Seminare 1957/8 im Spiegel der Abschlußberichte, Erzbischöfliches Landseelsorgeamt, Landjugend.

106 DAW, JA Kirchliche, Bestand, Dokumentation, K3, Konferenz der Dekane und Dekanatsjugendseelsorger des Bistums Würzburg am 28 November 1952.

107 DAW, LJ, K1, Monatsbericht, September 1957, Herbert Sippel.

108 Ibid., October 1957.

109 HAEK, Gen 23.68.7, Rückblick über die bisherige Arbeit des Katholischen Landvolkdienstes in der Erzdiözese Köln, 8 April 1958.

110 "Ist die Landjugend religiös?," KZK, 15 March 1959, 16A.

111 "Ist unserer Landjugend noch fromm? Eine Umfrage des Bielefelder Meinungsinstituts über die religiöse Einstellung Jugendlicher von 15 bis 24 Jahren," KZK, 1954, 317A.

CHAPTER 6

1 DJK Archiv, "Zur Gründung des DJK Verbandes Rhein-Weser" (von Jugendpfarrer Müller), Altenberg, 18 June 1953, file: Trennung. The inventory of this archive was not cataloged. In instances where a file was labeled, I have provided the name of the file. Otherwise, the documents will simply be listed under the heading DJK.

2 HAEK, Gen 26.49.3, Stohr an Frings, Mainz, 20 September 1957.

3 HAEK, Gen 23.11.10, "Privatklage des Verbandsfußballfachwartes des DJK-Zentralverbandes Heessen/Westfalen, Privatkläger gegen Hochwürden Herrn

Bundesjugendseelsorger Willi Bokler, Düsseldorf, Carl-Mosterts Platz, Jugendheim, Beschuldigter" (von Josef Brilla aus Heessen/Westfalen), 1 March 1958, and "Abschrift DJK Zentralverband, Verbandsfußballfachwart J Brilla, Heessen/Westfalen," 9 November 1957.

4 For one example within a prominent Catholic newspaper, see Gottfried Brock, "Das Elend der Deutschen Jugendkraft: Hohe Zeit, unbequeme Dinge beim Namen zu nennen," *Rheinische Merkur*, 1958. *Die Allgemeine Sonntagszeitung* also printed this article on 16 March 1958. See also Guido Zoeller, "DJK braucht Befriedung," *Rheinische Merkur*, 24 April 1959.

5 DJK Archiv, Willi Daume an Adenauer, Dortmund, 16 August 1960.

6 HAEK, Gen 23.11.5, Martin Söll an Caspar Schulte, 13 August 1959, and Deutsche Jugendkraft, Kath. Verband für Leibesübungen, Gelsenkirchen an Frings, 17 December 1949.

7 On the network of *Vereine* in Westphalia, see Wilhelm Damberg, *Abschied vom Milieu? Katholizismus im Bistum Münster und in den Niederlanden, 1945–1980* (Paderborn, 1997); Doris Kaufmann, *Katholisches Milieu in Münster, 1928–1933: Politische Aktionsformen und geschlechtsspezifische Verhaltensräume* (Düsseldorf, 1984).

8 Heinz-Egon Rösch, *Sport um der Menschen willen: 75 Jahre DJK Sportverband, "Deutsche Jugendkraft," 1920–1995* (Aachen, 1995). This work, produced by the DJK itself, provides the only account of the organization over its entire seventy-five-year history. For the prehistory of the DJK, see Willi Schwank, *Kirche und Sport in Deutschland von 1848–1920* (Hochheim am Main, 1979) and *Vorgeschichte und Gründung des katholischen Sportverbandes "Deutsche Jugendkraft," Geschichte der DJK*, no. 2 (Düsseldorf, 1990). See DJK Archiv, Diplomarbeit am Fachbereich Leibeserziehung des Johannes Gutenberg-Universität zu Mainz, Karin Reth, Juli 1980, "Kirche und Sport in der Weimarer Republik, Dargestellt am Beispiel der Gründung und Entwicklung des katholischen Sportverbandes DJK von 1920 bis 1925."

9 BAM, NL Ballhorn, F. Ballhorn, "Die Deutsche Jugendkraft in Münster" (n.d., but probably 1933).

10 JHD, Referat, Willy Bokler, Jahreskonferenz, Führerschaft des BDKJs, 1954, 12.

11 Martin Söll, ed., *Geist und Wesen der DJK: Reden und Aufsätze von Prälat Mosterts und Prälat Wolker in der Deutschen Jugendkraft* (Düsseldorf, 1960).

12 Ibid., 25.

13 Ibid., 35.

14 Ibid., 36.

15 Paul Hastenteufel, *Katholische Jugend in ihrer Zeit*, vol. 2, 1919–1932 (Bamberg, 1989), 376.

16 Rösch, *Sport um der Menschen willen*, 20.

17 Ibid., 20–21.

18 Christoph Kösters, *Katholische Verbände und moderne Gesellschaft: Organisationsgeschichte und Vereinskultur im Bistum Münster, 1918–1945* (Paderborn, 1995), 136–38.

19 DJK Archiv, "Zum Vertrag zwischen der Deutschen Turnerschaft und der Deutschen Jugendkraft" and "Vertrag," Berlin-Charlottenburg, 15 June 1932.

20 JHD, Haus Altenberg, "Bischöfliche Hauptstelle für katholische Jugendseelsorge und Jugendorganisation in den Deutschen Diözesen, Dezember-Bericht, 1945," 10. See also DJK Archiv, file: DJK und DSB, Willy Schulze, "Übersicht zur Geschichte der DJK, 2. Teil 1945–1954," Beitragsvorschlag zum Werkbuch.

21 DJK Archiv, "Ergebnis der Sportrundfrage vom 31.1.1946."

22 DJK Archiv, file: Konferenzen 46/47/48, "Sportkonferenz am 21.7.1946 in Düsseldorf."

23 JHD, Haus Altenberg, "Bischöfliche Hauptstelle für katholische Jugendseelsorge und Jugendorganisation in den deutschen Diözesem, Dezember-Bericht, 1945, an die Diözesen," 10–11.

24 See Rösch, Sport um der Menschen willen, 38. See also JHD, "Die erste Hauptkonferenz der katholischen Jugendseelsorge und Jugendorganisationen in den deutschen Diözesen, 29.4. bis 3.5. 1946 in Bad Soden-Salmünster, Bericht an die Diözesen," 24–25.

25 DJK Archiv, "Sportkonferenz am 21.7. 1946 in Düsseldorf."

26 The negotiations to found the DSB were painstaking. The Socialist organizations had insisted that all clubs were to remain neutral, that is, without political or religious affiliation. Wolker suggested a compromise: if the DSB were to accept denominational clubs, the DJK would "renounce its own special association." A British observer noted sarcastically, "But compromise does not come easy to the German character" (PRO, FO 1050/1096, "German Sports Organizations and the Erste Arbeitstagung des 'Ausschuss für Leibesübung,'" report by Mr. K. R. Walsh, Arnsberg).

27 Eduard Strych, Der westdeutsche Sport in der Phase der Neugründung, 1945–1950 (Schorndorf, 1975).

28 JHH, 2.28, Ludwig Wolker, "Um das Ethos im deutschen Sport: Referat des Prälaten Wolker auf der Zonensportratstagung am 13. Juni in Köln," Referat 1947.

29 Ludwig Wolker, Jugendkraft: Vom Ziel und Aufbau des Sportes in Katholischer Gemeinschaft (Altenberg, 1948).

30 Ute Schmidt, Zentrum oder CDU: Politischer Katholizismus zwischen Tradition und Anpassung (Opladen, 1987); Noel Cary, The Path to Christian Democracy: German Catholics and the Party System from Windhorst to Adenauer (Cambridge, 1996).

31 HAEK, Gen 23.11, Caspar Schulte, "Offener Brief an Prälat Wolker über die Wiederbelebung der DJK."

32 Ibid. See also JHH, 1.3225, Erinnerungen des Herrn Prälates Dr. Kaspar Schulte über die Wiedererstehung der DJK nach dem Zusammenbruch 1945, Paderborn, 24 October 1959.

33 At least no copies of a written response are in Catholic archives.

34 DJK Archiv, "Zur Gründung des DJK Verbandes Rhein-Weser."

35 HAEK, Gen 23.11.5, DJK, Kath. Verband für Leibesübungen, Gelsenkirchen an Frings, 17 December 1949.

36 JHH, 1.3225, Pfarrer Rath an Hengsbach, Dortmund, 10 October 1950.

37 DJK Archiv, file: Konferenzen 46/47/48, "Verbreitungsgebiet der Spiel- und Sportgemeinschaft kath. Vereine Rhein-Weser der DEUTSCHEN JUGENDKRAFT," 17 February 1949.

38 Kolping, das Zentralpräsidium der Deutschen Kolpingsfamilie, Antrag an die Zentralversammlung der Deutschen Kolpingsfamilie, Antrag no. 11, gez. Ridder, Generalpräses, 25 November 1954.

39 Kolping, Jugendreferat, Bundesführungsrat, BDKJ, 1953–9, "Um die andere Kanzel: eine notwendige Auflkärung," Abschrift aus dem "Anzeiger für die kath. Geistlichkeit," no. 3/1955.

40 JHH, 1.3225, Pfarrer Rath an Hengsbach, Dortmund, 10 October 1950. "So um das Jahr 1934/35 habe ich in Jugendkraftreden trotz der Gefahr, die von der Stapo drohte, häufiger auf die Phrase von Baldur von Schirach hingewiesen. Es sagte, soweit ich weiß: 'Es gibt keine katholische Bauchwelle und keine evangelische Kniewelle.' "

41 JHH, 1.3225, Pfarrer Rath an Meerkülter, 21 June 1948.

42 JHH, 1.3224, Pfarrer Rath, Dortmund, 2 July 1948, and Rath an Meerkötter, Dortmund, 21 June 1948.

43 Wolfgang Schroeder, *Katholizismus und Einheitsgewerkschaft: Der Streit um den DGB und der Niedergang des Sozialkatholizismus in der Bundesrepublik bis 1960* (Bonn, 1992) and *Gewerkschaftspolitik zwischen DGB, Katholizismus und CDU, 1945 bis 1960: Katholische Arbeiterführer als Zeitzeugen in Interviews* (Cologne, 1990).

44 Strych, *Westdeutsche Sport.* See also Lorenz Peiffer, ed., *Die erstrittene Einheit: Von der ADS zum DSB, 1948–1950. Bericht der 2. Hoyaer Tagung zur Entwicklung des Nachkriegssports in Deutschland* (Duderstadt, 1989).

45 DJK Archiv, Kiwitt an Wolker, 15 October 1952. Kiwitt never specified, however, what these lectures entailed.

46 DJK Archiv, Wolker an Kiwitt, Altenberg, 22 October 1952.

47 HAEK, Gen 23.11.5, DJK, Gelsenkirchen an Frings, Anlage, 17 December 1949.

48 JHH, 1.3225, Wolker and Sempels an den Hochwürdigsten Episkopat an die Führungsstellen in katholischer Gemeinschaft am 2. Adventssonntag 1957.

49 PRO, FO 1030/166, British report, 1947.

50 DJK Archiv, file: Bischöfe, Jaeger an Wolker, 14 February 1949.

51 PRO, FO 1013/2113, subject: Effects of the Nieheim incident, Church v. Freie Presse, Kreis Resident officer LK Höxter an Government Structure offices, HQ, RB Dortmund.

52 BAM, A26, Kiwitt an Wissing, 10 June 1952.

53 See Damberg, *Abschied vom Milieu?*, on this point. See also Chapter 1.

54 Keller did not state directly that his support for Rhein-Weser was based on these grounds. Documents from the Münster episcopate suggest, however, that he was particularly concerned about the control of the *Verbände* in his diocese. See, for instance, BAM, A26, Wissing an Kaplan Stürwald, 29 May 1953. See Wilhelm Damberg, "Zur 'Actio Catholica' und zum inneren Wandel des Milieus in den zwanziger und dreißiger Jahren" and "Gesellschaftlicher

Wandel und pastorale Planung: Das Bistum Münster und die Synoden von 1897, 1924, 1936 und 1958," in *Das Bistum Münster*, vol. 2, *Pastorale Entwicklung im 20. Jahrhundert*, ed. Werner Thissen (Münster, 1993), 18–39.

55 DJK Archiv, Keller an Wolker, 5 February 1952.

56 BAM, A26, DJK Keller an Tenhumberg (n.d., but probably 1960).

57 DJK Archiv, "Unser Weg: Eine Grundsatzerklärung des DJK-Zentralverbandes des Traditionsträgers des ehemaligen Reichsverbandes Deutsche Jugendkraft" (n.d., but probably the spring of 1958).

58 JHH, 1.3225, Pfarrer Rath an Hengsbach, Dortmund, 10 October 1950.

59 JHH, 1.3225, DJK Verband für Sportpflege in Katholischer Gemeinschaft EV an den Hochwürdigsten Episkopat und an die Führungsstellen in Katholischer Gemeinschaft, Altenberg, am 2. Adventssonntag 1951.

60 HAEK, NL Heinen, #33, "Verherrlicht Gott in eurem Leibe! Bekenntnistag 1948"; Ludwig Wolker, *Die Freude im Sport: Das Religiöse in den Leibesübungen der Gegenwart* (Buxheim, n.d.).

61 JHH, 1.2201.3, Ludwig Wolker, *Verherrlicht Gott in eurem Leibe!* (Altenberg, 1948), 6.

62 HAEK, Gen 26.49.1, aus dem Kirchlichen Amts-Blatt für die Diözese Rottenburg vom 21. März 1930, no. 4, vol. 13, 157, "Pius P.P.XI; Instruktion der Konzilarkongregation betreffend die Mode."

63 DJK Archiv, Grundsätze für den Frauensport (Handschrift oben, "von Pfr. Nünheu") (n.d.).

64 JHH, 1.3225, Entwurf einer Satzung für die Frauen DJK im DJK-Verband Rhein-Weser (n.d.).

65 HAEK, Gen 26.49.2, "Bundessportfest 1953." See also "Sport ist Spiel mit Regeln: Mädchenturnen und -gymnastik im Rahmen der 'Michaelswoche' vorgeführt," *Kölnischer Rundschau*, 25 September 1954.

66 DJK Archiv, file: Frauensport, "Bischöfliche Grundsätze für Leibesübungen katholischer Mädchen und Frauen in Schulen, Betriebe und Organisationen" (n.d., but after 1945). See also "Frauensport in katholischer Gemeinschaft, Verpflichtungen und Konsequenzen, Vortrag, gehalten anläßlich des 1. Verbandstages der DJK Frauensportgemeinschaft in Düsseldorf, am 15.1.1955 (von Dr. Lini Schneider, Beuel, Rhein)."

67 The term most commonly used was *weibliches Schauturnen*, which recurs throughout discussions of women's sports.

68 "Um das Problem, 'Mädchensport,'" *Die Jungführerin*, 1954, 170–75.

69 See the firsthand account of a "second-class" sports festival in DJK Archiv, file: Frauensport, "Ich sah ein Sportfest . . . Bericht über das Diözesansportfest von Aachen am 19./20. 54 in Rheydt."

70 JHD, 10.7, "Satzung der DJK-Frauensportgemeinschaft," Altenberg, 25 September 1953; HAEK, NL Böhler, cartoon, "Sport in der Jugenderziehung," "Grünes Licht für den Frauensport" (n.d., but probably 1955).

71 HAEK, Gen 26.49.1, Jaeger an Frings, Paderborn, 25 January 1955.

72 Ibid., Jaeger an Hebel, 25 January 1955.

73 See HAEK, Gen 26.49.3, Anlage 2, Betrf. Frauensport, no author, Cologne, 12 October 1953.

74 JHH, 1.3225, letter from Pfarrer Rath, n.d.

75 For one example, see ibid., Protokoll über die Sitzung des geschäftführenden Verbandsvorstandes am 2. Mai um 17.30 Uhr, 3 Mai 1952, Else Kiwitt.

76 Ibid., "Auszug aus dem Schreiben vom 30.9.1948 an die DJK-Spiel- und Sport-gemeinschaft Rhein/Weser."

77 JHH, 1.325, 1948.

78 Ibid.

79 HAEK, Gen 26.49.3, "DJK-Zentralverband—Verbandstag 1957, Entschliess-ungen."

80 BAM, A26, "Die DJK im Bistum Münster, Unterlagen für die Verhandlungen des Coordinierungausschusses," August 1959.

81 JHH, 1.3225, DJK, die DJK-Frauensportgemeinschaft im Bistum Essen an den Verbandsvorstand des DJK-Zentralverbandes, Dortmund (n.d., but probably late December 1957).

82 In 1953 Kiwitt claimed that Rhein-Weser consisted of 222 Vereine with 35,000 members. See DJK Archiv, Kiwitt an Wolker, 31 July 1953. Another account stated that Rhein-Weser contained 50,000 members; the Hauptverband, more than 95,000. See DJK Archiv, "Deutsche Jugendkraft—Bundesverband für Sportpflege in katholischer Gemeinschaft" (n.d., but probably from the late 1950s).

83 Karl Rohe, Vom Revier zum Ruhrgebiet: Wahlen, Parteien, Politische Kultur (Essen, 1986).

84 KZG, NLLW, II, 7a, Wolker an Schulte, Altenberg, 31 January 1955.

85 DJK Archiv, "Zur Charakterisierung der Lage beim Zentralverband" (n.d., no author, but probably August 1960).

86 DJK Archiv, Ludwig Roll an den DJK-Hauptverband, 10 April 1957; Werner Bolte an den DJK-Hauptverband, 9 April 1957.

87 DJK Archiv, "Zur Charakterisierung der Lage beim Zentralverband" and "Stand der Übertrittsverfahren vom DJK-Zentralverband zum DJK-Hauptver-band, Stichtag: 1. November 1960."

88 HAEK, Gen 23.11.8, "Vereinbarung zwischen der Deutschen Kolpingsfamilie und der Deutschen Jugend-Kraft, Verband Rhein-Weser," Köln, 15 April 1953, gez. Dr. Bernhard Ridder, Generalpräses, A. Kiwitt, Verbandspräses.

89 "Vergeben, jedoch nicht vergessen," Sturm und Steuer, 1959.

90 DJK Archiv, Martin Söll an Jaeger, 3 June 1959.

91 HAEK, Gen 26.49.4, "Zivilisation: Gefängnis oder Lebensraum (Dr. Hans Pelzner in der Vereinszeitung eines der größten deutschen Sport-Vereine)."

92 See "Herr Jedermann lebt viel zu bequem," Bremer Nachrichten, 3 March 1956. See also HAEK, Gen 26.49.4, "Gesundheitslage—Gesellungstrieb—Wachs-tumsprobleme—Ruckgang der Vitalität in unserer Jugend" aus Zehnjahresplan fördert Übungstattenbau (bearbeitet von Carl Diem, Jan. 1955).

93   See details in BAM, NL Ballhorn.

94   Mark Roseman, "National Socialism and Modernisation," in *Fascist Italy and Nazi Germany*, ed. Richard Bessel (Cambridge, 1996), 197–229.

95   BAM, A26, DJK, Keller an Tenhumberg (n.d. but probably 1960).

96   Arnold had also served as president of DJK-Bundesverbandes until his death in the late 1950s.

97   DJK Archiv, Willi Daume an Willy Bokler, Dortmund, 20 July 1960, and Bokler an Daume, 16 August 1960, with appended letter to Adenauer.

98   DJK Archiv, Johannes Sempels, Willy Bokler, Heinz Diekmann, Caspar Schulte, and Heinrich Tenhumberg an den Hochwürdigsten Deutschen Episkopat, 21 April 1961.

99   Rohe, *Vom Revier zum Ruhrgebiet*.

100 JHH, 1.3225, "Es gibt keinen christlichen Handstand: Die Kirche benötigt keine eigenen Sportverbände," *Sportbund, Nordrhein-Westfalen*, no. 12.

CONCLUSION

1   See Maria Höhn, *GIs and Fräuleins: The German-American Encounter in 1950s West Germany* (Chapel Hill, 2002), 175–76; Hans-Peter Schwarz, *Die Ära Adenauer: Gründerjahre der Republik, 1949–1957* (Stuttgart, 1981), 439–46; Arnold Sywottek, "Wege in die fünfziger Jahre," in *Modernisierung im Wiederaufbau: Die westdeutsche Gesellschaft der 50er Jahre*, ed. Axel Schildt and Arnold Sywottek (Bonn, 1993), 34–35; Uta Poiger, *Jazz, Rock, and Rebels: Cold War Politics and American Culture in a Divided Germany* (Berkeley, 2000).

2   See René Rémond, *L'anticléricalisme en France, de 1815 à nos jours* (Paris, 1976) and *Religion et société en Europe* (Paris, 1998); Gérard Chalry and Yves-Marie Hilaire, *Histoire Religieuse de la France contemporaine, 1930–1988* (Toulouse, 1988).

3   For a sweeping, recent account that depicts the current state of French Catholicism in an absolutely dismal light, see the work by French sociologist of religion Danièle Hervieu-Léger, *Catholicisme: La Fin d'un Monde* (Paris, 2003); for the transformations within rural France, see pp. 112–14.

4   See, in particular, Urs Altermatt, *Katholizismus und Moderne: Zur Sozial- und Mentalitätsgeschichte der Schweizer Katholiken im 19. und 20. Jahrhundert* (Zürich, 1989).

5   On the crisis in Dutch youth work, see Wilhelm Damberg, *Abschied vom Milieu? Katholizismus im Bistum Münster und in den Niederlanden, 1945–1980* (Paderborn, 1997), 567–74.

6   Ibid., 584–609. For an excellent overview of these changes in the Netherlands, see James Carleton Kennedy, "Building New Babylon: Cultural Change in the Netherlands during the 1960s" (Ph.D. diss., University of Iowa, 1995). This has appeared in print as *Nieuw Babylon in Aanbouw: Nederland in de Jaren Zestig*, 3d ed. (Amsterdam, 1999). See also John Coleman, *The Evolution of Dutch Catholicism, 1958–1974* (Berkeley, 1978), on this transition. For the political transfor-

mation, see Paul Luyks, "The Netherlands," in *Political Catholicism in Europe, 1918–1965*, ed. Tom Buchanan and Martin Conway (Oxford, 1996).

7 Rodney Stark and Roger Finke, *Acts of Faith: Explaining the Human Side of Religion* (Berkeley, 2000), 274.

8 On American Catholicism, see Steven Avella, *This Confident Church: Catholic Leadership and Life in Chicago, 1940–1965* (South Bend, 1992), 3. See also Chester Gillis, *Roman Catholicism in America* (New York, 1999); Mary Jo Weaver and R. Scott Appelby, *Being Right: Conservative Catholics in America* (Bloomington, 1995); Edward Kantowicz, *Modern American Catholicism, 1900–1965: Selected Historical Essays* (New York, 1988); Dean Hoge, ed., *Young Adult Catholics: Religion in the Culture of Change* (South Bend, 2000).

9 The literature here is voluminous. For the best and most recent overview, see Peter Steinfels, *A People Adrift: The Crisis of the Roman Catholic Church in America* (New York, 2003).

10 For a more thorough examination of these debates, see Steve Bruce, *God Is Dead: Secularization in the West* (Oxford, 2002); on the failure of the New Age and Eastern religions, see pp. 75–105, 118–39.

11 Damberg, *Abschied vom Milieu?*, 419.

12 Michael Ebertz, *Erosion der Gnadenanstalt? Zum Wandel der Sozialgestalt der Kirche* (Frankfurt, 1999), 75, 82, 91, 114.

13 One of the stumbling blocks in the debates about secularization has been over whether models of secularization apply only to Western Europe, Canada, Australia, and New Zealand or to the rest of the world. I would restrict such theories only to these regions: the 1990s and 2000s have seen the resurgence of religion, and in particular, Christianity and Islam, in Africa, Asia, and the Middle East.

14 See the brief discussion in Karl-Joseph Hummel, "Tatsachen—Deutungen—Fragen—Wohin steuert die Katholizismusforschung?," *Herder Korrespondenz* 57, no. 8 (2003): 398–403.

SELECTED

BIBLIOGRAPHY

ARCHIVAL SOURCES

Archiv der Deutschen Jugendkraft, Düsseldorf
Archiv des Deutschen Caritasverbandes (ADCV), Freiburg
   III.055 Zentralrat des DCV
Archiv Haus Altenberg
Bischöfliches Jugendamt Würzburg
   Kontenplan, Ordner 1-91
Bistumsarchiv Münster
   NL Franz Ballhorn
   NL Keller (A6)
Bund der Deutschen Katholischen Jugend, Cologne
Bund der Deutschen Katholischen Jugend, Düsseldorf, Jugendhaus Düsseldorf
Bundesarchiv Koblenz
   B268/79, 630–32, 95–100 (Bundesjugendring)
   Zsg.1—182/1 (1955–57) (Informationen des D. Bundesjugendringes)
Catholic University Archives, Washington, D.C.
   National Catholic Welfare Conference
      Exchange Programs, Box 29
   NL Alois Muench
Christliche Arbeiterjugend, Essen
   Aktenordner (1946–62), Statistik (approx. 100 Ordner)
Diözesanarchiv Würzburg
   BDKJ Jubiläumsausstellung (1987)
   Bestand: Dokumentation—Jugendarbeit, Kirchliche (K1–9)

Bestand: Dokumentation—Landvolk/LJ Kath. (K1–3)

Bestand: Dokumentation—Werkvolk, KAB, CAJ (K1–3)

Bischöfliches Jugendamt (K1–2)

Gestapo Akten

Monika Klinkhammer-Schalke Sammlung (K1–3) (includes oral histories, photographs)

NL Oskar Neisinger

NL Max Rößler

Dokumentationsstelle des BDKJ im Erzbistum Paderborn im Jugendhaus Hardehausen

Dom- und Diözesanarchiv, Mainz

NL Albert Stohr

Historisches Archiv des Erzbistums Köln

CR II, 22.17, 1–5 (Kolping)

CR II, 22.37, 1–5 (Katholische Aktion)

CR II 2, 19, 3–18 (Protokolle der Bischofskonferenzen)

Generalia II

Gen 23.2, 1–13 (Arbeitervereine)

Gen 23.4 (Marianische Kongregation)

Gen 23.6, 1–2 (Weibliche Jugend)

Gen 23.11, 1(a–b)–11 (Männliche Jugend)

Gen 23.11a, 1–4 (Männliche Jugendpflege)

Gen 23.11c, 1–2 (Jugendheime)

Gen 23.11d (Häuser des Jungmännerverbandes)

Gen 23.11e, 1–2 (Organisationen und Statuten im Jugendverband)

Gen 23.24, 1–2 (Verband Neudeutschland)

Gen 23.27 (Quickborn)

Gen 23.30 (Sittlichkeitsvereine, Damenmoden und Sitten)

Gen 23.33, 1–9 (Film und Funk)

Gen 23.40 (Mädchenschützverein)

Gen 23.42, 1–4 (Staatliche Jugendpflege)

Gen 23.67 (Schallplatten)

Gen 23.68, 1–8 (Landvolkseelsorge)

Gen 23.68a (Landvolk-Hochschule)

Gen 26.49, 1–4 (Turnen und Sport)

Gen 27.5 (Teilnahme Jugendl. An sittengefährlich. Vergnügen)

Gen 32.30, 1–5 (Seelsorgefragen)

Gen 32.30a (Seelsorgeamt)

NL Wilhelm Böhler (Zeitschriftensammlung)

NL Frings

Seelsorgeamt Heinen

    #32 Unterlagen zur Seelsorge der männlichen und weiblichen Jugend

    #33 Drucksachen zur Jugendseelsorge

    #34 Jugendseelsorge

#35 Jugendseelsorge
#36 Jugendseelsorge (Männliche Jugend)
#49 Katholiche Verbände und Vereine
#84 Ausarbeitungen
#90 Anzahl der Kapläne im Erzbistum
#96 Kommissionsentwürfe zur Vorbereitung der Diözesansynode 1954
#105, 6 Peregrinatio Mariae Durch das Erzbistum Köln: Berichte und
    Korrespondezen über Vorbereitung, Durchführung und Wirkungen
#114, 7 Herz-Maria Predigten
Katholische Frauengemeinschaft, Düsseldorf
    NL Hermann Klens
Kolpinghaus, Cologne
    Folders left behind and ordered by Theo Rempe
    Unordered documents
Kommission für Zeitgeschichte, Bonn
    NL Willy Bokler
    NL Johannes Maasen
    NL Neudeutschland
    NL Ludwig Wolker
Konrad-Adenauer Stiftung, St. Augustin
    NL Josef Rommerskirchen
National Archives, Washington, D.C.
    Historical Division
    Office of Research
    Public Opinion Barometer Reports
    RG 59 (State Department Decimal Files)
    RG 260 (Office of Military Government, United States)
    RG 466 (Office of the High Commissioner for Germany)
Pfarrarchiv Walberberg
Public Records Office, Kew
    FO/1006/319
    FO/1013/2112, 2120, 2128, 2129, 2130, 2131, 2133, 2132, 2141, 2146, 2148, 2150,
        2151, 2176
    FO/1049/436, 778, 779, 896, 1503, 1504
    FO/1050/12, 13, 82, 1076, 1077, 1079, 1081, 1082, 1083, 1092, 1094, 1096, 1251,
        1288, 1451, 1535, 1536, 1537, 1588, 1589, 1590, 1591, 1592, 1602, 1610, 1611,
        1612, 1613, 1670
U.S. Army Military History Institute, Carlisle Barracks, Carlisle, Pennsylvania
Zentralkomitee der Deutschen Katholiken, Bad Godesberg

NEWSPAPERS

(1947–62, unless otherwise indicated)
Die Befreiung

Der Brunnen
Deutsche Jugend
Der Fährmann
Der Jungführer
Die Jungführerin
Kirchenzeitung für das Erzbistum Köln
Mann in der Zeit
Michael (1947–55)
Der Pflug
Der Rheinische Merkur
Der Sämann
Der Scheideweg
Stimmen der Zeit
Unser Weg
Voran
Die Wacht

INTERVIEWS

Christel Beilmann, Witten, December 1995
Bernd Börger and Frau Börger, Düsseldorf, 1994, 1995
Elfriede Bonnländer, Weyersfeld, June 1996
Heidi Carl-Neisinger, Würzburg, April 1996
Paul Gail, Euskirchen, November 1995
Erika Kösters, Essen, November 1995
Felix Raabe, Bad Godesberg, November 1995
Josef Rommerskirchen, Bonn, November 1995

BOOKS, ARTICLES, AND DISSERTATIONS

Abrams, Lynn, and Elizabeth Harvey, eds. Gender Relations in German History: Power,
    Agency, and Experience from the Sixteenth to the Twentieth Century. Durham, N.C., 1997.
Affolderbach, Martin, and Steinkamp, Hermann, eds. Kirchliche Jugendarbeit in
    Grundbegriffen: Stichworte einer ökumenischen Bilanz. Düsseldorf, 1985.
Altermatt, Urs. "Katholische Subgesellschaft: Thesen zum Konzept der
    'Katholischen Subgesellschaft' am Beispiel des Schweizer Katholizismus." In
    Zur Soziologie des deutschen Katholizismus, edited by Karl Gabriel and Franz-Xaver
    Kaufmann, 145–65. Mainz, 1980.
——. Katholizismus und Moderne: Zur Sozial- und Mentalitätsgeschichte der Schweizer
    Katholiken im 19. und 20. Jahrhundert. Zürich, 1989.
Amery, Carl. Die Kapitulation oder der deutsche Katholizismus heute. Rheinbek, 1963.
Anderson, Margaret Lavinia. "Historiographical Review: The Limits of
    Secularization: On the Problem of the Catholic Revival in Nineteenth-Century
    Germany." Historical Journal 38, no. 3 (1995): 647–70.

Angerhausen, Julius. "Die Christliche Arbeiter-Jugend, die deutsche CAJ." *Trierer Theologische Zeitschrift* 63 (1954): 280–88.

Arbeitskreis für kirchliche Zeitgeschichte, Münster. "Katholiken zwischen Tradition und Moderne: Das katholische Milieu als Forschungsaufgabe." *Westfälische Forschungen* 43 (1993): 588–654.

Aretz, Jürgen. *Katholische Arbeiterbewegung und Nationalsozialismus: Der Verband katholischer Arbeiter- und Knappenvereine Westdeutschlands, 1923–1945.* Mainz, 1978.

Avella, Steven. *This Confident Church: Catholic Leadership and Life in Chicago, 1945–1965.* South Bend, 1992.

Barber, Benjamin. *Jihad versus McWorld.* New York, 1995.

Bauernkämper, Arnd. "Landwirtschaft und läandliche Gesellschaft in der Bundesrepublik in den 50er Jahren." In *Modernisierung im Wiederaufbau: Die westdeutsche Gesellschaft der 50er Jahre,* edited by Axel Schildt and Arnold Sywottek, 188–200. Bonn, 1993.

Baumgartner, Alois. "Die Auswirkungen der Liturgischen Bewegung auf Kirche und Katholizismus." In *Religiös-kulturelle Bewegungen im deutschen Katholizismus seit 1800,* edited by Anton Rauscher, 121–36. Paderborn, 1986.

———. *Sehnsucht nach Gemeinschaft: Ideen und Strömungen im Sozialkatholizismus der Weimarer Republik.* Paderborn, 1977.

Baumgartner, Siegfried, and Bernd Börger. "Die Entstehungsgeschichte des BDKJ." In *25 Jahre BDKJ,* ed. Bundesvorstand der Deutschen Katholischen Jugend (BDKJ), 7–28. Düsseldorf, 1973.

Bax, Erik. *Modernization and Cleavage in Dutch Society: A Study of Long Term Economic and Social Change in the Netherlands.* Brookfield, 1975.

Beilmann, Christel. *Eine katholische Jugend in Gottes und dem Dritten Reich: Briefe, Berichte, Gedrucktes, 1930–1945.* Wuppertal, 1989.

Berger, Peter, ed. *The Desecularization of the World: Resurgent Religion and World Politics.* Grand Rapids, 1999.

Berger, Walter. *Ad personam Ludwig Wolker.* Buxheim, 1975.

———, ed. *Worte von Ludwig Wolker.* Buxheim, 1975.

Biemer, Günter. *Der Dienst der Kirche an der Jugend: Grundlegung und Praxisorientierung.* Freiburg, 1985.

Biemer, Günter, and Werner Tzscheetzsch, eds. *Jugend der Kirche: Selbstdarstellung von Verbänden und Initiativen.* Freiburg, 1988.

Blackbourn, David. *Marpingen: Apparitions of the Virgin Mary in Nineteenth-Century Germany.* New York, 1994.

Blaschke, Olaf. "Das zweite Konfessionelle Zeitalter? Ein Deutungsangebot für Katholizismus- und Sozialhistoriker." *Geschichte und Gesellschaft* 26 (2000): 25–52.

Blaschke, Olaf, and Frank-Michael Kuhlemann, eds. *Religion im Kaiserreich: Milieus, Mentalitäten, Krisen.* Gütersloh, 1996.

Bleistein, Roman, ed. *Kirchliche Jugendarbeit: Angebot oder Anbiederung?* Düsseldorf, 1976.

———. "Kommentar zum Synodenbeschluß: 'Ziele und Aufgaben kirchlicher Jugendarbeit.'" In *Kirchliche Jugendarbeit: Angebot oder Anbiederung?,* edited by Roman Bleistein, 99–112. Düsseldorf, 1976.

Blessing, Werner. " 'Deutschland in Not, Wir im Glauben . . .' Kirche und Kirchenvolk in einer katholischen Region, 1933–1949." In *Von Stalingrad zur Währungsreform: Zur Sozialgeschichte des Umbruchs in Deutschland*, edited by Martin Broszat, 3–111. Munich, 1989.

Blom, J. C. *Verzuiling in Nederland, 1850–1925.* Amsterdam, 1981.

Blum, J. H. C., and J. Talsma. *De Verzuiling Voorbij: Godsdienst, Stand en Natie in de lange Negentiende Eeuw.* Amsterdam, 2000.

Bokler, Willy. "Lebensbewegung der Kirche: Katholische Jungmännergemeinschaft—KJG." In *Ein Haus für junge Menschen: Jugendhaus Düsseldorf, 1954–1994. Beiträge zur Geschichte der katholischen Jugendarbeit in Deutschland*, edited by Bernd Börger and Karin Kortmann, 145–48. Düsseldorf, 1994.

Bokler, Willy, and Heinz Fleckenstein. *Die sexualpädagogischen Richtlinien: Probleme der praktischen Theologie.* Mainz, 1967.

Böll, Friedhelm. *Auf der Suche nach Demokratie: Britische und deutsche Jugendinitiativen in Niedersachsen nach 1945.* Bonn, 1995.

Börger, Bernd. "Vielfalt als Wesensmerkmal der Einheit: Das Umfeld der Bischöflichen Hauptarbeitsstelle für Katholische Jugendseelsorge und Jugendorganisation." In *Ein Haus für junge Menschen: Jugendhaus Düsseldorf, 1954–1994. Beiträge zur Geschichte der katholischen Jugendarbeit in Deutschland*, edited by Bernd Börger and Karin Kortmann, 72–79. Düsseldorf, 1994.

———, ed. *Sie hielten Stand: Sturmschar im Katholischen Jungmännerverband Deutschlands.* Düsseldorf, 1989.

Börger, Bernd, and Karin Kortmann, eds. *Ein Haus für junge Menschen: Jugendhaus Düsseldorf, 1954–1994: Beiträge zur Geschichte der katholischen Jugendarbeit in Deutschland.* Düsseldorf, 1994.

Brandt, Hans Jürgen. *Schalke 91: Eine Katholische Arbeiterbewegung im Ruhrgebiet mit Tradition, 100 Jahre Pfarrei St. Josef Gelsenkirchen-Schalke.* Paderborn, 1991.

Brandt, Harm-Hinrich. *"Ein tüchtiges Organ des Handels- und Fabrikantenstandes": Die Industrie und Handelskammer Würzburg—Schweinfurt in 150 Jahren.* Würzburg, 1992.

Braun, Hans. "Demographische Umschichtungen im deutschen Katholizismus nach 1945." In *Kirche und Katholizismus, 1945–1949*, edited by Anton Rauscher, 9–25. Munich, 1977.

Briesen, Detlef, Gerhard Brunn, Rainer Elkar, and Jürgen Reulecke, eds. *Gesellschafts- und Wirtschaftsgeschichte Rheinlands und Westfalens.* Cologne, 1995.

Broszat, Martin, ed. *Von Stalingrad zur Währungsreform: Zur Sozialgeschichte des Umbruchs in Deutschland*, 2d ed. Munich, 1989.

———. *Zäsuren nach 1945: Essays zur Periodisierung der deutschen Nachkriegsgeschichte.* Munich, 1990.

Brown, Callum. *The Death of Christian Britain: Understanding Secularization, 1800–2000.* London, 2001.

Bruce, Steve. *God Is Dead: Secularization in the West.* Oxford, 2002.

———. *Religion in the Modern World: From Cathedrals to Cults.* Oxford, 1996.

———, ed. *Religion and Modernization: Sociologists and Historians Debate the Secularization Thesis*. Oxford, 1992.

Brücher, Bodo. *Die Sozialistische Jugendbewegung Deutschlands: Politisch-pädagogisches Konzept und Realität sozialistischer Jugend- und Erziehungsarbeit in den Nachkriegsjahren.* Werther, 1995.

Bund der Deutschen Katholischen Jugend. *Bundesordnung des BDKJ von 1948.* Düsseldorf, 1948.

———. *Bundesordnung des BDKJ von 1955.* Düsseldorf, 1955.

———. *Bundesordnung des BDKJ von 1962.* Düsseldorf, 1962.

Cardijn, Josef. *Das Apostolat der jungen Arbeiter.* Feldkirch, 1956.

Carter, Erica. *How German Is She? Postwar West German Reconstruction and the Consuming Woman.* Ann Arbor, 1997.

Cary, Noel. *The Path to Christian Democracy: German Catholics and the Party System from Windthorst to Adenauer.* Cambridge, 1996.

Conze, Werner, and M. Rainer Lepsius, eds. *Sozialgeschichte der Bundesrepublik Deutschland: Beiträge zum Kontinuitätsproblem.* Stuttgart, 1983.

Damberg, Wilhelm. *Abschied vom Milieu? Katholizismus im Bistum Münster und in den Niederlanden, 1945–1980.* Paderborn, 1997.

———. "Katholizismus im Umbruch: Beobachtungen zur Geschichte des Bistums Münster in den 40er und 50er Jahren." In *Ecclesia Monasteriensis: Festschrift für Alois Schröer zum 85. Geburtstag,* edited by Reimund Haas, 385–403. Münster, 1992.

———. "Kirchliche Zeitgeschichte Westfalens, der Schweiz, Belgiens und der Niederlande: Das katholische Beispiel." *Westfälische Forschungen* 42 (1992): 445–65.

Dillenberger, John, and Claude Welch. *Protestant Christianity Interpreted through Its Development.* New York, 1954.

Diözesanleitung des CAJ-Diözesanverbandes Münster, ed. *Christliche Arbeiter-Jugend, 1947–1987: Dokumentation 40 Jahre CAJ im Bistum Münster.* Münster, 1987.

Doering-Manteuffel, Anselm. *Die Bundesrepublik Deutschland: Aussenpolitik und innere Entwicklung, 1949–1963.* Darmstadt, 1993.

———. "Deutsche Zeitgeschichte nach 1945: Entwicklung und Problemlagen der historischen Forschung zur Nachkriegszeit." *Vierteljahrshefte für Zeitgeschichte* 4 (1993): 1–29.

———. *Katholizismus und Wiederbewaffnung: Die Haltung der deutschen Katholiken gegenüber der Wehrfrage, 1948–1955.* Mainz, 1981.

Doering-Manteuffel, Anselm, and Kurt Nowak, eds. *Kirchliche Zeitgeschichte: Urteilsbildung und Methoden.* Stuttgart, 1996.

Düwell, Kurt, and Wolfgang Köllmann, eds. *Rheinland-Westfalen im Industriezeitalter: Beiträge zur Landesgeschichte des 19. und 20. Jahrhunderts.* Vols. 1–4. Wuppertal, 1983–85.

Ebertz, Michael. *Erosion der Gnadenanstalt? Zum Wandel der Sozialgestalt der Kirche.* Frankfurt, 1999.

Engelbrecht, Jörg. *Landesgeschichte Nordrhein-Westfalen.* Stuttgart, 1994.

Evertz, Wilfried. "Im Spannungsfeld zwischen Staat und Kirche." In *Studien zur Kölner Kirchengeschichte*, edited by Historisches Archiv des Erzbistums Köln. Siegburg, 1992.

Fehrenbach, Heide. *Cinema in Democratizing Germany: Reconstructing National Identity after Hitler*. Chapel Hill, 1995.

Filsinger, Dieter, and Martin Fahlbusch. "Katholische Junge Gemeinde." In *Jugend der Kirche: Selbstdarstellung von Verbänden und Initiativen*, edited by Günter Biemer and Werner Tzscheetzsch, 96–98. Freiburg, 1988.

Frese, Matthias, and Michael Prinz, eds. *Politische Zäsuren und gesellschaftlicher Wandel im 20. Jahrhundert: Regionale und vergleichende Perspektiven*. Paderborn, 1996.

Frie, Ewald. *Caritativer Katholizismus in Deutschland im 19. und 20. Jahrhundert: Literatur zur Erforschung seiner Geschichte aus den Jahren 1960 bis 1993*. Freiburg, 1994.

Frohn, Hans-Werner. *Arbeiterbewegungskulturen in Köln, 1880–1933*. Essen, 1997.

Fromm, Erich. *Arbeiter und Angestellte am Vorabend des Dritten Reiches: Eine sozialpsychologische Untersuchung*. Stuttgart, 1967.

Gabriel, Karl. *Christentum zwischen Tradition und Postmoderne*. Freiburg, 1994.

——. "Die Katholiken in den 50er Jahren: Restauration, Modernisierung und beginnende Auflösung eines konfessionellen Milieus." In *Modernisierung im Wiederaufbau: Die westdeutsche Gesellschaft der 50er Jahre*, edited by Axel Schildt and Arnold Sywottek, 418–30. Bonn, 1993.

——. "Katholizismus und katholisches Milieu in den fünfziger Jahren der Bundesrepublik: Restauration, Modernisierung und beginnende Auflösung." In *Vatikanum II und Modernisierung: Historische, theologische und soziologische Perspektiven*, edited by Franz-Xaver Kaufmann and Arnold Zingerle, 67–83. Paderborn, 1996.

Gabriel, Karl, and Franz-Xaver Kaufmann, eds. *Zur Soziologie des deutschen Katholizismus*. Mainz, 1980.

Gauly, Thomas M. *Katholiken: Machtanspruch, Machtverlust*. Bonn, 1991.

——. *Kirche und Politik in der Bundesrepublik Deutschland, 1945–1976*. Bonn, 1990.

Gehrmann, Siegfried. *Fußball—Vereine—Politik: Zur Sportgeschichte des Reviers, 1900–1940*. Essen, 1988.

Generalsekretariat des Zentralkomitee der Deutschen Katholiken, ed. *Der Christ in der Zeit—72. Deutscher Katholikentag, 1948, 1949*.

Geyer, Michael, and Konrad Jarausch, eds. *Shattered Past: Reconstructing German Histories*. Princeton, 2003.

Gillis, Chester. *Roman Catholicism in America*. New York, 1999.

Gillis, John. *Youth and History: Tradition and Change in European Age Relations, 1770–Present*. London, 1981.

Goch, Stefan. *Sozialdemokratische Arbeiterbewegung und Arbeiterkultur im Ruhrgebiet: Eine Untersuchung am Beispiel Gelsenkirchen, 1848–1975*. Düsseldorf, 1990.

Goedde, Petra. *GIs and Germans: Culture, Gender, and Foreign Relations, 1945–1949*. New Haven, 2003.

Goldhammer, Karl-Werner. "Der Kampf der NSDAP gegen die Katholische Jugendarbeit in Unterfranken." *Würzburger Diözesangeschichtsblätter* (1975): 657–84.

——. *Katholische Jugend Frankens im Dritten Reich: Die Situation der katholischen Jugendarbeit unter besonderer Berücksichtigung Unterfrankens und seiner Hauptstadt Würzburg.* Frankfurt, 1987.

Gotto, Klaus. "Die deutschen Katholiken und die Wahlen in der Adenauer-Ära." In *Katholizismus im politischen System der Bundesrepublik, 1949–1963,* edited by Albrecht Langner, 7–32. Munich, 1978.

——. "Zum Selbstverständnis der katholischen Kirche im Jahre 1945." In *Politik und Konfession: Festschrift für Konrad Repgen zum 60. Geburtstag,* edited by Dieter Albrecht, 465–81. Berlin, 1983.

Götz von Olenhusen, Irmtraud. *Jugendreich, Gottesreich, Deutsches Reich: Junge Generation, Religion und Politik, 1928–1933.* Cologne, 1987.

——, ed. *Katholikinnen und Protestantinnen im 19. und 20. Jahrhundert.* Stuttgart, 1995.

——. *Wunderbare Erscheinungen: Frauen und katholische Frömmigkeit im 19. und 20. Jahrhundert.* Paderborn, 1995.

Greschat, Martin. " 'Rechristianisierung' und 'Säkularisierung': Anmerkungen zu einem europäischen konfessionellen Interpretationsmodell." In *Christentum und politische Verantwortung: Kirchen im Nachkriegsdeutschland,* edited by Jochen-Christoph Kaiser and Anselm Doering-Manteuffel, 1–24. Stuttgart, 1990.

Griech-Polelle, Beth A. *Bishop von Galen: German Catholicism and National Socialism.* New Haven, 2002.

Grossmann, Thomas. *Zwischen Kirche und Gesellschaft: Das Zentralkomitee der deutschen Katholiken, 1945–1970.* Mainz, 1991.

Grypa, Dietmar. *Die Katholische Arbeiterbewegung in Bayern nach dem Zweiten Weltkrieg, 1945–1963.* Paderborn, 2000.

Hanson, Sharon. "The Secularization Thesis: Talking at Cross Purposes." *Journal of Contemporary Religion* 12, no. 2 (1997): 159–79.

Hanssler, Bernhard. "Der Pluralisierungsprozeß im deutschen Katholizismus und seine gesellschaftlichen Auswirkungen." In *Katholizismus im politischen System der Bundesrepublik, 1949–1963,* edited by Albrecht Langner, 103–21. Munich, 1978.

Harrington, Joel, and Helmut Smith. "Confessionalization, Community, and State Building in Germany, 1555–1870." *Journal of Modern History* 69 (1997): 77–101.

Harvey, Elizabeth. *Youth and the Welfare State in the Weimar Republic.* Oxford, 1993.

Hastenteufel, Paul. "Grenzen und Möglichkeiten der kirchlichen Jugendarbeit im Zeitalter der modernen Technik: Eine Analyse der Entwicklung des BDKJ unter Geschichtspunkten personalbestimmter Pädagogik." Ph.D. diss., Munich, 1962.

——. *Katholische Jugend in ihrer Zeit.* Vol. 1, 1900–1918, and vol. 2, 1919–1932. Bamberg, 1988, 1989.

Hegel, Eduard. *Das Erzbistum Köln zwischen der Restauration des 19. Jahrhunderts und der Restauration des 20. Jahrhunderts 1815–1962.* Cologne, 1987.

Hehl, Ulrich von. "Der deutsche Katholizismus nach 1945 in der zeitgeschichtlichen Forschung." In *Christentum und politische Verantwortung: Kirchen im Nachkriegsdeutschland,* edited by Jochen-Christoph Kaiser and Anselm Doering-Manteuffel, 146–75. Stuttgart, 1990.

——. *Katholische Kirche und National Sozialismus im Erzbistum Köln, 1933–1945.* Mainz, 1977.

——. "Umgang mit katholischer Zeitgeschichte: Ergebnisse, Erfahrungen, Aufgaben." In *Staat und Parteien: Festschrift für Rudolf Morsey zum 65. Geburtstag*, edited by Karl Dietrich Bracher, 379–95. Berlin, 1992.

Hehl, Ulrich von, and Konrad Repgen, eds. *Der deutsche Katholizismus in der zeitgeschichtlichen Forschung*. Mainz, 1988.

Heinemann, Elizabeth. *What Difference Does a Husband Make? Women and Marital Status in Nazi and Postwar Germany*. Berkeley, 1997.

Hellfeld, Matthias von. *Bündische Jugend und Hitlerjugend: Zur Geschichte von Anpassung und Widerstand, 1930–1939*. Cologne, 1987.

Hellfeld, Matthias von, and Arno Klönne. *Die betrogene Generation: Jugend in Deutschland unter dem Faschismus*. Cologne, 1987.

Hervieu-Léger, Danièle. *Catholicisme: La Fin d'un Monde*. Paris, 2003.

Hiepel, Claudia, and Mark Ruff. *Christliche Arbeiterbewegung in Europa, 1850–1950*. Stuttgart, 2003.

Hobsbawm, Eric, and Terence Ranger, eds. *The Invention of Tradition*. New York, 1983.

Hoebink, Hein. "Gebietsreform." In *Nordrhein-Westfalen: Landesgeschichte im Lexikon*, 138–43. Düsseldorf, 1993.

Hoeren, Jürgen. *Die katholische Jugendpresse, 1945–1970: Daten und Fakten zur Entwicklung*. Münster, 1974.

Höffner, Joseph. *Industrielle Revolution und religiöse Krise: Schwund und Wandel des religiösen Verhaltens in der modernen Gesellschaft*. Opladen, 1961.

Hofmann, Karl. *Eine Katholische Generation zwischen Kirche und Welt: Studien zur Sturmschar des Katholischen Jungmännerverbandes Deutschlands*. Augsburg, 1992.

Hoge, Dean, ed. *Young Adult Catholics: Religion in the Culture of Change*. South Bend, 2000.

Höhl, Gudrun. *Forschungen zur Deutschen Landeskunde: Fränkische Städte und Märkte in geographischen Vergleich: Versuch einer funktionell-phänomenologischen Typisierung dargestellt am Raum von Ober, Unter-Mittelfranken*. Bad Godesberg, 1962.

Höhn, Maria. *GIs and Fräuleins: The German-American Encounter in 1950s West Germany*. Chapel Hill, 2002.

Holzem, Andreas. "Dechristianisierung und Rechristianisierung: Der deutsche Katholizismus im europäischen Vergleich." *Kirchliche Zeitgeschichte*, no. 11 (1998), 69–93.

Hummel, Karl-Joseph. "Tatsachen—Deutungen—Fragen—Wohin steurt die Katholizismusforschung?" *Herder Korrespondenz* 57, no. 8 (2003): 398–403.

Hürten, Heinz. *Deutsche Katholiken, 1918–1945*. Paderborn, 1992.

——. "Deutscher Katholizismus unter Pius XII: Stagnation oder Erneuerung?" In *Vatikanum II und Modernisierung: Historische, theologische und soziologische Perspektiven*, edited by Franz-Xaver Kaufmann and Arnold Zingerle, 53–65. Paderborn, 1996.

——. *Kurze Geschichte des deutschen Katholizismus, 1800–1960*. Mainz, 1986.

Hüttenberger, Peter. *Nordrhein-Westfalen und die Entstehung seiner parlamentarischen Demokratie*. Siegburg, 1973.

Jurgens, Birgit. *Zur Geschichte des BDM von 1923 bis 1939*. Frankfurt, 1994.

Kaiser, Jochen-Christoph. "Konfession und Provinz: Problemfelder der preußischen Kirchenpolitik in Westfalen." In *Westfalen und Preußen: Integration und Regionalismus*, edited by Karl Eppe and Michael Epkenhaus, 168–87. Paderborn, 1991.

Kaiser, Jochen-Christoph, and Anselm Doering-Manteuffel, eds. *Christentum und politische Verantwortung: Kirchen im Nachkriegsdeutschland.* Stuttgart, 1990.

Kammann, Bruno. *Carl Klinkhammer: Ruhrkaplan, Sanitätssoldat, und Bunkerpastor, 1903–1997.* Essen, 2001.

Kater, Michael. *Different Drummers: Jazz in the Culture of Nazi Germany.* New York, 1992.

Kaufmann, Doris. *Katholisches Milieu in Münster, 1928–1933: Politische Aktionsformen und geschlechtsspezifische Verhaltensräume.* Düsseldorf, 1984.

Kaufmann, Franz-Xaver. *Religion und Modernität: Sozialwissenschaftliche Perspektiven.* Tübingen, 1989.

Kaufmann, Franz-Xaver, and Arnold Zingerle. *Vatikanum II und Modernisierung: Historische, theologische und soziologische Perspektiven.* Paderborn, 1996.

Keller, Erwin. *Conrad Gröber, 1872–1948: Erzbischof in schwerer Zeit.* Freiburg, 1981.

Keller, Michael. *Katholische Aktion: Eine systematische Darstellung ihrer Idee.* Paderborn, 1933.

Kenkmann, Alfons. *Wilde Jugend: Lebenswelt grosstädtischer Jugendlicher zwischen Weltwirtschaftskrise, Nationalsozialismus und Währungsreform.* Essen, 1996.

Kennedy, James. *Nieuw Babylon in Aanbouw: Nederland in de Jaren Zestig.* Amsterdam, 1999.

Kinz, Gabriele. *Der Bund deutscher Mädel: Ein Beitrag zur Außerschulischen Mädchenerziehung im Nationalsozialismus.* Frankfurt, 1990.

Klaus, Martin. *Mädchen im Dritten Reich: Der Bund Deutscher Mädel.* Cologne, 1983,

Klöcker, Michael. "Das katholische Milieu: Grundüberlegungen—in besonderer Hinsicht auf das Deutsche Kaiserreich von 1871." *Zeitschrift für Religions- und Geistesgeschichte* 44 (1992): 241–62.

———. *Katholisch von der Wiege bis zur Bahre: Eine Lebensmacht im Zerfall?* Munich, 1991.

Klöcker, Michael, and Tworuschka, Monika. *Frau in den Religionen.* Weimar, 1995.

Klönne, Arno. *Jugend im Dritten Reich: Die Hitlerjugend und ihre Gegner.* Munich, 1995.

———. "Jugendprotest und Jugendopposition: Von der HJ-Erziehung zum Cliquenwesen in der Kriegszeit." In *Bayern in der NS-Zeit*, edited by Martin Broszat, vol. 4, pt. C, 527–620. Munich, 1983.

Kocka, Jürgen. "1945: Neubeginn oder Restauration?" In *Wendepunkte deutscher Geschichte, 1848–1945*, edited by Carola Stern and Heinrich August Winkler, 141–68. Frankfurt, 1979.

Köhler, Joachim. "Katholische Aktion und politischer Katholizismus in der Endphase der Weimarer Republik." *Rottenburger Jahrbuch für Kirchengeschicht* 2 (1983): 141–53.

Köhler, Joachim, and Damian van Melis. *Siegerin in Trümmern: Die Rolle der katholischen Kirche in der deutschen Nachkriegsgesellschaft.* Stuttgart, 1998.

Kolinsky, Eva. *Women in West Germany: Life, Work, and Politics.* Oxford, 1989.

Koonz, Claudia. *Mothers in the Fatherland: Women, the Family, and Nazi Politics*. New York, 1987.

Köster, Markus. *Katholizismus und Parteien in Münster, 1945–1953: Kontinuität und Wandel eines politischen Milieus*. Münster, 1993.

Kösters, Christoph. "Carl Mosterts." In *Zeitgeschichte in Lebensbildern: Aus dem deutschen Katholizismus des 19. und 20. Jahrhunderts*, edited by Rudolf Morsey, Jürgen Aretz, and Anton Rauscher, 7:9–25. Mainz, 1998.

——. *Katholische Verbände und moderne Gesellschaft: Organisationsgeschichte und Vereinskultur im Bistum Münster, 1918–1945*. Paderborn, 1995.

Kühr, Herbert. "Katholische und evangelische Milieus: Vermittlungsinstanzen und Wirkungsmuster." In *Wirtschaftlicher Wandel, religiöser Wandel und Wertwandel: Folgen für das politische Verhalten der Bundesrepublik Deutschland*, edited by Dieter Oberndörfer, 245–61. Berlin, 1985.

Lacquer, Walter. *Die Deutsche Jugendbewegung*. Cologne, 1962.

Langner, Albrecht, ed. *Katholizismus im politischen System der Bundesrepublik, 1949–1963*. Munich, 1978.

——. *Katholizismus, Wirtschaftsordnung und Sozialpolitik, 1945–1963*. Munich, 1980.

Lehmann, Hartmut, ed. *Religion und Religiosität in der Neuzeit: Historische Beiträge*. Göttingen, 1996.

——. *Säkularisierung, Dechristianisierung, Rechristianisierung im neuzeitlichen Europa: Bilanz und Perspektiven der Forschung*. Göttingen, 1997.

Lehnert, Detlef, and Klaus Megerle. "Identitäts- und Konsensprobleme in einer fragmentierten Gesellschaft: Zur politischen Kultur in der Weimarer Republik." In *Politische Kultur in Deutschland: Bilanz und Perspektiven*, edited by Dirk Berg-Schlosser and Jakob Schissler, 80–95. Opladen, 1987.

Lepsius, M. Rainer. "Parteiensystem und Sozialstruktur: Zum Problem der Demokratisierung der deutschen Gesellschaft." In *Wirtschaft, Geschichte und Wirtschaftsgeschichte: Festschrift zum 65. Geburtstag von F. Lütge*, edited by Wilhelm Abel, 371–93. Stuttgart, 1966.

Lester, Toby. "Oh, Gods! An Explosion of New Religions Will Shake the 21st Century." *Atlantic Monthly*, February 2002, 37–45.

Liedhegener, Antonius. *Christentum und Urbanisierung: Katholiken und Protestanten in Münster und Bochum, 1830–1933*. Paderborn, 1997.

——. "Katholisches Milieu in einer industriellen Umwelt am Beispiel Bochum: Strukturen und Entwicklungslinien, 1930–1974." In *Politische Zäsuren und gesellschaftlicher Wandel im 20. Jahrhundert: Regionale und vergleichende Perspektiven*, edited by Matthias Frese and Michael Prinz, 545–95. Paderborn, 1996.

——. "Marktgesellschaft und katholisches Milieu: Katholiken und katholische Regionen in der wirtschaflichen Entwicklung des Deutschen Reiches, 1895–1914." *Historisches Jahrbuch* 113 (1993): 283–354.

Liedhegener, Antonius, and Johannes Horstmann. *Konfession, Milieu, Moderne: Konzeptionelle Positionen und Kontroversen zur Geschichte von Katholizismus und Kirche im 19. und 20. Jahrhundert*. Schwerte, 2001.

Lindemann, Hans-Eckhard. *Historische Ortskerne in Mainfranken: Geschichte—Struktur—Entwicklungen.* Munich, 1989.

Lindmüller, Peter. *Remscheid und Solingen im industriegeographischen Entwicklungsvergleich.* Bochum, 1986.

Linton, Derek. *Who Has the Youth, Has the Future: The Campaign to Save Young Workers in Imperial Germany.* Cambridge, 1991.

Löhr, Wolfgang, ed. *Hirtenbriefe und Ansprachen zu Gesellschaft und Politik, 1945–1949.* Würzburg, 1985.

Lönne, Karl-Egon. "Katholizismus 1945: Zwischen gequälter Selbstbehauptung gegenüber dem Nationalsozialismus und Öffnung zur pluralistischen Gesellschaft." In *Ende des Dritten Reiches—Ende des Zweiten Weltkriegs: Eine perspektivische Rückschau,* edited by Hans-Erich Volkmann, 745–69. Munich, 1995.

———. "Literaturbericht: Katholizismusforschung." *Geschichte und Gesellschaft* 26 (2000): 128–70.

Loth, Wilfried. "Integration und Erosion: Wandlungen des katholischen Milieus in Deutschland." In *Deutscher Katholizismus im Umbruch zur Moderne,* edited by Wilfried Loth, 266–81. Stuttgart, 1991.

———. *Katholiken im Kaiserreich: Der politische Katholizismus in der Krise des wilhelminischen Deutschlands.* Düsseldorf, 1984.

———. "Milieu oder Milieus? Konzeptionelle Überlegungen zur Katholizismusforschung." In *Politische Deutungskulturen: Festschrift für Karl Rohe,* edited by Othmar Habert and Tobis Korenke, 123–36. Baden Baden, 1999.

———. "Soziale Bewegungen im Katholizismus des Kaiserreiches." *Geschichte und Gesellschaft* 17 (1991): 279–310.

Luyks, Paul. "Versäulung in den Niederlanden: Eine kritische Betrachtung der neueren Historiographie." *Jahrbuch des Zentrums für Niederlande-Studien* 2 (1991): 39–51.

Maase, Kaspar. *Bravo Amerika.* Hamburg, 1992.

———. *Grenzenloses Vergnügen: Der Aufstieg der Massenkultur, 1850–1970.* Frankfurt, 1997.

Martin, David. *A General Theory of Secularization.* Oxford, 1978.

McLeod, Hugh. *Religion and the People of Western Europe, 1789–1989.* Oxford, 1997.

———. *Secularisation in Western Europe, 1848–1914.* New York, 2000.

Meyer, Sibylle, and Eva Schulze. *Von Liebe sprach damals keiner: Familienalltag in der Nachkriegszeit.* Munich, 1985.

Misner, Paul. *Social Catholicism in Europe from the Onset of Industrialization to the First World War.* New York, 1991.

Mitchell, Maria. "Materialism and Secularism: CDU Politicians and National Socialism, 1945–1949." *Journal of Modern History* 67 (1995): 278–308.

Moeller, Robert. *Protecting Motherhood: Women and the Family in the Politics of Postwar West Germany.* Berkeley, 1993.

———, ed. *West Germany under Construction: Politics, Society, and Culture in the Adenauer Era.* Ann Arbor, 1997.

Mooser, Josef. *Arbeiterleben in Deutschland, 1900–1970: Klassenlagen, Kultur und Politik.* Frankfurt, 1984.

Morsey, Rudolf. *Die Bundesrepublik Deutschland: Entstehung und Entwicklung bis 1969.* Munich, 1995.

Morsey, Rudolf, and Konrad Repgen, eds. *Adenauer-Studien.* Vols. 1–5. Mainz, 1971– 86.

Mosshammer, Ottilie. *Werkbuch der katholischen Mädchenerziehung.* Freiburg, 1951.

Muench, Alois. *Theologische Grundgedanken zur Katholischen Landvolk-Bewegung: Akademische Ansprache anläßlich der Verliehung des Ehrendoktorates der Kath.—Theo. Fakultät der Universität Münster.* Regensburg, 1948.

Neisinger, Oskar. *Flugblätter: Katholische Jugend im Widerstand gegen den Nationalsozialismus.* Würzburg, 1982.

Nienhaus, Frank. "Transformations- und Erosionsprozesse des katholischen Milieus in einer ländlich-textilindustrialisierten Region: Das Westmünsterland, 1914–1968." In *Politische Zäsuren und gesellschaftlicher Wandel im 20. Jahrhundert: Regionale und vergleichende Perspektiven,* edited by Matthias Frese and Michael Prinz, 597–629. Paderborn, 1996.

Niethammer, Lutz, ed. *"Hinterher merkt man, dass es richtig war, dass es schiefgegangen ist": Nachkriegs-Erfahrungen im Ruhrgebiet.* Berlin, 1983.

Nipperdey, Thomas. *Religion im Umbruch: Deutschland, 1870–1918.* Munich, 1988.

Nolan, Mary. *Visions of Modernity: American Business and the Modernization of Germany.* New York, 1994.

Nothnagle, Alan. *Building the East German Myth: Historical Mythology and Youth Propaganda in the German Democratic Republic, 1945–1989.* Ann Arbor, 1999.

Pahlke, Georg. *Trotz Verbot nicht Tot: Katholische Jugend in ihrer Zeit.* Vol. 3, *1933–1945.* Paderborn, 1995.

Pahlke, Georg, and Wilhelm Pohlmann, eds. *Jugendhaus Hardehausen: 40 Jahre, 1945– 1985.* Paderborn, 1985.

Pauck, Wilhelm. *The Heritage of the Reformation.* Chicago, 1950.

Paul, Gerhard, and Klaus-Michael Mallmann. *Milieus und Widerstand: Eine Verhaltensgeschichte der Gesellschaft im Nationalsozialismus.* Bonn, 1995.

Pauleser, P. Saturnin. *Schönheit, Liebe und Glück.* Würzburg, 1955.

Peiffer, Lorenz, ed. *Die erstrittene Einheit: Von der ADS zum DSB, 1948–1950: Bericht der 2. Hoyaer Tagung zur Entwicklung des Nachkriegssports in Deutschland.* Duderstadt, 1989.

Peukert, Detlev. *Die Edelweißpiraten: Protestbewegungen jugendlicher Arbeiter im Dritten Reich.* Cologne, 1980.

———. *Grenzen der Sozialdisziplinierung: Aufstieg und Krise der deutschen Jugendfürsorge, 1878– 1932.* Cologne, 1986.

———. *The Weimar Republic: The Crisis of Classical Modernity.* New York, 1991.

Pirker, Theo. *Die verordnete Demokratie: Grundlagen und Erscheinungen der Restauration, 1945–1949.* Frankfurt, 1972.

Poiger, Uta. *Jazz, Rock, and Rebels: Cold War Politics and American Culture in a Divided Germany.* Berkeley, 2000.

Pollack, Detlef. "Funktionen von Religion und Kirche in den politischen Umbrüchen des 20. Jahrhunderts: Untersucht anhand der politischen Zäsuren von 1945 und 1989 in Deutschland." *Kirchliche Zeitgeschichte,* no. 1 (1999), 64–105.

Pommerin, Reiner, ed. *The American Impact on Postwar Germany*. Providence, 1995.

Quink, Cornelia. "Milieubedingunen des politischen Katholizismus in der Bundesrepublik." In *Politische Kultur in Deutschland: Bilanz und Perspektiven*, edited by Dirk Berg-Schlosser and Jakob Schissler, 309–21. Opladen, 1987.

Raabe, Felix. "Am Ende einer Epoche: Das BDKJ-Bundesfest 1965." In *Ein Haus für junge Menschen: Jugendhaus Düsseldorf, 1954–1994. Beiträge zur Geschichte der katholischen Jugendarbeit in Deutschland*, edited by Bernd Börger and Karin Kortmann, 175–80. Düsseldorf, 1994.

Raem, Heinz-Albert. *Katholischer Gesellenverein und Deutsche Kolpingsfamilie in der Ära des Nationalsozialismus*. Mainz, 1982.

Rauscher, Anton, ed. *Kirche und Katholizismus, 1945–1949*. Munich, 1977.

———. *Religiös-kulturelle Bewegungen im deutschen Katholizismus seit 1800*. Paderborn, 1986.

———. *Soziallehre der Kirche und katholische Verbände*. Cologne, 1980.

Reardon, Bernard. *Liberal Protestantism*. Stanford, 1968.

Reese, Dagmar. *Straff aber nicht Stramm: Herb aber nicht Derb: Zur Vergesellschaftung von Mädchen durch den Bund Deutscher Mädel im Sozialkulturellen Vergleich Zweier Milieus*. Weinheim, 1989.

Reineke, Augustinus. *Jugend zwischen Kreuz und Hakenkreuz: Erinnerungen und Erlebnisse: Ereignisse und Dokumente*. Paderborn, 1987.

Repgen, Konrad. "Die Erfahrung des Dritten Reiches und das Selbstverständnis der deutschen Katholiken nach 1945." In *Die Zeit nach 1945 als Thema kirchlicher Zeitgeschichte*, edited by Victor Conzemius, 127–79. Göttingen, 1988.

Reulecke, Jürgen. "Jugend und 'Junge Generation' in der Gesellschaft der Zwischenkriegszeit." In *1918–1945: Die Weimarer Republik und die nationalsozialistische Diktatur*, edited by Dietrich Langewiesche and H. E. Tenroth, 86–110. Munich, 1989.

———, ed. *Rückkehr in die Ferne: Die deutsche Jugend in der Nachkriegszeit und das Ausland*. Weinheim, 1997.

Riechert, Karen. "Der Umgang der katholischen Kirche mit historischer und juristischer Schuld anlässlich der Nürnberger Hauptkriegsverbrecherprozesse." In *Siegerin in Trümmern: Die Rolle der katholischen Kirche in der deutschen Nachkriegsgesellschaft*, edited by Joachim Köhler and Damian van Melis, 18–41. Stuttgart, 1998.

Righart, Hans. *De katholieke Zuil in Europa: Het Onstaan van Verzuiling onder Katholieken in Oostenrijk, Zwiterserland, Belgie en Nederland*. Amsterdam, 1986.

Rocholl-Gärtner, Ingeborg. *Anwalt der Frauen: Hermann Klens: Leben und Werk*. Düsseldorf, 1978.

Rohe, Karl. "Parteien und Parteiensysteme in Nordrhein-Westfalen: Traditionen und Mentalitäten nach 1945." In *Nordrhein-Westfalen: Fünfzig Jahre Später*, edited by Wolfram Köhler, 8–26. Essen, 1996.

———. "Parteien und Sozialstruktur: Zum Problem der Demokratisierung der deutschen Gesellschaft." In *Deutsche Parteien vor 1918*, edited by Gerhard A. Ritter, 56–80. Cologne, 1973.

————. "Politische Traditionen im Rheinland, in Westfalen und Lippe: Zur Politischen Kulture Nordrhein-Westfalen." In *Nordrhein-Westfalen: Eine politische Landeskunde*, edited by Die Landeszentrale für politische Bildung Nordrhein-Westfalen, 14–34. Cologne, 1984.

————. *Vom Revier zum Ruhrgebiet: Wahlen, Parteien, Politische Kultur*. Essen, 1986.

————. *Wahlen und Wählertraditionen in Deutschland: Kulturelle Grundlagen deutscher Parteien und Parteiensysteme im 19. und 20. Jahrhundert*. Frankfurt, 1992.

Rölli-Alkemper, Lukas. *Familie im Wiederaufbau: Katholizismus und bürgerliches Familienideal in der Bundesrepublik Deutschland, 1945–1965*. Paderborn, 2000.

Rommerskirch, Erich. "Neudeutschlands Geschichte 1919–1939 im Spiegel seiner Zeitschriften Leuchtturm und Die Burg." In *Löschte den Geist nicht aus: Der Bund Deutschland im Dritten Reich: Erlebnisberichte*, edited by Rolf Eilers. Mainz, 1985.

Rösch, Heinz-Egon. *Sport um der Menschen willen: 75 Jahre DJK Sportverband, "Deutsche Jugendkraft," 1920–1995*. Aachen, 1995.

Roseman, Mark. "National Socialism and Modernisation." In *Fascist Italy and Nazi Germany*, edited by Richard Bessel, 197–229. Cambridge, 1996.

————. *Recasting the Ruhr, 1945–1958: Manpower, Economic Recovery, and Labour Relations*. New York, 1992.

————, ed. *Generations in Conflict: Youth Revolt and Generation Formation in Germany, 1770–1968*. Cambridge, 1995.

Roth, Heinrich, ed. *Katholische Jugend in der NS-Zeit, unter besonderer Berücksichtigung des Katholischen Jungmännerverbandes, Daten und Dokumente*. Düsseldorf, 1959.

Ruff, Mark Edward. "Der 'Bruderzwist' der DJK: 'Integralisten' und 'Modernisierer' in einem Katholischen Sportverband." In *Katholiken und Protestanten in den Aufbaujahren der Bundesrepublik*, edited by Thomas Sauer, 148–69. Stuttgart, 2000.

Ruhl, Klaus-Jörg. *Frauen in der Nachkriegszeit*. Munich, 1988.

————. *Verordnete Unterordnung: Berufstätige Frauen zwischen Wirtschaftswachstum und konservativer Ideologie in der Nachkriegszeit, 1945–1963*. Munich, 1994.

Rupieper, Hermann-Josef. *Die Wurzeln der westdeutschen Nachkriegsdemokratie: Der amerikanische Beitrag, 1945–1952*. Opladen, 1993.

Rüther, Martin. *Arbeiterschaft in Köln, 1920–1945*. Cologne, 1990.

————. *Zwischen Zusammenbruch und Wirtschaftswunder: Betriebsratstätigkeit und Arbeiterverhalten in Köln, 1945 bis 1952*. Bonn, 1991.

Ryba, Josef. *Schonungen: Geschichte eines fränkischen Dorfes*. Würzburg, 1966.

Sauer, Thomas, ed. *Katholiken und Protestanten in den Aufbaujahren der Bundesrepublik*. Stuttgart, 2000.

Scharl, Emmeram. "Organisationsformen der Katholischen Landvolkbewegung in der Bundesrepublik." In *Das Dorf*, no. 9/10 (1957), 129–36.

Schatz, Klaus. *Zwischen Säkularisation und Zweitem Vatikanum: Der Weg des deutschen Katholizismus im 19. und 20. Jahrhundert*. Frankfurt, 1986.

Schellenberger, Barbara. *Katholische Jugend und Drittes Reich: Eine Geschichte des Katholischen Jungmännerverbandes 1933–1939 unter besonderer Berücksichtigung der Rheinprovinz*. Mainz, 1975.

————. "Ludwig Wolker, 1887–1955." In *Zeitgeschichte in Lebensbildern: Aus dem deutschen*

Katholizismus des 19. und 20. Jahrhunderts, edited by Rudolf Morsey, Jürgen Aretz, and Anton Rauscher, 5:134–46. Mainz, 1982.

Schelsky, Helmut. *Die skeptische Generation: Eine Soziologie der deutschen Jugend.* Düsseldorf, 1957.

Schewick, Burkhard van. *Die katholische Kirche und die Entstehung der Verfassungen in Westdeutschland, 1945–1950.* Mainz, 1980.

Schieder, Wolfgang, ed. *Religion und Gesellschaft im 19. Jahrhundert.* Stuttgart, 1993.

Schildt, Axel. *Moderne Zeiten: Freizeit, Massenmedien und "Zeitgeist" in der Bundesrepublik der fünfziger Jahre.* Hamburg, 1995.

Schildt, Axel, and Arnold Sywottek, eds. *Modernisierung im Wiederaufbau: Die westdeutsche Gesellschaft der 50er Jahre.* Bonn, 1993.

Schilson, Arno. "Die Liturgische Bewegung: Anstöße—Geschichte— Hintergründe." In *Den Glauben feiern: Wege liturgischer Erneuerung*, edited by Klemens Richter and Arno Schilson, 11–48. Mainz, 1989.

Schissler, Hanna, ed. *The Miracle Years: A Cultural History of West Germany, 1949–1968.* Princeton, 2001.

Schlund, Erhard. *Die Katholische Aktion: Materialien und Akten.* Munich, 1928.

Schmidt, Eberhard. *Die verhinderte Neuordnung, 1945–1952.* Frankfurt, 1970.

Schmidt, Ute. *Zentrum oder CDU: Politischer Katholizismus zwischen Tradition und Anpassung.* Opladen, 1987.

Schmidtchen, Gerhard. *Protestanten und Katholiken: Soziologische Analyse konfessioneller Kultur.* Bern, 1973.

Schmitt, Karl. *Konfession und Wahlverhalten in der Bundesrepublik Deutschland.* Berlin, 1989.

Schroeder, Wolfgang. *Gewerkschaftspolitik zwischen DGB, Katholizismus und CDU, 1945 bis 1960: Katholische Arbeiterführer als Zeitzeugen in Interviews.* Cologne, 1990.

———. *Katholizismus und Einheitsgewerkschaft: Der Streit um den DGB und der Niedergang des Sozialkatholizismus in der Bundesrepublik bis 1960.* Bonn, 1992.

Schulte-Umberg, Thomas. *Profession und Charisma: Herkunft und Ausbildung des Klerus im Bistum Münster, 1776–1940.* Paderborn, 1999.

Schulze, Matthias. *Bund oder Schar—Verband oder Pfarrjugend? Katholische Jugendarbeit im Erzbistum Paderborn nach 1945.* Paderborn, 2001.

Schwab, Martin. *Kirche Leben und Gesellschaft Gestalten: Der Bund der Deutschen Katholischen Jugend (BDKJ) in der Bundesrepublik Deutschland und der Diözese Würzburg, 1947–1989.* Würzburg, 1997.

———. *Kirchlich, Kritisch, Kämpferisch: Der Bund der Deutschen Katholischen Jugend (BDKJ), 1947–1989.* Würzburg, 1994.

Schwalbach, Bruno. *Erzbischof Conrad Gröber und die deutsche Katastophe: Sein Ringen um eine menschliche Neuordnung.* Karlsruhe, 1994.

Schwank, Willi. *Kirche und Sport in Deutschland von 1848–1920.* Hochheim am Main, 1979.

———. *Die Turn- und Sportbewegung innerhalb der katholischen Kirche Deutschlands im 19. und 20. Jahrhundert unter besonderer Berücksichtigung der Gesellen- und Jugendvereine.* Lahnstein, 1978.

———. *Vorgeschichte und Gründung des katholischen Sportverbandes "Deutsche Jugendkraft."* *Geschichte der JK*, no. 2. Düsseldorf, 1990.

Schwarte, Norbert, and Jürgen Reulecke. "Fernweh und Grossfahrten in der bündischen Jugend der Nachkriegszeit." In *Rückkehr in die Ferne: Die deutsche Jugend in der Nachkriegszeit und das Ausland*, edited by Jürgen Reulecke, 151–67. Weinheim, 1997.

Schwarz, Hans-Peter. *Die Ära Adenauer: Gründerjahre der Republik, 1949–1957*. Stuttgart, 1981.

Scott, Joan. *Gender and the Politics of History*. New York, 1988.

Söll, Martin, ed. *Geist und Wesen der DJK: Reden und Aufsätze von Prälat Mosterts und Prälat Wolker in der Deutschen Jugendkraft*. Düsseldorf, 1960.

Sperber, Jonathan. "Kirchengeschichte or the Social and Cultural History of Religion?" *Neue Politische Literatur* 43 (1998): 13–35.

———. *Popular Catholicism in Nineteenth-Century Germany*. Princeton, 1984.

Spitznagel, Peter. *Wähler und Wahlen in Unterfranken, 1919–1969: Versuch einer Analyse der Wählerstruktur eines Regierungbezirkes auf statistischer Grundlage nach den Erhebungen der Volkszählungen 1925, 1950, 1961 und 1970*. Paderborn, 1979.

Spotts, Frederic. *Kirchen und Politik in Deutschland*. Stuttgart, 1976.

Stachura, Peter. *The German Youth Movement, 1900–1945: An Interpretation and Documentary History*. London, 1981.

Stark, Rodney, and Roger Finke. *Acts of Faith: Explaining the Human Side of Religion*. Berkeley, 2000.

Stark, Rodney, and Laurence Iannaccone. "A Supply-Side Reinterpretation of the 'Secularization' of Europe." *Journal for the Scientific Study of Religion*, September 1994, 230–53.

Statistisches Landesamt Nordrhein-Westfalen, ed. *50 Jahre Wahlen in Nordrhein-Westfalen, 1919–1968*. Düsseldorf, 1969.

Steinfels, Peter. *A People Adrift: The Crisis of the Roman Catholic Church in America*. New York, 2003.

Steinkamp, Hermann. *Jugendarbeit als soziales Lernen: Ziele und Aufgaben kirchlicher Jugendarbeit: Zum Beschluß der Gemeinsamen Synode der Bistümer in der Bundesrepublik Deutschland*. Mainz, 1977.

———. "Neue Akzente in der kirchlichen Jugendarbeit? Ein Kommentar zu zwei programmatischen Entwürfen." *Katechetische Blätter* 98 (1973): 193–207.

Steinmaus-Pollak, Angelika. *Das als Katholische Aktion organisierte Laienapostolat: Geschichte seiner Theorie und seiner kirchenrechtlichen Praxis in Deutschland*. Würzburg, 1988.

Strych, Eduard. *Der westdeutsche Sport in der Phase der Neugründung, 1945–1950*. Schorndorf, 1975.

Swatos, William H., Jr., and Daniel V. A. Olson. *The Secularization Debate*. Oxford, 2000.

Tenfelde, Klaus. "Die Entfaltung des Vereinswesens während der industriellen Revolution in Deutschland, 1850–1873." In *Vereinswesen und Bürgerliche Gesellschaft in Deutschland*, edited by Otto Dann, 51–114. Munich, 1984.

———. "Historische Milieus—Erblichkeit und Konkurrenz." In *Nation und Gesellschaft in Deutschland*, edited by Paul Nolte and M. Hettling, 247–68. Munich, 1996.

———. "Zur Sozialgeschichte der Arbeiterbewegung im Ruhrgebiet 1918 bis 1933." In *Rheinland-Westfalen im Industriezeitalter: Beiträge zur Landesgeschichte des 19. und 20. Jahrhunderts*, edited by Kurt Düwell and Wolfgang Köllmann, 2:333–48. Wuppertal, 1983.

Tent, James. *Mission on the Rhine: Reeducation and Denazification in American-Occupied Germany*. Chicago, 1982.

Thurmair, Georg. *Ein Priester der Freude: Das Leben des Prälaten Ludwig Wolker*. Buxheim, 1957.

Troeltsch, Ernst. *Protestantism and Progress: The Significance of Protestantism for the Rise of the Modern World*. Philadelphia, 1986.

Turner, Ian, ed. *Reconstruction in Post-War Germany: British Occupation Policy and the Western Zones, 1945–55*. Oxford, 1989.

Volk, Ludwig. *Akten deutscher Bischöfe über die Lage der Kirche, 1933–1945*. Vols. 4–6. Mainz, 1981, 1983, 1985.

Volkmann, Hans-Erich, ed. *Ende des Dritten Reiches—Ende des Zweiten Weltkriegs: Eine perspektivische Rückschau*. Munich, 1995.

von der Osten, Petra. *Jugend- und Gefährdetenfürsorge im Sozialstaat: Auf dem Weg zum Sozialdienst katholischer Frauen, 1945–1968*. Paderborn, 2003.

Walter, Franz. "Milieus und Parteien in der deutschen Gesellschaft." *Geschichte in Wissenschaft und Unterricht* (1995): 479–93.

Weichlein, Siegfried. *Sozialmilieus und politische Kultur in der Weimarer Republik: Lebenswelt, Vereinskultur, Politik in Hessen*. Göttingen, 1996.

Weiss, Otto. "Religiöse Geschichte oder Kirchengeschichte? Zu neuen Ansätzen in der deutschen Kirchengeschichtsschreibung und Katholizismusforschung—Ein Forschungsbericht." *Rottenburger Jahrbuch für Kirchengeschichte* 17 (1998): 289–312.

Weiss, Wolfgang. "Forschungsperspektiven zum Problemkreis 'Kirche und ländliche Gesellschaft in Mainfranken.'" *Würzburger Diözesangeschichtsblätter* (1990): 304–20.

Wilson, B. R. *Religion in Secular Society*. London, 1966.

———. *Religion in Sociological Perspective*. Oxford, 1982.

Wirtz, Heiner J. *Katholische Gesellenvereine und Kolpingsfamilien im Bistum Münster, 1852–1960, "Gott zur Ehre und den Gesellen zum Vorteil."* Münster, 1999.

Wittstadt, Klaus. "Ein Bischof in schwerer Zeit: Das Wirken Bischof Matthias Ehrenfried im Dritten Reich." *Würzburger Diözesangeschichtsblätter* (1995): 407–20.

———. "Perspektiven einer kirchlichen Erneuerung—Der deutsche Episkopat und die Vorbereitungsphase des II. Vatikanums." In *Vatikanum II und Modernisierung: Historische, theologische und soziologische Perspektiven*, edited by Franz-Xaver Kaufmann and Arnold Zingerle, 85–106. Paderborn, 1996.

———. *Würzburger Bischöfe, 742–1979*. Würzburg, 1979.

Wolker, Ludwig. *Jugendkraft: Vom Ziel und Aufbau des Sportes in Katholischer Gemeinschaft*. Altenberg, 1948.

———. *Verherrlicht Gott in eurem Leibe!* Altenberg, 1948.

Wollasch, Andreas. *Der Katholische Fürsorgeverein für Mädchen, Frauen und Kinder, 1899–1945: Ein Beitrag zur Geschichte der Jugend- und Gefährdetenfürsorge in Deutschland.* Freiburg, 1991.

Wothe, Franz-Josef. "Gegenwartsfragen der Familienerziehung: Kritische Würdigung der familienpädagogischen Tradition in Adolf Kolping." Ph.D. diss., Munich, 1938.

Wuthnow, Robert. "Recent Patterns of Secularization: A Problem of Generations." *American Sociological Review* 41 (1976): 856–67.

Yonke, Erich. "The Catholic Subculture in Modern Germany: Recent Work on the Social History of Religion." *Catholic Historical Review* 80 (1994): 534–45.

Zeiger, Ivo. "Um die Zukunft der katholischen Kirche in Deutschland." *Stimmen der Zeit* 141 (1947/48): 241–52.

Zentralkomitee der Deutschen Katholiken, ed. *Kehrt um und glaubt—Erneuert die Welt, 87. Deutscher Katholikentag Düsseldorf, 1. bis 5. September 1982.* Paderborn, 1982.

———. *Kirche und Landvolk: Arbeitstagung des Zentralkomitees der Deutschen Katholiken, Würzburg, Herbst 1955.* Paderborn, 1955.

Zorn, Wolfgang. "Die Struktur der Rheinischen Wirtschaft in der Neuzeit." *Rheinische Vierteljahrsblätter* (1963): 37–62.